The Mountain and the Politics of Representation

Liverpool Studies in the Politics of Popular Culture

Sociologists and other scholars are reporting a resurgence of interest in popular culture. To engage with popular culture is to engage in any number of debates about power, ideology, hegemony, (dis)order, resistance and reproduction. The purpose of this series is to engage with these concepts, not as abstract ideas circulating in the grand corridors of government and academe, but rather, as Raymond Williams (1958) once put it, as ideas which are manifest in the everyday lives of 'ordinary' people.

This series looks at popular culture in its broadest sense, including topics such as celebrity and reality TV, popular culture and youth, race and diversity, Internet culture, television, music, cinema, social media, games, comedy, popular literature, comics and graphic novels, radio, subcultures, countercultures and celebrity cultures, advertising and consumerism, sports, and more. Proposals are welcome from across the disciplines and subject fields of sociology, cultural sociology, cultural studies, sociology of identity and community, popular music studies, youth studies, fashion studies, gender studies, and sport and leisure studies.

Series editors:
Brett Lashua, University College London
Stephen Wagg, De Montfort University

The Mountain and the Politics of Representation

Edited by
Martin Hall
and
Jenny Hall

LIVERPOOL UNIVERSITY PRESS

First published 2023 by
Liverpool University Press
4 Cambridge Street
Liverpool
L69 7ZU

British Library Cataloguing-in-Publication data
A British Library CIP record is available

ISBN 978-1-83764-506-0

Typeset by Carnegie Book Production, Lancaster
Printed and bound by CPI Group (UK) Ltd, Croydon CR0 4YY

Contents

Acknowledgements   vii

Contributors   ix

Introduction   1
       Martin Hall and Jenny Hall

I. COMMODIFICATION AND THE MOUNTAIN

1. Scripted Summits: Book History, Mountaineering, and the Experiences of Janet Adam Smith (1905–1999)   17
       Fiona Mossman

2. Tommy Caldwell's *The Push*: Climbing, Edgework and Media Perception of Risk   37
       Martin Hall

3. Thinking *with a* Mountain: A Narratological and Rhetorical Analysis of the Haptic Sublime in Jon Krakauer's Mountaineering Memoirs   57
       David Lombard

4. Transforming the Dirtbag Label in Kentucky's Red River Gorge   73
       James Maples and Michael Bradley

5. Decolonising Mountain Writing: Gender, Race and the Mini-Memoirs of the Digital Age   91
       Sarah Ives

II. INTERSECTIONAL REPRESENTATION IN MOUNTAINEERING

6. Bengal's Encounter with the Himalayas: Mountaineering
Beyond Conquest   115
   Anandarup Biswas

7. "Upon the whole I expect he took me for an aventurière":
British Women Grand Tourists' Accounts of Mountains
and Mountaineering   133
   Emma Gleadhill

8. "The Woman Business": Dorothy Pilley's *Climbing Days*   151
   Sarah Lonsdale

9. Wanda Rutkiewicz and Ewa Matuszewska: Deliberations on
the Auto/Biographical *Na jednej linie* [*On One Rope*]   169
   Agnieszka Kaczmarek

10. Julie Tullis: Gender and the Emotional Labour of Climbing
the "Mountain of Mountains"   189
    Jenny Hall

III. EMBODYING THE MOUNTAIN

11. The Total Mountain: Nan Shepherd and the Virtual Qualities
of Landscape   211
    Ben Garlick

12. The Representation of Play in Joe Simpson's *Touching the Void*
and Paratexts   233
    Anna Holman

13. Walking Mountains: Zen Practice and Ecological Awareness
in Peter Matthiessen's *The Snow Leopard*   251
    Christopher Kocela

14. Fatherhood, Emotional (Dis)Entanglements and Adventurous
Masculinities: Ben Fogle on Everest   269
    Paul Gilchrist

15. Politics of Representation in Mountaineering: Conclusion   289
    Jenny Hall and Martin Hall

Index   297

Acknowledgements

"I don't mind not getting to the top…It really doesn't matter…I had reached the clouds and climbed through them, going up and coming down…we had…survived; we had a future. This time I was content." (Tullis, 1987, p. 300)

Martin

I would first like to thank my wife, Victoria Hall, for enthusiastic and never-ending support in my writing and my climbing. Thanks also go to my colleagues at York St John University with whom I discussed the book, my climbing partners with whom I venture into the mountains and to my dad, for showing me the outdoors in the first place. And thanks, of course, to Jenny for being an amazing collaborator, colleague and friend.

Jenny

Difference is at the heart of this book and it is the authors who have contributed their diverse and insightful research that I thank. Thanks also to the series editors Stephen Wagg and Brett Lashua and my husband and climbing partner Louis Hume for their support. Finally, thank you Martin for inviting me to join in your vision to create this book – one day I hope we get to climb 'real' mountains too.

Contributors

Dr Martin Hall completed his PhD in British and European art cinema in 2013 and began teaching full-time at York St John University in 2014 where he is now a Senior Lecturer and the Course Leader for the Film and Media Studies programmes. His research centres on art, poetics and independence in the cinema, having written on Truffaut, Polanski, Antonioni and extensive work on Woody Allen. His current work is focused on climbing and mountaineering in the cinema, beginning with a conference paper on "Physical Achievements: Movement and the Human Body in the Climbing Film", a forthcoming chapter titled "A poet who climbed or a climber who writes poetry: The Poetry of cinema and movement in the Rock Climbing documentary" for the Cambridge Scholars edited volume, *The Art of Fact: The Place of Poetics Within Documentary Filming.*

Dr Jenny Hall is a Senior Lecturer at York St John University, United Kingdom and a cultural geographer interested in tourism, adventure sports and heritage. Her research explores embodiment, gender and emotional experiences in adventure environments from a feminist social justice perspective. More recently she has been exploring sustainability and spatial justice in historic cities. Jen is a Fellow of the Royal Geographical Society and Treasurer of Geographies of Leisure and Tourism Research Group. Jen is a mountaineer, ultra-mountain runner and member of her local mountain rescue team.

Anandarup Biswas teaches English Literature in Shibpur Dinobundhoo College, affiliated to the University of Calcutta where he is an Associate Professor. His research interests include travel writing and literature and the environment. His doctoral research is on Eric Rolls and Australian environmentalism. He has received the Australia-India Council Fellowship to visit reputed Australian universities for research activities. He is also the recipient of a University Research Fellowship from the University of Calcutta. His abiding interest in travel and travel writing has inspired him to pursue a research project funded by the University Grants Commission. The project explores the writings of Bengal's pilgrims to the Himalayas in the colonial period. An avid trekker, Anandarup enjoys walking and photographing in the Himalayas. Some of his walks and trips have been transformed into travel writing pieces for reputed Bengali travel magazines.

Dr Michael J. Bradley is an Associate Professor and currently serves as Chair in the Department of Agriculture and Tourism at Arkansas Tech University. His professional and academic interests include natural resource and wildlife tourism; recreation and tourism as economic development tools, and tourism related to beer, wine, and spirits. Dr Bradley's scholarship includes 45 peer reviewed publications, 216 professional publications and reports, 280 presentations, and serves on various national, state, and local boards related to outdoor recreation and natural resources. In his free time he enjoys visiting state parks and other natural areas, fishing, hunting, and coffee on the back porch. You can follow him on LinkedIn and Instagram @mikeisoutside.

Dr Ben Garlick is a Senior Lecturer in Geography at York St John University, where he has been based since 2017. Prior to this, he was based at the University of Edinburgh, where he worked towards his PhD in Geography, examining the historical geographies of bird of prey conservation in Scotland during the mid- and latter-twentieth century. His research interests concern the relationship between humans, animals and landscape, particularly in the context of conservation. He has written on the subject of landscape in relation to the protection of the Scottish osprey (*Pandion haliaetus*) and the haunted, entangled experiences of the environment produced through encounters between humans and this nationally threatened species. More recently he has turned to focus on landscape and human-nature relations in the work of authors such as Nan Shepherd and John Berger.

Dr Paul Gilchrist is Principal Lecturer in Human Geography, School of Applied Sciences at the University of Brighton, UK. He has researched, written and lectured primarily on the geographies of sport and leisure for two decades. Paul's work has appeared in many academic journals and books and his research has been funded by the British Academy and Arts and Humanities Research Council. He is a founding convenor of the Political Studies Association's Sport and Politics Study Group and joint Series Editor of the Advances in Leisure Studies book series published by Taylor & Francis. His doctoral research, completed in 2009, was on the cultural politics of heroism in British mountaineering and in 2013 he edited a special issue of *Sport in History* (Vol. 33, issue 3) on "Gender and British climbing histories". His most recent publication was in the *International Journal of the History of Sport* (2020) special issue on "Women and mountaineering" on the rise of charitable and postfeminist celanthropic activisms in climbing.

Emma Gleadhill a social and cultural historian based in Melbourne, Australia. Her research interests are in gender, material culture and travel. Her work uses a methodology which is informed by material culture, literary and design theory, tourism studies and the influential work of thinkers like Walter Benjamin and Susan Stewart to provide new perspectives on the history of the travel souvenir. She published her first academic monograph *Taking Travel Home: The Souvenir Material Culture of British Women Tourists, 1770–1830* in 2022. The book provides a historic analysis of the relationship between British women tourists and the objects they brought home during the late eighteenth and early nineteenth century. Ultimately, it argues that the rise of the souvenir during the period is representative of female agency, as women used their souvenirs to form spaces in which they could create and control their own travel narratives.

Anna Holman earned her PhD in Theater, Dance, and Performance Studies from the University of California, Santa Barbara in 2023. She received an MA at the University of British Columbia and a BA from Butler University. Her research includes climbing as performance, representations of climbing in theater and documentary film, and the performance of identity. Originally from Idaho, she enjoys spending time in the mountains hiking, backpacking, snowboarding and climbing.

Dr Sarah Ives is a broadly trained sociocultural anthropologist with a focus on gender and representation and the racial politics of climate change. She is the author of the book *Steeped in Heritage: The Racial Politics of South African Rooibos Tea* (2017), as well as numerous book chapters and peer-reviewed articles in journals such as *Gender, Place and Culture* and *American Anthropologist*. As a Mellon and Fulbright scholar, she received her doctorate in anthropology from Stanford University and her MA in geography from the University of Washington. She taught for four years in Stanford's Department of Writing and Rhetoric and Department of Anthropology and currently teaches cultural anthropology at City College of San Francisco.

Dr Agnieszka Kaczmarek is an Assistant Professor in the Department of Modern Languages at the University of Applied Sciences in Nysa, Poland (UAS). Her current interests concern twentieth- and twenty-first-century Polish and American literature, with a focus on nature and mountain-travel writing. In 2013, she published her doctoral dissertation entitled *Little Sister Death*, which constitutes the analysis of William Faulkner's *The Sound and the Fury* while bearing in mind the philosophies of death as presented by Max Scheler, Martin Heidegger, and Emmanuel Levinas. She has also published articles on Charles Dickens, Mark Twain, Harold Pinter, Thomas Merton, Edward Abbey, Eva Hoffman, Wanda Rutkiewicz, Arlene Blum, Bill Bryson, and Cormac McCarthy. She has also received a Fulbright Senior Award (2020–2021) to conduct research at California State University, Bakersfield.

Christopher Kocela is Associate Professor of English at Georgia State University where he teaches contemporary US literature, theory and popular culture. He is the author of *Fetishism and Its Discontents in Post-1960 American Fiction* and his essays and articles have appeared in the journals *Postmodern Culture, Genders, Comparative Literature and Culture,* and *LIT,* as well as in critical studies on the work of Thomas Pynchon, David Foster Wallace and Tim O'Brien. His current research examines intersections between Eastern thought (especially Buddhism) and the depiction of racial and gender difference in contemporary US fiction and life writing.

David Lombard is a research fellow at the Belgian National Fund for Scientific Research (F.R.S.-FNRS) and a PhD candidate in literary studies at the ULiège and KU Leuven (joint degree), where he is a researcher at the Interdisciplinary Center for Applied Poetics (CIPA), Intersections, and the Leuven English Literature Research Group. Besides, he was a visiting scholar at the University of Texas at Austin (fall 2022) and the Ohio State University (spring 2023) in the United States. Since 2018, he has been mainly working and publishing in the fields and areas of contemporary American literature and culture, life writing, theories of the sublime, Henry David Thoreau and American transcendentalism, the environmental humanities, rhetorical narrative theory, comparative literature, and the health humanities. He is the author of the book *Techno-Thoreau: Aesthetics, Ecology and the Capitalocene* (Macerata: Quodlibet, 2019), which served as an extended pilot study for his broader PhD project on the sublime and the rhetorics and narrations of self and environment in the contemporary American ecobiographical memoir (2020–2024), and his essays and book reviews have been published in academic journals such as *Épistémocritique*, *Miranda*, the *Journal of Arts and Media Studies*, the *Metacritic Journal for Comparative Studies and Theory*, *Local Environment*, *The Trumpeter*, and *Acta fabula*.

Dr Sarah Lonsdale is a Senior Lecturer in the Department of Journalism at City, University of London. Her latest book *Rebel Women Between the Wars* was published in 2020. She specialises in interwar women writers and journalists, with the above book including a biographical chapter on Dorothy Pilley.

Dr James N. Maples is a Professor of Sociology and Director of the Division of Regional Economic Assessment and Modelling (DREAM) at Eastern Kentucky University. His work examines the economic impact of sustainable tourism in rural and transitional economies, particularly those in Central Appalachia. His authoritative history of the Red River Gorge climbing community, *Rock Climbing in Kentucky's Red River Gorge: An Oral History of Community, Resources, and Tourism* was published in 2021 by West Virginia University Press.

Fiona Mossman is a Research Librarian at the Scottish Courts and Tribunals Service. She is a graduate of the University of Edinburgh, where she earned both an undergraduate MA in English Literature in 2016 and a postgraduate MSc in Book History and Material Culture in 2020. She has held posts in libraries in Oxford, Cambridge and Edinburgh, and her research interests embrace library history, literary studies and the cultures of the book. She also writes fiction and spends her free time seeking adventure as a mountaineer, skier and climber.

Introduction

Martin Hall and Jenny Hall

Considered to be the most literary of sports and leisure pursuits (McNee, 2017; Rak, 2021) mountaineering and mountain climbing have been prolifically documented through a range of media including the mountain memoir since the mid-1850s (Gifford, 2013). In this volume, we explore a burgeoning tradition of mountaineering literature, of cinema and of memoir to appreciate difference, beyond the habitual heroic, white male, adventurer that dominates screens and bookshelves. The authors offer both contemporary and historical embodied representations that show how mountaineering has been practised, constructed and commodified in multifaceted ways. Through exploring multidimensional axes of social differentiation from gender, race, class and age to dis/ability and sexuality, the book will demonstrate how commodification is embodied through representation in mountaineering literature, media, film and memoir in mountaineering spaces. Amongst our aims, this book intends to understand how multiple social dimensions overlap and work to produce independent systems of exclusion and inclusion that focus on untraditional ways of being a mountaineer. This volume contributes to the emerging field of mountain studies and particularly the discussion on diversity and difference in publicly consumable mountaineering representations. However, we, the authors, do acknowledge the dominance of Western academic voices and subjects in this volume and would call upon scholars to take seriously issues of inclusion across multiple axes of social distinction.

An attention towards representation in popular culture helps us to appreciate forms such as the memoir, and its closeness to (and association with) film and other media forms. The mountaineering memoir has a long and rich tradition, with adventure literature becoming legendary and further popularised through Hollywood movies. In *Memoir: A History*, Ben Yagoda makes the salient point that, "Memoir has become the central form of the culture" (2009, p. 35), the culture here being that of mountaineering. It is this centrality that is significant, indeed foundational, to this book. Through promulgating the powerful message that these books and films and paratexts expound, we problematise the neoliberal commercialisation of these highly sensitive mountain spaces and places through textual sources. In doing so, we challenge the dominant narrative of consumption in these leisure and tourism spaces and how we engage with sensitive mountain environments and their communities.

This collection draws together interdisciplinary scholarship across literary, historical, film studies and social sciences to help us think through how the representation of mountaineering in popular culture shapes mountaineering spaces and places and its implications. Since the earliest explorations by scientific geographers such as Alexander von Humboldt, mountains have held a brutal attraction inspiring terror, fascination and scientific curiosity, generating imaginative and material ideas concerning altitudinous locations and human experience over the last two centuries (Cosgrove & della Dora, 2009). One of the lesser-known aspects of von Humboldt's work are his written observations about his bodily reactions to the environment and how he embodied experiences of nature (Debarbieux, 2009). Strikingly, this tradition of the adventurer narrating embodied stories of mountaineering pervades in a burgeoning mountaineering literature, with over 2,000 mountaineering books in the British Library alone (Schaumann, 2020), written largely by the climbers themselves, who bear witness and "record their triumphs and tragedies" (Isserman, Weaver and Molenaar, 2008, p. x). These histories are almost uniquely singular and paradoxical, due in part to the team effort required to ascend the mountain, in contrast to the selective storytelling that constructs a mountaineering identity where "modern man stands alone on the summit, autonomous from other men and dominant over nature" (Hansen, 2013, p. 2). Schaumann (2020, p. 234) shows how nineteenth-century authors constructed a narrative of climbing achievement that was "bound in the political, racial and ethical ramifications of the frontier experience" that fails to recognise the rich cultural history of indigenous peoples, a factor that pervades today in the contested space of Himalayan mountaineering (Purtschert, 2020). Furthermore, the mountaineering memoir is almost exclusively representative of male achievements, with 94 percent of all memoirs being written by men (analysis focused on French and British authors, Moraldo, 2013), and, as a homosocial, masculinist and colonial endeavour, mountaineering is well documented as elitist and exclusionary pursuit (Gifford, 2013; Hall & Brown, 2022; Hunt, 2019) as Anandarup Biswas, Emma Gleadhill, Jenny Hall, Helen Mort, Sarah Lonsdale and Sarah Ives illustrate in this volume.

Since Ortner (1999) first conceptualised that mountaineering had been founded upon a cultural ideology epitomised in heroic white masculinities, the gendered nature of mountaineering has remained resistant to change (Hansen, 2013; Rak, 2021). In part, such resistance has been attributed to individual sovereignty, where man has the power to exercise authority over social and natural environments (Hansen, 2013). Hansen (2013) theorised how the liberalising political forces of modernity, during the 1850s, were tightly connected with the development of colonising scientific and nation-building adventure in mountainous regions. Performing individual sovereignty in mountaineering is "a story told over and over in best-selling books and films shown at film festivals around the world" (Rak, 2021, p. 34). Developing this, Rak shows how mountaineering as a gendered space intersects across multiple dimensions of exclusion, such as race and class:

> Sovereignty has a body in mind, but the properties of that body go unmentioned. This is why the discourse of mountaineering gender has been tied to political exercises of sovereignty over territory such as colonialism, or as the exercise of Romantic ideas about sovereignty when the mountains become places of leisure and adventure for certain classes. Ultimately, sovereignty is the reason why mountaineering came to depend heavily on the gendering of sovereign bodies as normatively white, European, able-bodied, male and heroic, without mentioning gender very much at all. (2021, p.34)

An interrogation of how commodifying forces of representation intersect and are then embodied is central to this volume. The mountaineering memoir has constructed a shared cultural ideology through narrating existential sense-making processes. These processes are transformative for mountaineers and for the host communities and spaces with which they interact. These stories are "the interpretation of the Seen or the reconstruction of the Unseen … [it is] … the art of confirming conjecture as to what is beyond … sight from 'signs' within view" (Winthrop Young, 1920, pp. 370 – 371). Previously and elsewhere, sociological explorations (Allen Collinson, Crust & Swann, 2019; Lewis, 2000) and a geographical turn to materiality (Brown, 2017; Bunn, 2022; Hall & Brown, 2022; Rickly-Boyd, 2012) have explored embodied experiences in mountain-eering, but this volume works to contend that mountaineering literature can be read as the expression of bodily knowledge passed down through stories told both verbally and physically.

However, the memoir is not an innocent genre in that it creates a sensorial regime that is embodied in the practices of mountaineering (Manning, 2007). Sensory expression represented through various media is politicised, codified and adheres to social norms that grade bodies (Ahmed, 2010; Hall & Brown, 2022). From this sensorial and physically embodied perspective, thinkers such as McNee (2017) have suggested that haptic understandings of mountaineering have a heritage born in the Victorian era. Driven by a more visceral experience of living and doing, climbing mountains was fuelled by a growing professionalisation of the medical world and an interest in the material workings of the human body which produced a turn to the haptic sublime, in which famous Victorian writer and mountaineer Leslie Stephen (1871) argued that to know a mountain one must climb it. Sensorial politics are manifest in the very nature of telling stories by whatever means. Class, gender and race all function to fix the sense of how the Westernised sport of mountaineering is conducted through the masculinised body-politics of how something 'should' be climbed. For example, Lewis (2000) notes that traditional styles of rock climbing in the UK have been dominated by the notion of climbing something 'cleanly' or without changing the nature of the rock by attaching permanent fixtures or manmade bolts to protect a climbing route. The early Victorian mountaineers were masters at categorising, codifying and classifying the space of mountaineering, which, this book argues, continues to be foundational to what, why and how mountains ought to be climbed. This is epitomised in what is still considered to be a mountaineering classic, Stephen's 1894 book *The Playground of Europe*. Stephen's visceral account of his mountaineering exploits in the Alps established extreme sporting or touristic adventures as a form of play – terminology that is widely used today to describe adventure tourism and sporting activities.

Our methodological approach aims to interrogate how mountaineering literary and media culture impact bodies, spaces and places; to nuance how commodification intersects across social categories and is embodied in multi-dimensional ways. Firstly, in "Part I: Commodification and the Mountain" the book interrogates the commodification of mountaineering, mountains and mountain pursuits. Subsequently, in "Part II: Intersectional Representation in Mountaineering", we question to what extent mountaineering texts create, rather than mirror reality, and how sustainable this literary genre is across multiple dimensions of social distinction (Miller & Mair, 2019; Rak, 2021; Watson, 2018). And finally, with 'Part III: Embodying the Mountain', our contributors explore the embodied relationship between mountaineering feats and the commodifying forces of media representation on embodied experiences through autobiographical literature. The volume explores these questions by interrogating how mountain and mountaineering texts, including those that are translated and adapted across media, have the power to influence the ethical consciousness of athletes, authors, filmmakers and crucially their audiences (Gifford, 2013). We examine how the influence of these texts has been harnessed, such as Chin and Vasarhelyi's Oscar and BAFTA-awarding winning film, *Free Solo* (2018), and what the social, cultural and ethical ramifications are on mountaineering spaces and places. As such the volume elucidates upon the representation and prominence of mountaineering, in its broadest meaning, through both the memoir and its associated paratexts.

Part I: Commodification and the Mountain

Mountaineering and climbing have become extraordinarily popular lifestyle sports. More generally, mountain-going has been one of the fastest growing leisure activities of the past thirty years. An estimated "10 million Americans go mountaineering annually" (Macfarlane, 2004, p. 17) and in the United Kingdom 2.48 million people participate in recreational rock climbing and mountaineering (Mintel, 2018). The American Alpine Club, in their annual State of Climbing Report noted that in 2018 there were "7.7 million" American climbers (2019, p. 6), "2,500 licenced USA climbing athletes" (2019, p. 10). In 2017, "climbing contributed $12,450,000,000 to the economy" (2019, p. 13), where in the UK, the British Mountaineering Council (BMC) membership currently stands at 80,000 individuals and 320 clubs. This wealth of attention and interest in the mountain, however, is underpinned by masculinist traditions and heroic ideologies which remain significant today.

Within the remit of the first part of this volume, the authors engage with various ideas encompassing the problematic commodification of mountains and mountaineering, from Maples and Bradley's work on "Dirtbags", examining the climber's place in rural economies and local resident perceptions of climber identities; to David Lombard's "Thinking for the Mountains", where he suggests that mountaineering memoirs provide new and more sustainable perspectives on the experience of sublime mountains as impacted by mass tourism; and Martin Hall's exploration of the influences of mediated perceptions of mountain spaces, places and pursuits.

Beginning this part, Fiona Mossman seeks to put the mountaineering memoir and other forms of writing in a "book historical" perspective to understand the use of books in mountaineering, and the extent to which these activities conditioned one another. The work focuses on the mountaineer Janet Adam Smith, whose explicit engagement with mountaineering and its literature as a reader, writer, collector, reviewer and translator of many mountaineering memoirs makes her a useful figure in this investigation. The chapter investigates how a mountaineer uses their books in personal, social, practical and imaginative meaning-making, both on and off the mountain, arguing that mountaineering books create, condition and thus commodify mountaineers' interactions with both mountains and other texts.

In Chapter Two, Martin Hall interrogates perceptions of risk as they adapt and adjust in relation to experience and mediation. In exploring the phenomenological success of a film like *Free Solo*, it is arguably the edgework in this "death-defying" film which has brought it the previously unseen success and indeed the "cultural significance" that has distinguished it from other climbing films. The chapter explores Peter Donnelly's definition of one of the fundamental characteristics of climbing as "the maintenance of a tension balance between difficulty and risk" (2003, p. 294) and views climbing film through the lens of Stephen Lyng's suggestion that "the voluntary pursuit of activities that involve a high potential for death, serious physical injury, or psychic harm – activities that I have termed as edgework – has acquired special cultural significance in the contemporary western world" (Lyng, 2008, p. 107).

In the following chapter, David Lombard evaluates, through a close narratological and rhetorical analysis of Jon Krakauer's mountaineering memoirs, the affordances and limits of using notions such as the "haptic" and "toxic" – sexist and/or elitist – sublime to represent mountains.

These notions are then also related to concepts pertaining to the field of environmental humanities such as Stacy Alaimo's "trans-corporeality", which emphasises that humans are constantly "intermeshed" with the non-human world, thus providing an appropriate framework to examine the emotional and affective dimensions of representations of sublime mountains (2010, p. 2).

James Maples and Michael Bradley, with Chapter Four, then examine the climber's place in rural economies and local resident perceptions of climber identities in those economies. The 'dirtbag' lifestyle remains in the climbing community's ethos even as the label becomes dated; recent studies by Maples and Bradley in several states indicate that climbers today are a valued source of economic impact in rural communities, including parts of Central Appalachia, where climbers have been recognised by some as a sustainable form of economic growth which supports transitioning away from resource extraction. In Chapter Five, Sarah Ives follows this up, focusing specifically on Instagram and on what she terms the "Mini-Memoirs" which the format affords. Groups such as @browngirlsclimb, @nativesoutdoors, @melaninbasecamp, and @brownpeoplecamping are attempting to use Instagram to widen the range of voices and, significantly, affect whose images are heard and seen in the climbing world. To explore the role of social media in creating new forms of mountain writing, the chapter demonstrates how writing in conventional formats, such as nonfiction books and magazines, has configured mountains as white, male spaces (Finney, 2014; Kosek, 2006; Spence, 1999). The threads of commodification which bind these authors together concern how our desire to tell a story catalyses the processes of commodification, which is embodied in a multitude of different ways.

Through historical and contemporary mountaineering experiences, these chapters coalesce to demonstrate how the commodification of storytelling is founded within heroic white, class-based, masculine ideologies.

Part II: Intersectional Representation in Mountaineering

Part II foregrounds a heterogeneity of voices within the mountain memoir. This diverse collection of authors explores how race, class and gender matter and what they can show us concerning inclusion in mountaineering representation. In Chapter Six Anandarup Biswas asks what drove a group of young men (and later, women) who were poles apart from privileged, White European mountaineers eager to establish their supremacy over nature and fellow climbers, to risk everything for climbing an Everest or a Kanchenjunga. Was it the same, intrepid, albeit arrogant, spirit of adventure that made colonial mountaineers conduct their assaults? The chapter engages with an understanding of mountaineering in the age of nation building that had been driven by an expeditionary zeal which was justified by the post-Enlightenment, colonial urge to explore and possess the uncharted territories of the earth. Bengal's attitude to the Himalayas, as he argues, was not tempered by the Western spirit of conquest, even though Western modernity shaped its cultural practices in many other ways. By tracing the long history of Bengal's encounter with the Himalayas in the form of pilgrims, scholars and walkers, and by considering the rich and diverse literature inspired by Himalayan travel, Biswas argues that Bengal's climbers and travellers sought to achieve goals that were in fact different from those aspired to by the conquest-driven climbers of the West.

With Chapter Seven, Emma Gleadhill analyses the ways in which contingent meanings of femininity emerged and gained legitimacy through women's efforts to record their mountaineering experiences in their journals and take specimens from their vertical feats. Women could enlist these texts and objects as prompts to tell stories of their bold explorations long after returning home. Eighteenth-century women's accounts of mountaineering have not yet been considered in light of subsequent women's mountaineering memoirs, but the inclusion of this chapter in the volume is to suggest that there is more continuity between the two than has been acknowledged. A historical view reveals the aesthetic and cultural work that mountains have long performed as women have described them in ways designed to communicate messages about mountain environments and themselves.

Sarah Lonsdale follows this up with Chapter Eight, exploring Dorothy Pilley's account of her first experience of climbing in the Alps in the summer of 1920 and suggesting that this book defiantly places a woman, in breeches, sweating and panting in a physically dangerous environment amidst the "unshaven" manly mountaineers of the interwar period. It also, unusually, reveals a woman meditating on the beauty and vastness of "the wild", attempting to understand the urge to propel oneself to the limits of physical strength to participate in it. The chapter engages with how the memoir expresses this woman's sense of being out of place, an intruder, and only of use to supply a hairpin to help unblock a male mountaineer's pipe. This memoir of early post-First World War climbing, published in 1935, Lonsdale suggests, is so much more than a technical log of new routes, equipment used and peaks conquered, of which there were dozens published during the interwar period; Dorothy Pilley's *Climbing Days* (1965) is a radically feminist text which chronicles the first "manless" rope ascent of an Alpine peak at a time when women mountaineers, who climbed without male guides or leaders, were characterised as "insane" and "a disgrace" in the leading mountaineering publication of the age, the *Alpine Journal* (1929, p. 423).

In Chapter Nine, Agnieszka Kaczmarek addresses Wanda Rutkiewicz's *Na jednej linie [On One Rope]*, questioning which genre the book demonstrates and attempting to clarify the authorship of the autobiographical account. To the Polish readership, recently more and more interested in mountain-travel literature, the salient primary source of information on Wanda Rutkiewicz's mindset as well as the events regarding the momentous ascent of Everest she is remembered for has been this account. First edited in 1986, Kaczmarek explores why it continues to be a contentious book. Jenny Hall then concludes the section with Chapter Ten in which she explores the emotional politics of risk in mountaineering literature through Julie Tullis's memoir *Clouds from Both Sides* (1986), offering insight into how Tullis navigated this environment so successfully and the emotional tactics she developed, by necessity, to do so. Through the lens of emotional politics Julie's experiences offer insight into the different ways she represents her mountaineering achievements and the emotional labour she experienced. This deepens our understanding of how women negotiate power-laden relations in high-altitude environments to create different spaces of adventure. The implications for identifying inequalities offer insight for diversifying the mountain memoir by problematising this "singular white history" and call for different heritages in mountaineering to be recognised (Hunt, 2019, p. 3).

This section explores how early women mountain tourists played a role in the development of the "imaginative constructions of the mountain and the activity of mountaineering in relation to the self" and works to emphasise the absence of women mountaineers from mountaineering literature in the twentieth century. Excluding difference has had a long tradition and this intersectional analysis will show how mountaineering is conducted in very different ways when a diversity of voices are represented.

Part III: Embodying the Mountain

The book's third part then seeks to challenge the prevailing narrative and the conception of how the body is represented and thus performs in the mountains, the body becoming socially and culturally imbued with semiotic meaning sedimented through its textual heroic antecedents. Garlick interrogates the embodied experiences and forces which are produced by immersion in the mountains through analysing the affective forces of Nan Shepherd's work. Kocela explores Matthieson's *Snow Leopard* (1978) through Zen philosophy and challenges anthropocentric approaches to mountains to build greater embodied ecological awareness. Anna Holman suggests that the space for future mountain narratives is performed on the mountaineer's body itself and offers a different kind of spatiality and temporality that incorporates new ways to imagine mountain spaces and places.

In Chapter Eleven, Ben Garlick develops the notion of "the total mountain" introduced within Nan Shepherd's *The Living Mountain*, in concert with the lyrical evocations of landscape found throughout Shepherd's prose and poetry, rooted in her own experiences of northeast Scotland's environment. It figures her writing as offering, after Brian Massumi (2002), a series of "exemplars", or "parables", that both articulate and sensitise us to the affective qualities of space. The chapter presents Shepherd's concept of "the total mountain" as framing an alternative ontology of the mountainous as situated, excessive and alive with potential. Chapter Twelve, by Anna Holman, then analyses how Joe Simpson's book, *Touching the Void* (1988) and its paratexts create mountains of the mind through the multivariant mediums of literature, film and drama. In so doing the chapter posits that the phenomenological mountain, the actual mountain and the mountain which holds space for future narratives, is performed on the mountaineer's body. In Chapter Thirteen Kocela examines the representation of mountaineering as a form of ecological Zen practice in Peter Matthiessen's *The Snow Leopard*; he contends that Matthiessen's memoir draws heavily on the de-anthropocentric representation of mountains "walking" and "flowing" in Zen master Dōgen's "Mountains and Waters Sutra" (1243), which Matthiessen first read while editing his *Dolpo* journals for publication between 1976 and 1978.

In Chapter Fourteen Paul Gilchrist extends the analysis of the incommensurability of parenthood and mountaineering and the particular vitriol given to "mountaineering mothers" (Frohlick, 2006; Gilchrist,

2007) through close textual reading of a memoir that is one of few to explicitly address the subject of fatherhood, family and a life of extreme adventuring. The chapter draws upon and analyses the memoir, *Up: My Life's Journey to the Top of Everest* (2018), written by British TV personality and adventurer Ben Fogle and his wife Marina Fogle. This dual-voiced memoir narrates Ben Fogle's boyhood dream of summiting Everest, whilst revealing the emotional process of a grieving father confronting a recent stillbirth and missing his remaining children.

In an employment of varied and multifarious perspectives, the chapters in this volume are curated with the clear intention of engaging with multitudes of difference through numerous power geometries. In questioning the scope of mountain literature, this book nuances dominant narratives of consumption within leisure and tourism spaces by contributing novel accounts of mountain environments and the communities associated therein.

Bibliography

Ahmed, S. (2010) "Happy objects", in Gregg, M. and Seigworth, G.J. (eds) *The Affect Theory Reader*. Durham, NC: Duke University Press, pp. 29–51.

Brown, K.M. (2017) "The haptic pleasure of ground feel: The role of textured terrain", *Health & Place*, 46, pp. 307–314.

Bunn, M. (2022) "The Edgeworker's Habitus: Climbing and Ordinary Risks", in Świtek, B., Abramson, A. and Swee, H. (eds) *Extraordinary Risks, Ordinary Lives: Logics of Precariousness in Everyday Contexts*. Cham: Palgrave Macmillan, pp. 177–201.

Cosgrove, D. and della Dora, V. (2009) *High Places*. London: I.B. Tauris & Co. Ltd.

Debarbieux, B. (2009) "Between pure reason and embodied experience", in Cosgrove, D. and della Dora, V. (eds) *High Places*. London: I.B. Tauris & Co. Ltd., pp. 87–105.

Dōgen, E. (2010) "Mountains and Waters Sutra", in Tanahashi, K. (ed.) *Treasury of the True Dharma Eye: Zen Master Dōgen's Shobo Genzo*. Boston: Shambhala, pp. 154–164.

Finney, C. (2014) *Black Faces, White Spaces: Reimagining the Relationship of African Americans to the Great Outdoors*. Chapel Hill: The University of North Carolina Press.

Fogle, B. (2018) *Up: My Life's Journey to the Top of Everest*. London: William Collins.

Free Solo (2018) Directed by Jimmy Chin, Elizabeth Chai Vasarhelyi [DVD]. USA: National Geographic.

Frohlick, S. (2006) "'Wanting the children and wanting K2': The incommensurability of motherhood and mountaineering in Britain and North America in the late twentieth century", *Gender, Place & Culture*, 13(5), pp. 477–490.

Gifford, T. (2013) "Early women mountaineers achieve both summits and publication in Britain and America", in Gomez Reus, T. and Gifford, T. (eds) *Women in Transit through Literary Liminal Spaces*. London: Palgrave Macmillan, pp. 91–106.

Hall, J. and Brown, M.K. (2022) "Creating feelings of inclusion in adventure tourism: Lessons from the gendered, sensory and affective politics of professional mountaineering", *Annals of Tourism Research*, 97, 103505. https://doi.org/10.1016/j.annals.2022.103505.

Hansen, P.H. (2013) *The Summits of Modern Man*. Cambridge, MA: Harvard University Press.

Hunt, R. (2019) "Historical geography, climbing and mountaineering: route setting for an inclusive future", *Geography Compass*, 13(4), Article e12423.

Isserman, M., Weaver, S. and Molenaar, D. (2008) *Fallen Giants: A History of Himalayan Mountaineering from the Age of Empire to the Age of Extremes*. Newhaven, CT: Yale University Press. http://www.jstor.org/stable/j.ctt1nqb0n.

Kosek, J. (2006) *Understories: The Political Life of Forests in Northern Mexico*. Durham, NC: Duke University Press.

Lewis, N. (2000) "The climbing body, nature and the experience of modernity", *Body & Society*, 6(1), pp. 58–80.

Lyng, S. (2008) "Edgework, Risk, and Uncertainty", in Zinn, J.O. (ed.) *Social Theories of Risk and Uncertainty: An Introduction*. London: Wiley Blackwell.

Manning, E. (2007) *Politics of Touch: Sense, Movement, Sovereignty*. Minneapolis, MN: University of Minnesota Press.

Massumi, B. (2002) *Parables for the Virtual: Movement, Affect, Sensation*. Durham, NC: Duke University Press.

Matthiessen, P. (2008) *The Snow Leopard* [1978]. New York: Penguin.

McNee, A. (2017) *The New Mountaineer in Late Victorian Britain: Materiality, Modernity, and the Haptic Sublime*. London: Palgrave Macmillan.

Miller, M.C. and Mair, H. (2020) "Between space and place in mountaineering: navigating risk, death, and power", *Tourism Geographies*, 22(2), pp. 354–369.

Mintel (2018) Leisure Review – UK – December 2018. http://academic.mintel.com/display/859751/.

Moraldo, D. (2013) "Gender relations in French and British mountaineering. The lens of autobiographies of female mountaineers, from d'Angeville (1794-1871) to Destivelle (1960–)", *Journal of Alpine Research | Revue de géographie alpine*, 101–1. https://doi.org/10.4000/rga.2027.

Ortner, S. (1999) *Life and Death on Mount Everest*. Princeton: Princeton University Press.

Pilley, D. (1965) *Climbing Days* [1935]. London: Secker and Warburg.

Powers, P. (2019) State of Climbing Report, American Alpine Club. Available at: http://americanalpineclub.org/state-of-climbing-report (Accessed: 10 October 2022).

Purtschert, P. (2020) "White masculinity in the death zone: transformations of colonial identities in the Himalayas", *Culture and Religion*, 21(1), pp. 31–42, DOI: 10.1080/14755610.2020.1858546.

Rak, J. (2021) *False Summit: Gender in Mountaineering Nonfiction*. London: McGill-Queen's University Press.

Rickly-Boyd, J.M. (2012) "Lifestyle climbing: Toward existential authenticity", *Journal of Sport & Tourism*, 17(2), pp. 85–104, DOI: 10.1080/14775 085.2012.729898.

Rutkiewicz, W. and Matuszewska, E. (2010) *Na jednej linie [On One Rope]*. Warszawa: Wydawnictwo Iskry.

Schaumann, C. (2020) *Peak Pursuits: The Emergence of Mountaineering in the Nineteenth Century*. New Haven, CT: Yale University Press. https://doi.org/10.2307/j.ctv138wr6d.

Shepherd, N. (2011) *The Living Mountain* [1977]. Edinburgh: Canongate.

Simpson, J. (2004) *Touching the Void: The True Story of One Man's Miraculous Survival*. Revised. Perennial.

Stephen, L. (1871) *The Playground of Europe*. London: Spottiswoode and Co.

Spence, D. (1999) *Dispossessing the Wilderness: Indian Removal and the Making of the National Parks*. Cary, NC: Oxford University Press.

Tullis, J. (1987) *Clouds from both Sides*. 2nd edn. London: Grafton Books.

Watson, B. (2018) "Thinking intersectionally and why difference (still) matters in feminist leisure and sport research", in Mansfield, L., Caudwell, J., Wheaton, B., and Watson B. (eds) *The Palgrave Handbook of Feminism and Sport, Leisure and Physical Education*. London: Palgrave Macmillan, pp. 313–334.

Winthrop Young, G. (1920) *Mountain Craft*. London: Kessinger Publishing.

Yagoda, B. (2009) *Memoir: A History*. London: Riverhead Books.

I. COMMODIFICATION
AND THE MOUNTAIN

Chapter 1

Scripted Summits

Book History, Mountaineering, and the Experiences of Janet Adam Smith (1905–1999)

Fiona Mossman

Mountains, standing above the rest of the landscape, hard places to live in or to cultivate, have long been sites of religious, scientific and cultural significance across the world. As parts of the natural environment, they are often portrayed as unchanging, untamed, uncaring. But, as Simon Schama notes, "Even the landscapes that we suppose to be most free of our culture may turn out, on closer inspection, to be its product" (2004, p. 9). Every interaction with "nature" is coded by the ways in which nature is understood and discussed, as many scholars have pointed out (Debarbieux et al., 2015; della Dora, 2016; Grebowicz, 2021; Macfarlane, 2003). A significant part of the cultural encoding of mountains and the activity of mountaineering is through books, and in particular, the mountaineering memoirs that emerged at the same time as mountaineering itself. This is the starting point for this chapter, which aims to investigate how books condition our mountain experiences in practice, in the context of mountaineering.

Mountaineering, as one particular way of experiencing the mountain world, is distinctive among many other sports and leisure activities in its symbiotic relationship to books. This chapter seeks to use the methods of book history to understand the uses of books (including but not limited to the act of reading) in mountaineering, and the extent to which these activities conditioned each other. To do so, I will focus on one particular mountaineer, Janet Adam Smith, a woman-of-letters whose mountaineering began in earnest in 1929 and whose passion for both mountains and books was lifelong. Born to an intellectual Scottish family, educated at Oxford, living through two world wars, the enfranchisement of women in Britain and European post-war recovery, Janet Adam Smith (who wrote under her maiden name) was among the first women openly able to earn a degree and to work at the BBC, where she became an editor and reviewer at *The Listener*. Though she left the BBC upon her marriage in 1935, she later held jobs at *The Criterion* and *The New Statesman* and published biographies of Robert Louis Stevenson and John Buchan along with edited volumes of poetry. She also wrote a mountaineering memoir, *Mountain Holidays*, and translated several mountaineering books, including a co-translation of the bestselling *Annapurna* (1952) by Maurice Herzog with her friend and fellow mountaineer Nea Morin. Together with her husband, poet, fellow mountaineer and schoolteacher Michael Roberts (1902–1948), she amassed a collection of mountaineering books, of which about 200 were donated to the University of Oxford to form part of the Oxford Mountaineering Library (OML). Her explicit engagement with mountaineering and its literature in various roles makes her a useful figure in this investigation. Her identity provides an approach into the issues of class, gender, ethnicity and nationality which operate, materially and aesthetically, in the worlds of mountains and books, while her status as an "average" rather than pioneering climber goes some way towards diversifying the narrative of mountaineering and focusing on continuity, rather than disruption, in the sport's history.

She is also well-placed in the history of what will be referred to here as the mountaineering book or the mountaineering memoir, which was established and influential during her lifetime. These books, which took shape alongside mountaineering itself in what became known as the "Golden Age" of mountaineering, 1854–1865, are first-person, non-fictional accounts, with textual roots in the writing of science, the sublime and the Romantic poets, and often with material analogues to guidebooks and travelogues. In the books that mediated the mountain, the values and assumptions of the mountaineer-authors found a form that, while far from universal, is nonetheless very significant when it comes to understanding the cultural and social place of mountaineering. Where Europe's mountains had previously been nameless and feared, in the writing of eighteenth- and nineteenth-century scientists, travellers and poets the summit became scripted, becoming both the goal and the definition of mountaineer and mountain alike. This can be found in the accounts of those who climbed in the name of science, such as Horace Bénédict de Saussure's *Voyages dans les Alpes*; in the aesthetics of the sublime that reconfigured Europe's wild places from places of negative fear and unknowability into places of positive "delectable horror" (Schama, 2004, p. 449); and subsequently with the Romantic poets who carved out an imaginative space that enabled mountaineering to be both an act of culture as well as an act of science and self-expression (Bainbridge, 2020). It was the Victorian mountaineers, however, who gave shape to the mountaineering memoir, alongside their first ascents. These books, as McNee explains, shared a "celebration of adventure, physical challenge, and the measured but unflinching acceptance of an element of risk" (2016, p. 16), and it was their influence that future mountaineering memoir writers wrote from and responded to.

These mountaineering memoirs fulfilled several roles. On a practical level, mountaineering books allowed the dissemination of the author's scientific results or sporting ethos, alongside benefits to finance and reputation. They also served the function of proof, testifying that the conceptual space of the summit had been reached, which was, as Gifford points out, a key reason for mountaineering's literary nature (2013, p. 92). A textual record allowed the author/mountaineer to script *themselves* onto the summit. This practice transforms the act of mountain-climbing into a readable history, without which the summit would not hold its imaginative power. As Leslie Stephen put it in *The Playground of Europe*:

> The Schreckhorn will probably outlast even the British Constitution and the Thirty-nine Articles: so long as it lasts, and so long as Murray and Baedeker describe its wonders [...] its first conqueror may be carried down to posterity by clinging to its skirts. (1871, pp. 73–74)

So long as Murray and Baedeker and their successors write their guidebooks, indeed, but also so long as those books are read. These mountaineering books influenced many future adventurers, for example the bestselling *Scrambles Amongst the Alps* by Edward Whymper (1871). Acknowledging its effect on his own mountaineering, Arnold Lunn wrote in 1957 that "no book made more converts to mountaineering than the famous *Scrambles*" (1912, p. 61). The mountaineer who read mountaineering texts often produced their own, such as Lunn and, indeed, Adam Smith.

To investigate mountaineering through the lens of book history, we must acknowledge the book as "a text, an object, a transaction and an experience" (Howsam, 2015, p. 3), in dialogue with other systems: economic, social, political and cultural. Following Robert Darnton, this can be understood as a communications circuit, which runs full cycle from writer to publisher, bookseller and reader, where the reader can connect to a new cycle as writer. This cycle "transmits messages, transforming them en route, as they pass from thought to writing to printed characters and back to thought again" (Darnton, 2015, p. 234). The mountaineering book communication circuit is remarkable in the swiftness of its cycle: readers of mountaineering books were very often the authors of new mountaineering books, and the rise of mountaineering as a leisure activity was intimately linked to its texts. For mountaineers who read, in particular the mountaineering exploits that inspired the reader's next climbs, but also for readers of poetry and other reading matter, this cycle includes the experience of the mountain. The experience of the mountain then contributes to the experiences of reading and writing, and thus it functions as an extra component of Darnton's cycle, pointing outside, to a world that is at once beyond the book and conditioned by the book. In the following sections, I will investigate how one particular mountaineer used her books both on and off the mountainside, and how this affected the meaning of both the books and the mountains.

The Mountain Book in the Lowlands

If mountaineering is, as it was at least in part for Janet Adam Smith, a way of escaping the "problems and preoccupations of your lowland life" (1932, p. 351), then what was the effect of bringing the mountaineering book into the home – bringing the mountain, as it were, indoors? The evidence within Adam Smith's book collection and her mountaineering memoir provides not a complete record of reading – such a thing being all but impossible – but a partial and fascinating glimpse into how books can become part of a mountaineer's life. I will be using this evidence to demonstrate how books become part of the historical record, propelling mountaineering through the imaginative space that reading and writing take up; how books can be interpersonal objects, inscribed with individual memories and social currency; and how they relate to both the mountaineer's identity, and the fact of the mountain itself, which is a necessary reference for the type of book that we can call the mountaineering memoir.

In *Mountain Holidays*, Adam Smith notes that "the right place for the mountain classics is by one's own fire on autumn evenings, and not in one's Alpine luggage" (1946, p. 95). Here, we can start to see how the place of reading is significant when it comes to mountain memoirs. The right place, both for Adam Smith and others, is defined in opposition to being on the mountain: static, familiar, in your own home, preferably beside the comfortable, cheerful fireplace. It is also defined in time: time that is for leisure (the evening), but leisure time that is not being used to go on a mountain holiday (autumn, or the "winter reading" [1946, p. 96] that she also mentions). Historians of reading have argued that the space in which a book is read interpenetrates the experience and meaning of the book to its reader: "the sights, the sounds and even the smells of such reading places interpenetrated 'the emotional and cerebral affects of the text'" (Colclough, 2011, p. 100). For Adam Smith, what is particularly notable about her reading of mountaineering texts at home is that they are able to combine "the world of rock and ice" with "the world of men" (1946, p. 95). She notes the "beautiful emblems, title-pages, and dedications" of the mountaineering books of the "Ladies" which she began to collect, highlights Douglas Freshfield as "the humanist of the Alps", and celebrates George Yeld's "delight in poetry and flowers" (1946, p. 95). Evidently she valued the books that enabled her to align the mountains with a certain type of "civilisation", mediated via the Victorian mountaineers' textuality and inflected with her own tastes. While safe at home, this type of reading experience gains potency by contrasts: travelling while staying put, experiencing danger from a place of safety, with the emotional and cerebral effects of the text putting the inhuman mountain in the context of an imaginative space mediated by the book.

Reading is only part of the experience of the book, and when we examine Adam Smith's mountaineering collection, we can find all sorts of examples of her engagement. Clipped newspaper stories on Everest expeditions are inserted into two books of the same subject (Bodleian Libraries, *Forerunners to Everest* and *Ascent to Everest*), which suggests a way of linking the reading of the books to the current moment or a future history. Another document inserted into a book reveals the ways in which Adam Smith acknowledged and aided the historical record: tucked into her copy of *The Indian Alps and How We Crossed Them, by a Lady Pioneer* is a letter from Auckland Public Library requesting assistance in identifying the "lady pioneer", Nina Elizabeth Mazuchelli, and notes for a reply (Bodleian Libraries, *The Indian Alps*), implying not only reading of but reading around the text to find out Mazuchelli's identity.

Adam Smith's work as a reviewer can also be seen amongst her books, as notes and articles are interleaved in many of them: the

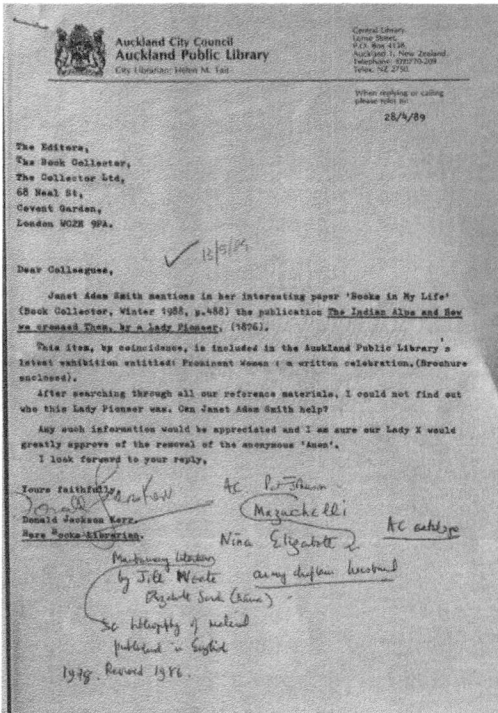

Figure 1.1: The letter inserted into Janet Adam Smith's copy of *The Indian Alps and how we crossed them*
Source: The Radcliffe Science Library, Bodleian Libraries, University of Oxford, Shelfmark: OML/Himalayas:MAZ

mountaineering memoir, for her as for so many others, was part of her profession and her income, and this, too, changes the experience of the book. For Adam Smith as a reviewer, she helped to transmit the values written into these texts. We can see her admiration for the Victorian books of her father when, many years on from her first encounter with them, she wrote a review praising *The Puma's Claw* in 1959 in terms that recall Leslie Stephen: she praises it for displaying the "spirit of a cheerful Alpine holiday" that recaptured for the mountaineer-authors and their readers "the high Victorian zest of the men who made the Alps their playground" (1959, p. 378). In her role of authority as the reviewer, she frames these Alpine classics as the apogee of mountaineering writing for those who might not have as extensive a background in the subject as she has. Her involvement in the communications circuit of mountaineering books fitted many different roles, and through her own reading experiences she helped to shape other peoples' encounters with the texts and mountains that she then wrote about.

But it is less the historical record than the personal one that is written all over Adam Smith's books. "I do have to bring in a lot of personal and family memories when I talk about my books, because they have been so much in the mainstream of my life" (1988, p. 2) she said in her talk on her book collecting, emphasising the links between books and memory and books and relationships. These relationships imbued some of her most treasured mountaineering books with particular meaning: a "fragile first edition" of Whymper's *Scrambles*, together with Tyndall's *Hours of Exercise in the Alps* and Stephen's *Playground*, she remembers fondly as having been introduced to her by her father, George Adam Smith (1988, p. 2). She inherited these books and others that had family significance, such as a limited edition book called *The Pioneers of the Alps*, a gift from fellow-mountaineer C.E. Mathews to her parents on the occasion of their wedding (1988, p. 2), and it was these memories and relationships that she highlighted as being special to her in her collection of books. Carrying on the traditions of books as material signs of important relationships, she and her husband exchanged many such gifts, including Whymper's

Figure 1.2: Janet Adam Smith in
front of a bookcase
Source: Adam Roberts

Ascent of the Matterhorn (a popular version of *Scrambles*); Keats' letters, accompanied by crampons; and when they were engaged, the "jewel in the collection", William Windham's *Account of the Glaciers or Ice Alps in Savoy* (1988, pp. 5–6). Sometimes these relationships are inscribed into the book, reminding us of how printed books, designed to be replicated, become unique in the hands of their owners and readers: the copy of *The High Alps in Winter* by pioneering winter climber Elizabeth Le Blond (one of the "Ladies") held by the OML contains the inscription "Janet Roberts with love from Michael 1.III.42" (Bodleian Libraries). For Adam Smith, reading these texts would have been not just an exercise in reading the words of an author but also a way of remembering the people with whom she associated these books. The book becomes a way of bringing the place, the people and the relationships together, proving that "every book", like every mountainside, "is a potential meeting place" (Mole, 2019, p. 108).

Reading, collecting and adding to these books allowed Janet Adam Smith to remember the people and places that were linked to her via these physical objects. They also helped her to demonstrate her own self-identity as a mountaineer, even while not on the mountain. For example, Adam Smith's understanding of herself as both a woman and a mountaineer can be seen when she notes that she takes "special pleasure" in owning many books by the lady pioneers and their less aristocratic successors, where many of the latter, "Dorothy Pilley, Miriam Underhill, Micheline Morin, Nea Morin, have been my friends" (1988, pp. 11–12). The knowledge of the women who have preceded her informs her own identity and ambitions: "if I, who had fallen heir so easily to the territory they had won for women climbers, could claim a tenth of their independence, initiative and courage, then I could be well pleased with myself" (1946, p. 127). Adam Smith's mountaineering rarely centres on her experience of womanhood: for example, her only reference to having her first child in 1937 was that she was relieved to find that "being a mother didn't spoil one's balance" (1946, p. 170). However being a mother did, in the end, impact both her climbing activities and her attitude to risk, turning the focus away from intense mountain days and towards "pleasant scramble[s]" (1982, p. 154). By contrast her friend, co-translator and fellow-mountaineer Nea Morin built her mountaineering and rock-climbing activities around her femininity, setting new records in all-female groups with her practice of *cordée féminine*. Adam Smith partook in this practice after her husband's death in 1948, but in general her mountaineering was in mixed parties. Her solo mountaineering trips in Scotland in the early 1930s were deliberate exercises in equipping herself with the skills needed to be a capable mountaineer and an equal partner (1946, p. 19), and after a lifetime in the mountains she "claimed that [...] she'd never been discriminated against" (Noble, 1994, p. 26). While playing down both traditional gender roles and a feminism of exceptionalism, Adam Smith was nonetheless very aware of the debt she owed to the female climbers who had preceded and accompanied her, and she frames this historical record in a personal way through her mountaineering books.

While the place of reading may be in the comfort of one's own home, where researching the book's author and inserting newspaper cuttings can be done with ease, the place that the mountaineering memoir depends upon and refers to is never out of view: the mountain itself. For the reader of the mountaineering memoir, this experience of the place of the mountain in the book can be one of memory or one of antici-pation. Returning from her first Alpine trip in 1929 to find that the *Alpine Journals* and mountaineering books in her parents' house "were no longer just part of the furniture of home", Adam Smith "spent hours on the floor beside them, picking out, of course, all those which referred to the Rimpfischhorn and the Zinalrothorn" (1946, p. 16), mountains that she had recently climbed, where reading combined with remembered experience.

These books also helped to shape the future goals of the mountaineers. Their maps promised the reader accuracy in relation to the mountain's terrain, while the way in which they described and inscribed what was worth pursuing shaped what mountaineers' desire: for example, David Roberts, Reinhold Messner, Joe Simpson and Robert Macfarlane all cite *Annapurna* as the inspiration for their own mountaineering, and the epic, heroic qualities of Herzog's narrative was a large part of that influence (Macfarlane, 2003; Rak, 2007). Nea Morin, meanwhile, fulfilled an ambition to climb the east face of the Grépon in a climb with Adam Smith in 1995, having read about the first ascent in Geoffrey Winthrop Young's *On High Hills* (1968, p. 187). This, then, is what is notable about the books of mountaineering: in a communications circuit that encompassed many of the same people at various stages of the book's journey, as readers became writers and writers became reviewers, the mountain was an external, impersonal actor. The mountains led to the books, and the books in turn led to the mountains.

The Book on the Mountain

The mountaineer and the book of the mountain are both defined by reference to the mountain, and when the location of book and reader is taken out of the lowlands and set into the highlands, these physical and material realities interfuse with the book's meanings. The place where both the activity of the mountaineer and the experience of the book could occur, the mountain, is impersonal, atextual, natural, yet part of the cultural, social, economic and political world, as books are. Embracing a wider purview of both "the book" and "the mountaineer", the experiences of readers on the mountains will be explored, where the book as purely material or purely immaterial becomes extremely significant, where the social and personal meanings of the book are enhanced, and where the vagabond reader, the "poacher" (Chartier, 2015, p. 254) across the fixed boundaries of landscape and textscape, becomes integral to an understanding of how the mountain and the book make meaning in the book culture of mountaineering.

Here, I take the "experience" to be both reading and more nebulous activities of the book. In King's study of soldiers' uses of books in the First World War we get a sense of the possibilities:

> Unopened, it could be a symbol of the familiar or everyday world beyond the war. The act of reading, skimming, or holding it, meanwhile, offered a soldier a way of occupying the mind and preventing the intrusion of unwanted thoughts, particularly in situations where physical movement was limited, such as periods of prolonged bombardment. (2014, p. 376)

A holiday in the Alps obviously does not have the same connotations as a soldier's experience of war, but in the meanings that the book gains in the relationship between book, place and experience, we can see that "textual significance is not necessarily fixed and spatially transcendent, but is formed in the moment and at the site of encounter" (Keighren, 2006, p. 529). When the site of encounter is a mountain, with its steep and dangerous slopes, its culturally scripted beauty, its local communities, and its new railways, huts and infrastructure that have been built for mountain activities, the reader's encounter with the book becomes affected conceptually, materially, socially and personally.

Reading was and is a common mountain experience. In huts and inns, reading matter is strewn around for the visitor to avail themselves of while visitors' books allow mountaineers to write and peruse the experiences of the mountaineering community. While some of these reading experiences can be comfortable, if there is a warm shelter and an armchair involved, by and large reading while on a mountaineering trip is a matter of discomfort. Stuck in a hut on a bad weather day, reading visitors books' and safety notices became a way of staving off the boredom, as Adam Smith describes: "spinning it out with only a few pages at a time" as "the benches got harder and harder" (1946, p. 45). Another twentieth-century female climber, Gwen Moffat, writes of a similar experience in a Scottish bothy: "After breakfast it rained again. Under the persistent gaze of the bothy mouse – who sat in dark corners with his eyes on stalks – we read a book about Borneo and sympathized with the writer in the monsoon" (2013, p. 90). The places of the reader and the book's subject become linked by the senses, and a Scottish downpour creates a link with a tropical monsoon.

For Adam Smith, this interfusing of mountain and book has a place in her mountaineering memoir, as she writes that: "*Roderick Hudson* will always be associated for me with waiting for fine weather at the Jungfraujoch, and my copy of *The Golden Bowl* still bears the marks of my drenching and battering on Suilven" (1946, p. 67). The time, place, and weather of the situation became part of the book's experience and associated meanings, while at the same time the book's physical aspects can change, conspicuously and irrevocably, thanks to their encounter with the mountain. Books, as book historians point out, are physical objects; they can get wet, and while on a mountaineering trip, their physicality is hard to overlook. Adam Smith, whose early mountaineering experiences – conditioned by her parents' practices – involved the luxuries of a fixed base at a hotel, balls to attend, a wardrobe for dresses, and a shelf for her books (1946, p. 32), became far more aware of books in relation to weight and necessity as she took up a different kind of mountaineering with Michael Roberts, where they traversed the Alps rather than staying at a fixed base. She turned up at Zermatt on her first Alpine trip with Roberts with "the one-volume *War and Peace*, and the Clarendon Press Shelley" which weighed, as she frames it in her mountaineering memoir, "about as much as a pair of crampons or a dozen tins of sardines" (1946, p. 32) – their physicality suddenly foregrounded.

So while books became intimately understood as objects with weight in the context of a mountaineering expedition, it could also be the mountaineers themselves who made changes to the book's physical form.

This was the case with Adam Smith's "dishonourably battered" copy of Ball's *Guide to the Western Alps*:

> before each holiday we would carefully fillet the sections we needed, perhaps 32 pages of the total 600, and encase them in the covers of a book – probably a discarded review copy – whose contents had been brutally removed. Fellow-climbers in Alpine huts would look awed or puzzled when we produced books with such titles as *Beet's Guide to the Sky* or *Political Thought from Sieyes to Sorel* and planned our next day's climb from the contents. (1988, p. 6)

Adam Smith and Roberts are far from the only mountaineers to react to the physicality of the book in a way that undermined the book's form in favour of the mountain's demands. While caught on the Aonach Eagach ridge in Scotland, Moffat noticed a tiny fire on the opposite hill, the Aonach Dubh: "We learnt later that someone was stranded on a ledge, and burning his guide book to attract attention" (2013, p. 162). The book as an object could cause problems, weighing down rucksacks and requiring filleting and splitting, but in this case, its physicality was life-saving. The obvious yet underappreciated concern of book historians of the book's status as an object becomes a very intense truth in the often dangerous and uncomfortable landscapes traversed by mountaineers.

However, while the book is material, the experience of reading can in fact divorce the text from its embodiment. This is the experience of reading from memory, and it comes up frequently in Adam Smith's own mountaineering memoir. She describes climbing the Rimpfischorn in 1929, while reciting Keats's "Odes", "Kubla Khan", "Lycidas", "L'Allegro" and some Shakespearean sonnets to herself, "for these are my usual stand-by for upward plods, far better than counting steps" (1946, pp. 12–13). These poems have already been memorised and can be called to mind to aid the mountaineer through their journey, but the mountain landscape also acts on these readings, suggesting associations. Seeing the dawn on Monte Rosa prompts Adam Smith to recall Shakespeare's couplet: "Night's candles are burnt out, and jocund day/stands tiptoe on the misty mountain tops", where mountain beauty and poetry are linked by that "same breathless catch at the heart, that same purity of joy" (1946, p. 13). Adam Smith started memorising poetry as a child and the immaterial text still bears a link to its physicality in the way that she remembers it "as it appeared in the book from which I memorised it" (2005, pp. 30–31) as well as taking on new inflections in the locations where it is later called to mind. She recommended memorisation, but with her characteristic emphasis on pleasure rather than morality or utility: "stock up the attics of your mind with enjoyment for the future" (1963, p. 20), advice that came from her own experience and where her multiple, repeated readings of memorised poems were shaped by a lifelong practice of reading in many different locations, including while moving on the mountain.

The mountain makes reading difficult, but for those mountaineers who manage to read – materially or immaterially – being on the mountain augments texts' meanings in their new situations. Moffat, benighted on a mountain when staying awake meant staying alive, also used a memorised text, telling her companion "the complete story of *The Well of Loneliness*" (2013, p. 341). However, while this new context reconfigures the significance of this book – it is now a lifeline, used alongside word games for two people to survive the night – it did not lose its prior social, historical and personal connotations on the impersonal mountain. *The Well of Loneliness*, controversial when it was published in 1928 for its representation of lesbianism (Love, 2000, p. 116), retains its reputation and history, and in this case is implicated in Moffat's identification with counter-cultural climbers of the 1940s and 1950s. The effect of a particular mountaineer reading a particular book in a mountain setting will vary, of course, with the reader, the book and the mountain. For Adam Smith, we see a recognition of the socially agreed meanings of books – in this case, highbrow and lowbrow reading – being affected by the mountain: Roberts's tastes, she writes, "become more elementary the higher he goes", while she maintains "that Stendhal and Henry James can be read with least distraction, and with added appreciation of their civilized refinements, in the intervals of a mountain holiday" (1946, pp. 66–67). Mountaineers bring their own ways of reading, conditioned by education and social mores, with them to the mountains.

While the holidays were conceived of as escapes, Figure 1.3 is a "set photograph" with "a beer bottle and the *Petite Anthologie Surréaliste* as stage properties" taken while Roberts was avoiding working on a review for Auden and Garrat's *Poet's Tongue* (1946, pp. 64–65), and Figure 1.4 shows Adam Smith holding a copy of *The Listener* in front of the Matterhorn, both of which demonstrate that for these particular mountaineers, their writing work co-existed to some extent with their leisure activities – similar to how their book-collecting habits demonstrated their identity as mountaineers while in the lowlands. There is no getting away from the implication of both book and mountain in the affairs of other people, whether that is lowland

Figure 1.3: Michael Roberts at Val d'Isère, 1935
Source: Adam Roberts

life or shared communities of mountaineers. This, indeed, is often the point. Adam Smith says of reading George Yeld's *Scrambles in the Eastern Graians* that it "gave us a perspective, linked us with our predecessors in these delightful terrains" (1988, p. 6), and of a book inherited from her mountaineering mentor, W.P. Ker, she was thrilled to find pencilled notes in the back that showed that he had slept in the very same hut that she was sleeping in that night (1946, p. 115). Adam Smith's reading also connected the landscape directly with the mountaineers of the past, as when she climbed the Matterhorn – "no one who has read and re-read Whymper can climb the top stretch unmoved" – or when she saw the Brouillard ridge in terms of Young's narrative (1946, pp. 126 & 89). At the Chanrion hut, she noted that it had "Saussure's *Voyages dans les Alpes* on its shelves—the book Ruskin had asked to be given on his fifteenth birthday" (1946, p. 74), claiming kinship with a past reader as well as past mountaineers.

Many of the same answers might be given as to why a person might go to the mountains as they might read a book: for knowledge, for

Figure 1.4: Janet Adam Smith with *The Listener* in front of the Matterhorn, 1929
Source: Adam Roberts

utility, for self-understanding, for pure pleasure. But to take a book to the heights is in itself an act of meaning-making. Whether is it Nea Morin's son with a "paperback Spinoza" on a three-person climb in Wales in 1957 (Morin, 1968, p. 158), or James Forbes, over a hundred years before, studying glaciers in the Alps "established in some mountain shelter with his books" (2011, p. 14), mountaineers have taken books to the mountains throughout the activity's history. They have cursed the book's physicality and responded to the mountain's demands: a book is filleted for convenience, or it is burned by a stranded mountaineer to attract attention. Reading matter is turned to in huts to alleviate boredom, shared reading and writing become acts of history and community, and moments of reading in the mountains become charged with associations and new memories, while retaining their lowland significances. Adam Smith, as mountaineer and reader, can use both the transportable book and the transporting landscape to enact her identity and her interrelationship with the natural world and the social world, which in turn act on each other to enhance the reader's vagabond nature, the book's physicality, and the meaning of book and mountain in context of each other.

Conclusion

On contemporary relationships between people and mountains, Victoria della Dora writes that "mountains linger between commodification and their persisting power to inspire awe" (2016, p. 227), detailing the risk-seeking culture of extreme sports spawned from mountaineering, and the myriad ways that these are disseminated: books, yes, but joined by film, television and headcam footage shared on social media. Examining the ground of those who have gone before us can help us to understand our own historical moment, here on the "warming flipside of the Industrial Revolution" where in writing about mountains, and nature writing in general, "the tenor and urgency [...] has shifted beyond our individual emotions" (Aalto, 2020, p. 15). In the writings of mountaineers, the mountain has been many things: a sacred way, a playground, fearsome, beautiful, conquerable, connective, a testing ground for the self, impersonal, unknowable and unrelentingly physical. Mountain writing has put its readers in the imagined or real positions of conqueror, of consumer of the mountain experience and the sublime, and of a mind and body connected with the mountain and its elements. But it is not just in the story we tell ourselves about our environment, it is also about how we position and receive that story, and in the book history of mountaineering it is the social, imaginative and the physical aspects (in terms of the book's materiality, the location of its experience and the mountaineer's embodiment in regards to both) that stand out. When we understand the communications cycle in its entirety, with the mountain as an extra actor in the development of the book, we can reach the same insight: that nature and culture are far more implicated in each other's creation than their oppositional definitions would imply. Mountaineering offers both isolation and community, selfhood and transcendence of self, mundanity and profundity. In its bookishness, especially, it offers both nature and culture.

Books are hybrid creations: as much physical object as text, as much an experience as a transaction, when seen through a book-historical lens they appear as networks of people, place and materials, where both chance and decision conspire in the many meanings that they bring to each of us. Examining the impact of the mountaineering book and the practices of the bookish mountaineer, I have attempted to add to ongoing conversations in the realms of both mountain studies and book history. Books are one of the oldest and most influential forms of mountain media and taking a book-historical perspective which includes the book's communications circuit and experiential significance helps us to see how and why these books were so important in the formation and dissemination of mountaineering as an activity. For book history, studying the book culture of a sporting community that has such a long and varied relationship with books, a holistic investigation of text, object, transaction and experience of the book within this community is possible, and we also find a renewed appreciation of the importance of place. While Adam Smith's experiences are unique, her practices have parallels, historical analogues and suggestive similarities with other mountaineers, and she is not the only one to have noticed that books and mountains have a longstanding and complex relationship. Through the lens of this particular mountaineer, we can see how the mountains create the book, the book creates the mountain, and – for those who explore both – particular contexts and reconfigurations occur when people, mountains and books come together.

Bibliography

Aalto, K. (2020) *Writing Wild: Women Poets, Ramblers and Mavericks Who Shape How We See the Natural World.* Portland, OR: Timber Press.

Adam Smith, J. (1932) "Highland Rocks and Ridges", *The Listener*, 8(191), pp. 350–351 [Online]. Available at: https://link-gale-com.ezproxy.is.ed.ac.uk/apps/doc/GM2500068097/LSNR?u=ed_itw&sid=LSNR&xid=461679f9 (Accessed: 29 June 2020).

Adam Smith, J. (1946) *Mountain Holidays* London: J.M. Dent and Sons Ltd.

Adam Smith, J. (1959) "High Enjoyment", *New Statesman*, 57(1461), pp. 377–378 [Online]. Available at: https://search-proquest-com.ezproxy.is.ed.ac.uk/docview/1306900103?accountid=10673 (Accessed: 22 July 2020).

Adam Smith, J. (ed.) (1963) *Faber Book of Children's Verse.* London: Faber and Faber.

Adam Smith, J. (1982) "A Family Century in the Alpine Club", *Alpine Journal*, 87(331), pp. 142–158 [Online]. Available at: http://www.alpinejournal.org.uk/Contents/Contents_1982_files/AJ%201982%20142-158%20Adam%20Smith%20Memoir.pdf (Accessed: 30 June 2020).

Adam Smith, J. (1988) *Books in My Life: The Collection of Janet Adam Smith and Michael Roberts.* England, s.n.

Adam Smith, J. (2005) *An Autobiography: 1905–1926.* London: PIP Printing [Privately Printed].

Bainbridge, S. (2020) *Mountaineering and British Romanticism: The Literary Cultures of Climbing, 1770-1836* [Online]. Oxford: Oxford University Press. Available at: https://ebookcentral.proquest.com/lib/ed/detail.action?docID=6181454 (Accessed: 10 July 2020).

Bodleian Libraries, *Forerunners to Everest: the story of the two Swiss expeditions of 1952 (Catalogue entry)* [Online]. Available at: http://solo.bodleian.ox.ac.uk/permalink/f/1qavhip/oxfaleph016069252 (Accessed: 23 July 2020).

Bodleian Libraries, *The ascent of Everest (Catalogue entry)* [Online]. Available at: http://solo.bodleian.ox.ac.uk/permalink/f/1o7ipr7/oxfaleph012399911 (Accessed: 23 July 2020).

Bodleian Libraries, *The high Alps in winter: or, mountaineering in search of health (Catalogue entry)* [Online]. Available at: https://solo.bodleian.ox.ac.uk/permalink/f/89vilt/oxfaleph011210114 (Accessed: 23 July 2020).

Bodleian Libraries, *The Indian Alps and how we crossed them: being a narrative of two years' residence in the eastern Himalaya and two months' tour into the interior (Catalogue entry)* [Online]. Available at: http://solo.bodleian.ox.ac.uk/permalink/f/1qavhip/oxfaleph016069543 (Accessed: 23 July 2020).

Bradshaw, P. (2012) "Living at Our Full Compass: Michael Roberts and the Poetry of Mountaineering", *The Alpine Journal*, pp. 229–237.

Chartier, R. (2015) "Communities of Readers", in Levy, M. and Mole, T. (eds) *The Broadview Reader in Book History*. Ontario: Broadview Press, pp. 251–266.

Colclough, S. (2011) "Representing Reading Spaces", in Crone, R. and Towheed, S. (eds) *The History of Reading*. London: Palgrave Macmillan.

Darnton, R. (2015) "What is the History of Books?", in Levy, M. and Mole, T. (eds) *The Broadview Reader in Book History*. Ontario: Broadview Press, pp. 231–250.

Debarbieux, B., Rudaz, G., Todd, J.M. and Price, M.F. (2015) *The Mountain*. Chicago, IL: University of Chicago Press.

della Dora, V. (2016) *Mountain: Nature and Culture*. London: Reaktion Books.

Forbes, J.D. (2011) *Travels through the Alps of Savoy and Other Parts of the Pennine Chain: With Observations on the Phenomena of Glaciers* [Online]. Cambridge: Cambridge University Press. Available at: https://doi.org/10.1017/CBO9781139096942 (Accessed: 22 July 2020).

Gifford, T. (2013) "Early Women Mountaineers Achieve Both Summits and Publication in Britain and America", in Gómez Reus, T. and Gifford, T. (eds) *Women in Transit through Literary Liminal Spaces* [Online]. London: Palgrave Macmillan, pp. 91–106. Available at: https://doi.org/10.1057/9781137330475 (Accessed: 26 June 2020).

Grebowicz, M. (2021) *Mountains and Desire: Climbing vs. the End of the World*. London: Repeater.

Howsam, L. (2015) "The Study of Book History", in Howsam, L. (ed.) *The Cambridge Companion to the History of the Book* [Online]. Cambridge: Cambridge University Press, pp. 1–13. Available at: http://dx.doi.org/10.1017/CCO9781139152242.002 (Accessed: 3 August 2020).

Keighren, I.M. (2006) "Bringing Geography to the Book: Charting the Reception of Influences of Geographic Environment", *Transactions of the Institute of British Geographers*, 31(4), pp. 525–540 [Online]. Available at: http://www.jstor.com/stable/4639993 (Accessed: 29 June 2020).

King, E.G. (2014) "E. W. Hornung's Unpublished 'Diary', the YMCA, and the Reading Soldier in the First World War", *English Literature in Transition 1880–1920*, 57(3), pp. 361–387 [Online]. Available at: https://link-gale-com. ezproxy.is.ed.ac.uk/apps/doc/A372883478/AONE?u=ed_itw&sid=AONE& xid=5d6e6493 (Accessed: 4 August 2020).

Love, H. (2000) "Hard Times and Heartaches: Radclyffe Hall's The Well of Loneliness", *Journal of Lesbian Studies*, 4(2), pp. 115–128 [Online]. Available at: doi://10.1300/J155v04n02_08 (Accessed: 29 July 2020).

Lunn, H.K. (1912) "A Journey", in Lunn, A.H. (ed.) *Oxford Mountaineering Essays*. London: Edward Arnold, pp. 93–106.

Macfarlane, R. (2003) *Mountains of the Mind: A History of a Fascination*. London: Granta.

McNee, A. (2016) *The New Mountaineer in Late Victorian Britain: Materiality, Modernity, and the Haptic Sublime*. Cham: Springer International Publishing.

Moffat, G. (2013) *Space Below My Feet*. London: Weidenfeld & Nicolson.

Mole, T. (2019) *The Secret Life of Books: Why They Mean More than Words*. London: Elliott and Thompson.

Morin, N. (1968) *A Woman's Reach: Mountaineering Memoirs*. London: Erye & Spottiswoode.

Noble, T. (1994) "Report of the Second Festival of Mountaineering Literature", in Gifford, T. and Smith, R. (eds) *Orogenic Zones: The First Five Years of the International Festival of Mountaineering Literature*. Wakefield: Bretton Hall, pp. 25–26.

Rak, J. (2007) "Social Climbing on Annapurna: Gender in High-altitude Mountaineering Narratives", *English Studies in Canada*, 33(1), pp. 109–146 [Online]. Available at: https://search-proquest-com.ezproxy.is.ed.ac.uk/docview/ 205819790?accountid=10673 (Accessed: 12 June 2020).

Schama, S. (2004) *Landscape and Memory*. London: Harper Press.

Stephen, L. (1871) *The Playground of Europe*. London: Longmans, Green, and Co.

Whymper, E. (1871) *Scrambles Amongst the Alps*, John Murray [Online]. Available at: https://archive.org/details/scramblesamongst00whym (Accessed: 27 July 2020).

Chapter 2

Tommy Caldwell's *The Push*

Climbing, Edgework and Media Perception of Risk

Martin Hall

All my life I've constantly refined my own sense of risk by considering not just the obvious factors – exposure, weather, rock quality, run out – but also ego, motivation, mental health, and the inevitable peer pressure (which exists, even if everyone tries to deny it). I seemed naturally able to metabolise fear; I love to suffer (elective suffering, that is) and I had excellent stamina. But I saw risking my neck on dangerous crimes are selfish, disrespectful of how my getting hurt or killed would affect my family and friends. I worried about doing something I didn't feel was morally right enough to cash in on fame and notoriety. (Caldwell, 2017, p. 334)

Introduction

This chapter aims specifically to interrogate perceptions of risk as they adapt and adjust in relation to experience and mediation. Central to this interrogation is the role of the viewer when exploring the notion of "perceived" risk and in particular the differences in spectatorship when the viewer is either "informed" or not. This chapter primarily focuses on Tommy Caldwell's book *The Push* (2017) as a catalyst for this interrogation into risk perception, beginning by exploring how Caldwell, a world-class free climber, engages with his own personal and subjective perception of professional risk. Similarly, in exploring the phenomenological success of a film like *Free Solo* (2018), it is arguably the edgework in this "death-defying" film which has brought it the previously unseen success and indeed the "cultural significance" that has distinguished it from other climbing films. Peter Donnelly has even defined one of the fundamental characteristics of climbing as "the maintenance of a tension balance between difficulty and risk" (2003, p. 294) but does acknowledge that all the major controversies in climbing have been "concerned with maintaining this tension balance" (p. 296). Stephen Lyng has defined much of the key work in this area such as when he proposed that "the voluntary pursuit of activities that involve a high potential for death, serious physical injury, or psychic harm – activities that I have termed as edgework – has acquired special cultural significance in the contemporary western world" (Lyng, 2008, p. 107).

Risk

It has been suggested, and often by climbers themselves, that "the majority of rock climbers" express motivations and experiences driven not by risk but a sense of "flow" (Rickly-Boyd, 2012, p. 86), a state which psychologist Mihaly Csikszentmihalyi describes as one in which "people are so involved in an activity that nothing else seems to matter" (1990, p. 4). Rickly-Boyd in fact builds a case that safety, or at least a sense of safety in one's climbing is essential in the ability to achieve flow, suggesting that "at least security with one's gear and partner's abilities is essential to the deep focus that results in flow" (Rickly-Boyd, 2012, p. 86). Tommy Caldwell, in his own book, *The Push*, questions the truth in this perception of climbing as edgework, suggesting that for him, climbing is quite conversely, particularly safe. He instead deems the media the culprits in producing articles about the sport with 'absurd inaccuracies, while also portraying climbing as a sport for roulette-wheel-spinning maniacs' (Caldwell, 2017, p. 421). However, *Mountains of the Mind* (2003) author Robert Macfarlane perpetuates this idea of danger-seeking, considering the role played by socio-cultural change, suggesting this pursuit is a reactionary one, when he proposes in his dialogue for Jennifer Peedom's 2017 film, *Mountain*, that as "life becomes safer, we look for danger".

For Lyng, edgework and flow do differ. Acknowledging the "distortion in one's experience of space and time, feelings of transcendence, and a state of focussed attention" which comes with flow, Lyng argues that in contrast, "edgework generates a heightened sense of self that subjects describe as a form of self-realization or self-actualization" (2008, p. 119). Beyond this, it is true to say that a large part of the success of these sportspeople is to be attributed to this ability to deal with risk and the fact that they "are better able to remain calm and centered, which to the untutored observer makes them appear curiously nonchalant" (David Dornian, 2003, p. 283). It is the untutored observer which this chapter considers when exploring the representation of risk primarily in Caldwell's *Push* but also in its cinematic adaptation, *The Dawn Wall* (2017), and in associated cinematic texts. This question of the knowing and unknowing viewer is key in the exploration of these kinds of phenomena. Certainly, the point which this chapter aims to make is one of perception and representation in terms of Stuart Hall's seminal work on "encoding/decoding" in which he explores the notion that audiences actively decode messages according to their particular social identity. In his work on "misunderstandings", wherein viewers do not decode the particular embedded meaning from visual language, Hall proposes that they most likely occur when "The viewer does not 'speak the language', figuratively if not literally: he or she cannot follow the complex logic of argument of exposition; or the concepts are too alien" (Hall, 1973, p. 15).

Commercialisation

Part of the issue with the way in which these sports are perceived by specialist and non-specialist audiences, is in terms of the way in which they have been commercialised. These sports are no strangers to commercialisation; as Stephen Poulson has observed, "many people see no incompatibility between an adventure experience and corporate culture" (2016, p. 26). Or such as, in the same vein, when Joanne Kay and Suzanne Laberge describe "the self-conscious performances" in Warren Miller's skiing film *Freeriders* (1998) as exemplifying "quintessential capitalist kitsch, offering the viewer only a commodified tracery of the spontaneous gesture" (2003, p. 393). This has indeed been explored elsewhere, by scholars such as Thomas Raymen, who has written about how Parkour and other perceived "sub-cultural" sports are founded upon neoliberal consumer capitalist forces that drive us to "cool individualism" (2018).

This rings truest in looking at the film of Tommy Caldwell and Kevin Jorgenson's climbing of the "Dawn Wall". Caldwell eventually became enormously unhappy with the role which the mainstream media played in this, to him, a very personal achievement, pointing out that even before the climb began, "a handful of people form a semi-circle around us, some snapping photos. This kind of thing never happens in our insular little climbing world. I smile bashfully. Out of politeness I shake a few hands, and then, like a skittish deer, I jog to my van" (Caldwell, 2017, p. 393). This overwhelming media interest came to a head once the climbers were on the wall, with Caldwell pointing the finger at even his own reliance upon the media as a problem. He describes the following situation:

> First Facebook, then the small-time paparazzi, now this. Not to mention that we have a film crew with us. What a circus. I say nothing. And then, before I know it, I'm fully wrapped up in surfing the web, mouth breathing at my screen. We go an hour without saying a word.
>
> Wait a second, this is so messed up! I put down my phone and try to make conversation. Keven and Brett both answer me in monosyllables, then look back down at their phones. (Caldwell, 2017, p. 393)

Similarly, Caldwell's point aligns the mediation of these sports with notions of sponsorship and athletes' responsibilities thereto. Horst Eidenmüller's paper on "The Law and Economics of Extreme Sports Sponsoring" explores this is great depth and he too observes that in consuming these extreme sports, we as spectators are "wired by the media to the performing athletes, creating a pernicious feedback loop of ever more risk seeking and taking in a stressful environment" (Eidenmüller, 2019, p. 4). In this sense, then, there is a self-fulfilling prophecy at work wherein the more risk-taking and perceived "adventure" taking place, the more likely it is to produce a desire to engage with more content of this kind. Authors Holyfield, Jonas and Zajicek have also similarly engaged with this idea of "adventure" in a piece suitably titled "Adventure without Risk Is Like Disneyland" (2005, p. 173). These authors, focusing in this case on white water rafting, quote from an interview with an average customer on a river guiding trip who says, "let's do something fun, something that is really going to scare us" (2005, p. 180). Tommy Caldwell's inclusion of the media in his own endeavour in free climbing the "hardest" route up El Cap has been criticised, despite some calling it "perhaps the most difficult free climb ever attempted" (Wilkinson, 2015). In particular, "Spending two to three weeks on the route, surrounded by camera crews, fixed lines, and other media accoutrements; getting goodies brought up to you by friends... Doesn't something about all that seem a little out of place in the middle of El Capitan?" asked Chris Kalman, a climber, on his blog Fringe's Folly (Kalman, 2015). "Where, I repeat, is the adventure?" (Ibid.). Clearly the repeated idea of tension balance reappears here, and for Kalman, this tension in risk versus reward (adventure) is softened, diluted or even erased altogether by the mediation of the event; quite pointedly, this is heralded by the presence of cameras. Holyfield, Jonas and Zajicek too engage with this idea of tension, where, for them, "Providing white water adventure to those who otherwise would not experience the river sometimes creates significant tension between the twin imperatives for safety and uncertainty" (2005, p. 181). Whether there is a pleasure to be found in this pursuit of risk or not, it is clear that doing, or for the purpose of this chapter, reading something or watching something that is "really going to scare us" (p. 180) is a big part of our regular lives. Deborah Lupton succinctly observes this ever-present fear as, in her own terms:

> Contemporary experts and popular cultures tend to represent risk as negative, something to be avoided. So too, much of the academic literature on risk represents individuals in late modernity as living in fear, constantly dogged by feelings of anxiety, vulnerability and uncertainty in relation to the risks of which they are constantly made aware. (2013, p. 203)

Evidently, whilst the media interest in these pursuits is damaging and almost suffocating at times, it has, to a certain extent, begun to transform this "insular little climbing world" into a global phenomenon (Caldwell, 2017, p. 393).

Audiences

What emerges, in a sense, surrounding the central concern of perception, is the point that there is a certain amount of pre-knowledge, or at least, assumed knowledge, required to fully comprehend what we are experiencing in these written and filmed memoirs, or else there is a distinct chance that audiences will experience what Stuart Hall termed "misunderstandings". In this case, these misunderstandings ally themselves to the idea of safety and thus to the perception of the level of risk. Here again, this "untutored viewer" engages in a very different mode of specta-torship in engaging with these texts. In this sense, then, it is enormously important that the audience for these films be taken into keen consid-eration when trying to understand the texts themselves, exploring what Judith Mayne has perceptively called "the need to understand just how and why ideological systems interpellate their subjects so effectively" and to study "how film-goers become subjects, how the various devices and components of the cinema function to create ideological subjects" (1993, p. 14). Films of this kind tend to be celebrated by the climbing community and as such as the more populist[1] texts which have provoked this study have some ability to transcend these humbler origins; they call particular attention to themselves.

As a useful analogue, historically, the "cult cinema" is often categorised as a community, and scholars similarly exclaim the attraction of these kinds of "cult films" as being characterised by their active and lively communal followings. In fact, it seems that this is an enormous part of the climbing film too. One might look simply towards the International Alliance for Mountain Film who state themselves that their goal is "to promote, enhance and conserve mountain cinematography" (2022). The IAMF are an alliance which consists of 27 members of which 26 are "Mountain Film" festivals and one "Mountain Film Museum", across twenty countries. The IAMF also celebrated *Free Solo* as a bastion of this film genre, suggesting that "Never before, has mountain cinema attracted such large audiences. The work of the IAMF and its members is a long-term contribution to increasing public attention to mountain film. This is a fantastic prize for the mountain world!" (IAMF, 2019).

In addition, one of the most significant communal followings with regards to climbing films, comes in the guise of festival film tours – from the Banff Mountain Film Festival, the Kendal Mountain Festival, and London Mountain Film Festival to the European Outdoor Film Tour and the Reel Rock film festival. Award-winning climbing filmmakers Josh Lowell and Peter Mortimer, who most notably directed *The Dawn Wall* amongst many others, having promoted the release of their own climbing films, began a tour of similar films focused on climbing:

---

[1] That is to say, the texts which have been viewed by non-specialist audiences, outside of the climber-specific contexts. For the sake of this study that constitutes *Free Solo* and *The Dawn Wall*.

Lowell and Mortimer realized the huge demand for exciting live events in the outdoors community and combined forces to create The Reel Rock Film Tour in 2006. In 2018 the REEL ROCK Tour included over 500 screenings world-wide and was seen by more than 75,000 people. This year's Reel Rock 14 Tour promises to be even bigger and better! (Reel Rock, 2019)

Considering the dual concepts of spectatorship and differing notions of perception, one can observe that the simplicity in *Free Solo*, for example, speaks to its success, in that it is perceived by many in the same way. The reality, then, pertains more to the phenomenological understanding of these texts, as Malin Wahlberg suggests: "Cinematic representations are epistemologically related to the spectator's language, ideological beliefs, and aesthetic sensibilities or the unconscious thought processes such as desire and expectation" (Wahlberg, 2008, p. 123).

In a sense, then, with the conflicting notion of the knowing and the uninitiated viewer, this idea of competing perceptions begins to make sense of the conception of spectatorship as a form of commodification and allows us to explore the impact this has on the phenomenological experience. Therefore, one might expect that, if the spectator needs the right "language" to properly and thoroughly enjoy these films, when the concept is more universal, as in *Free Solo*, the audience is simply bigger. Interestingly, 2018 was not the first time that Honnold had taken part in a "free soloing" documentary. One important consideration here is the suggestion that watching, for example, *Honnold 3.0*, a 2007 Sender Films documentary, would be more difficult for non-climbing audiences without the knowledge required of climbing skills and cultures, to enjoy. Here Honnold solo climbs three of Yosemite National Park's biggest peaks, El Cap, Half Dome and Mount Watkins, within just 24 hours, being not just the first person to climb these three peaks solo, but also setting a speed climbing record along the way. The reality here is that Alex "solos" these climbs but does not "free solo" them. Honnold "daisy solos" these climbs, meaning that he takes with him two short loops of webbing or strap chord with carabiners on either end. Rather than using a rope, he simply clips himself into the wall at various points using these "daisy chains" to secure himself to existing bolts on the rock face. There is, however, always a point where Alex is not clipped to anything and is therefore effectively "free soloing". The argument here might be that this type of climbing is too complicated and not so readily perceived by both skilled and unskilled audiences alike. *Free Solo* does the typical Hollywood thing in that it is perceived by everyone in the same way. This knowingness, or "insider knowledge", cannot be disregarded as a component of success here. One sees a clear resonance of this in one of the more telling quotations from Chin and Vasarhelyi's film wherein Tommy Caldwell, a fellow internationally regarded free climber, suggests that this knowingness, this, to some extent, required vocabulary, plays a large part in the perception of what Alex Honnold was doing, suggesting that "people who know a little bit about climbing are like, yeah he's safe, he says he's got it. People who know exactly what he's doing are *freaked out*!" Ultimately, this tension balance is a matter of fine-tuning to find the right mixture of adventure and risk for the spectator. However, some critics have accused the *Free Solo* directors of going too far, or perhaps tipping the scales for the wrong reasons: "Vasarhelyi and Chin milk this death-defying endeavour for all the suspense they can" (Benson-Allott, 2019, p. 68). This is yet another process of commodifying risk. Benson-Allot goes on to make clear the element of "marketing" ingrained in this kind of spectatorship relationship which she keenly identifies as a "contract":

> The film's marketing materials, however, prominently feature Chin and Vasarhelyi questioning their decisions, "Is it ethical to film someone as he risks his life?" Vasarhelyi asks in *The New York Times* op-doc that she and Chin created about *Free Solo*. They then sidestep their responsibility, contending, "That is, in part, a question for our audiences." (2019, pp. 70–71)

Motivation

When defining "risk", then, and re-stating Donnelly's notion of the "tension balance between difficulty and risk" (2003, p. 294), one must consider for whom these behaviours are seen as risky. Writing of Mary Douglas's approach to the study of risk, Deborah Lupton points out the following:

> Risk, for Douglas, is a contemporary Western strategy for dealing with danger and Otherness. Much of her writings on risk seek to explain why it is that some dangers are identified as 'risks' and others are not. Her main explanations revolve around the importance for social groups, organizations or societies to maintain the boundaries

between self and Other, deal with social deviance and achieve social order. (Lupton, 2013, p. 52)

Thus, it is a question of perspective and position. By the same token Caldwell often points out these differing perceptions of risk and safety. In *The Push* he points out his own calculated position on "risk" when he writes that "Early on I was learning that risk and recklessness are two entirely different things. We were never raised to be thrill seekers and adrenaline junkies" (Caldwell, 2017, p. 30).

Not to mention the notion that, indeed, these are professional athletes who are acclimatised as much to height as they are to risk. For these professionals, the notion of risk is seen differently than it is for non-specialist audiences:

> The exposure had become comfortable, like mounting a fast motorcycle and then taking it for a slow speed. The feelings of fear had passed years ago, replaced by only a twinge of excitement. High on the walls is my rightful place in this world. (Caldwell, 2017, p. 194)

Horst Eidenmüller has argued that, in reference to Sebastian Haag and Andrea Zambaldi's deaths in a climb on Nepal's Shishapangma that "Personal ambition, cognitive biases, sponsor expectations and media interest had created a powerful death trap", and goes on to refer to a further "seven athletes who died in the last 10 years on three different continents when practicing extreme sports" (2019, p. 2). Whilst this opens up the exploration of the particularly significant element of "sponsor expectations" the question of why athletes pursue the inherent risk we see is one of interest. This chapter doesn't seek to ask why climbers seek out risk; in fact, this author is not convinced that they do. In solidarity with Caldwell's book wherein the climber points out that for him, "climbing was about taking a stimulating and potentially dangerous environment and then using our heads, our attentiveness, and our skills to make it safe" (Caldwell, 2017, p. 30), this chapter is concerned only with the awareness and mediation of that perceived risk by uninitiated spectators. However, as the question of "why" is so ready on so many lips, it does shed some light on the desire to understand why risk has come so spectacularly evident in climbing literature and cinema.

Exploring the ideas of motivation, too, is integral to this idea of negotiating risk and reward. George Mallory's now enormously famous quote, when asked why he climbed Mount Everest, was to retort, "Because it was there" (1923). Tommy Langseth and Øyvind Salvesen are scholars who have sought to investigate the relationship between risk and motivation in a fascinating study. In their article on "Rock Climbing, Risk and Recognition" for the journal *Frontiers in Psychology*, they argue to the contrary that "climbers do not climb because the mountain 'is there' but because other people 'are there,' that means that we will explore the social component of risk-taking behavior in regard to climbing" (2018, p. 1). From this perspective, then, it is therefore a matter of perception and mediation that can be read as driving this pursuit for risk. Although, the authors propose that "a climber accepting that recognition is a driving force behind her or his action would be accepting the motivation does not come from 'within'" (2018, p. 6). Herein lies an interesting question: "why" do climbers seek out this risk? For Caldwell, in his own writing on the mediation of risk in his personal climbing achievements, the endeavour to better oneself and improve upon previous levels of success and achievement in climbing is not necessarily a matter of taking more and more risk but in fact seeking to prove his "worth" to others, thus reiterating Langseth and Salvesen's idea of climbing "because other people 'are there'" (2018, p. 1). Caldwell wrote, in regards to further challenging himself and tackling the "most difficult climb ever attempted", that:

> This route was a notch harder than any of the others I had previously done on El Cap. It would be a new level for my climbing, and prove to others, and to myself, that I could still be a professional climber. I'd demonstrate that I was in control of my life again. (2017, p. 156)

Perhaps here, then, even Caldwell is buying into the spectatorship in as much as he desires to be seen and recognised – thus legitimised – for his achievements, and in this sense Caldwell too is commodifying this risk. As early as 1923 commentators were noticing the risk associated with this pursuit of the mountains and they too questioned the motivation of non-specialist climbers venturing into the mountains. One *New York Times* columnist, in a piece calling out the "hazards of the Alps", questions why tourists were mounting the peaks of Chamonix, suggesting that "it is considered a reproach for an athletic man or woman not to venture the ascent of Mont Blanc" (Hazard, 1923). The author does pose, but tellingly does not answer, the question of "can climbing in the Alps ever be considered accident-proof?" But nonetheless, whilst decrying the increasing mortality rate amongst people scaling the mountains the author does in fact reinforce the notion of risk and reward, observing, in reference to the beauty and splendour of the local landscape, whilst most tourists elect to view the mountain range from the safety of the valleys, "this is not to say that the thrill of braving the hazards of the ascent and looking down on the tiny chalets of Chamonix and far and wide over the field of mountains is not the finer emotion" (Hazard, 1923). Risk vs reward thus is almost reified here and certainly elevated in creating a somewhat hegemonic distance between mere tourists and the superhuman mountaineers prepared to take on danger in order to reap a greater and more significant reward: in some sense living a better life than mere mortals, reinforcing the sovereignty afforded to specific bodies – white male, European, Western bodies. To this same end, Jennifer Jordan in her 2010 book of Dudley Wolf's mountaineering, *The Last Man on the Mountain: The Death of an American Adventurer on K2*, establishes Wolf's death on KS by quoting Charles S. Houston's 1938 K2 diary in which he writes:

> Is it not better to take risks...than die within from rot? Is it not better to change one's life completely than to wait for the brain to set firmly and irreversibly in one way of life and one environment? I think it is...taking risks, not for the sake of danger alone, but for the sake of growth, is more important than any security one can buy or inherit. (Quoted in Jordan, 2010, p. 143)

What is interesting in this sense of negotiating the precarious balance between risk and adventure purely as an entertainment phenomenon is that whilst one might initially consider that the responsibility lies squarely on the shoulders of the audience – of spectators, in fact – it ought to be understood that the filmmakers and media outlets in and of themselves hold a greater deal of responsibility in marketing the reception of these pursuits; they too commodify the sport or leisure activity. To an extent, films like *Free Solo* and *Dawn Wall*, texts which phenomenologically have risen above the constraints of an "insular little climbing world" (Caldwell, 2017, p. 393) might more usefully be read as "media events". This of course is a term reserved for television viewing in particular, events which Daniel Dayan and Elihu Katz describe as "the festive viewing of television [...] those historic occasions [...] that are televised as they take place and transfix a nation or the world" (Dayan and Katz, 1992, p. 1). But if we suppose to transpose this phrase into cinema language the idea of the spectacle, and indeed "festive" viewing of these films, becomes pointed. This is particularly so if one sees these films within the context of the festival viewing space so integral to the success of the genre. Similarly, Freddie Wilkinson, writing about Caldwell's *Dawn Wall* for *The New York Times* in 2015, said that "the anticipation and spectacle surrounding it – an adventure that, thanks to cellphones, social media and the Internet, has been shared by millions of people – surpass anything imaginable in Mr. Harding's[2] day" (Wilkinson, 2015). This experience, enhanced by technological developments, delivers to spectators the phenomeno-logical experience of the thrill and an experience of the sublime, but, as the uninitiated, only from a safe distance. Furthermore, for Wilkinson, "technology and the media may bring viewers closer than ever before to these intense endeavors, but in Mr. Harding's day, they could have the curious effect of dehumanizing both the personalities and the experience" (2015). What is interesting to engage with here is the point that there is a responsibility to be shared in creating the tension of risk in order to demonstrate a kind of marketable spectatorial experience for audiences. It is in fact the "death-defying" nature of *Free Solo* that makes it so attractive a viewing experience. In fact, in his book about Honnold's free solo climb, Mark Synott points out that "by 2015, it wasn't just possible for profes-sional climbers to keep their fans appraised of their exploits in real time; it was expected. Endorsement contracts often included stipulations about social media: how often to post, which hashtags to use, and even creative guidelines" (Synott, 2018, pp. 198–199).

Responsibility

There is the sense that too much risk can of course be unsettling, and whilst that unsettling feeling is one that many spectators pursue and enjoy, as will be explored later in this chapter, the disease of these kinds of films is not without precedent. My own experience of watching Honnold free soloing the 3,000 ft, around 900 metres, of Yosemite National Park peak, El Capitan on the big screen in the cinema was received with squeals and screams from other cinema-goers. Indeed, one of the most significant

---

[2] Warren Harding was the first person to climb El Cap's "Dawn Wall", in 1970, using "aid climbing" techniques (hammering hardware into the wall to pull oneself upwards) as opposed to Tommy Caldwell's "free climbing" (using just hands and feet to move upwards with the rope and removable hardware for safety only) approach.

tropes of what can be termed "extreme cinema" "is its potential to elicit affect" (Kerner and Knapp, 2016, p. 156). Extreme cinema is seen more commonly as "films that have pushed against, if not breached conventions regarding treatment of sex and violence in the cinema" (Ibid., p. 1). This author does not intend to refer to climbing films' portrayal of risk as "violent" but does observe, in films such as *Free Solo* and *The Dawn Wall,* a clear push-back against, and to some extent a breach of, convention. What is interesting, however, is that in their exploration of *Extreme Cinema,* scholars Aaron Michael Kerner and Jonathan L. Knapp acknowledge the specificities of particular audiences in the reception of these kinds of films, pointing out that:

> Submitting the affective referent to the analytic gaze wields the potential to neutralize that which spawns sensation. Furthermore, the affective experience is hardly universal, and although we have perhaps over-"idealized" the affective as pan-cultural in certain instances, it is clear that it is subject to cultural, historical and personal mediation. (2016, p. 156)

This "personal mediation" as they experience it is cleanly aligned with the idea of the untutored observer in the climbing film, evidently impacting the notion of affect in differing spectators. In a sense it is important that the audience and the filmmaker, in purely metaphorical terms, "speak the same language".

Benson-Allott, in her exploration of *Free Solo* as tantamount to a "snuff film", accuses the filmmakers of violating a kind of spectatorial contract with the viewer in not acknowledging the central focus on death; as the author claims, "I could no longer trust Vasarhelyi and Chin to deliver the safe spectoral experience I'd expected" (Benson-Allott, 2019, p. 68). For Benson-Allott the seeking of risk for climbing films did not pay off, building the case for the argument here that more risk does not in fact equal more reward for spectators, and indeed those untutored observers in particular, are concerned. There is in fact a certain morbid curiosity ingrained in the human condition which might account for the interest in this kind of risk-taking cinema. To echo Tommy Caldwell's reaction to Honnold's climb from the film itself, on the one hand interest comes in the guise of viewers who believe Honnold is simply a sports person at the top of his profession doing what he does best, and on the other hand there are viewers, like Benson-Allott who see this as "threaten[ing] the viewer with psychic harm" (Benson-Allott, p. 73). Psychologically speaking, research does suggest that as humans we are predisposed to "potentially dangerous phenomena" (Scrivner, 2021, p. 1) and in particular, much like looking at a car crash, "This is true even when the phenomenon is unpleasant; indeed, pleasantness appears to be unrelated to interest-ingness" (Ibid.). More pointedly, in a paper exploring the measurement of morbid curiosity, Coltan Scrivner makes it clear that

> Morbid curiosity is colloquially described as an interest in or curiosity about unpleasant things, especially death. While psychologists have extensively explored how the mind deals with death (e.g., Solomon, Greenberg, & Pyszczynski, 2015) and curiosity has been investigated in a variety of research programs (e.g., Kidd & Hayden, 2015; Loewenstein, 1994), they have largely overlooked morbid curiosity as a topic of study. (2021, p. 2)

Though the field of psychology has largely overlooked the facets of morbid curiosity as an element of the human condition it is nonetheless important here. In fact, what makes Scrivner's work particularly salient for the focus of this chapter is his exploration of what he sees as the first psychological paper on morbid curiosity by Zuckerman and Litle in 1986, in which they developed the "Curiosity About Morbid Events (CAME) scale" (Zuckerman and Litle, 1986) on which, most interestingly, scores are "positively correlated with sensation seeking" (Scrivner, 2021, p. 2). In this case, then, from the perspective of climbing filmmakers in particular, there is indeed a reward to be found in seeking risk, particularly that of the risk of death. What these films need to do is to negotiate this risk, to toe the line as it were, in order to negotiate an experience wherein a viewer – and in order to attract a larger viewership and thus more financial success, an untutored viewer – can enjoy this pursuit of edgework without experiencing "psychic harm". This seems a particularly difficult balance; indeed, a balance which Lowell and Mortimer have well-struck in *The Dawn Wall*, but one which, for Benson-Allot at least, Vasarhelyli and Chin have misjudged with *Free Solo*. Benson-Allot does acknowledge the role of the filmmakers in her perfectly reasonable response to the film when she suggests that:

> Chin and Vasarhelyi defuse the issue of culpability in *Free Solo* by allowing Honnold to articulate ethics as a question of performance. He laments how "messed up" it would be for him to fall in front of his friends and their cameras, because "nobody wants to see that". (Benson-Allott, 2019, p. 70)

Whilst the film is evidently predominantly well-received with its enormous acclaim including an Oscar, a BAFTA, 7 EMMYs and more, this perspective is not unique to Benson-Allott. Exploring the spectacle of *Free Solo,* Joseph E. Taylor points out the absurdity that in the film, "no one will call Honnold selfish" (Taylor, 2020, p. 375). And it is not just audiences who fall foul of the perception of risk in these films. Sponsors too become, if not culpable, certainly responsible and have addressed this balance in the past. Sponsors are indeed responsible for this commodification of risk in their constant search for new resources to fuel the growth economics of consumer capitalism. Caldwell himself critiques this relationship between sponsorship and risk when he considers his younger partner on the wall, Kevin Jorgenson, observing in his behaviours that "Many more, in particular younger, athletes compete for sponsorships, and they have to take ever higher risks to catch the attention of (potential) sponsors and the general public" (2019, p. 3). It is obvious of course, that sponsored athletes do need to avoid activities that would harm their sponsors; in fact, as Eidenmüller has explored in particular relation to the economics of "extreme sports", "a great majority of sponsored athletes are bound by a 'moral clause'. Athletes must not behave in a way detrimental to their sponsor's interests, such as talking poorly about the product, modifying the product or covering the product" (Eidenmüller, 2019, p. 211). This has reared its head with climbing, most clearly when Clif Bar[3] dropped several climbers from their brand. In 2014 the brand released the following statement:

> We understand that some climbers feel these forms of climbing are pushing the sport to new frontiers. But we no longer feel good about benefitting from the amount of risk certain athletes are taking in areas of the sport where there is no margin for error; where there is no safety net. (Clif Bar, 2014)

What is interesting is the climbers' responses to sponsors withdrawing from contracts. Dean Potter, another famous free solo climber and a friend of Alex Honnold's who died wing suit flying in 2015 called the sponsors actions "a huge emotional blow" (Branch, 2014). Interestingly, whilst Clif Bar never gave a reason for their change in direction, Dean Potter accused the sponsor of reacting to Peter Mortimer and Nick

---

[3] Clif Bar & Company is an American company that produces energy foods and drinks.

Rosen's film *Valley Uprising* (2014) which details the history of climbing in the Yosemite Valley, including footage of free soloing. This speaks, of course, to the power and influence of these films and the effects which this delicate balance of negotiation between risk and "adventure". Giving credence to the complicated notion that more risk equals more reward, Alex Honnold's own response to the sponsor, in an op-ed for *Sports Illustrated*, was to suggest that sponsors refusing to support risky climbing behaviours like soloing could make the sport "more sterile" (Honnold, 2014a). For *The New York Times* Honnold engages more with the notion of personal policing and speaks to the ways in which he is skilled enough to compartmentalise the risk in his climbing, knowing his own limits and "drawing his own lines":

> soloing appeals to me for a variety of reasons: the feeling of mastery that comes from taking on a big challenge, the sheer simplicity of the movement, the experience of being in such an exposed position. Those reasons are a powerful enough motivation for me to take certain risks. But it's a personal decision, and one that I consider carefully before any serious ascent. (Honnold, 2014b)

Conclusion

What is more, engaging with this negotiated balance is something to which Caldwell gives a great deal of attention in his mountaineering memoir *The Push*. He gives great thought to the logical conclusion of greater risk: death at the hands of the mountain.

> Sport climbing is safe. Its controlled. It's great. But how far do you take it? He saw my drive and toughness and he feared that my ambitions would push me closer to the Alpine round and leave me to distant and dangerous summits. Too many climbers he'd known had died this way. (2017, p. 92)

Maybe much like these filmmakers, there is a more egocentric reasoning behind the pursuit of risk for these climbers. Much like the extreme cinema, where "distributors in fact have used 'extreme' as a marketing device" (Kerner and Knapp, 2016, p. 157) which ultimately encourages viewers to, as Kerner and Knapp put it, "read these films through a particular lens" (Ibid.) so too does the climbing film's mediation of "risk" encourage audiences to do the same. There is a real concern in the commodification of risk, as it pertains to spectatorship and phenomenological experiences. Filmmakers, authors, biographers, sponsors and even viewers are guilty of this force of commodification and yet what is missed often is the nuance in the differing experiences across diverse audiences when exposed to high-end professional athleticism. If one were to seek an answer to the unposed question of why it is that some of these films have indeed transcended the "insular little climbing world" (Caldwell, 2017, p. 393), the more successful commodification of risk is one compelling response and yet Caldwell's own book and the accompanying film speak to a different experience of risk, even if he is occasionally, as we have seen here, guilty of commodifying the risk experience himself.

For Caldwell, in his book he spends much time engaging with the "control", "heightened awareness" and even at one point the sense of "invincibility" (240) that risk affords him as a climber. But at least in negotiating his own culpability in the potentially dangerous hazards in this tightrope walking, in balancing the risk vs reward elements of climbing, it ultimately comes down to the pursuit of pleasure: "Perhaps more than most pursuits, climbing is self-glorifying and self-serving. As we ascend, we risk becoming our own gods" (Caldwell, 2017, p. 203).

Bibliography

Branch, J. (2014) "A Sponsor Steps Away from the Edge", *The New York Times*. Available at: https://www.nytimes.com/2014/11/16/sports/clif-bar-drops-sponsorship-of-5-climbers-citing-risks-they-take.html (Accessed: 25 May 2022).

Benson-Allott, C. (2019) "On Platforms: Watching without a Rope", *Film Quarterly*, 72(4), Summer. Available at: https://doi.org/10.1525/fq.2019.72.4.68 (Accessed: 25 May 2022).

Caldwell, T. (2017) *The Push: A Climber's Journey of Endurance, Risk and Going Beyond Limits*. London: Penguin Books.

"Clif Bar Releases Statement Regarding Dropped Athletes", (2014) *Climbing*. Available at: https://www.climbing.com/news/clif-bar-releases-statement-regarding-dropped-athletes/ (Accessed: 25 May 2022).

Csikszentmihalyi, M. (1990) *Flow: The Psychology of Optimal Experience*. New York: Harper Perennial.

Dayan, D. and Katz, E. (1994) *Media Events: The Live Broadcasting of History*. Cambridge, MA: Harvard University Press.

Donnelly, P. (2003) "The Great Divide: Sport Climbing vs. Adventure Climbing", in Rinehart E. and Syndor, S. (eds) *To the Extreme: Alternative Sports, Inside and Out*. New York, NY: State University of New York Press, pp. 291–305.

Dornian, D. (2003) "Xtreem", in Rinehart E. and Syndor, S. (eds) *To the Extreme: Alternative Sports, Inside and Out*. New York, NY: State University of New York Press, pp. 281–289.

Eidenmüller, H. (2019) "Setting up Dates with Death? The Law and Economics of Extreme Sports Sponsoring in a Comparative Perspective", *Marquette Sports Law Review*, 30(1), pp. 191–242.

Hall, S. (1973) "Encoding and Decoding in the Television Discourse, a Paper for the Council of Europe Colloquy on 'Training in the Critical Reading of Televisual Language'", University of Leicester. Available at: http://epapers.bham.ac.uk/2962/1/Hall,_1973,_Encoding_and_Decoding_in_the_Television_Discourse.pdf (Accessed: 25 May 2022).

"Hazard of the Alps" (1923) *The New York Times*, 29 August. Available at: https://www.nytimes.com/1923/08/29/archives/hazards-of-the-alps.html (Accessed: 25 May 2022).

Holyfield, L. and Zajicek, A. (2005) "Adventure without risk is like Disneyland", in Lyng, S. (ed.) *The Sociology of Risk-Taking*. London: Routledge, pp. 173–187.

Honnold, A. (2014a) "Climber Alex Honnold in op-ed: 'I draw the lines for myself'", *Sports Illustrated*, 20 November. Available at: https://www.si.com/edge/2014/11/20/clif-bar-climbers-sponsorship-alex-honnold (Accessed: 25 May 2022).

Honnold, A. (2014b) "The Calculus of Climbing at the Edge", *The New York Times*, 19 November. Available at: https://www.nytimes.com/2014/11/20/opinion/the-calculus-of-climbing-at-the-edge.html (Accessed: 25 February 2022).

IAMF (2019) "And the Winner Is… Free Solo!!!" Available at: https://www.mountainfilmalliance.org/and-the-winner-is-free-solo/ (Accessed: 25 May 2022).

Jordan, J. (2010) *The Last Man on the Mountain: The Death of an American Adventurer on K2*. New York, NY: W.W. Norton & Co.

Kalman, C. (2015) "What Nobody Is Saying About the Dawn Wall", *Fringe's Folly*, 5 January. Available at: https://fringesfolly.wordpress.com/2015/01/05/what-nobody-is-saying-about-the-dawn-wall/ (Accessed: 25 February 2022).

Kay, J. and Laberge S. (2003) "Oh Say Can You Ski: Imperialistic construction of freedom in Warren Miller's *Freeriders*", in Rinehart E. and Syndor, S. (eds) *To the Extreme: Alternative Sports, Inside and Out*. New York, NY: State University of New York Press, pp. 381–399.

Kerner, A. and Knapp, J.L. (2016) *Extreme Cinema: Affective Strategies in Transnational Media*. Edinburgh: Edinburgh University Press.

Langseth, T. and Salvesen Ø. (2018) "Rock Climbing, Risk, and Recognition", *Frontiers in Psychology*, 9. Available at: https://www.frontiersin.org/articles/10.3389/fpsyg.2018.01793/full (Accessed: 25 February 2022).

Lupton, D. (2013) *Risk and Pleasure*. London: Routledge.

Lupton, D. (2013) *Risk*. 2nd edn. London: Taylor & Francis Group.

Lyng, S. (2008) "Edgework, Risk, and Uncertainty", in Zinn, J.O. (ed.) *Social Theories of Risk and Uncertainty: An Introduction*. London: Wiley Blackwell.

Mallory, G. (1923) "A Member of Former Expeditions Tells of the Difficulties Involved in Reaching the Top – Hope of Winning in 1924 by Establishment of

Base Camps on a Higher Level", *The New York Times*, 18 March. Available at: https://graphics8.nytimes.com/packages/pdf/arts/mallory1923.pdf (Accessed: 25 May 2022).

Macfarlane, R. (2003) *Mountains of the Mind*. London: Granta.

Mayne, J. (1993) *Cinema and Spectatorship*. London: Routledge.

Poulson, S.C. (2016) *Why Would Anyone Do That? Lifestyle Sport in the Twenty-First Century*. New York: Rutgers University Press.

Raymen, T. (2018) *Parkour, Deviance and Leisure in the Late-Capitalist City: An Ethnography*. London: Emerald Publishing Limited.

Reel Rock (2019) "FAQs", Available at: https://www.reelrock.co.uk/faq-s (Accessed: 25 February 2022).

Rickly-Boyd, J.M. (2012) "Lifestyle climbing: Toward existential authenticity", *Journal of Sport and Tourism*, 17(2), pp. 85–104.

Scrivner, C. (2021) "The psychology of morbid curiosity: Development and initial validation of the morbid curiosity scale", *Personality and Individual Differences*, 183. Available at: https://doi.org/10.1016/j.paid.2021.111139 (Accessed: 25 May 2022).

Synnott, M. (2018) *The Impossible Climb: Alex Honnold, El Capitan, and the Climbing Life*. New York, NY: Dutton.

Taylor, J.E. (2020) "The Spectacle of *Free Solo*", *Environmental History*, 25(2), pp. 372–376. Available at: https://www.journals.uchicago.edu/doi/10.1093/envhis/emz088 (Accessed: 25 May 2022).

Wahlber, M. (2008) *Documentary Time: Film and Phenomenology*. Minneapolis, MN: University of Minnesota Press.

Wilkinson, F. (2015) "On the Dawn Wall, Climbing and Tweeting", *The New York Times*, 8 January. Available at: https://www.nytimes.com/2015/01/09/opinion/yosemites-challenge-in-the-facetime-age.html (Accessed: 25 May 2022).

Zuckerman, M. and Litle, P. (1986) "Personality and curiosity about morbid and sexual events", *Personality and Individual Differences*, 7, pp. 49–56.

Filmography

The Dawn Wall (2017) Directed by P. Mortimer and J. Lowell [DVD]. USA: Sender Films.

Free Solo (2018) Directed by J. Chin and E.C. Vasarhelyi [DVD]. USA: National Geographic.

Freeriders (1998) Directed by B. Sisselman [DVD]. USA: Warren Miller Entertainment.

Honnold 3.0 (2012) Directed by A. Lowther, J. Lowell, N. Rosen and P. Mortimer [DVD] USA: Sender Films.

Mountain (2017) Directed by J. Peedom [DVD]. USA: Peedom.

Valley Uprising (2014) Directed by P. Mortimer and N. Rosen [DVD] USA: Sender Films.

Chapter 3

Thinking *with a* Mountain

A Narratological and Rhetorical Analysis of the Haptic Sublime in Jon Krakauer's Mountaineering Memoirs

David Lombard

From the Mountain to the Haptic Sublime: Reducing Distance to Experience Minor Affects

Mountains are the epitomes of the natural sublime. From Longinus to Thomas Burnet and Joseph Addison, they were deemed sublime because of their size and greatness, which were commonly associated with the divine or sacred (Brady, 2013, p. 16; Shaw, 2017, pp. 28–38). Edmund Burke later influentially theorized and systematized the sublime as provoking "delightful horror" (Burke, 1998, p. 67) while Immanuel Kant and Friedrich Hegel claimed that mountains symbolized "massiveness" as well as the "infinite", 'inaccessible" and "unknowable" (Brady, 2013, p. 80; Shaw, 2017, p. 151). For most of these thinkers, literary description was the optimal means of expressing the ineffable features of the romanticized sublime experience while staying at a safe distance from the threatening material object. For example, Burke's landmark *A Philosophical Enquiry into the Origin of Our Ideas of the Sublime and Beautiful* (1757), and more specifically its section on "words", is an invitation to inquire into the ability of the literary imagination to produce emotions of awe and terror. Although outdated, Burke's typology of "aggregate", "simple abstract" and "compounded abstract" words urges readers to interpret poetic associations as imaginative attempts to describe the unpresentable and their ability to "affect [readers] often as strongly as the things they represent, and sometimes much more strongly" (Burke, 1998, p. 161).

In her influential *Mountain Gloom and Mountain Glory: The Development of the Aesthetics of the Infinite* (1959), Marjorie Hope Nicolson emphasizes the role of pre-Romantic poetic description in shaping a "new Sublime" of a godly and infinite nature, which can spiritually elevate the beholder of mountains by confronting her with the limits of her understanding (1959, p. 329; Shaw, 2017, p. 98). More recently, Gene Ray has referred to the pre-Romantic or late seventeenth-century enthusiasm for Nicolson's "new Sublime" as the "mountain sublime". The "mountain sublime", Ray (2005, p. 26) argues, occurred among the "English elite" and "within the context of latent and emergent imperialist competition", which might have contributed to establishing it as a conventional aesthetic view. This "elite passion for wild land" is also part of what historian William Cronon identifies as the "trouble with wilderness". In his eponymous provocative essay, Cronon (1995, p. 9) claims that many nineteenth- and early twentieth-century "elite urban tourists" tended to visit mountains and the wilderness for mere "recreation", as a way of "project[ing] their leisure-time frontier fantasies onto the American landscape" without further exploring its complexity. If this form of tourism is characteristic of an aesthetic shift from what historian Roderick F. Nash (2014) refers to as "antipathy" to "appreciation" of wilderness, this relationship is still problematic, especially in the current ecological context. Indeed, while the sublime and romantic poetry associated the divine with mountains or the wilderness, which contributed to the development of preservation ethics (Nash, 2014, pp. 44–45), they have nurtured a fraught relationship to overpowering mountains. More specifically, most traditional theories of the sublime suggest a purely visual and imaginative experience or distant mountain *view* which has influentially shaped the Western relationship with nature (Caracciolo, 2021, p. 299). Throughout the eighteenth and nineteenth centuries, the traditional mountain sublime did not mature into a more direct or collective experience, and it is still incompatible with the current context of the Anthropocene, in which the reality of nature can no longer be estranged from humanity and its culture (Vermeulen, 2020, pp. 37–40). If it is to become a viable aesthetic mode in the Anthropocene, Marco Caracciolo argues, the sublime needs to account for affects that move beyond the confines of the experience of awe and horror (2021, pp. 299–300).

According to Sianne Ngai, such affects could be "minor affects", namely "animatedness, envy, irritation, anxiety, stuplimity, paranoia, and disgust", which she uses to examine "a multiplicity of other representational and theoretical dilemmas" (2005, p. 37). This essay attempts to examine descriptions of minor affects such as tedium, pain and euphoria as parts of contemporary sublime moments. More precisely, it interprets these minor affects as emerging through the "haptic sublime", a recent avatar of the sublime coined by Alan McNee which has replaced the distant contemplation of the traditional sublime by a direct and embodied experience of landscapes, or a haptic experience of mountain *terrain* (as opposed to mountain *view*) that is felt in muscles, skin, lungs, and heart (2016, p. 4). The affects produced by haptic sublime moments are analysed as "*narrative affect[s]*" in Jon Krakauer's mountaineering memoirs, namely "body-based feelings" that are "attached to formal dimensions of texts such as metaphor, plot structure, and character relations", and therefore contribute to understanding the complex or "coconstitutive" relationship the author develops with his environment (Houser, 2014, pp. 3–8, emphasis in original).

The Anthropocene has shed light on notions of scale and environmental responsibility and, like the sublime, is customarily linked to senses of excess, overwhelm and disorientation (Purdy, 2015, p. 421). The memoir, as an inevitably human-centred and "actively constructive" genre which "must refer to an extra-textual reality" by means of narrative technique such as self-questioning (Couser, 2011, pp. 55–74), is a privileged site to investigate the revisions of the sublime and the variety of affects it produces. What is more, some contemporary mountaineering memoirs such as Jon Krakauer's *Into Thin Air* (1996), as McNee (2016, p. 221) remarks, reconsider sublime mountains in a more anthropogenic context insofar as they are concerned by the "rampant commercialism, egotism, and ruthlessness that characterize modern [...] mountaineering, and [its] consequences for the mountain environment". In fact, these memoirs echo the genre of what ecocritic and ecofeminist Stacy Alaimo terms "material memoir" in that the self "is coextensive with the environment" and "trans-corporeal" although they do not engage with "scientific and medical information", as the memoirs Alaimo analyses do. In haptic sublime experiences, contact with and understanding of environments are obtained through hard physical effort which allows the climbers to better apprehend the impenetrable difficulty of the sublime. The haptic sublime is therefore more focused on the repositioning of the "mountain sublime" in a state that places the human as, if not "intermeshed" with the non-human environment – which Alaimo (2010, p. 2) has termed "trans-corporeality" – then more physically connected with it.

Such an approach aligns with the call of literary scholars and ecocritics such as Ngai (2005), Houser (2014), Timothy Morton (2018), and Caracciolo (2021) to encompass and comprehend a wider range of (minor and negative) affects such as disgust and discord but also the presumably inexpressible affects linked to the sublime, which are produced or intensified by ecological change. The haptic sublime explores such broader affective dimensions insofar as the haptic involves various sensory systems which (re)position our experience in a greater degree of intimacy and produce a wider array of feelings. McNee's conceptualisation of the "haptic sublime", however, suggests an ableist perspective on haptic experience since it is restricted to people who are not disabled and can make full use of most if not all their limbs, an issue that McNee does not address in his account. In spite of this regrettable bias, interpreting descriptions of the haptic sublime can encourage humans to start thinking *with a* mountain, that is to reflect on affects mountaineering produces and on what they mean to the experience of the sublime and to the relationship between self and environment that it constructs.

As a recreational hunter and naturalist, Aldo Leopold struggled with tensions that echo mountain sublime rhetoric. For instance, when pondering over the idea of killing wolves to increase the number of deer in mountains, he "see[s] the green fire die" in the eyes of the dead "old wolf" he has just shot, suggesting that the inconvenient presence of wolves in mountains, almost perceived as invasive by hunters, is fundamental to the ecosystem balance of the grander mountain environment (1970, pp. 140–41). Leopold's famous phrase "think like a mountain" promotes an arguably biocentric or ecologically "anthropocentric" (Fromm, 1993, p. 48) view of ecosystems which invites humans to adopt the behaviour of mountains, but it also makes "use of simile" and therefore "locates the reader in figurative language as an appropriate and compatible dwelling to occupy, to linger in, in order to pursue this thought process" (Holdefer, 2020, p. 28). In a similar fashion but without simile, this essay argues that some memoirs which do not necessarily include figurative language (but, for example, self-questioning passages and the use of epigraphs) suggest that the practice of mountaineering or climbing can lead to a comparable reflection to the one Leopold conveys by means of his experience of hunting. In other words, by moving on to the more recent and less alienating haptic sublime in our relation to natural environments, which is, as this essay attempts to show in the next section, envisioned in Krakauer's mountaineering memoirs, such a materialist project of "transcorporeality" could emerge.

While embracing the basic premise of "econarratology" that "understandings of narrative change as the environment changes", this chapter undertakes a narratological and rhetorical analysis of descriptions of the sublime in Jon Krakauer's mountaineering writings to demonstrate that it is not the sublime that is "no longer relevant theoretically" but that it is the narrative of the sublime which needs to be changed as our environmental context is altered and ecological awareness is raised (James and Morel, 2020, p. 1; Brady, 2013, p. 185). Informed by recent insights from rhetorical (eco)narratology, this chapter proceeds to what rhetorical narrative scholars James Phelan and Peter J. Rabinowitz have termed "theory-practice", or "inquiries in which theory aids the work of interpretation even as that work allows for further developments in theory" (Phelan, 2017, p. 4). In other words, it uses the lens of the sublime in close readings to illustrate the theoretical limits and affordances of the haptic sublime for exploring minor affects produced by physical encounters with environments, which also highlights the relevance of these notions in both theories and understandings of the sublime. Considering the close relationship between econarratological themes and Alaimo's concept of trans-corporeality inasmuch as it appeals to "embodied cognition" – or "the idea that cognition is dependent upon the experience of the physical body in an environment" – and "enactivism" – or "the idea that consciousness arises via a body's interaction with its environment" – this essay suggests that descriptions of mountains and climbing that deploy haptic sublime rhetoric complicate the affective dimension of mountaineering and thus our understanding of the relationship between self and (mountain) environments (James and Morel, 2020, pp. 10–12).

Jon Krakauer's Mountaineering Memoirs: Exploring the Affective Dimension of Haptic Sublime Moments

Jon Krakauer's two chapters entitled "The Stikine Ice Cap" from his bestseller *Into the Wild* (1996), which is devoted to Christopher McCandless's hiking adventures in North America and Alaska in the 1990s, develop the haptic dimension of the sublime. The first chapter begins with two quotes on rock climbing, one from John Menlove Edwards's "Letter from a Man" in which he claims that his mind "was wanting something more, something *tangible*" and the other from Thoreau's *Journal* (1837–1861), in which wilderness aesthetics and the natural sublime unambiguously prevails as he ascends an "unhandselled, awful, grand" mountainous landscape which could "never become familiar" (Krakauer, 1996, p. 133, emphasis added).[1] The chapter's main difference from the rest of the creative nonfiction book, which makes it belong to a particular category of autobiography or memoir, is that the author and narrator, Krakauer, replaces the protagonist, McCandless, as he identifies with his resentment toward his father, which is confusingly conflated with a desire to make the father proud.[2] As a result of this troubling relationship, Krakauer explains, he developed in his youth a coping mechanism in what first appears as a frontiersman's self-reliant desire to defeat the terrifying and dangerous wilderness and the traditional mountain sublime:

> I devoted most of my waking hours to fantasizing about, and then undertaking, ascents of remote mountains in Alaska and Canada—obscure spires, steep and frightening, that nobody in the world beyond a handful of climbing geeks had ever heard of. (134)

However, climbing turned out to enrich his imagination as he comments on his experience in a much more positive approach that defies the fraught Burkean and natural sublimes:

> Some good actually came of this. By fixing my sights on one summit after another, I managed to keep my bearing through some thick postadolescent fog. Climbing *mattered*. The danger bathed the world in a halogen glow that caused everything—the sweep of the rock, the orange and yellow lichens, the texture of the clouds—to stand out in brilliant relief. Life thrummed at a higher pitch. The world was made real. (134)

Krakauer does not establish a firm ontological border between the human (himself) and the nonhuman (the so-called "unhandselled" [Krakauer, 1996, p. 133] mountain landscape). Unlike what the traditional sublime suggests, he seeks a committed and less observational relationship with the mountain which eventually transforms the "frightening" into

---

[1] As José Sánchez Vera notes, the term "unhandselled" was "coined by Emerson and used by Thoreau" and refers to "nature as untouched, unused or unproven by the human being" (2015, p. 50).

[2] Vera uses Sidone Smith and Julia Watson's term "auto/biography" to define Krakauer's "mode of narrative that inserts a personal narrative within a biography" (Vera, 2015, p. 42; Smith, 2001, p. 184).

"brilliant relief". Lastly, Krakauer's ascent is a coming of age experience which got him through a "postadolescent fog" because he concludes that "the world was made real" through his transformational experience. This comment contrasts with a claim he makes in an earlier book, *Eiger Dreams: Ventures Among Men and Mountains*, that "constructions of the imagination have a way of blurring with reality" since, in this case, his idealisation of what climbing mountains had meant for him or for other mountaineers and poets did not influence his epiphany (1997, p. 5).

The ascent of the "Devils Thumb", a challenging Alaskan mountain for every climber, leads Krakauer to further introspection as he reflects upon solitude and gets an introductory taste of the haptic sublime. At first, Krakauer seems persuaded that climbing for him is what John Menlove Edwards, from whom he quotes twice in the chapter, terms a "psycho-neurotic tendency" or a form of "refuge from the inner torment that framed his existence" (p. 135). Then, Krakauer's opinion on solitude and human interactions evolves, specifically because of a decisive encounter with a woman named Kai Sandburn:

> I had convinced myself for many months that I didn't really mind the absence of intimacy in my life, the lack of real human connection, but the pleasure I'd felt in this woman's company—the ring of her laughter, the innocent *touch* of a hand on my arm— exposed my self-deceit and left me hollow and aching. (p. 137, emphasis added)

Through intimate and physical contact with Kai, Krakauer realises his "self-deceit", or that isolation in mountains may not be the healthiest way of dealing with personal issues. When back climbing the Devils Thumb, he acknowledges that "alone, [...] even the mundane seem[s] charged with meaning" as the peaks are "infinitely more menacing than they would have been [had he been] in the company of another person" (p. 138). As his "emotions [are] similarly amplified" with "periods of despair" that get "deeper and darker", time spent alone in the mountains has "enormous appeal" but also seems uncomforting since he later feels "abandoned, vulnerable, [and] lost" (pp. 138–41).

However, when Krakauer reaches the "Witches Cauldron Glacier", the climbing experience turns into what he describes as a "trancelike state" that "settles over your efforts", "a clear-eyed dream" which makes you forget "the accumulated clutter of day-to-day existence" for a brief moment as "an overpowering clarity of purpose" and the "seriousness of the task at hand" gradually install (pp. 142–43). Such a conclusion results from demanding haptic efforts that eventually make his bodily movements automatic in what becomes an entirely embodied experience of the mountainside:

> All that held me to the mountainside, all that held me to the world, were two thin spikes of chrome molybdenum stuck half inch into a smear of frozen water, yet the higher I climbed, the more comfortable I became. Early on a difficult climb, especially a difficult solo climb, you constantly feel the abyss pulling at your back. To resist takes a tremendous conscious effort; you don't dare to let your guard down for an instant. [...] But as the climb goes on, you grow accustomed to the exposure, you get used to rubbing shoulders with doom, you come to believe in the reliability of your hands and feet and head. You learn to trust your self-control. (142)

This climbing moment, which provides him with "something resembling happiness", is what differentiates the haptic from the traditional sublime, as well as from Edwards's "psycho-neurotic" attitude (143). Krakauer's experience has affinities with McNee's "haptic sublime" inasmuch as it is "transformed by an infusion of physical exercise and hazardous contact with mountain landscapes, and by a heightened concern with materiality" (2016, p. 149). Krakauer's "trancelike state" and his use of a terminology traditionally associated with the sublime – words like "difficult", "tremendous", "exposure" – are also reminiscent of McNee's argument that the "physical connection" is "directly responsible for creating a powerful, even transcendent emotional experience in the climber", who does not necessarily use the term "sublime" but describes an experience that is undoubtedly sublime (2016, p. 149). Contrary to the Burkean distant and fraught experience of mountain landscapes, Krakauer's climbing moment exemplifies the haptic sublime experience because of its "aesthetic of mastery, of overcoming a threat or difficulty" rather than of pondering over or submitting to its perceived divinity (2016, p. 151). Besides, Krakauer's sublime is not centred around the sense of sight but, rather, "involve[s] the whole body" (2016, p. 153). As he overcomes the sense of overwhelm produced by the overpowering mountain, it is Krakauer's "clarity of purpose" that becomes "overpowering", which suggests that, unlike traditional sublime moments, "the human subject's sense of agency and power is reinforced rather than diminished by the experience of danger and physical suffering" (Krakauer, 1996, pp. 142–143; McNee, 2016,

p. 158). The choice of the word "happiness" to characterise the experience also echoes McNee's interpretation of the term in Albert F. Mummery's account of "The Aiguilles des Charmoz and de Grepon" as an expression of the haptic sublime or as the surprisingly comforting and exhilarating feeling that the climber experiences after a difficult ascent (2016, p. 159). If the perception of the Burkean or natural sublime seems to be an inevitable stage in the climber's sublime moment, Krakauer's approach evokes what McNee identifies as a determining factor of the haptic sublime, namely "the effect of diminishing interest in the sublime object, and even to a certain extent in the perceiving subject, concentrating instead on the processes by which sublime affect is produced" (2016, p. 161). By surpassing the spiritually elevating moment, Krakauer's climb becomes, through intense and risky physical contact, a "finely attuned instrument for making sense of [the mountainous] landscape" (2016, p. 175).

The second "Stikine Ice Cap" chapter also starts with two quotations: one from John Muir's *Mountains of California* (1882) which highlights the "uncontrollable there is" in climbers (Krakauer, 1996, p. 145), and the other from Donald Barthelme's *The Dead Father* (1975), which portrays a complex father-son relationship centred on a son who seems deeply affected by his unloving paternal upbringing. The structure and form of the different chapters, which all include one or two epigraphs, are meant to set the tone of the storyline. If the first Ice Cap chapter conveys the author's desperate need to find meaning and comfort in the act of climbing, the second one details the trauma through which he suffered in his troubling relationship with his father, which negatively impacted his perception of climbing. This contextualisation of Krakauer's unstable father-son relationship also constitutes a narrative technique, a backstory as well as a hypodiegetic story inasmuch as it helps both Krakauer, who experienced a similar trauma, and the reader to identify or sympathize with Chris McCandless while contributing to the romanticisation of the story (Vera, 2015, p. 59). At the end of the chapter, Krakauer compares his climbing experience with Chris McCandless's last moments in Alaska as they "were similarly affected by the skewed relationships [they] had with [their] fathers" and had a "similar agitation of the soul" (p. 155). Chris's sister, Carine McCandless, also published her memoir *The Wild Truth* (2014) in which she points out Chris's unstable family life as the main determining factor that urged him to embark on his life-ending journey in Alaska. Since Krakauer's first climb of the Devils Thumb was unsuccessful, this contextualisation is used by the author to justify his hard-headed and reckless behaviour as he depicts himself as a sore loser who made the decision to give it another try during which he finally reached the summit. Initially, his description of the summit is again reminiscent of the Burkean horror insofar as it "was a surreal, malevolent place", but he then feels "euphoria" and an "overwhelming sense of relief" when he returns, which was followed by "an unexpected melancholy" (pp. 153–154). As the descent is not exactly part of the sublime experience, it is a significant stage for Krakauer because it ensures its completion by provoking a necessary feeling of relief. This essay's interpretation of the descent contrasts with literary scholar Anne C. McCarthy's "Red Bull Sublime" and view of the descent of the Everest in *Into Thin Air* as "almost taken for granted as an inevitable, but far less interesting, part of the process" (2017, p. 546). Indeed, there are similarities between Krakauer's melancholy and the positive aspects of the (haptic) sublime experienced after the descent since, as philosophers Emily Brady and Arto Haapala have argued, both the sublime and melancholy involve feelings of pain, fear, or "loneliness" which are then overcome and replaced by "the exhilaration of our capacity to cope with an impending obstacle" for the sublime and the comeback "to the sweetness of particular memories" for melancholy (Brady and Haapala, 2003). In Krakauer's case, there is reluctance and then refusal to concede to fear or pain or to be discouraged by danger, which finally provides him with heightened self and environmental awareness. Whether this ascent turned out to be a positive haptic sublime experience, in which overwhelming relief prevails over the overpowering mountain landscape, he cannot but admit that it was a life-threatening act motivated by "hubris" (p. 155). As Krakauer concludes, "it changed almost nothing", "but [he] came to appreciate that mountains make poor receptacles for dreams" (155). From this significant climb (and descent), Krakauer realises that the sublime may have instilled mountain landscapes with an excess of poetic or spiritual meaning. His personal haptic experience of the Devils Thumb was an opportunity to, through physical effort, gain understanding of the *material* mountain landscape that exists beyond the spirituality and imaginative literary descriptions of the traditional sublime. Ironically, it is Krakauer's story and descriptions that could provoke a similar sentiment in readers.

While traditional theories of the sublime have focused on a spiritually elevating experience of the sublime, they have stimulated a view of (mountain) landscapes as admittedly perilous but also, especially when conflated with frontier ideology, as challenges to be overcome. Krakauer refers to this conflation in *Eiger Dreams* by quoting famous rock climber John Gill who claims that in order "to be a boulder", one needs "to be on the frontier, to discover things" (p. 17). In his reading of Slavoj Žižek's take on the sublime, Shaw rightfully notes that "the sublime does indeed verge on the ridiculous" because "it encourages us to believe that we can scale the highest mountains" and "become infinite" whereas "all the time it is drawing us closer to our actual material limits: the desire to outstrip earthly bonds leads instead to the encounter with lack, an encounter that is painful, cruel, and some would say comic" (Shaw, 2017, p. 10). While canonical theories of the sublime celebrate ideas of greatness and infinity, the ridiculous sublime demystifies the act of climbing high mountains, underlining its lack of "powerful moral and political resonances" and making the climber "ridiculous" in his belief that mountains are accessible and that climbing them will lead to moral elevation (Ngai, 2010, p. 950). Ultimately, this experience could culminate in what Ngai calls the "stuplime" because "the ridiculous" occurs when the climber faces not "the infinite but [...] finite bits and scraps of material in repetition" which produce "sudden excitation and prolonged desensitization, exhaustion, or fatigue" (2005, pp. 271–272). More importantly, such a view of the sublime that urges us to "scale" high mountains is here at the origin of Krakauer's haptic sublime experience, but it results in a more humbling moment which does not border on the ridiculous. In his memoir *Into Thin Air* (1997), in which he recounts the disastrous 1996 Mount Everest expedition during which eight mountaineers passed away, Krakauer conveys that self-determination, or obduracy as he understands it, as well as an idealistic perception of mountains led the climbers to turn a blind eye on other dead climbers' corpses:

> Few of the climbers trudging by had given either corpse more than a passing glance. It was as if there were an unspoken agreement on the mountain to pretend that these desiccated remains weren't real—as if none of us dared to acknowledge what was at stake here. (1999, 111)

Adopting an approach reminiscent of what he describes in the Ice Cap chapters, Krakauer further argues that "adrenaline" was not what motivated the climbers but very much what resembles the haptic sublime conversion of pain to euphoria and relief:

The ratio of misery to pleasure was greater by an order of magnitude than any other mountain I'd been on; I quickly came to understand that climbing Everest was primarily about enduring pain. And in subjecting ourselves to week after week of toil, tedium, and suffering, it struck me that most of us were probably seeking, above all else, something like a state of grace. (1999, 140)

The repetitive, tedious and painful movements and physical efforts, here expressed by means of the rhetorical device of amplification through the dramatic repetitions of "week after week of toil, tedium, and suffering" are significant components of the climb. They echo McNee's understanding of the haptic sublime, although they involve not only the haptic but all of the "lower" sensory systems such as the kinaesthetic and the vestibular, which have been traditionally, at least in Western history, "dedicated to manual labor and the basic feeding and care of the body" (Howes and Classen, 2014, p. 67). A weakness in McNee's theory is therefore his omission of these sensory systems—that the term "haptic" fails to represent—which complicate and enrich Krakauer's embodied experience. To a lesser degree, Krakauer's description is reminiscent of Ngai's "stuplime", especially because it converts repetitive tedious efforts into the shocking result of a "state of grace", which is the haptic sublime's pleasurable outcome.[3] The moment of "stuplimity", Ngai explains, stems from a correlation of shock or astonishment with boredom which is caused by exhausting repetitions and permutations, a rhetorical and narratological strategy which enables the reader to develop minor feelings beyond traditional templates of awe or horror. For example, Ngai uses Gertrude Stein's modernist novel *The Making of Americans: Being a History of a Family's Progress* (1925), in which "repeating is [...] the dynamic force by which new beginnings, histories, and genres are produced and organized" (2005, p. 262). In addition to "stuplimity", this "state of grace" and the satisfaction it provides seem to obscure if not obliterate notions of vulnerability and mortality as "mortality had remained a conveniently hypothetical concept, an idea to ponder in the abstract" and climbing a way of "idealiz[ing] risk-taking"

---

[3] McCarthy discusses this specific "state of grace" passage in her article "Reading the Red Bull Sublime" as representative of the "higher meaning" climbers instill into the act of ascending while the process of descending appears as tedious and banal (2017, p. 546). My analysis focuses instead on the transformation of the "enduring pain" into "pleasure" since it is more relevant in my interpretation of Krakauer's haptic sublime experience.

and "steal[ing] a glimpse across [the] forbidden frontier" of mortality (Krakauer, 1999, pp. 282–87).

Despite his idealisation of risk and personal accomplishment, Krakauer ambiguously alternates in the "Stikine Ice Cap" chapters as well as in *Into Thin Air* between "an emphasis on self-reliance" and his difficulty bearing loneliness (1999, p. 11). For example, a recurrent technique in Krakauer's writings is, as this essay has shown, to include epigraphs at the beginning of his chapters. This practice is again repeated in *Into Thin Air*, in which some of the quotes evoke loneliness, like in Thomas F. Hornbein's *Everest: The West Ridge* (1965), or a need to rely on one's own competence and survival skills more than on other people, like in Krakauer's mentor David Roberts's *Moments of Doubt: And Other Mountaineering Writings* (1986). Besides, while he acknowledges that being guided by Sherpas, who basically did everything from cooking to carrying their equipment, through the Everest trip was "hugely unsatisfying" (p. 176), Krakauer comes to, when he is back in the United States, (re)appreciate intimacy with his wife and the undemanding, "ordinary pleasures of life at home" which "generated flashes of joy that bordered on rapture" (p. 282). As this passage and the climb of the Devils Thumb showcase, positive emotions of relief and joy are often used by Krakauer to characterise the aftermath of his haptic sublime experience, and they are also frequently conflated with a renewed appreciation of simplicity. For instance, in his essay "Descent to Mars", he describes his return to the surface after exploring the Lechuguilla Cave in Mexico as "electric, surreal, almost overwhelming" and providing him with a relieving "whoop of joy" and "a newfound appreciation of the ordinary" (2019, p. 65). Still, this relieving moment of "rapture" occurs after the climb or the descent, thus suggesting again that physical efforts and suffering are prerequisites for the positive outcomes of the haptic sublime. Krakauer's descriptions of haptic moments, however, present this demanding bodily experience of the mountain landscape and the resulting positive emotions of relief, joy and melancholy as vectors of constructive meaning. If the haptic sublime experience does not (yet) culminate in explicit concerns over environmental disruption, it does lead to a connection with materiality which can be characterised as trans-corporeal. In other words, Krakauer's bodily experience of mountain terrain produces a *different* aesthetic engagement than visual contemplation from afar, and thus necessitates a move – at once conceptual, embodied and affective – beyond the traditional frame of the natural sublime.

Conclusion: Thinking with a Mountain, or the Limits and Affordances of the Haptic Sublime in the Contemporary Memoir

The current context of global ecological crisis compels us to rethink the relationship between self and material environments. Since the sublime has been a prevalent case study for the exploration of the mind-body-environment relationship, its recontextualisation and consequential redefinition have become paramount. This chapter's analysis of the haptic sublime in Jon Krakauer's mountaineering works have suggested that the contemporary memoir is a suitable genre for outlining the foundations of such a project because of the narrative strategies and scenarios it employs, which are inevitably human-centred and personal and refer to landscapes that physically exist outside the actual literary text. Despite its unfortunate ableist bias, and its conceptual vagueness inasmuch as the term "haptic" does not inevitably involve all the human sensorial systems, McNee's revision of the sublime contributes to enriching our understanding of the sublime and to reevaluating its relevance in affect studies and affective ecocriticism since the (narrative) affects it can deploy – ranging from "tedium" and "pain" to "joy", "euphoria" and "melancholy" – complicate the affective dimension of the self-environment relationship.

In an essay entitled "Embrace the Misery" published in a recent collection of re-edited articles, Krakauer conveys a sense of resignation as he reflects upon the meaning of climbing in an era of global crisis and in relation to Albert Camus's *Myth of Sisyphus* (1942):

> As a gray-haired alpinist, you've spent more than half a century struggling on high escarpments, inventing purpose out of hardship, and conjuring meaning from otherwise senseless acts. For Sisyphus to be contented as he toils beneath his rock doesn't strike you as far-fetched. But when you contemplate the uncertain future and the Sisyphean tribulations it's apt to impose, actual joy seems a little too much to hope for. All things considered, you'd settled for stoical resolve. (2019, p. 178)

The sublime has for ages served poets and mountaineers alike to make sense of the ineffable or impenetrable. Contrary to what Krakauer seems to suggest, his "senseless acts" or risky haptic experiences of mountain rocks and landscapes go beyond Sisyphus's content with his daily meaningless struggle. Krakauer humbly, and possibly unconsciously, reminds us that commitment entails contact, that the sublime experience has to be direct and not distant for it to become (eco)critically meaningful and useful. Thinking *with a* mountain will require less of the spiritual mystique surrounding climbing and the traditional sublime, and substantially more of this "stoical resolve" to foster the awareness that haptic sublime moments have to offer.

Bibliography

Alaimo, S. (2010) *Bodily Natures: Science, Environment, and the Material Self.* Bloomington, IN: Indiana University Press.

Brady, E. (2013) *The Sublime in Modern Philosophy: Aesthetics, Ethics, and Nature.* New York, NY: Cambridge University Press.

Brady, E. and Haapala, A. (2003) "Melancholy as an Aesthetic Emotion", *Contemporary Aesthetics*, 1. Available at: https://quod.lib.umich.edu/c/ca/7523862.0001.006/--melancholy-as-an-aesthetic-emotion?rgn=main;view=fulltext (Accessed: 19 June 2023).

Burke, E. (1998) *A Philosophical Enquiry Into the Origin of Our Ideas of the Sublime and Beautiful.* Edited by A. Phillips. Oxford: Oxford University Press.

Caracciolo, M. (2021) "Being Moved by Nature in the Anthropocene: On the Limits of the Ecological Sublime", *Emotion Review*, 13(4), pp. 299–304. doi: 10.1177/17540739211040079.

Couser, G.T. (2011) *Memoir: An Introduction.* New York: Oxford University Press.

Cronon, W.J. (1995) "The Trouble with Wilderness; or, Getting Back to the Wrong Nature", in *Uncommon Ground: Rethinking the Human Place in Nature.* New York, NY: W.W. Norton & Co., pp. 69–90.

Fromm, H. (1993) "Aldo Leopold: Aesthetic 'Anthropocentrist'", *ISLE: Interdisciplinary Studies in Literature and Environment*, 1(1), pp. 43–49.

Holdefer, C. (2020) "Necessary Wonder: Promises and Pitfalls of Enchantment", in Meillon, B. (ed.) *Dwellings of Enchantment: Writing and Reenchanting the Earth.* Lanham, MD: Lexington Books, pp. 23–32.

Houser, H. (2014) *Ecosickness in Contemporary U.S. Fiction: Environment and Affect.* New York, NY: Columbia University Press.

Howes, D. and Classen, C. (2014) *Ways of Sensing: Understanding the Senses in Society.* New York, NY: Routledge.

James, E. and Morel, E. (2020) "Introduction: Notes Toward New Econarratologies", in James, E. and Morel, E. (eds) *Environment and Narrative: New Directions in Econarratology.* Columbus, OH: The Ohio State University Press.

Krakauer, J. (1996) *Into the Wild.* New York, NY: Anchor Books.

Krakauer, J. (1997) *Eiger Dreams: Ventures Among Men and Mountains.* New York, NY: Anchor Books.

Krakauer, J. (1999) *Into Thin Air: A Personal Account of the Mount Everest Disaster.* New York, NY: Anchor Books.

Krakauer, J. (2019) *Classic Krakauer: Essays on Wilderness and Risk*. New York, NY: Anchor Books.

Lombard, D. (2019) *Techno-Thoreau: Aesthetics, Ecology and the Capitalocene*. Macerata: Quodlibet.

McCandless, C. (2014) *The Wild Truth*. New York, NY: HarperCollins.

McCarthy, A.C. (2017) "Reading the Red Bull Sublime", *Publications of the Modern Language Association of America*, 132(3), pp. 543–557. doi: 10.1632/pmla.2017.132.3.543.

McNee, A. (2016) *The New Mountaineer in Late Victorian Britain: Materiality, Modernity and the Haptic Sublime*. London: Palgrave Macmillan.

Morton, T. (2018) *Being Ecological*. Cambridge, MA: The MIT Press.

Ngai, S. (2005) *Ugly Feelings*. Cambridge. MA: Harvard University Press.

Ngai, S. (2010) "Our Aesthetic Categories", *PMLA/Publications of the Modern Language Association of America*, 125(4), pp. 948–958. doi: 10.1632/pmla.2010.125.4.948.

Nicolson, M.H. (1959) *Mountain Gloom and Mountain Glory: The Development of the Aesthetics of the Infinite*. Ithaca, NY: Cornell University Press.

Peeples, J. (2011) 'Toxic Sublime: Imaging Contaminated Landscapes,' *Environmental Communication*, 5(4), pp. 373–392. doi: 10.1080/17524032.2011.616516.

Phelan, J. (2017) *Somebody Telling Somebody Else: A Rhetorical Poetics of Narrative*. Columbus, OH: The Ohio State University Press.

Purdy, J. (2015) *After Nature: A Politics for the Anthropocene*. Cambridge, MA: Harvard University Press.

Ray, G. (2005) *Terror and the Sublime in Art and Critical Theory: from Auschwitz to Hiroshima to September 11*. New York, NY: Palgrave Macmillan.

Shaw, P. (2017) *The Sublime*. London: Routledge.

Smith, S. (2001) *Reading Autobiography: A Guide for Interpreting Life Narratives*. 1st edn. Minneapolis: University of Minnesota Press.

Vera, J.S. (2015) "Thoreau as an Oblique Mirror: Jon Krakauer's *Into the Wild*", *American Studies in Scandinavia*, 47(1), pp. 40–60. doi: 10.22439/asca.v47i1.5160.

Vermeulen, P. (2020) *Literature and the Anthropocene*. London: Routledge.

Chapter 4

Transforming the Dirtbag Label in Kentucky's Red River Gorge

James Maples and Michael Bradley

Located in a rural impoverished region of Eastern Kentucky and Central Appalachia (United States), the Red River Gorge has often been considered a hidden gem. Climbing memoir author Chris Chaney notes, "when you drive in the Red River Gorge through the small unincorporated towns of Nada, Slade, and Pine Ridge, you don't automatically recognize the wealth of recreational opportunities hiding under the trees and below the flat horizons of the Cumberland Plateau" (Chaney, 2019, p. 7). These wild areas remained largely unknown to outdoor recreation users until the 1960s when concerns over a proposed dam vaulted the region to national recognition (Maples, 2021). Soon, protestors, activists and visitors swarmed to the Red River Gorge, "to see the place the Army was going to destroy with water" (Collins, 1975, p. 275).

Chris Chaney's climbing memoir *In the Red* (2019) recounts the unlikely story of rock climbing in Kentucky's Red River Gorge (herein the Red), exploring how climbers find a sense of belonging and completion through climbing there. Chaney represents one of very few people empowered to write a true memoir of the Red's climbing community as he is a local resident and a climber. As a result, the memoir was written for both climbers looking to experience Chaney's time in the Red (in the same vein as many climbing memoirs are written) while locals would

Unless otherwise cited, quotes in this chapter are from interviews conducted 2016–2021 in the Red River Gorge. The authors have provided residents stilling living in the Red River Gorge pseudonyms to protect their anonymity among a very small community.

appreciate titbits of history and Chaney's connection to place. As a Powell County native, Chaney understands the unique experience of living in Central Appalachia's hollers and hills.[1] He also understands the pull of the Red: "While the Appalachian community where I grew up continually drives me away looking for opportunity...the Red River Gorge always draws me back. It is my spiritual magnetic north" (Chaney 2019, p. 13). Chaney's early interests in the isolated pleasure of the Red led him to explore most every foot of it. Yet his hikes and climbs found few local faces there: "In the years before, during, and after my time as an active rock climber I didn't encounter many of my fellow Eastern Kentuckians in the cliff-shadows of the Red River Gorge" (Chaney, 2019, p. 9). He notes that it "was rare to run into people from Powell, or Wolfe, or Menifee, or Lee Counties. And when I did it seemed they disappeared almost as soon as I found them" (Chaney, 2019, p. 9).

Chaney's identity as a climber is complicated in that it binds him with an outsider label. Residents long steered clear of the Red's wilderness areas and those who engaged these areas for outdoor recreation. Chaney argues this was triggered by residents' fight for a proposed dam in the 1960s. Climbers coincidentally arrived as protests rose, leading locals to label climbers as outsiders, hippies and dirtbags in the region. Limited interactions between climbers and residents further allowed locals to imbue climbers with the mystique of violating cultural norms. Perceptions would only begin to change as local businesses began accepting climbers as clientele and research debunked their myths about climber demographics.

Memoirs provide a valuable opportunity to look backwards in history and place events into the context of place and time. Seemingly unimportant events can be understood within a greater narrative, providing insight on the impacts of decisions made and paths chosen. Like memoirs, the stories conveyed from one generation to the next generate their own memories. Children are taught the stories and experiences of previous generations through family stories, lived lessons and morality tales. In the Red's case, two competing memories existed: that of the climber envisioning themself as a dirtbag and the local community's perception of the dirtbag label as a negative connotation. In the end, discussions between the two sides

---

[1] "Holler" is an Appalachian term used to describe communities in remote, rural areas. These areas are often bound on more than one side with natural features such as mountains or rivers. Hollers are also a point of place attachment and using the term is understood to be synonymous with ideas like "home" or "where I'm from".

following the advent of sport climbing greatly diminished the competitive memories, blurring them together as the climber becomes part and parcel with the Red.

This chapter follows a history where Chaney's memoir weaves into the history of this community. It explores how residents initially branded visiting climbers as outsiders, hippies and dirtbags over five decades, but, and more importantly, how ongoing efforts have deconstructed these perceptions to create a collaborative narrative of the region. This chapter explores how climbing memoirs in general understand the dirtbag label before breaching into a concise history of the Red's climbing community in the shadow of a proposed dam. Longstanding myths established about visitors and the norms of using the Red during this time were reinforced as self-evident truths decades later with the appearance of climbers at Miguel's Pizza, a restaurant located inside a former commune. However, as a handful of local businesses embraced climbers and the Red's value as a climbing destination became evident, local perceptions slowly changed. The release of an economic impact study in 2017 led further business owners to drop their guard to climbers, leading to a rapid increase in the acceptance of climbers as a part of the local community. Now, as the history of the Red continues to unfold, storylines are adopting a collaborative narrative.

Climbing Memoir and the Dirtbag

Climbing memoirs place seemingly unrelated stories into a skilfully woven historical context, providing meaning and clarity to the lived experience. Steve Roper's (1998) *Camp 4* and Glen Denny's (2016) *Valley Walls* envelop the authors' climbing experiences within the history of Yosemite and America's Golden Age of Climbing. Lynn Hill's (2003) *Climbing Free* and Miriam Underhill's (1971) *Give Me the Hills* explore how gender and outdated patriarchal beliefs stand between women who climb and their goals. Alex Honnold's (2016) and Alexander Huber's (2010) memoirs both examine the free-solo climbing life when the rope is removed. Climbing memoirs also use tragedy and death as context. Tommy Caldwell's (2017) memoir, *The Push*, links his climbing life to the aftermath of a death while on an expedition. Catastrophic accidents, such as the 1996 Everest disaster (Boukreev and DeWalt, 1997; Krakauer, 1997), have also spurred memoirs looking to explain the past through select moments.

Climbing as a lived form of life, up to the point that one's life spent climbing is perhaps embodied within one's ability to climb, is a frequent premise in climbing memoirs. *Climbing as life* represents an existence filled with purpose largely because climbing is present (Rickly, 2016; Rickly, 2017). This idea is plainly embedded even in memoir titles. David Roberts (2005) uses the subtitle "A Climbing Life Reexamined" to denote the important connection between life and climbing. This theme is frequently revisited in the reflective nature of nearly every climbing memoir's backward glance: that one's existence is best remembered through challenges at the crag, while everything else (relationships, careers and other lived experiences) take a back seat.

Of note here is the *dirtbag*: a climber wholly dedicated to climbing such that they eschew all other opportunities (Rickly, 2012). Perhaps best chronicled in *Dirtbag: The Legend of Fred Beckey* (O'Leske, 2017), the dirtbag chooses poverty in exchange for more time to climb. They identify ways to stretch and reduce expenditures to supplement their climbing lifestyles. Similarly, comforts and relationships (beyond climbing relationships) simply melt away to hone one's internal focus on climbing. The dirtbag is also no longer isolated to climbing. It now has overflowed into most any form of outdoor recreation wherein the user abjures the ideals entailing a normal life lived for accomplishments in the wilderness. Similar terms like *hiker trash* are now used to indicate one has centralised outdoor recreation as the central purpose of one's existence (Fondren, 2015).

Dirtbags have no clear etymological origins although it is often attached to Yvon Chouinard and Yosemite's climbing community in the 1950s. Yosemite's Golden Age revolved around historic climbers like Royal Robbins, Warren Harding, Tom Frost, Chuck Pratt, Dean Caldwell and Chouinard (Roper, 1998). The community had divergent philosophies on climbing; Robbins, for example, was an aesthete in shirking permanent protection inserted in the rock face, while his frenemy Warren Harding promulgated hammering in permanent gear along routes to get to the top. Over time, these competing philosophies converged to appreciate the value of both perspectives, with Royal conceding the situational value of Harding's approach on the Dawn Wall in 1970 in his own memoirs (2009). However, they remained unified in scrimping to extend their stay in Yosemite, even as park rangers gradually cracked down on their violations. Throughout, this community utilised *dirtbag* as a term of endearment and affirmation of one's dedication to climbing.

Flooding and Climbing in the Red

The history of climbing in the Red, in some ways, begins in the history of flooding in the Red. Eastern Kentucky is prone to flooding and has a storied history of deluges causing rivers to swell, top their banks, and plunge fields, roads and homes deep into the water. Over the last century, counties linked to the Red (Powell, Wolfe, Lee, Menifee) have seen extreme floods resulting in loss of life, property and opportunities, including a very recent 2021 flood in Lee which submerged much of downtown Beattyville along the banks of the Kentucky River (Maples, 2021). Following a devastating 1962 flood in Powell County's Clay City, the US Corps of Engineers (COE) released plans to construct a dam and reservoir on the north Fork of the Red River to limit localised flooding. The COE plan would flood approximately 1,400 privately held acres as well as 2,000 acres on the Daniel Boone National Forest (Kentucky Afield Radio, 2016). As a result, much of the Red would become a water recreation and retention pond.

Residents and politicians strongly supported the proposed dam. The collective feeling was that it would prevent future devastating flooding in the region (Shrake, 1968). A 1963 COE public meeting in Stanton (Powell County) on the dam proposal recorded no dissent. The next step was to delist the Red River as a protected wild and scenic river. This step slowed things until 1966, by which time regional and national resistance had fomented against the dam. In February 1966, Carroll Tichenor, Dorris Tichenor, Bill Holstein, Jim Kowalski and others founded the Cumberland Chapter of the Sierra Club. This chapter represented the primary resistance against the dam, while residents counter-organised the Red River Dam Association in support of the proposed dam.

At a follow-up 1967 COE meeting in Stanton, the Cumberland Chapter registered its public dissent against the dam, and this began a downward slide for the proposal. Although unable to secure support from other national organisations, the Cumberland Chapter successfully arranged for journalists from the Louisville Courier-Journal to hike with Supreme Court Justice William O. Douglass to the site of the proposed dam (Kentucky Afield Radio, 2016). This so-called Protest Hike drew greater attention to the dam and its impacts on the natural features of the region. Soon, Kentucky Governor Louie Nunn and Senator John Sherman Cooper both withdrew their support, eventually leading President Nixon to stop forward progression on the dam (Maples, 2021). A follow-up proposal in the early 1970s temporarily resurrected the dam proposal, but this soon broke apart. In later decades, the Red River would return to holding a scenic and wild river status, meaning that any future attempts to dam the river would be difficult. And it was amid this period the earliest climbers in the Red began putting on their harnesses and exploring what the Red had to offer.

The modern history of climbing in the Red unofficially begins possibly as early as the 1950s via Bluegrass Grotto, a spelunking organisation with ties to The University of Kentucky (Chaney, 2019; Maples, 2021). There are actually very few caves in the Red. Cavers were instead focused on its practical offerings as an above-ground practice site. Imagine for a moment, practising caving techniques for the first time *below* ground. There, it is dark, muddy and damp. It is also difficult to have one's instructor nearby and observing the process to ensure techniques are done safely. The Red's cliffs offered a perfect solution. There, cavers could install permanent bolts in the rocks and attach lines from these points to practice rappelling, abseiling and even chimney work in some spots. Not surprisingly the earliest documented climbing route in the Red was Caver's Route at Tower Rock, likely installed in the early to mid-1960s by members of Bluegrass Grotto (Maples, 2021).

Among these cavers were also several persons interested in climbing, among them Ron Stokley. Ron had caving experience from around the region (including Mammoth Cave in Central Kentucky) but was interested to climb in the Red. He soon connected with Dieter Britz, already an experienced mountaineer, who was in Lexington, KY for his postdoctorate at the University of Kentucky. The two soon collaborated with Bob Stokes to complete the Red's earliest fully documented climbing-only routes at locations like Chimney Top Rock (a location Chaney spends nearly a full chapter discussing in detail). Ron also acted as the leader of the first local climbing organisation in the Red, the Cumberland Climbers, which officially started 8 September 1969 (Maples, 2021). Although over one hundred members joined the Cumberland Climbers in the early years, there were only around a dozen or so actual climbers. The remainder were environmentalist and activists who were part of the Sierra Club's Cumberland Chapter, linking (in the eyes of locals) the environmentalists and activists against the dam directly to the climbers.

Ron and Dieter remember very few interactions with locals perhaps beyond getting gasoline in Slade. Ron shared, "(t)here were not many shops as I recall. Most of the time we took everything with us that we would need. I only recall dealing with a mechanic's shop once in an emergency situation" in which someone removed the spark plug wires from their Corvair engine to jumpstart a nearby road grader. Dieter had similar experiences:

> I don't remember encountering locals much, except one time, [Floyd] Ledford [after whom the Ledford Route, the Red's first fully-reported climbing route circa 1969 was named], invited us in and gave us water. And one time, as I drove up in fall, to camp with my wife among those great fall colours, a local asked me 'How's your hammer hanging' as I slowly drove past.

Similar to Ron, Dieter had been assisted by a local resident on a car issue: "Another time the clutch in our Rambler Ambassador got stuck, and another local, came up and said 'Havin trouble, buddy?'. I explained, and he asked me if I had a screwdriver. I did, and he fixed the problem." There were even few interactions with the Daniel Boone National Forest Service workers. Ron felt this might be due to the Sierra Club's lack of interactions with the Forest Service following the dam's defeat.

The Appearance of the Post-dam Dirtbag

The negative application of the dirtbag label developed in stages in the Red through conditions created by the failed dam proposal. First was a period of transition from the dam to a relative lack of interaction between climbers and residents. The fallout from the dam was a mix of passioned loathing and indifference. Local business owner Ella Carroll expressed her concerns about outsiders meddling in the affairs of the Red's local residents: "Everything was fine down here for a long time – we were going to get our dam and flood control and everything. Then some danged outsiders had to pipe up" (Rutherford, 1972, p. 23). Ella went on to explain that residents understood what needed to be done and knew what was best for the area without outside input. Moreover, she felt the people fighting the dam wouldn't be there or even care when the next flood came. More frequent, however, were the long looks at local businesses as climbers came through. The coincidental link between environmental activism and climbing had established them as being outsiders to the residents. Or as Chris remembered it: "(t)hose who supported the dam and the Red River Lake weren't thrilled about the Sierra Club and others who came in and

meddled in local affairs" (Chaney, 1999, p. 8). Interestingly, climbers felt
very little of this malice: Ron Stokley and Dieter Britz recalled having very
few interactions with locals after the dam protests concluded. The Forest
Service simply continued with business as usual, communicating with
climbers to ensure natural features were protected when impacts rarely
proved an issue. As such, the feelings that climbers were outsiders was
effectively an internal dialogue among local residents of this generation.
This would remain a theme for decades for future climbers: a sense of
emotional distance grew between locals and climbers reinforced by
minimal interactions between the two sides.

The influx of visitors also mixed with inclusion of environmental
activists linked to the dam protests. Environmental activists were rendered
by residents as being synonymous with the greater political temperature
of the era to reinforce the idea that hippies and protestors were present
in the Red. Recall the late 1960s and early 1970s in the United States
were a period of social revolution. The term hippie was often used as an
oversimplification of persons participating in this time of change. Chaney
vividly remembers the perception that the Red "was populated by dirty
hippies and ruffians" was prevalent throughout his interactions with other
residents (Chaney, 1996, p. 8).

Logically, climbers' behaviours also labelled them as being different
than the local population. Rock climbing has never been a cultural activity
for Appalachians. Adam, a Beatyville native, sums up his perspective on
climbing: "They're crazy. They're nuts…Gray's Arch one time, I was
watching them rappel, they were jumping from a cliff onto a little tiny
rock just like it was nothing…I'm not that brave." Buried within that
recent (2016) interview quote, one can already see a separation presented
between locals and climbers and what is a normal way to use the Red. A
more normal use of resources would be All Terrain Vehicles (ATVs), which
are popularly used by residents for hunting, farming, transportation and
recreation. As a point of comparison, had climbers been on ATVs instead
of hauling rope bags and carabiners, then climbers (or rather ATV users)
likely would have been largely accepted by the local community from day
one. Moreover, climbers are quite recognisable based on their distinct rope
packs, the clinking of metal carabiners in their bags, their clothing, and
their talk. This made the labelling process that much easier.

Second, climbing occurred in a forbidden zone where their activities and
engagements were deemed deviant by residents (Jamal and Hollinshead,
2001). Despite its predilection with flooding the Red, locals remained

largely wary of it. Lifelong Wolfe County resident Jenny shared a story from her childhood about territorialisation. "As a child and teenager growing up in Wolfe County, we were pretty much forbidden to go (to the Red)." Her family members would go fishing in the Red, but "would come up on these little villages of people and there would be drinking and drug activity involved and that stopped the locals from going. Ever since then the locals have told their kids not to go because it was a bad place." Here the theoretical process of territorialisation occurs, as acceptable norms for a particular area are dictated to residents. Ellen of Estill County tells a similar story about access to the Red: "I really didn't know about the Red River Gorge until I was in middle school, and then I was allowed to go to certain places (in the Red) by myself and with friends." When asked, both agreed that much of what individuals locally knew (both now and then) about visitors in the Red was largely handed down across generations and subject to a healthy injection of myth. Taking a distrustful view of those who used the Red for recreation was really a cultural norm for the area. There was also probably a smidge of power and influence involved in the territorialisation, as taking efforts to control the activities of the young in the community could arguably keep them within the major cultural norms of the time.

Third was the premise that the dam, even in its failure, had brought and would continue to bring in more visitors. Common local logic felt that news of the Red's amazing wilderness spaces would prove too much for tourists' intemperance, and that an influx of tourism would destroy the region. In the 1970s, local resident Lionel Johnson saw the proposed dam's failure as an augury of the Red's doom: "The single most adverse impact on the area as a result of the new dam and reservoir won't be the water, but the additional people they will bring to the Gorge" (Rutherford, 1972, p. 23). This is relatable to extensive research exploring how resident populaces see new faces (such as immigrants) entering a particular area (Cervantes, Alvord and Minjivar, 2018; Panichella and Ambrosini, 2018; Tummala-Narra, 2020).

Interestingly, this same concern for an influx of tourists and visitors to the Red was a similarity between residents and climbers, although this message was never adequately communicated to the other sides. This tone washed over into several publications from this era, including the Red's second climbing guide, written by Frank Becker, which stated in its introduction that the book's real purpose was to document the history of the place before it was lost, noting the Red was "doomed to impoundment. Though it is likely that the lake will directly affect the climbing routes, it will certainly deteriorate the aesthetic experience of climbing" (Becker, 1974, preface). Guides over the next decade would continue this messaging. Today, guides still include concerns over climber impacts and list ways to ensure those can be reduced.

By the end of the 1970s, the foundations for negatively labelling climbers had been set: they were established as outsiders, the Red had been compartmentalised into acceptable/unacceptable territories, and there was clear (or at least self-reinforcing evidence) that this new horde of visitors would not stop coming to the area. A handful of environmentalists from the dam protests remained in the region. A Buddhist retreat would open in nearby Clay City in the mid-1980s while a communal living area developed in Slade. Throughout, locals remained convinced that climbers were different from those who lived in and around the Red, with the outsider, dirtbag and hippie labels remaining quite sticky. Chrissy, from Beattyville, added "(t)here's quite a few (climbers) that come into the area" and described climbers as "(k)inda hippy-ish, all natural folks....Earthy, that describes them." She went on to talk about her memories of a climber she recently saw in the Red: "There was a man sitting at the bottom of one of the cliffs with a bongo drum and dog and no one else around." But perhaps the strongest evidence would come following the advent of sport climbing in the mid-1980s and the increasing presence of climbers at a business, Miguel's Pizza. There, a swelling horde of brightly clothed to sometimes semi-nude climbers could be seen primitive camping and holding bonfires well into the evenings. And this could be seen by any local resident as they drove alongside the restaurant on one of the main highways through the area.

Embracing the Dirtbag Ethic at Miguel's

Chaney's memoir includes a long list of encounters with new faces and friends related to his adventures in the Red, but one of the most poignant is his encounter with Stephen. He meets Stephen one winter while exploring a crag in the Red.

> As I hiked along the deserted trail below a towering cliffline movement up near the base of the wall caught my attention. I looked up and saw a gangly person, seemingly male, wearing a baclava covering his face, and walking sort of away from me...

[i]t was my own private bigfoot sighting right here in the Red River Gorge. (Chaney, 2019, pp. 40–41)

As it turns out, Stephen had moved from Cincinnati, Ohio to live in the woods while working on the route Halloween. The two struck up a friendship of sorts and Chaney agreed to return the next day to climb with Stephen. Chaney's mom was not excited to hear about the chance encounter nor that her son would be climbing with a "bigfoot" person he'd met in the woods, and this harkens back to similar concerns by local residents about exactly who would be found out there in the Red's wilderness.

The Red was attracting a new set of tourists to the region as the 1970s gave way to future generations of climbers. Amid the rise of sport climbing, the Red transitioned from a fairly isolated community of trad climbers to a nationally known (and soon globally renowned) sport climbing community (Mellor, 2001). This community centred itself around Miguel's, an ice cream parlour turned pizza shop right on the edge of the Red. Climbers bolting routes in the Red needed a nearby base of operations so they could effectively live in the Red. Miguel's existed on a communal property and the owners, Miguel and Susan Ventura, began making bread for climbers. Before long, they allowed camping in the back yard and cemented their place in the Red's climbing history.

Life at Miguel's took on a tribal essence not dissimilar to the Yosemite Camp 4 ethic. Climbers lived for extended periods in Spartan conditions, pinching pennies to extend their stay. Both conditions (e.g., lack of available showers) and climbing itself rendered Miguel's new residents dirty and unkept by modern standards. And inside the camps, a largely young contingent of lifestyle climbers did everything from wax bombs (loud and bright explosions of burning wax) to bonfires late into the night. By day, residents driving through the area could see the tents as well as climbers in various states of dress moving in and out of Miguel's. To those living at Miguel's, their lives were pursuing that essence of living to climb. To local residents, it reinforced daily the idea that climbers were different, outsiders and perhaps even a bit scary. However, Miguel's also creates one of the early instances where local residents and climbers could exist in a shared space, and this idea of shared spaces would gradually change how locals understood climbers.

Sharing spaces with others can change perceptions. For example, Knappert and associates (2020) found that interacting and having personal contact with refugees positively impacts how one sees migrants in general. Similarly, Turner and Brown (2008) explored how children's short-term attitudes toward refugees could be changed through educational programmes exposing them to refugee experiences. In exploring a wide berth of research on perceptions of immigrants, Rétiová and associates (2021) found evidence that being exposed to persons deemed as outsiders meant the lines between in and out groups theoretically should begin to blur and the gaps between the two groups dwindle. So, too, was the case with residents and climbers.

Miguel's was home to many legendary climbers over the years. Tim was one of several important climbers who could be regularly found at Miguel's living in an abandoned house dubbed The Love Shack in response to climbers sleeping nearly naked there in Kentucky's hot summers. Tim remembers that residents did visit Miguel's to eat and that he, unlike other climbers, interacted with them: "I had a much different relationship with the locals than most other climbers. I made friends with lots of them." He also felt that locals weren't bothering the climbers: "I also never remember locals harassing climbers either. There was friction with the oil companies in the southern region early on", partly caused by establishing the Pendergrass-Murray Recreational Preserve, but less so locals actually causing problems. Rather, the persistent idea of climbers as outsiders remained, leading locals more often to watch them from afar. This would continue until accepted residents began thinking of climbers in terms of clientele. Tim represents one of these important collective efforts by a handful of climbers to begin communicating with residents, gradually breaking the silence between the two sides.

By the turn of the century, three more businesses in the region embraced climbers as clientele: Lago Linda, Land of the Arches, and Koops. Each was important in providing legitimacy to the climbing community in its own way. First, Lago Linda created a lodging option in the newly expanding southern region of the Red. At the time, Lago Linda was owned by Linda Black. Linda and her husband Doug had settled on the property in the 1990s as a retirement location. They tried several business options, including a horse-riding camp, but found purchase when Kenny Barker became their first steady climber clientele in 2003 while he was establishing routes in the region. Over time, more climbers came, and within years, Linda's became a common place to leave campers and camper vans all climbing season. Linda remembered that local residents still felt climbers were a failure as clients: "What are you doing? You'll close down!" she remembered them telling her. Within a matter of years, a local gas station up the street began similarly courting climbers as clientele while climbers also began attending local tourism org meetings in Lee County.

David Terrill is the owner of Land of the Arches and is a long-time resident of Wolfe County. As a child, David had relocated to Ohio as part of the Great Migration but returned to work with his grandparent's farm to help support his family. There, David learned how to operate a farm. As a young adult, David would again relocate to Ohio to work in manufacturing but would return to Wolfe County to retire. He purchased the land that would become Land of the Arches. He constructed a large hanger which turned into several temporary business ventures: a roller rink, a flea market, a boxing arena, and even a horse show venue. By this time (around 2006) climbers were expanding well into Wolfe County at Muir Valley, a climbing preserve. David then opened his property as a campground for the climbing community for $5 a night. They soon flocked to the property given its convenient location near Muir Valley. In the coming years, the Red River Gorge Climbers' Coalition would begin hosting their annual Rocktoberfest event at Land of the Arches. Again, through interacting with a local business, climbers earned legitimacy.

Last is Koops General Store, located near The Motherlode in Lee County. The Motherlode represents likely the most famous climbing area in the Red and has become a world famous climbing area. Koops' clientele is decidedly centred on residents: they sell anything one might expect at a local convenience store as well as gasoline. However, their proximity to the region's established ATV trail system makes them a common destination for this community. Davis from Beattyville puts it like this: "Get fuel, grab a sandwich, recharge, and hit it again." Davis describes Koops as the focal point for a growing ATV community in the area. Koops provides a location for the community to meet for ATV trips around the area, as well as tables for conversations over thick cut bologna sandwiches. Residents recognise ATVs as a form of adventure tourism (which has, of recent, become a buzz word in local and state government) and the economic activity that follows tourism. Dustin from Beattyville shared that "[t]ourism is one of the only economic developments in this area, so any way we can get people to come here, the better". Dustin adds that "commercially, I just see [ATVs] taking off now. Adventure tourism is just starting to develop now, which is good. We need it." This support for ATVs has created an opening for climbers, too.

Given Koops' proximity to The Motherlode, climbers have also made the general store a frequent stopping point in an area otherwise lacking retail opportunities. Climbers would stop for snacks, but later began asking about leaving cars there as parking is at a premium in most crags. Later came rental lockers for storing gear and belongings to risk the potential for car break-ins. This created an opening, too, for climbers and local ATV users to begin communicating with each side, whether chatting over an ATV under repair or swapping stories over Ale-8s, a local soft drink.

In April 2016, James Maples and Brian Clark presented some of their recent findings (see Maples, 2017) about the Red's climbing community to local business owners (particularly rental cabin owners) in Lee County. Lee County is home to Beattyville as well as two climbing preserves managed by the Red River Gorge Climbers' Coalition. At this talk, Maples noted the disbelief among local resident attendees as he described climbers as well-educated with correspondingly high incomes, particularly when compared to the low wages often found in Kentucky. Brian felt the meeting was a turning point for residents, where a crucial second wave of business owners embraced the community, making them accepted visitors.

> The residents have embraced rock climbing and in turn this sport has brought life, energy, and money back into the region. There are many people who have moved to this area in eastern Kentucky to be close to the steep sandstone cliffs and just as many that just want to be in this area because of the culture that has been building over the past couple of decades.

By this time, the barriers between locals and climbers had steadily diminished.

Conclusion

Chaney notes the importance of being in the Red as a form of recovery and recharging: "Everyone has their reasons for coming to the Red, and most come as empty vessels wanting to be filled by the wonder and beauty of the place" (Chaney, 1999, p. 8). Climbers sojourn to the Red with increasing frequency as locals feared in the 1960s and 70s, while local residents continue to send their roots deep. Since then, climbers have spread further and further from the Red with each generation such that, today, the bulk of climbing there is no longer even in the Red River Gorge proper. Along the way, climbers established a system of support by select members of the community who demonstrated climbers as a viable form of economic activity in a very poor region. These relationships created conversations with locals, leading to the Red we know today, and will continue to shape the region and the story of the future.

Chaney's memoir also leaves space for future Red River Gorge climbers to recount and share their collective and individual memories. Following Maples' (2021) oral history of the Red River Gorge climbing community, several climbers who lived that history have begun writing their own memoirs. This includes some of the community's earliest members (from around the time of the proposed Red River Dam) sharing informal memories online with the community and Maples also sharing these memories through YouTube history videos. In remembering and stating the Red's importance in his own life, Chaney has now inspired others to reflect on this same premise. New historical challenges (such as the very recent proposed development of a destination resort in the Red) has also prompted climbers to reflect on their experiences there, mirroring some of the same reactions found in the fight against the 1960s dam proposal.

As new authors undertake writing their own memoirs, it will be interesting to see how the community addresses conflicting memories about historical moments. Internal differences (such as having different philosophies or even techniques in climbing) have previously created duelling perspectives on events within the community. Disagreements may be further influenced in Maples' oral history being treated as a formal record of the community, forcing memoir authors to frame their experiences within that recorded history. Internal divisions within the community (such as traditional versus sport climbers) may also have differing perspectives on the same events. Additional questions include what forms these memoirs will take. Chaney self-published his memoir, and given the ease and prevalence for doing this, it seems reasonable others may take this opportunity. However, other climbers have taken to sharing individual memories in online communities or even via publicly accessible reports. Still others have written poems, and more recently documentaries have been created on specific moments in the Red's climbing history (such as Mike Wilkinson's 2021 YouTube documentary on the legacy of Muir Valley). What remains unseen (for now) are the stories of those who will live these changes and hopefully write their experiences in new memoirs on the Red River Gorge.

Bibliography

Boukreev, A. and DeWalt G.W. (1997) *The Climb: Tragic Ambitions on Everest.* New York, NY: St Martin's.

Caldwell, T. (2017) *The Push: A Climber's Search for the Path.* London: Penguin.

Cervantes, A.G., Alvord, D. and Menjivar, C. (2018) "'Bad Hombres': The Effects of Criminalizing Latino Immigrants through Law and Media in the Rural Midwest", *Migration Letters*, 15(2), pp. 182–196.

Chaney, C. (2019) *In the Red: Adventures in Kentucky's Red River Gorge.* Stanton, KY: Ascensionist Press.

Collins, R.F. (1975) *A History of the Daniel Boone National Forest, 1770–1970.* Lexington, KY: Daniel Boone National Forest Service.

Denny, G. (2016) *Valley Walls: A Memoir of Climbing and Living in Yosemite.* San Francisco, CA: Yosemite Conservancy.

Fondren, K. (2015) *Walking on the Wild Side: Long-distance Hiking on the Appalachian Trail.* New Brunswick, NJ: Rutgers University Press.

Hill, L. (2003) *Climbing Free: My Life in the Vertical World.* New York, NY: Norton.

Honnold, A. (2016) *Alone on the Wall.* New York, NY: Norton.

Huber, A. (2010) *The Mountain Within: The True Story of the World's Most Extreme Free-Ascent Climber.* New York, NY: Skyhorse.

Jamal, T. and Hollinshead, K. (2001) "Tourism and the forbidden zone: the underserved power of qualitative inquiry", *Tourism Management*, 22, pp. 63–82.

Krakauer, J. (1997) *Into Thin Air: A Personal Account of the Mt. Everest Disaster.* New York, NY: Anchor Books/Doubleday.

Kentucky Afield Radio (2016) "Kentucky's Red November". Available at: https://www.youtube.com/watch?v=zM30OdwUckA (Accessed: 12 April 2022).

Maples, J.N. (2021) *Rock Climbing in Kentucky's Red River Gorge: An Oral History of Community, Resources, and Tourism.* Morgantown, WV: West Virginia University Press.

Maples, J. N., Sharp, R.L., Clark, B., Gerlaugh, K. and Gillespie, B. (2017) "Climbing out of Poverty: The Economic Impact of Rock Climbing in Eastern Kentucky's Red River Gorge", *Journal of Appalachian Studies*, 23(1), pp. 53–71.

Mellor, D. (2001) *American Rock: Region, Rock, and Culture in American Climbing.* Woodstock, VT: Countryman Press.

O'Leske, D. (Director) (2017) *Dirtbag: The Legend of Fred Beckey.* [Film]. Patagonia.

Panichella, N. and Ambrosini, M. (2018) "Between Fears, Contacts and Family Dynamics: The Anti-Immigrant Attitudes in Italy", *Int. Migration & Integration*, 19, pp. 391–411.

Rickly, J. (2016) "Lifestyle Mobilities: A Politics of Lifestyle Rock Climbing", *Mobilities*, 11(2), pp. 243–263.

Rickly, J. (2017) "'I'm a Red River Local': Rock Climbing Mobilities and Community Hospitalities", *Tourist Studies*, 17(1), pp. 54–74.

Rickly, J. (2012) *On Lifestyle Climbers: An Examination of Rock Climbing Dedication, Community, and Travel*. PhD dissertation, Indiana University, Bloomington.

Robbins, R. (2009) *To Be Brave*. Ojai, CA: Pink Moment Press.

Roberts, D. (2005) *On the Ridge Between Life and Death: A Climbing Life Reexamined*. New York, NY: Simon & Schuster.

Roper, S. (1998) *Camp 4: Reflections of a Yosemite Rockclimber*. Seattle, WA: Mountaineers Books.

Rutherford, G.O. (1972) "The Saga of the Red River Gorge", *American Forests Magazine*, 78 (February), pp. 20–23.

Shrake, E. (1968) "Operation Build and Destroy", *Sports Illustrated*, 1 April. Available at: https://www.si.com/vault/issue/42933/47 (Accessed: 12 April 2022).

Taylor, J. (2010) *Pilgrims of the Vertical: Yosemite Rock Climbers & Nature at Risk*. Cambridge, MA: Harvard University Press.

Tummala-Narra, P. (2020) "The fear of immigrants", *Psychoanalytic Psychology*, 37(1), pp. 50–61.

Underhill, M. (1971) *Give Me the Hills*. New York, NY: Dodd Mead.

Wilkinson, M. (2021) "The Muir Valley Legacy". Documentary. Available at: https://www.youtube.com/watch?v=cbV1XDDeNV8 (Accessed: 12 April 2022).

Chapter 5

Decolonising Mountain Writing

Gender, Race and the Mini-Memoirs of the Digital Age

Sarah Ives

As a social phenomenon the climb is not over till the tale is told. – Mitchell, 1983, p. 72

One photo of a woman climbing changed my perception of what I could or couldn't do, and I can only hope that my photography does the same. – Irene Yee, 2019, p. 83, Instagram handle, @she_explores

A pair of climbers roped together battle biting winds and blinding snow as they make their way slowly up an impossibly steep ridge, the risk of death ever imminent. Finally, they conquer the peak and pose for a victory picture. Sometimes they suffer from frostbite; sometimes they miraculously save a fellow climber; sometimes fellow climbers succumb to deadly falls. Often, they return home to write about it. Popular mountain memoirs have for decades constructed a particular notion of adventure connected to a particular notion of masculinity: white, cisgender and heterosexual (Rak, 2021; Michel, 2019). While the precise language used in mountain writing shifted from overtly colonial and militaristic during the Victorian era to spiritual and transcendent in the 1970s, the idea of who belongs – and who does not – in the mountains has remained strikingly similar.

This mountaineering literature foregrounds erasure. As Mark David Spence notes in his history of the US National Park Service, "outdoor enthusiasts viewed wilderness as an uninhabited Eden that should be set aside for the benefit and pleasure of vacationing Americans...[and] the exclusion or removal of native peoples" (1999, p. 4). The idea of reserving mountains for the white and privileged was echoed and amplified by many of the "founding fathers" of conservation and environmental movements in the United States. Gifford Pinchot, for example, often paired his admiration of mountains and forests with his advocacy for human eugenics. In *Our National Parks*, a 1901 essay collection written to promote tourism in parks, John Muir writes, "As to Indians, most of them are dead or civilized into useless innocence" (cited in Purdy, 2015). Edward Abbey, considered an iconic figure in nature writing, espoused virulently anti-immigrant views because he wanted to preserve open and uncrowded spaces from "culturally-morally-genetically impoverished people" (Kosek, 2006, p. 161).

These ideas have woven their way into mountain memoirs, but the consequences do not end there. Popular media are the primary means by which images and stereotypes about the outdoors are disseminated and perpetuated (Martin, 2004). As Carolyn Finney notes, "Racialization and representation [in the media] are not passive processes; they also have the power to determine who actively participates in environment-related activities and who does not; which voices are heard in environmental debates and which are not" (2004, p. 3). After all, Julie Cruikshank observes, "people delineate their understandings in stories" (2005, p. 20). Mountain memoirs have force in part because of their persistence: while each story is unique, the themes and actors remain remarkably alike. The "authentic" mountain voice mirrors the typical autobiographer and memoirist: "a unified, transcendent subject" (Coslett et al., 2000, p. 2). In other words, "privileged white male writers" (Ibid.).

This chapter explores how some people are challenging traditional mountain memoirs through a new form of self-representation: the social media app Instagram. With about two billion active users worldwide, social media have dramatically altered the way people interact, learn about current events, and represent themselves to the world (Miller et al., 2016).[1] Social media, scholars argue, are distinct from other forms of media because of their unique affordances, such as the "visibility and

---

[1] Instagram has not made its user numbers public since it crossed the one billion mark in 2018. However, news organisations cite sources who state the company passed two billion active users in 2021.

persistence of content, the association of connections, and the editability of content" (Costa, 2018, p. 472). Social media about climbing and other outdoor activities are no exception. A collection of groups and individuals has begun to use this forum to challenge the hegemony of privileged white male mountain writers. With Instagram handles such as @melanin-basecamp, @she_explores and @fatgirlshiking, they are rewriting the content *and* format of mountain memoirs, and more centrally, who the protagonists are. By creating their own accounts and fostering their own audiences, they are able to tell these stories *directly*, without gatekeeping by publishers or editors.

In the wake of Russian interference in the 2016 US presidential election, vaccine misinformation, and the storming of the US Capitol in 2021, discussions of social media and the dangers of fake news have taken centre stage. These are critically important conversations; however, rather than focusing on the truth or falsity of Instagram posts, I will demonstrate how social media allow members of historically marginalised communities to tell their own stories and challenge traditional mountain writing and the exclusive, toxic and even violent culture it can perpetuate. By conceptualising Instagram as a form of mini-memoir, I address how shifting and expanding the idea of what "counts" as mountain writing has the potential to be more inclusive and equitable.

I examined 40 Instagram accounts with a combined total of 42,013 posts and 2,349,021 followers. I started with accounts featured in news stories about "climbing" and "representation", and then expanded my analysis to accounts tagged or referenced by the original accounts, as well as to accounts recommended by Instagram's algorithm. In my analysis, I recorded each account's number of followers, types of photographs posted and narrative descriptions accompanying the photographs. Because I was interested in the dialogic nature of Instagram, I also read "Comments" sections below images. The accounts I analysed ranged from weekend climbers to professional athletes and mountain photographers with over 100,000 followers. I read the posts as texts, in parallel with my reading of "traditional" mountain writing in books and articles.[2] I used thematic analysis to identify patterns through a process of data familiarisation,

---

[2] The field of online ethnography is relatively new, and virtual/digital research methods have come under rigorous debate in the last decade (Abidin, 2020; Abidin and de Seta, 2020; Ardévol, 2012; Caliandro, 2014; Murthy, 2008; Pink et al., 2015). However, I analysed the accounts as public writing and did not conduct interviews.

coding, theme generation and revision (Braun and Clarke, 2006). Because the majority of these Instagram accounts come from North America, I will place them in conversation primarily with North American mountain writers.

Claiming, reclaiming and redefining language is key to decolonising mountains. Language around mountains and the people who visit or inhabit them is highly contested, with long, complicated genealogies. I have chosen to use the language that Instagram users themselves employ as it relates to gender, sexuality, race and ethnicity. I have also made the conscious choice to use the words "nature", the "environment", and the "outdoors" interchangeably and alongside "mountains" because part of the decolonising project central to many of the accounts I analysed includes challenging what counts as authentic, valued climbing or mountaineering experiences. These Instagram "memoirs" describe how representation matters, but also that representation alone is not enough. The regularity of posts and the ability to connect with others online allow these mini-memoirs to attach ideas about representation with calls to action: they attempt to change both the *narratives* and *politics* surrounding mountains. Like memoirists before them, they write from their personal knowledge and memories. Yet unlike the long form of a book, essay or magazine article, they write in short, regular bursts. Posts remain emergent and adaptable, the memoirs always ongoing and still-to-be-written.

The "Authentic Climber"

> Mountaineering is still foundational to the maintenance of a narrow version of masculinity, and that masculinity is the preserve of a certain kind of man, writ large in the hundreds of accounts of classic mountaineering expeditions, from the nineteenth century to the latest IMAX film about Mount Everest. – Rak, 2021, p. 5

Early European and Euro-American mountaineering literature was a product of the age of imperialism. The language in many of these accounts echoes that of colonial military campaigns. Expeditions used "siege-style" tactics to do "battle with a mountain", and writers connected mountain heroism to war heroism. In the Victorian era, mountaineers attempted to codify gender, like they did flora and fauna, by altitude: the higher the altitude, the more masculine the space (Reidy, 2015). During the shift to "alpine-style" climbing in the 1970s, stories of self-realisation and being "one with nature" moved to the forefront. Yet, scholar Julie Rak contends, the protagonists in mountain writing merely exchanged 'one kind of climbing masculinity for another' (2021, p. 59). Both masculinities necessitated privilege. As anthropologist Sherry Ortner writes, "One of the dominant discourses of mountaineering...positions itself as critical against 'bourgeois' existence, even as the sport demands the resources made possible by such an existence" (1999, p. 35).

Attempts to erase this privilege span from Thoreau's discussion of "living deliberately" and "Spartan-like" in the woods of Walden Pond to narratives about "dirtbag" climbers forsaking material possessions to eat from dumpsters and dedicate their lives to rocks. Yet these narratives were and are inherently exclusionary: Native Americans could not "live deliberately" on lands stolen from them; slaves had few opportunities to "live deliberately" anywhere. Geographer Jake Kosek describes how the idea of "salvation through a return to nature" foregrounds ideas of purity – both environmental and racial – and the "ability of whites to benefit from nature's curative powers depended on the absence of, and distance from, those with darker skin" (2006, p. 158). Exclusionary notions of nature spilled over and informed ideas about climbing and climbers. For centuries, debates about what constitutes "real climbing" excluded many from participating in mountaineering culture, except as "servants or members of the interested public" (Rak, 2021, p. 5). These ideas were deeply embodied. In other words, the physique of the climber – white, male, able-bodied – served as the measure of belonging, and "anyone who does not have such a body is either not an authentic mountain climber in the first place, or they must prove that they can be a worthy substitute" (Rak, 2021, p. 40).

With this policing, Rak argues that many were written out of the narrative, "because their way of doing things, or *being* in the world, are of no account" (Ibid.). In his influential 1865 book, *Man and Nature*, George Perkins Marsh "accorded 'man' a direct responsibility for the care and governing of 'her' well-being" (Kosek, 2006, p. 73). Nature was female, a space for (white) men to claim sovereignty (Kolodny, 1975). Conversely, women were not granted sovereignty over their bodies because they were seen as closer to nature than men were (Ortner, 1974). In other words, women cannot "conquer" nature because they "are" nature.

Femininity in mountain writing was defined in contrast to the authentic climber. In her account of a women's expedition to Annapurna,

Arlene Blum wrote of past experiences: "I went on a guided climb of Mount Waddington in British Columbia and was informed by our climbing guide that 'there are no good women climbers. Women climbers either aren't good climbers, or they aren't real women'" (1980, p. 1). Blum describes how men often told women that they were not strong enough to carry heavy loads or emotionally capable of handling the stress of climbing. Rak writes extensively about gender in mountaineering literature in her 2021 book, *False Summit*. She argues that most writing about women used "an ideology of liberal inclusion" – or simply added women to the list of "greats". She calls it a "hopeful strategy" that fails to address the sexism that prevented equal opportunities.

This sexism persisted in part because women and people of colour were seldom given the opportunity to write memoirs and were rarely interviewed in men's accounts. Instead, they were relegated to supporting roles, at best. Stereotypes are rampant in classic mountain texts, including Jon Krakauer's *Into Thin Air*, a book that sold close to three million copies. According to Rak, Krakauer depicts women as sexual distractions, a challenge to the "brotherhood of the rope" that might affect the ability of men to concentrate on climbing. Other stereotypes pervaded: women who climb were bad mothers, or they were infantilised, mere tourists shepherded up mountains. Women cannot be strong; they cannot be agents; and, significantly, they cannot "be Krakauer's rivals as chroniclers" (Rak, 2021, p. 214). In other words, women cannot write their own mountain memoirs.

With "the era of commercialization" in mountaineering in the 1990s, debates about who was and was not an "authentic climber" intensified. According to Rak, mountain writing framed diversity as a threat that represented climbing in decline. The many "firsts" by women, people of colour, and the disabled were described as "stunts", not as authentic climbs by climbers overcoming enormous odds. In her 2005 memoir, Blum describes a 1981 article in *Outside Magazine* written by David Roberts that asked: "Has Women's Climbing Failed?" The article stated that women often climb for the wrong reasons, one of which was to prove something about women. A 2015 article in *National Geographic* encapsulates this sentiment:

> The Everest game has intensified beyond mere mountaineering adventure; it is a notch in the belt, a pursuit of Guinness Book-ish records for being the first woman, the first black man (a South

African), and, more recently, the first black South African woman
to summit ...."For the true climber, the story and the experience,
exemplified by the way you go up the mountain, is more important
than getting to the summit," says Conrad Anker, an American
mountaineer who has climbed Everest. "For commercial expeditions,
it's more about getting to the summit". (Parker, 2015)

Tess Coslett and her co-authors (2000) assert that there has been a
longstanding feminist interest in the autobiographical because it connects
the personal and political and brings the gendered construction of subjectivities to the forefront. There are many examples of mountain memoirs
by women, including writing by famed Japanese climber Junko Tabei
and other "first" women climbers such as Sharon Wood. These memoirs
push back against the ideas expressed in Robert's *Outside* article and
Parker's *National Geographic* piece. The climbing magazine *She Sends*,
founded in 2003, centred women's experiences. But this writing rarely
receives the same attention as books such as Krakauer's *Into Thin Air*.
Alternative narratives of the Everest disaster, such as Lene Gammelgaard's
Climbing High: A Woman's Account of Surviving the Everest Tragedy,
have "been overlooked or even erased" (Rak, 2021, p. 216).[3] Instead,
autobiographies and memoirs have been typified by the (masculine)
privilege of self-possession (Marcus, 2004). While social media does
not necessarily challenge the privilege of self-possession, its format and
audience interaction can foreground the personal and political in ways
that books and magazines cannot.

From Books and Articles to Instagram

Before social media became widespread, people communicated through
media in two primary ways: publicly through broadcast media, such as
television, radio and newspapers, or privately through one-to-one conversations. The internet began to break down this public/private divide with
group emails, chatrooms, blogs, and eventually Instagram (Miller et al.,

---

[3] An exception to the idea of women's writing being overlooked is *Alpinist*, a magazine
dedicated to mountain literature and mountaineering ascents. The magazine began to
foreground underrepresented voices under the editorship of Katie Ives (note that Ives
is the author's sister). These articles often received widespread attention in the alpine-
climbing world and sparked at-times heated discussions.

2016). These changes in communication informed early ideas of digital optimists (Castells, 1997). Scholars such as Donna Haraway (2004) describe how high-tech culture challenges antagonistic dualisms, such as male/female, civilised/primitive, culture/nature that "have all been systematic to the logics and practices of domination of women, people of colour, nature…all [those] constituted as others" (p. 35). Digital optimists emphasised how the internet could enable the constitution of new forms of collective and individual gender identities. While in retrospect ideas of "free-floating online identities, detached from real-world bodies, have proved short-lived", forums such as Instagram provide space to reflect experiences that have been historically trivialised or ignored (Miller et al., 2016, p. 114). In this section, I describe social media, and Instagram in particular, as a different kind of space for self-representation.

Sites such as Instagram have certain signatures: they are easily copied and disseminated; they leave a digital footprint in archives; and they are instantly searchable and potentially viewed by millions (boyd, 2010). Instagram also encourages direct interaction through features such as "comments" and "likes". Scholars of the internet argue that one of its most enduring inequities is the gender divide (Dixon et al., 2014). Yet Instagram has challenged this pattern, with more women users than men (Auxier and Anderson, 2021). The app has significant racial and ethnic diversity as well: a Pew Center Survey of Instagram use in the United States found that about half of "Hispanic" (52%) and "Black Americans" (49%) say they use the platform, compared with smaller shares of "White Americans" (35%). Overall, 40 percent of adults in the United States have Instagram accounts (Ibid.).

With 59 percent of users logging on every day, Instagram weaves its way into people's lives, as they view the accounts of celebrities alongside those of family and friends (Auxier and Anderson, 2021). In the early days of the internet, people often differentiated between the "virtual" and the "real", but now "it is very evident that there is no such distinction – the online is just as real as the offline" (Miller et al., 2016, p. 7). As such, we should no longer view social media as simply a form of media or communication, but a "place where many of us spend part of our lives" (Ibid.). The Instagram accounts I analysed want to change that "place".

#RepresentationMatters

Some will say we are not there. Untrue. I will say that you haven't always wanted us to be seen. – @urbanclimbr, posted on 3 February 2021

The first time I saw a woman with brown skin sport climbing outside was on Instagram. She was radiant, smiling from ear to ear … I didn't realize what an impact that image meant for me and my climbing. – @browngirlsclimb, posted on 22 March 2018

Scholars describe the idea of "debriefing" as the moment when a private physical accomplishment becomes a public, social topic of discussion (Rak, 2021). Many Instagram accounts "debriefed" about how a lack of representation permeated their experiences in the mountains. In response, they worked to make their private accomplishments public through their posts. Miya spoke about how *she* could change representation through Instagram. She posted an image of herself with the caption:

Why don't I see more afros, sizes, shapes, and ambitions of all walks of life? Why don't more people of color know how great this sport is?…Will they be more motivated if we saw more people like us being successful, confident, and sponsored?…the easiest thing to do is be who I'd like to see more in the climbing community. (Posted on @browngirlsclimb on 18 January 2017)

For many, "making visible" is key to the mini-memoirs they post. "Here's our new goal," @melaninbasecamp's website states, "to increase the visibility of outdoorsy black, indigenous, people of color, to increase our representation in the media, advertising and in the *stories* we tell ourselves about the Outdoors" (2021, emphasis added). "A woman of color has been featured in every cover I have taken," @ladylockoff wrote on 15 August 2020, "and if that's not leaving something better behind me in the world, I don't know what is." She described herself as the author of a new mountain story with new protagonists.

Featuring new protagonists often involves redefining "authentic climbs". The mini-memoirs of Instagram included everything from first ascents of major peaks to family hikes in urban parks. As @sabrinachampman80 writes, "I don't want mainstream media to tell me what achievement looks like or what elite looks like. I want to define it for myself" (posted on

@she_explores on 12 August 2020). Champman is describing her experience in the documentary, *The Titan Project,* the first major crowdfunded film about a black woman sport climber – a film which premiered live on Instagram and Facebook. *The Titan Project* stands in contrast to mainstream films such as the Academy Award winning documentary, *Free Solo,* which featured Alex Honnold climbing El Capitan in Yosemite without ropes. "Stop Making Movies About White Guys Doing Cool Shit," wrote Anaheed Saatchi in an article for @melaninbasecamp (posted on 2 April 2019). "Free Solo took up so much screen time, so much cultural space, that I am left feeling as though none of the work around diversity in the outdoor industry is ever going to pan out if we keep bolstering straight, cis-gendered, white men as demigods." The post drew so much vitriol and so many racial slurs that @melaninbasecamp disabled the "Comments" feature overnight. One commenter responded:

> I think a lot of the negative reactions to this article boil down to what *constitutes a good story.* If you think that a good climbing story can only be about an ascent that's never been done before because of difficulty, remoteness, danger, etc [*sic*], then trying to include diverse climbers is seen as 'lowering the bar' but that's not the only factor that makes a good story. (Posted by @s.jamison, emphasis added)

The Titan Project focuses on Champman's climb, but also on her experiences as a black woman climber. She is attempting to shift what 'constitutes' a good story.

Many Instagram posts relay a common theme: one reason that climbing remains so hostile and unwelcoming – a place only for the privileged – is that the community defines authentic climbs as occurring only in epic locations. These kinds of climbs are not available to all. @eyeabearclimbs described how she did not have access to climbing gyms, rock walls or even trees growing up. Instead, her mountain memoir began with climbing kitchen cabinets (posted on 28 July 2019). These posts highlight the barriers many experienced when trying to enter the mountains. Climbing is expensive; it remains a "boys club"; and finding mentors is challenging for women, and women of colour in particular. Many women also feel at risk of sexual and physical assault when they put themselves in "male dominated spaces in the wilderness" (@BrownGirlsClimb, posted on 23 August 2019). These narratives paint mountains as places of fear and violence, not serenity and transcendental meaning.

Rewriting mountain narratives also involves redefining climber bodies in an intersectional way (Crenshaw, 2011). As @wishison wrote, "I dream of a climbing community where communities like mine are normalised, and where it's safe from racism, sexism, ableism, queerphobia, and other oppressive systems and behaviors. (Just like it's normal to check out knots, spot each other, and to not climb on wet sandstone)" (posted on @BrownGirlsClimb on 10 July 2019). Others posted about motherhood and climbing, "I make boob juice at the top of a mountain. What's your superpower?" wrote @eckoalecl, accompanied by images of her breast-feeding (posted on 12 September 2019). Still others lamented about parenting and childcare during COVID or their decisions to freeze embryos, decidedly different mountain stories than a conquest of Everest. They described menstruation while climbing, as well as body shaming and eating disorders.

Rather than relegating mothers to the sidelines – a bit part in a mountain siege, or worse a "bad mother" for leaving her child behind – Instagram posts celebrated post-partum bodies, even if that meant sharing details that many women hide. "When I got home [from a run] my shorts were soaked but my mind was happy," wrote @bethrodden. Her son "looked at me and said, 'what happened to your shorts?' I looked down, and looked back him, smiled and said very matter of factly, 'mom's pelvic floor never fully recovered after having you, so I pee when I run.'" The narrative was accompanied by a photograph of her wet shorts. "I feel like pee is the last thing I should be ashamed of since climbing through urine soaked cracks on El Cap is seen as a badge of honor and something that makes us climbers better than the normal person" (posted on 26 August 2020). She wanted to make her story part of the climbing narrative, a badge of honour: "I'm just going to keep posting these until it becomes normal instead of brave" (@bethrodden, posted on 18 December 2020).

The narrative around bodies extends beyond binary notions of men/women. Many posts raised the visibility of transgender and nonbinary climbers. In response to the idea of "firsts" as mere stunts, unbecoming of the authentic climber (unless they are white men, such as Alex Honnold), @inheadlights posted an image of a story about a first ascent by a non-binary climber:

> It might still feel strange to emphasize the importance of things like first transgender ascents or first non-binary ascents or a [first ascent] by a woman, but—here we are. And don't @ me because

I've heard arguments for both sides, and surely, so have you… But there's still a really cool historical aspect of a route that deserves recognition, and to be the first of *anything* does hold a special meaning. (Posted on 15 February 2021)

The post recognises an audience – "don't @ me", she writes, meaning don't send her combative comments – but explicitly attempts to control the narrative by foregrounding her own interpretation: firsts matter because they celebrate overcoming enormous odds, they represent "the possible" for many searching for mentors, and they re-write the protagonists of mountain writing.

Others paired first ascents by white men with historical contexts typically left out of these stories:

It is challenging for me to fully appreciate significant moments in climbing's history and know that these opportunities were not available to all, and that some were fighting for their lives—for basic human rights—at the time that others had the privilege to be blissfully selfish and invest in a sport. (Posted @meliseymo on 2 April 2019)

In other posts, @meliseymo pairs first ascents with events happening at the time, such as laws allowing people to be fired because of their sexuality, Rosa Parks and the bus boycott, and the Indian Relocation Act. The mountain story takes a decidedly different tone when framed in this way. She celebrates climbing through posts about her own experiences in the mountains, but she also argues that climbing cannot exist in a vacuum: white male mountain memoirs that are disconnected from politics and social justice were and are possible only because of the author's power and privilege.

Representation Is Not Enough

P.s. WE LIVE, HIKE, AND CLIMB ON STOLEN LAND. --@ BrownGirlsClimb, posted on 1 November 2017

In their discussion of feminism and autobiography, Coslett et al. (2000) describe the idea of testimony as a first-person account in the legal framework, but also in the religious sense: testimony involves bearing witness to conversion. Combining the legal and the religious, a feminist understanding of testimony could involve speaking about untold or *unheard* experiences. Unlike confession, listeners of testimony are encouraged to identify with the "victim" position – innocent and passive – rather than "discover the perpetrator in themselves as well" (Ibid., p. 11). The Instagram posts I analysed appear to do both – "convert" people to their way of seeing the world by telling their stories, while also asking people to interrogate their own complicity in racism, sexism, homophobia and ableism. These testimonies counter the patriarchy and privilege embedded in conventional mountain memoirs. While images are powerful, however, many posts specifically called out the limits of representation. It is one thing to portray happy or determined images of women and people of colour climbing, it is another to recognise that many do not feel safe in the mountains – not because they fear falls or avalanches, but because they fear violence and discrimination. As Cristal Cisneros wrote on @she_explores, "There's a big push to diversify the outdoors, but people don't understand that you have to make sure that those outdoor spaces are safe" (posted on 11 January 2021).

When some posted about discrimination in the mountains, they were told to be quiet and "just climb". But "just climbing" isn't possible when you are fighting for your life. As @nikkik_smith wrote:

> Why can't climbing…just be about climbing?" * This comment is used constantly when anyone from an underrepresented group talks about their experiences in climbing or the outdoors. * How can climbing be about climbing when a black climber has to worry about being harassed, attacked, or murdered while driving to a climbing area…No activity can be just about that activity when it's [sic] participants live in fear while participating. (Posted on 28 May 2020)

@Meliseymo compared her own experiences to the Instagram posts of her "white and white presenting peers" that were full of photographs of adventures in the mountains. "I don't know how many times this needs to be said: it is a privilege to ignore politics and enjoy the outdoors," she posted on 22 June 2018. In 2021, she compared their boasts about mountain exploits to the current era:

> Your successes happen at a time when protests for Black lives to matter are at a peak, when Black &/or Indigenous people are

disproportionately dying from covid19, when many are evicted and put out on the street, when many have lost loved ones. Are your... big wall ventures really that impressive if you had to be so privileged that you are virtually untouched by the pandemic and civil rights movement? (Posted on 5 May 2021)

Many accounts included mountain stories not only about their lives, but also about the lands on which they were hiking or climbing. Decolonising the outdoors was not just a project of foregrounding the visibility of *people* who had been left out of the narrative, but also of foregrounding the histories of the *mountains* themselves. These histories included acknowledging the Indigenous people who lived on or were dispossessed of those lands. Some accounts highlighted Indigenous names of mountains, while others focused on the long history of Indigenous climbers. @victoriabuschman combines these goals in her 25 November 2020 post:

Did you know that Inuit are some of the original adventurers, climbers, and mountaineers in the Arctic? We've been at it for thousands of years, before these activities were ever conceptualized as sports...Inuit have climbed up and rappelled off thousand foot sea cliffs all across our homelands, sometimes without ropes, in order to collect eggs from thick-billed murre and other seabird colonies. We still do this...The outdoors can often feel like places we don't exist or don't belong, but this couldn't be further from the truth! Our knowledge and skills have made it possible for other athletes and adventurers to come to our homelands and have amazing experiences. I don't doubt you've seen lots of glossy outdoor magazines with pictures and stories about our homelands without ever seeing or hearing about us. Next time you see a @ natgeo feature from the Arctic, consider that it's likely not the first time someone's been somewhere or doing something. Inuit have a long history of being pretty wild. I hope to live up to that someday... (Posted on @BrownGirlsClimb)

@victoriabuschman is signalling the erasure of Indigenous people in the past and the present. Central to this erasure is the idea of naming. As Alexandra Stern (2005, p. 121) writes, when European colonists and scientists encountered places that were new to them, they "classified flora and fauna while surveyors plotted terrain, attaching their surnames to plants and places and alternately erasing and raiding Native American tribal lexicons". Naming acted as a rite of possession. Instagram accounts such as @NativeOutoors and @BrownGirlsClimb attempt to shift that nomenclature by including Indigenous land acknowledgements with their climbing images or by geotagging the land with the Indigenous name rather than with the "colonial name": Chomolungma instead of Everest. @heyflashfoxy asks followers to take land acknowledgements one step further:

> Always take the time to ask: 'Who's Land Am I On?' Before climbing in a new area, learn about whose land it is, if there is indigenous presence there (or if it is a place of cultural and spiritual significance to one or more tribes). If available, check out the Cultural Centers, tribal websites and support native businesses. (Posted on 14 October 2019)

Issues around naming persist into the present. If books about mountains cement the fleeting experience of a climb into a social phenomenon digested and interpreted by millions of readers, the *names of climbing routes themselves* can inscribe the violence of racial and gendered exclusion onto the walls of mountains: "She Got Drilled." "Pussy Whipped." "Parade of Whores." "Slant Eye." "Case of the F*gs." "Kool Krux Klimbing." "Slave fingers." Expedition accounts and climbing guides that casually list "Smell of Fat Chick" as a "511.b trad climb" solidify who belongs in the mountains. Instagram accounts call out these names and the effects they have on feelings of safety and belonging. They call for a re-naming. As Saatchi (2020, p. 38) states, "Language provides affected communities with the ability to name injustice. Words reinforce direct action. We can't cease this dialogue until we've infiltrated the top tiers of the corporations, publications, gyms, events, nonprofits and all the other entities that build our modern climbing cultures…Climbing is political because everything is political." Woven between images of mountains and scenic climbs are photos of people voting, participating in the Women's March, and raising their fists at Black Lives Matter demonstrations.

Using the Tools of Instagram

I'm too exhausted from fighting racism at work, at the climbing gym, and in outside spaces to write anything on here. So here is a picture of me bouldering in Santa Fe over the weekend. – @ felinefavia (posted on 4 June 2020)

Photographs, Dunaway (2005) writes, can shape our imagination about how landscapes should be. Through an accumulated narrative of thousands of daily Instagram posts over the course of years, the accounts I analysed used photographs, links to other accounts, and hashtags to shape the mountain landscape. For some accounts, images of a person of colour or transgender woman or breastfeeding mother on a mountain provided a powerful counternarrative to prevailing ideas about authentic climbers. Other accounts emphasised collaboration, dialogue, education and mentorship. Many used Instagram to describe how their own politics and understanding of climbing and the climbing community could be adaptive to changing situations and to feedback from people engaging with material in their "Comments" sections. These "tools" of Instagram demonstrate social media's potential to upend the status quo.

"Did this photo of climbing get your attention?" asked @marina_ inaway under a scenic image. "Maybe you thought things were back to 'normal'! But no, I'm here to ask this: How will you bring the Black Lives Matter movement to your community?" (Posted on 10 April 2021). The image challenges representation in climbing, but the story posted under it attempts to engage the viewer in action. Many accounts highlighted that pretty pictures on Instagram do not tell the whole story. Under a smiling photograph of herself on the rock, @tradprincess paints a very different picture in her written description:

> This is a post I'm honestly uncomfortable making. I'm doing it because I've gathered a large social media following and I feel like it's the responsible thing to do. A girl I've been mentoring for a couple of years was raped…She thought she wasn't strong enough. She said she wished she was strong like me. Wow. Let me admit something I couldn't even talk about out loud until a couple of years ago. Something that still makes me scream, talk, and even cry in my sleep. I was taken advantage of when I was 15…Don't compare your real life experiences to some bitch on Instagram who likes to take neat climbing photos. (Posted on 30 August 2020)

At the end of the post, she includes seeming incongruous words: #climbingphotography, #climbing_photos_of_instagram, and other hashtags. A smiling photograph might have been used to get a user's attention, but why pair a heart-wrenching story of rape with such innocuous hashtags?

The use of hashtags – or # – at the end of posts is a common part of mountain stories. A hashtag is a label that helps people who are interested in a topic find similar content. Including a hashtag in a post makes the post visible in a larger conversation on Instagram or beyond, as demonstrated by the #MeToo campaign against sexual harassment and assault. Rentschler (2015) calls these group conversations "hashtag feminism". Hashtags are prominent on the accounts I analysed and include ones that highlight representation, broader social justice movements, or generic climbing conversations in a way that help to re-write those narratives with a variety of images and points of view, such as the @tradprincess example above (See Table 1).

Increasing Representation	#girlstraintoo, #browngirlslift, #womenwhoclimb, #girlsboulder; #fatgirlshiking, #diversifyoutdoors, #blackgirlmagic, #unlikelyhiker, #sheexplores, #herwild, #wildernessbabes, #mom, #adventuremamas, #girlswhoclimb, #outdoorwomen, #unlikelyhiker, #climblikeagirl, #OutdoorAsian, #brownpeoplecamp
Social Justice	#chicanamovement, #stophomophobia, #stopracism, #endsexism, #queer, #smashthepatriarchy, #publiclandscarenativelands
Generic Climbing	#climbing, #climber, #climbing_pictures_of_ instagram, #mountainlife, #liveclimbrepeat, #vanlife

Table 1: Examples of Hashtags

The idea of collective dialogue embodied by hashtags permeates Instagram posts. Indeed, dialogue is built into the app with its "Comments" feature. Readers can talk directly to the author of the "mountain memoir", and those conversations become embedded in the memoir itself. Conversations also cover logistical issues, such as organising affinity-based meetups and classes, supporting friends with fundraisers, organising climbing festivals, and making climbing gear accessible to all climbers, including those who identify as disabled, fat and non-binary. These concrete steps are critical to shifting offline experiences in the climbing world:

> Why do we need [climbing festivals]? Because we need to see women and GNC [gender non-conforming] folks lead. Because we need to

see women and GNC folks have and present technical knowledge. Because we need a space where we are not constantly questioned to explain ourselves. Because we need to see ourselves [to] know it's damn possible. (@ladylockoff, posted on @heyflashfoxy on 28 January 2020)

Conclusion

Pictured: me laughing because I overheard someone say 'Instagram isn't an effective tool for social change.'" – @laura.edmondson, posted on 11 January 2021

Here is to every single woman who chooses to stay on this platform. Who, despite all the sh*t that is said about her, continues on to share her life and show up for us who may not be that resilient yet. Thank you for sharing your stories, bodies, and vulnerability. – @ladylockoff, posted on 8 March 2020

Social media scholar Marwick (2019) argues that feminist spaces online can help normalise a feminist gaze on the world. But are these spaces truly inclusive? Can they re-write mountain narratives online in a way that shifts experiences offline? In her famous 1988 essay, Spivak asks: "Can the Subaltern Speak?" She notes that either they cannot speak at all, or they are read only as the "other", defined by their oppression, their only agency found in their "resistance". In some respects, Instagram perpetuates much of the silence and marginalisation that occur offline. For example, access to the internet – and therefore Instagram – remains out of reach for many. Yet Roopika Risam (2015) describes how the prevalence of feminist hashtags highlights arguments that intersectional feminists have been making all along: there is no single, common cause within feminist movements, and social media has the potential to displace white, cisgender and heteronormative narratives. According to Marwick (2019), the ability to call out racism, classism, transphobia or ableism within feminist movements *and* find solidarity with others is a strength of today's social media landscape (Marwick, 2019).

That said, many pitfalls remain online, including the prevalence of trolling – or the posting of inflammatory comments – and concerns around mental health. Marwick argues that harassment online is widespread in part because of the same technical functionality that allows for the building of community. Sociologist Erving Goffman (1959) famously wrote that impression management works only if the audience is in sync with a person's self-perception. The same argument can be made online: if audiences disagree with the image someone presents on Instagram, the self-presentation is interrupted. "We live in this comparison culture with social media platforms that make it difficult for us not to compare ourselves to other people," @SofJin wrote. "Since we can see them all the time in that culture, it's very easy to hold ourselves to an external standard, you know, be it from another person, an algorithm, a set of analytics, and to lose track of your own reasons for doing the things that you love" (posted on @she_explores on 23 June 2021). Despite the pitfalls, people keep posting, and with each post, they are writing their own stories about the mountains and their place in them – because it "matters to be seen."

Bibliography

Auxier, B. and Anderson, M. (2021) "Social Media Use in 2021", *Pew Research Center* [online]. Available at: https://www.pewresearch.org/internet/2021/04/07/social-media-use-in-2021/ (Accessed: 30 June 2021).

boyd, d. (2010) "Social Network Sites as Networked Publics: Affordances, Dynamics, and Implications", in Papacharissi, Z. (ed.) *A Networked Self: Identity, Community, and Culture on Social Network Sites.* New York, NY: Routledge, pp. 39–58.

Blum, A. (1980) *Annapurna: A Woman's Place.* San Francisco, CA: Sierra Club Books.

Blum, A. (2005) *Breaking the Trail: A Climbing Life.* New York, NY: Scribner.

Castells, M. (1997) *The Power of Identity. The Information Age: Economy, Society and Culture Vol. II.* Oxford: Wiley-Blackwell.

Coslett, T., Lury, C. and Summerfield, P. (2000) *Feminism & Autobiography: Texts, Theories, Methods.* London: Routledge.

Costa, E. (2018) "Affordances-in-Practice: An Ethnographic Critique of Social Media Logic and Context Collapse", *New Media & Society*, 20(10), pp. 3641–3656.

Crenshaw, K. (2011) "Postscript", in Lutz, H., Vivar, M. and Supik, L. (eds) *Framing intersectionality: Debates on a multi-faceted concept in gender studies.* Burlington, VT: Ashgate, pp. 221–233.

Cruikshank, J. (2005) *Do Glaciers Listen? Local knowledge, colonial encounters, and social imagination.* Vancouver: UBC Press.

Dixon, L., Correa, T., Straubhaar, J., Covarrubias, L., Graber, D., Spence, J. and Rojas, V. (2014) "Gendered Space: The Digital Divide between Male and Female Users in Internet Public Access Sites", *Journal of Computer-Mediated Communication*, 19(4), pp. 991–1009.

Dunaway, F. (2005) *Natural Visions: The Power of Images in American Environmental Reform*. Chicago, IL: University of Chicago Press.

Finney, C. (2014) *Black Faces, White Spaces: Reimagining the Relationship of African Americans to the Great Outdoors*. Chapel Hill, NC: The University of North Carolina Press.

Haraway, D. (1991) *Simians, Cyborgs and Women: The Reinvention of Nature*. New York, NY: Routledge.

Kolodny, A. (1975) *Lay of the Land: Metaphor as Experience and History in American Life and Letters*. Chapel Hill, NC: University of North Carolina Press.

Kosek, J. (2006) *Understories: The Political Life of Forests in Northern Mexico*. Durham, NC: Duke University Press.

Martin, D. (2004) "Apartheid in the Great Outdoors: American Advertising and the Reproduction of a Racialized Outdoor Leisure Identity", *Journal of Leisure Research*, 36(4), pp. 513–535.

Marwick, A. (2019) "None of this is New (Media): Feminisms in the Social Media Age", in Press, A. and Oren, T. (eds) *The Handbook of Contemporary Feminism*. New York, NY: Routledge, pp. 309–332.

Michel, B. (2019) "Making Mount Kilimanjaro German: Nation building and heroic masculinity in the colonial geographies of Hans Meyer", *Transactions of the Institute of British Geographers*, 44(3), pp. 493–508.

Miller, D., Costa, E., Haynes, N., McDonald, T., Nicolescu, R., Sinanan, J., Spyer, J., Venkatraman, S. and Wang, X. (2016) *How the World Changed Social Media*. London: UCL Press.

Ortner, S. (1974) "Is female to male as nature is to culture?" in Rosaldo, M.Z. and Lamphere, L. (eds) *Woman, culture, and society*. Stanford, CA: Stanford University Press, pp. 68–87.

Ortner, S. (1999) *Life and Death on Mount Everest*. Princeton, NJ: Princeton University Press.

Parker, L. (2015) "Will Everest's Climbing Circus Slow Down After Disasters?" *National Geographic* [online]. Available at: https://www.nationalgeographic.com/science/article/150513-everest-climbing-nepal-earthquake-avalanche-sherpas (Accessed: 1 July 2021).

Purdy, J. (2015) "Environmentalism's Racist History", *The New Yorker*. Available at: https://www.newyorker.com/news/news-desk/environmentalisms-racist-history (Accessed: 11 October 2022).

Rak, J. (2021) *False Summit: Gender in Mountaineering Nonfiction*. Montreal: McGill-Queen's University Press.

Reidy, M. (2015) "Mountaineering, Masculinity, and the Male Body in Mid-Victorian Britain", *Osiris*, 30(1), pp. 158–181.

Risam, R. (2015) "Toxic Femininity 4.0", *First Monday*, 20(4).

Saatchi, A. (2020) "Your Climbing Is Political Whether You Like It or Not", *Alpinist*, 16, pp. 38–44.

Stern, A. (2005) *Eugenic Nation: Faults and Frontiers of Better Breeding in Modern America*. Berkeley, CA: University of California Press.

Complete list of accounts consulted

Alannah Yip (2021) Alannah Yip's profile. [Instagram]. Available from: https://www.instagram.com/alannah_yip. (Accessed: 15 July 2021).

Ashima Shiraishi (2021) Ashima Shiraishi's profile. [Instagram]. Available from: https://www.instagram.com/ashimashiraishi. (Accessed: 20 July 2021).

Backcountry Babes (2021) Backcountry Babes' profile. [Instagram]. Available from: https://www.instagram.com/backcountrybabes. (Accessed: 16 July 2021).

Beth Rodden (2021) Beth Rodden's profile. [Instagram]. Available from: https://www.instagram.com/bethrodden. (Accessed: 20 July 2021).

Brittany Leavitt (2021) Brittany Leavitt's profile. [Instagram]. Available from: https://www.instagram.com/Bleavitt8. (Accessed: 8 July 2021).

Brown Girls Climb (2021) Brown Girls Climb's profile. [Instagram]. Available from: https://www.instagram.com/browngirlsclimb. (Accessed: 2 July 2021).

Brown People Camping (2021) Brown People Camping's profile. [Instagram]. Available from: https://www.instagram.com/Brownpeoplecamping. (Accessed: 15 July 2021).

Caroline Gleich (2021) Caroline Gleich's profile. [Instagram]. Available from: https://www.instagram.com/carolinegleich. (Accessed: 25 July 2021).

Dr. Carrie Cooper, DPT (2021) Dr. Carrie Cooper, DPT's profile. [Instagram]. Available from: https://www.instagram.com/carriecooper_dpt. (Accessed: 1 August 2021).

Climb Like a Woman (2021) Climb Like a Woman's profile. [Instagram]. Available from: https://www.instagram.com/climblikeawoman. (Accessed: 27 July 2021).

Daila Ojeda Sanchez (2021) Daila Ojeda Sanchez's profile. [Instagram]. Available from: https://www.instagram.com/dailaojeda. (Accessed: 28 July 2021).

Emily Harrington (2021) Emily Harrington's profile. [Instagram]. Available from: https://www.instagram.com/Emilyaharrington. (Accessed: 15 July 2021).

Fat Girls Hiking (2021) Fat Girls Hiking's profile. [Instagram]. Available from: https://www.instagram.com/fatgirlshiking. (Accessed: 16 July 2021).

Fat Wander Babes (2021) Fat Wander Babes' profile. [Instagram]. Available from: https://www.instagram.com/fatwanderbabes. (Accessed: 16 July 2021).

Favia Dubyk (2021) Favia Dubyk. profile. [Instagram]. Available from: https://www.instagram.com/felinefavia. (Accessed: 12 July 2021).

Flash Foxy (2021) Flash Foxy's profile. [Instagram]. Available from: https://www.instagram.com/heyflashfoxy. (Accessed: 15 July 2021).

Steph Davis (2021) Steph Davis's profile. [Instagram]. Available from: https://www.instagram.com/highsteph. (Accessed: 20 July 2021).

Kathy Karlo (2021) Kathy Karlo's profile. [Instagram]. Available from: https://www.instagram.com/Inheadlights. (Accessed: 21 July 2021).

Irene Yee (2021) Irene Yee's profile. [Instagram]. Available from: https://www.instagram.com/ladylockoff. (Accessed: 15 July 2021).

Laura, Digital Educator (2021) Laura Edmondson's profile. [Instagram]. Available from: https://www.instagram.com/laura.edmondson. (Accessed: 15 July 2021).

Lynn Hill (2021) Lynn Hill's profile. [Instagram]. Available from: https://www.instagram.com/_linacolina_. (Accessed: 21 July 2021).

Maiza Lima (2021) Maiza Lima's profile. [Instagram]. Available from: https://www.instagram.com/maizalimarock. (Accessed: 19 July 2021).

Marina Inoue (2021) Marina Inoue's profile. [Instagram]. Available from: https://www.instagram.com/marina_inaway. (Accessed: 18 July 2021).

Marisa Romero (2021) Marisa Romero's profile. [Instagram]. (Available from: https://www.instagram.com/marisaromeroo. Accessed: 20 July 2021).

Melanin Base Camp (2021) Melanin Base Camp's profile. [Instagram]. Available from: https://www.instagram.com/melaninbasecamp. (Accessed: 8 July 2021).

Mémé (2021) Mémé's profile. [Instagram]. Available from: https://www.instagram.com/Meliseymo. (Accessed: 9 July 2021).

Midori Buechli (2021) Midori Buechli's profile. [Instagram]. Available from: https://www.instagram.com/midoriontherocks. (Accessed: 17 July 2021).

Natives Outdoors (2021) Natives Outdoors's profile. [Instagram]. Available from: https://www.instagram.com/NativesOutdoors. (Accessed: 8 July 2021).

Nikki Smith (2021) Nikki Smith's profile. [Instagram]. Available from: https://www.instagram.com/nikkik_smith. (Accessed: 17 July 2021).

Olivia Hsu (2021) Olivia Hsu's profile. [Instagram]. Available from: https://www.instagram.com/olicow. (Accessed: 19 July 2021).

Pasang Llamu Sherpa Akita (2021) Pasang Llamu Sherpa Akita's profile. [Instagram]. Available from: https://www.instagram.com/pasang_llamu_sherpa_akita. (Accessed: 20 July 2021).

Paulina Dao (2021) Paulina Dao's profile. [Instagram]. Available from: https://www.instagram.com/paulinadao. (Accessed: 8 July 2021).

Caitlin McNulty (2021) Caitlin McNulty's profile. [Instagram]. Available from: https://www.instagram.com/seecaitclimb. (Accessed: 11 July 2021).

She Explores (2021) She Explores' profile. [Instagram]. Available from: https://www.instagram.com/she_explores. (Accessed: 8 July 2021).

Nina Williams (2021) Nina Williams's profile. [Instagram]. Available from: https://www.instagram.com/Sheneenagins. (Accessed: 10 July 2021).

Sophia Danenberg (2021) Sophia Danenberg's profile. [Instagram]. Available from: https://www.instagram.com/sophiaclimbs. (Accessed: 15 July 2021).

Sunny Stroeer (2021) Sunny Stroeer's profile. [Instagram]. Available from: https://www.instagram.com/sstroeer. (Accessed: 22 July 2021).

Theresa Silveyra (2021) Theresa Silveyra's profile. [Instagram]. Available from: https://www.instagram.com/theresasilveyra. (Accessed: 10 July 2021).

Mary Catherine Eden (2021) Mary Catherine Eden's profile. [Instagram]. Available from: https://www.instagram.com/tradprincess. (Accessed: 10 July 2021).

"L." R E N E E (2021) "L." R E N E E's profile. [Instagram]. Available from: https://www.instagram.com/urbanclimbr. (Accessed: 9 July 2021).

Wai Yi Ng (2021) Wai Yi Ng's profile. [Instagram]. Available from: https://www.instagram.com/waiyi.hawaii. (Accessed: 15 July 2021).

II. INTERSECTIONAL REPRESENTATION IN MOUNTAINEERING

Chapter 6

Bengal's Encounter with the Himalayas

Mountaineering Beyond Conquest

Anandarup Biswas

This essay pursues the argument that the Bengali-speaking people of India have, since 1960, followed their passion for climbing the Himalayan peaks with a motivation rooted not in an urge to conquer, but to attain goals of a more private and even spiritual order. As I trace the difference between the spirit of conquest that drove several British mountaineers of the colonial era and the more modest, yet equally determined pursuit of mountaineering that propelled many civilian climbers from Bengal, I propose an alternate ethic of mountaineering carefully represented within a robust tradition of Bengal's literary travel writing. By examining the literature of Himalayan journeys in Bengali along with public lectures, diaries and personal interviews, I have attempted to demonstrate a distinct yet emergent discourse of surrender that builds itself on withdrawal rather than assertion of the self. For British travellers and climbers I have focused particularly on the writings of John Hunt, Francis Younghusband, George Mallory and others who climbed, directly or indirectly, for the interests of the empire, along with more reckless and adventure-seeking individuals like Frank Smythe, Bill Tilman and Eric Shipton. For Bengali writings I have relied largely on the writings of the climbers themselves, interviews and reports on climbing where first-hand narratives are not available. But the Himalayas have also attracted pilgrims and trekkers from Bengal who have penned their travel experiences from the middle of the nineteenth century. This essay also takes them into serious consideration. Locating the cultural tradition of representing the Himalayas within a complex, interwoven discourse that draws as much on ancient scriptures and Sanskrit epics as on Bengal's colonial encounters with Western literary forms, I try to establish a difference in outlook towards the Himalayas between Bengal's climbers and those of the empire.

Bengal's mountaineering history is customarily traced back to the successful climb of Mt Nandaghunti (20,820 ft) in the Garhwal region in 1960,[1] but a couple of important names turn up farther back in time. Gopendranath Dutta, an employee of the Geological Survey of India, walked alone for about 155 miles from Jogbani in Bihar to Namche Bazaar in Nepal to join Eric Shipton who was then camping at Namche for the famous 1951 expedition to Mt Everest. Shipton sent him to explore an alternate route to avoid the Khumbu icefall and Dutta eventually climbed what was later named the Island Peak (20,210 ft) in a solo attempt. It remains the first recorded mountaineering feat by any climber from Bengal. In the same year Debshankar Seal and Kalyan Roy made a couple of serious climbing attempts in Sikkim (Das, 2006). But even before climbers from Bengal started making their mark, trekkers and pilgrims had made countless journeys on foot to several inhospitable and hard-to-access Himalayan locations.

Bengal's encounter with the Himalayas goes a long way back in time, to the eleventh century, when Atiśa Dipamkara (982–1026), a scholar from Bikrampur (in present day Bangladesh), crossed the Himalayas and reached Tibet to preach Buddhism (Atiśa 2011). The trade routes among India, Tibet and China were historically known as major contact zones through which ideas were exchanged and merchandise traded. Despite these long and deep cultural and religious linkages, preparations for serious climbing attempts in West Bengal began only after the historic success of the Mt Everest expedition of 1953. Tenzing Norgay, who made history alongside Edmund Hillary, was a resident of the Tong Song Bustee in the northern district of Darjeeling (in West Bengal) and soon after the successful summit attempt on 29 May 1953 the people of Bengal, along with those of Nepal claimed that Tenzing was the son of their soil. Tenzing was in fact given two passports – by India and Nepal – and honoured with the George Medal from the Queen, something that he refused since India was then no longer a part of the British kingdom and free India did not allow its citizens to hold foreign titles (Ullman, 2003, p. 285; Hansen, 2013, pp. 251–252). The euphoria after Tenzing and Hillary's success spread like wild fire and the sport of climbing caught the fancy of

---

[1] The first major mountaineering attempt by an Indian was by Gurdayal Singh who summited Mt Trishul (23,360 ft) on 23 June 1951.

978-1474220538

Bengal's youth rather quickly. More importantly, it drew attention from circles of governance too. Within a year, the first mountaineering institute was established in Darjeeling under the aegis of Dr Bidhan Chandra Roy who was at that time the chief minister of West Bengal, with Tenzing as its Director of Field Training.

It was also Tenzing, rather than Hillary, who emerged as the more accessible of the two heroes, probably because of his modest social background and non-white lineage. Soon after the Himalayan Institute started its operation in the autumn of 1954, a group of Bengal's young men who were passionate about climbing and worshiped the two heroes enrolled themselves for training. When these men – including Sukumar Roy, Biswadeb Biswas and Dhruba Mazumder – having completed their training, felt stifled by the mundane routine of their middle-class lives in Calcutta, the idea of an expedition took shape in their minds. It was neither easy nor common for men like them to start thinking of a civilian mountaineering expedition. The very thought of climbing a 20,000 ft mountain for sport was new and alien to the profile of the Bengali-speaking middle-class families; they could easily relate to cricket or football or hockey, but not climbing. High-altitude climbing was not just uncommon, it appeared too exotic to be a realistic hobby in their social sphere. Not only were Sukumar and his friends discouraged in their immediate circles, but the concerned authorities in the Indian government too were also not without misgivings about the potential of these men as climbers (Ghosh, 2001).

Ironically, their experience at the Himalayan Mountaineering Institute was far from motivating: "Sukumar found that most of his fellow trainees were military officers who came only for a certificate. They were least interested in the Himalaya. For most of them the Himalaya was a steppingstone to bigger goals [like promotion in service], not the goal in itself" (Ghosh, 2001, p. 21). Disappointment was in store even in later, planning stages of the Nandaghunti expedition when neither Tenzing nor Brigadier Gyan Singh, who was then in charge of the Institute's operations, agreed to cooperate with equipment and Sherpa guides. Even the central ministry, though it gave its approval and encouragement to the expedition, did not lend any financial support. Appeals for private funding too were turned down until *Anandabazar Patrika*, a leading Bengali newspaper came forward with sponsorship.

Organising a civilian expedition in India was, understandably, difficult then: "The early expeditions were in low key, small in numbers never

ISBN-13
978 1526137111

exceeding ten, financed very frugally largely by the members themselves, anxious primarily to enjoy a mountain holiday, with equipment so basic and rudimentary as to be laughable by present day standards" (Jayal, 2006, p. 27). Lack of infrastructure and logistical support could be explained by the novelty of the sport in India and the serious financial costs it involved, but the social and political unwillingness to extend cooperation proved more detrimental to the growth of the sport among civilians. But despite being trammelled by severe constraints, the first group of climbers led by Sukumar did manage to summit Nandaghunti with borrowed equipment, used clothing and minimal climbing experience. What, then kept them going till the very end? In Gour Kishore Ghosh's (2001) still unmatched account of that expedition, the details of the climb appear incredible and improbable when one considers the earlier, preparatory phases of the expedition. A conversation like the one that follows, typically illustrates the indifference that the members confronted when they asked for funds:

-- Can you arrange for some funds? We are planning an expedition.

-- Expedition! What on earth is wrong with you? Are you guys out of your minds? Where will you go?

-- Nandaghunti.

-- What is that?

-- A peak in the Himalaya.

-- Forget it! Such a bogus idea! Better go to Ranchi.[2] We will collect some money for that trip! (Ghosh, 2001, p. 42)

In surpassing these constraints, the climbers from West Bengal secured a position of respect for mountaineering in the minds of future climbers too, who dared to nurture similar climbing goals. More importantly, though the representation of the expedition played a crucial role in making the unknown climbers almost household names. The immediacy and novelty of experience that the expedition's chronicler Gour Kishore Ghosh captured beautifully in his writings by collating interviews, journal

---

[2] The Central Institute of Psychiatry (formerly, Ranchi European Lunatic Asylum, founded in 1918), India's foremost facility and research institute for psychiatry, is located in Ranchi, a city in Eastern India. People often insensitively referred to a visit to Ranchi as a euphemism for treatment for mental disorder.

entries and personal, real-time experience, brought a sport not even remotely associated with the cultural identity of the Bengali youth closer to their hearts. Consequently, there was a noticeable rise in mountain-eering and rock-climbing camps. As mountaineer Sujal Mukhopadhyaya (1995, p. 178) records, the number of clubs in West Bengal such as the Asansol Trekkers Club (1961) and Jadavpur University Mountaineering and Hiking Club (1966) rose from six in 1960 to 85 in 1984. Expeditions too were arranged more often with the sport still coping with severe shortage of funds. In 1960, led by Gyan Singh, the first major attempt to climb Mt. Everest fell short by a mere 1,200 ft. Among the three-member summit team were geologist C.P. Bhora and Ajit Kumar Chowdhury. The team doctor, Sudhangshu Kumar Das, wrote the first account of a mountaineering expedition in Bengali, entitled *Everest Diary* (1962). In the following decades, some of the highest peaks in India including Neelkantha (21,770 ft), Satopanth (23,347 ft), Trishul (23,496 ft), and Kamet (25,595 ft) were attempted by climbers like Pranesh Chakraborty, Saibal Mitra and others. In 1967, the first women's expedition from Bengal, led by Dipali Sinha was organised to summit Mt Ronti (19,893 ft). In August 1970 three women from Calcutta – Sujaya Guha, Sudipta Sengupta and Kamala Saha – attempted to summit Mt Lalana (20,130 ft) in Himachal Pradesh. Five days after they summited the peak, Guha and Saha were swept off by a mountain stream. Only Sudipta Sengupta survived (Som, 2020). The more organised, bigger expeditions that were being conducted during this time also demonstrate the growing popularity of Himalayan high-altitude climbing. If one follows the records of climbing attempts from Bengal after 1960 it appears that in the second half of the twentieth century, among the 330 expeditions from Bengal about 203 were successful (Das, 2006).

But was it passion alone that motivated these climbers? I believe the standard goals of mountaineering as a sport were not the only incentives that encouraged them. On the contrary the goals that shaped the spirit of conquest in climbers like George Mallory, Charles Bruce, Hugh Ruttledge and several other mountaineers in the age of empire, were quite distinct from those that guided the pursuit of self-knowledge and spiritual introspection among Bengal's mountain enthusiasts. To understand the difference further, we first need to dig deeper into the roots of Bengal's cultural and religious association with the Himalayas.

The long and robust culture of walking in the Himalayan trails for pilgrimage is as old as Hinduism's sacred texts themselves. The final stage of life, called the *sannyas* or the reclusive phase, required life to be spent as a wandering mendicant (variously termed *parivrajaka, samana* and *bhikshu* in the Hindu and the Buddhist tradition), ideally, in the Himalayas (Singh, 2017, pp. 300–301). At the end of the great epic, the *Mahabharata* (5th century BCE), the five princes led by the eldest brother, Yudhisthira, undertake a long and arduous journey in the Himalayas on their way to *swarg* (heaven). During that journey they are tested for moral righteousness and their allegiance to *dharma* or the right way of life. The sixteenth-century text *Ain-i-Akbari* by Abul Fazal (1551–1602) mentions the holy cave of Amarnath in Kashmir which was known to be a Hindu pilgrimage site.

The first Himalayan travelogue in Bengali dates to 1865. *Tirtha Bhraman* (Pilgrimage Journeys) is a five-hundred-page record by Jadunath Sarbadhikary, a merchant from South Bengal who travelled in several places in North India between 1855 and 1857. Since then, Himalayan journeys, involving long walks in inhospitable terrains and inclement weather, have become subjects of travelogues which in turn evolved as exercises in soul-searching and self-exploration. The corpus of travel writing was enriched by many keen walkers (and writers) some of whom spent their lifetime traversing the Himalayan trails. The foremost of these travellers and travel writers include Jaladhar Sen (1860–1939), Pramod Kumar Chattopadhyay (1885–1979), Umaprasad Mukhopadhyaya (1902–1997) and Abadhut (1910–1978). The first generation of Bengal's climbers, as my reading suggests, felt closer affiliation with these pilgrim-writers than die-hard climbers. Dhruba Mazumder, a member of the Nandaghunti team, writes, "I wore the mantle of a pilgrim when my first encounter with the Himalaya took place" (Mazumder, 1988, p. 5). Other climbers were also comfortable with the idea of the Himalaya as a place of worship and themselves as pilgrims.

But mountaineering goals are not determined in terms of religious experiences alone. Adventure certainly had its place in the lives of these climbers, but it was rarely attended by the privilege and authority of the Western climber acting as a representative of the colonial or imperial power, directly or indirectly perpetuating the process of colonisation. Their zeal to gather knowledge about the Himalayas, was in principle, not different from gathering relevant information about a prospective colony that could be adequately exploited for commercial purposes. European travel from the onset of empire building was driven by an urge to know and possess new places (Hooker, 1854; Waddell, 1899). Producing knowledge about a place was tantamount to possessing it, as Edward Said has long since established: "To have such knowledge of such a thing [the Orient] is to dominate it, to have authority over it" (Said, 2001, p. 32). Modern travel writing studies have only started to revisit colonial travel writing as a hegemonic discourse produced consistently in accordance with the goals of the colonial machinery. "Travel", as Holland and Huggan (2003, p. ix) point out, has recently emerged as "a crucial epistemological category for the displacement of normative values and homogenizing, essentialist views". The authority and assumed supremacy of European travelogues too have come under serious scrutiny: "Central to the travel narrative, though less obvious than the presumption of physical autonomy, is the presumption that being a literate European abroad grants the prerogative and even obligation to represent with authority" (Burton, 2013, p. 27).

Working outside these privileges and hierarchies of power, the early climbers of Bengal had to take a giant leap forward in choosing an actual expedition over a leisured trek to a Himalayan pilgrimage site even though the latter was by no means a comfortable journey. For Sukumar, Biswadeb and Dhruba, nothing less than a real climb could quench their mountaineering desire. In Sukumar's thought the Himalayas were more than a mark that a sportsman could aim at. They offered unbounded freedom, unblemished in their timeless beauty and redemptive in their therapeutic, immersive silence. Sujal Mukherjee, a mountaineer of the same generation as Sukumar, writes: "What magic there is in these mountain rivers! . . . The triviality of human endeavours becomes evident and I feel humbled in their presence" (Mukherjee, 1995, pp. 14–15).

The association of the Himalayas with freedom, spirituality and peace of mind goes deep in the culture of Bengal's Himalayan encounters. From the 1890s travelogues in Bengali became increasingly self-referential with the Himalayas looming large as a symbol of divinity and salvation. Not only were individuals like Abadhut[3] eager to renounce all material comforts for a harsh, austere life of a monk, but others like Jaladhar Sen made frenzied journeys in the mountains to reconcile with a lifetime of grief. Even Swami Vivekananda (1863–1902) found Mayabati, a remote, inaccessible, wooded corner in the district of Almora in Kumaon, to be

---

[3] Abadhut's real name was Dulal Mukherjee. He spent several years in the Himalayas first in quest of a spiritual guru and then in some serious soul searching. He wrote many books based on his travels, of which *Nilkantha Himalaya* (1965) is chiefly about his Himalayan journeys.

the most suitable place for meditation and contemplation of *Advaitabad* or the philosophy of non-dualism. A renunciatory ethic controls the lives and writings of many of these travellers which, taken as a whole, presents a discourse of surrender. A brief extract from the writings of Umaprasad Mukhopadhyaya (2006, p. 232) may illustrate this:

> Among the gigantic mountains I saw myself as the Lilliputians of *Gulliver's Travels*! I felt as if I were a bubble in an ocean of infinite time. The qualities that I have so far valued in my earthly and civilized life seemed meaningless to me. Knowledge and ignorance seemed to overlap boundaries. I could understand only one thing – that I knew very little. Looking deep into the inner recesses of the mind I saw that there was not the slightest trace of either fear or worry or anxiety or love or affection or "*Maya*". It was an experience that lifted one over ambition, greed and the contradictions of ordinary life. The chain of earthly desires was snapped. My consciousness was, like the placid water of the lake, calm, free from turbulence.
>
> As I stood under the deep blue sky I was surrounded by the lofty walls of mountain ridges – a castle of inaccessible remoteness. Above the mountains the blue sky sent messages of liberation for the soul. It seemed that I was being entranced by some unknown tune resonating amidst infinite space. Motionless, unfathomable, calm, I found in it a deep feeling of peace in my mind.

Umaprasad's rhetoric of self-effacement leads us to the next part of my enquiry: how did the discourse of surrender take shape and how far were the climbers impacted by the literary representation of Himalayan travel by pilgrims and trekkers? Many of the foremost travel writers bore the legacy of Bengal's literary hybridity which scholars have traced back to the formation of the canon of modern Bengali literature in the late eighteenth and the early nineteenth century. As Rosinka Chaudhuri (2014) has argued, the formation of the modern canon in Bengali literature involved the exclusion of many writers like Bharatchandra (the late eighteenth-century court-poet) and Ishwarchandra Gupta (1812–1859), who were left out for their use of a relatively crude style and more traditional vernacular components like *kabi-gaan* (a form of Bengal's folk performance in which two poets engage in a verbal duel of songs which are supposedly rendered as impromptu compositions) and *aakhyan* (oral, narrative poems, usually dealing with mythological or religious themes). The more iconic founding voices of modern Bengali literature like Michael Madhusudan Dutta (1824–1873) and Rangalal Bandopadhyay (1827–1887) on the other hand were both educated in the colonial system and developed their literary career drawing heavily on their English and classical literary influences. "'Nothing can be better than Milton . . . I don't think it is impossible to equal Virgil, Kalidas and Tasso. Though glorious, they are still mortal poets. Milton is divine', wrote Michael Madhusudan Dutta while writing *Meghnad Badh Kavya* which he modeled on Milton's *Paradise Lost*" (cited in Ray, 1995, p. 8).

The travel writers writing in Bengali may be affiliated to this literary tradition showing varying degrees of influence, but their primary spiritual inheritance is unmistakably rooted in the more traditional bodies of religious knowledge. Ancient texts such as the *Vedas* and the *Upanishads* ascribed to the Himalayas spiritual properties, which, over centuries, had trickled into the lives and imaginations of visitors to the Himalayan pilgrimage sites. Swami Vivekananda, who played a lead role in the religious reformation in Bengal in the nineteenth century, unambiguously affirmed the spiritualism that the Himalayas symbolised. When he was asked by Sister Nivedita (1867–1911), his Irish-born disciple who championed the cause for women's education and dedicated her life to underprivileged women in Bengal, about the reason behind the Hindu devotee's kissing the ground before the holy image, he replied, "Is it not the same thing to kiss the ground before the image as to kiss the ground before these mountains (meaning the Himalaya)?" (Sunirmalananda, 1986, p. 24). Additionally, the mountain's mythic associations, nurtured by oral cultures, written scriptures and the great epics, make it easily identifiable as divine (Reader, 2015, pp. 83–88). Jaladhar Sen, one of Bengal's foremost Himalayan travel writers, also wrote about the Himalayas' divine appeal. His emphatic pronouncement, "the rugged beauty of the mountains, nature's myriad views, swiftly flowing rivers with their incessant music, the cool breeze – these are the gods I worship in my life" truly expresses the way the Himalayas became an object of both wonder and worship (Sen, 2009, p. 160).

Bengal's climbers too were steeped in the travel literature of the Himalayas, just as their earlier generation of travellers and writers absorbed and appropriated English writings in general and Romantic literature in particular. There are frequent records of climbers worshipping the Himalayas as the Hindu god Shiva or participating in rituals performed by the Sherpas. Bishwadeb Biswas notes how, on multiple expeditions, an obstacle was removed or an impasse resolved after a *puja* (a sacred prayer accompanied with the chanting of mantras) was performed with due solemnity and faith. During the Nandaghunti expedition, for example, only after a sacrificial goat was dedicated to the goddess Nanda Devi, were several hurdles (including finding the right routes) removed. Similar incidents during the Kabru expedition of 1964 strengthened the beliefs of climbers in the divine aura of the mountains. Approaching the mountains as a supplicant, offering prayers and chanting shlokas (scriptural verses) during an expedition were manifestations of an attitude that goes beyond the pride of a conquest. Thus Biswas writes:

> For the mountaineers the Himalaya is not just a lofty, impenetrable, suffocating obstacle of rock and snow, nor is it a combination of danger and ugly death. It is a source of self-knowledge and self-realisation. Mountaineering is not about crossing hurdles one after another in quest of victory wearing the mantle of a daring adventurer. We do not take part in an expedition to conquer a mountain. After a thoroughly exhaustive climb, reaching the summit, we rarely relish the moment because we have vanquished an enemy. We are rather overwhelmed by a supreme sense of joy and fulfillment of a long cherished desire. It is as if we are blessed with the benediction of the supreme Mahadeva after having surrendered ourselves completely at his feet. That is why the first thing we do on the summit is offer puja and pray for the well being of everyone. (Biswas, 2001, p. 17)

The humility and self-effacement in the urge to surrender to the mountain's divinity is quite the opposite of what many Western climbers expected from mountaineering in the age of empire. Attempts to climb Everest alone, in the early decades of the twentieth century, are frequently described in unambiguously aggressive terms. Thus John Hunt writes:

> ... this tussle between men and a mountain reaches beyond the scope of mountain climbing in its physical aspect. It seems to me to symbolize man's struggle to come to terms with the forces of nature; it speaks eloquently of the continuity of this struggle and of the bond between all those who have taken part in it. The opponent was not other parties, but Everest itself. (Hunt, 1954, p. 6)

For Younghusband (2000, p. 8) it was a celebration of the human spirit itself: "The mountain may be high. But he [man] will show that his spirit is higher. And he will not be content until he has it in subjection under his feet."

Aggression and the quest for personal glory alone, however, do not comprehensively cover the history of Western mountaineering at the time when climbing was not restricted to an individual or a team sport but became entwined with political hierarchies and national pride among European nations. Many Western climbers of the late twentieth century, including Peter Boardman, Hermann Buhl and Reinhold Messner, followed climbing methods that were not hierarchical like those of the British climbers who preceded them. Boardman's perceptive views on mountaineering particularly critiques the ideals of many Western climbers (1985). By the 1930s, as Scott Ellsworth (2020, p. 92) finds in his book, "High-altitude mountaineering was no longer just a matter of conquest. It had also become a bit player in global politics." He also sheds light on the motley group of climbers who, despite their European affiliations, could not be uniformly categorized: "Indeed, many of them had been considered to be failures during their lifetimes, misfits and odd ducks who never settled down, never got real jobs, never joined the ranks of everyday society" (Ellsworth, 2020, p. 2). This note of individualism, stretched to the point of idiosyncrasy, appealed to early climbers of Bengal. The likes of Frank Smythe and Eric Shipton for whom climbing success or failure did not matter as much as being thrilled by the "multi-coloured afterglow of sunset spreading over the vast mountain world" (Shipton 2014, p. 1155), inspired a love of the mountains more than an urge to conquer them.

Contrary to what Peter Hansen claims in his book *The Summits of Modern Man: Mountaineering After Enlightenment* about the Himalayas being "reappropriated" after the formation of the mountaineering institute in West Bengal, it reinforced with even greater emphasis the traditional spiritual values of the mountain on the one hand and the thrill and joy of climbing on the other. Instead of forging an ethic of national pride, discipline and masculinity, it continued to instil in a now trained group of climbers the desire to bring the mountains closer to their private lives – as part of their personal joys and disappointments rather than as agents for buttressing their national pride. Even today, the sense of personal adventure is the chief motivator. When I asked Satyarup Siddhanta, a leading climber of our time, what inspired him most to choose the difficult life of an adventure sportsman in India, he said he was drawn by the "spellbinding beauty" of Mount Everest even before he knew its exact height. Being "blown away by the adventure quotient" of a hill trek, he overcame many physical and financial challenges (he was asthmatic) to become the first Indian to climb the seven summits:

> [On 21 May 2016], after a lot of adventures and misadventures (from hanging inside a crevasse for 30 minutes, to seeing a Sherpa fall to his death, to having my Oxygen failing me for 30 minutes near the summit, to three cameras failing at the summit, to losing three friends on Everest on that day) I fluttered the national flag at the top of Mt Everest at 5.30 am Nepal time. I didn't conquer the mountain but the fear. (Siddhanta, 2022)

For Debasish Biswas, another climber who has successfully climbed five of the fourteen 8,000m peaks, the spirituality of the Himalaya is something he has never lost sight of:

> At the start of every expedition, we offer puja; the first thing we do after stepping on the summit of a mountain is offer our prayers to the gods. After all, the peaks are named after our gods – Chomolungma is the goddess mother of the earth, Annapurna is a devi in Hinduism, Makalu is another name for Mahakaal (which is one way of describing Shiva). I have seen many western climbers celebrate by hugging each other and sending messages to lower camps after a successful summit attempt. We start celebrating only after a *puja*. (Biswas, 2022)

Other climbers too remain unaffected by the agenda to demonstrate masculinity and muscle in an increasingly competitive sport.

Notwithstanding the fatal incidents of May 1996 that claimed the lives of a dozen people, the frequency of Bengal's attempts at high-altitude climbing continued to increase (Krakauer, 1997; Boukreev and Dewalt, 2002). In 2016 as many as eleven climbers from Bengal attempted to summit Mt Everest while two more climbed Lhotse and Dhaulagiri (Dutta, 2016). Organised expeditions conducted by professional agencies with assistance from experienced Sherpas, cutting edge technology and sophisticated equipment in India and Nepal eliminated many of the uncertainties that loomed large in the mind of early climbers. But funding, as Debashis Biswas writes in the first of his many books, was still a matter of concern. Funds were raised by many including his colleagues and his wife even sold her jewellery to obtain the hefty sum needed to participate in an Everest expedition in May 2010 (Biswas, 2013). Yet, even during one of his difficult climbs, he never loses sight of his limitation as a middle-class man whose community has never quite excelled in sports that required athleticism and physical stamina:

> Where did I stand in comparison with the vast, titanic mountains? ...
> [Yet], Here I was, an average Bengali of five and a half feet striving against another Debasish who would not retreat even an inch from his goal. (Biswas, 2014, p. 65)

An average Bengali of five and a half feet is an image of anything but an intrepid adventurer pushing his way through mountains and waves with unmitigated strength, fearlessly taking up the baton of discovery and exploration from an earlier generation of heroes. Yet Debasish and his long-standing partner in climbing, Basanta Singha Roy, have established themselves as heroes in their own ways. They did not necessarily have to recast the image of the middle-class Bengali-speaking *bhadralok*[4] who, since the encounter with Western modernity in the nineteenth century, became incrementally associated with intellectual pursuits but seldom with adventure sports. Ironically, that image does injustice to a community of people who have had a known culture of exercising and body-building (Chatterjee and Naha, 2014). Rabindranath Tagore himself tells us in his memoirs that as a boy he had to train with a wrestler in the wee hours of the morning before starting his lessons (Tagore, 1912, p. 21).

Despite their growing number of feats, sometimes clouds of bitter cynicism would also engulf mountaineers in West Bengal. When Chanda Gayan, a young climber who had achieved the unique feat of climbing Mt Everest (29,032 ft) and Mt Lhotse (28,102 ft) in the same expedition, went missing during her attempt to climb Kanchenjunga and Kanchenjunga West in 2014, many speculations were made. Newspapers reported that she had indeed been killed during an attempt even though Nepal's local laws refrained from naming someone as dead until their body was found (Giri, 2014). Rajib Bhattacharya, a member of her team, wrote in a leading Bengali daily describing the unfortunate circumstances in which Chanda fell victim to an avalanche during her summit attempt to Yalung Kang. "She was physically quite fit and I had no doubt that she could do the impossible," wrote Rajib, as he, along with the climbing fraternity

---

[4] A social category, the genealogy of which scholars trace back to the 1830s. It refers to the members of the educated middle class, usually Hindus, who from the colonial era on were influenced by ideas of European Enlightenment, rationalism and humanist thought (Hatcher, 2008; Ray, 1995).

of Bengal and India, found it hard to accept that Chanda had died (Bhattahcharya, 2014). Debasish Biswas would later describe Chanda's rise in the mountaineering circuit as nothing short of "meteoric" (Biswas 2016, p. 318). Because Chanda, like her contemporary climber Tushi Das, hailed from a modest background and her success as a climber was phenomenal, she also faced some amount of negative criticism including scepticism about her claim of doing two summits in a single go. Debashis strongly condemned such criticism:

> Most of us try to judge others according to our own standards. What is impossible for us to achieve is considered unachievable in general. More so if that person has the girl-next-door image. And the pride of those who have hardly ever climbed a mountain beyond an occasional attempt has been badly hurt by Chanda's success. The balloons of their vanity have been deflated summarily by this young girl of small frame. That is why they are even more jealous and cynical about her feat. They try to convince others that she has never climbed both Everest and Lhotse. (Biswas, 2016, p. 318)

But despite these adversities, climbers such as Chanda Gayan and Tushi Das did make it to the top. Their achievement reflects the tenacity and conviction among less-privileged climbers and their fame rests in no small measure on the important space that the literature of Himalayan travel has created in Bengali culture. Intimate stories of individual struggles have always shared the narrative space with actual descriptions of climbs. Instead of producing superhuman figures or the tin-pot heroes that crowd much of India's media, the writings of Debasish Biswas or Basanta Singha Roy present rare but inspirational accounts in unexaggerated, familiar terms.

I believe the living, flourishing tradition of literary travel writing in Bengali that has always provided an alternate perspective to view the Himalayas not as an enemy but as a divine presence has also lifted the glory of the sport beyond its more tangible laurels. This, as I have already hinted, makes their narratives fall in line with the writings of a separate breed of adventure loving mountaineers who, unlike the unrelenting men of the empire, did not climb the Himalaya directly to serve imperial interests. As Maurice Isserman and Stewart Weaver (2008, p. xi) argue, mountaineering in the age of empire cannot be understood as a linear narrative of conquest driven by imperial goals alone:

The expeditionary culture of the age of empire, perhaps best exemplified by the Everest expeditions of Mallory's day and some years thereafter, was a paradoxical thing. It was bound up with visions of imperial destiny that assumed the rule of white Europeans over darker-skinned Asians and drew many of its conventions from the hierarchical order of the English public school and the British Army. At the same time, it harbored individual climbers who were often misfits in their own societies, romantic rebels who found a spiritual purpose and freedom in the mountains unavailable to them through conventional pursuits at home.

The literature produced by Bengal's climbers, of which only a tiny bit could be explored in the scope of this essay, represented what was largely a pilgrim's reflective musings interspersed with occasional crescendos of frenzied awareness of the thrill and excitement of mountaineering. For them, the Himalayas remained a shared symbol of life's deeper goals, more spiritual than material, more private than could be shared in public life. Little wonder therefore that when, towards the end of his life in 1931, Rabindranath Tagore voiced his weariness with life's unrelenting demands, he chose to express himself through the metaphor of Mt Everest:

> For one who is getting close to eighty years of age, it is like climbing up the top of Mt. Everest – you can hardly feel the numbing, freezing silence at the top with the rush of warm blood in your bodies. I am too tired of carrying out life's errands to respond to your requests. (Tagore 1974, p. 298)

In 1939 when Tagore wrote this in a letter to Amiya Chakravarty[5], Mt Everest was yet to be climbed successfully. But the nuances of the image already go beyond the stereotypes of achievement that the summit quickly came to symbolise in popular imagination after 1953. Tagore's metaphor runs deeper than Everest's immediate associations with success and achievement. It recapitulates the mountain's potential to inspire a sense of reclusive, renunciatory indifference that its spirituality embodies. The literature of Himalayan journeys by Bengal's climbers, trekkers and pilgrims frequently reinforces that realisation.

---

[5] Amiya C. Chakravarty (1901–1986) was an eminent scholar, critic and poet besides being a close associate of Rabindranath Tagore. He accompanied Tagore as a friend and secretary during his tour of Russia.

Bibliography

Atiśa (2011) *Atiśa and Tibet: Life and Works of Dipamkara Śrijñāna*, trans. Chattopadhyaya, A. Delhi: Motilal Banarsidass Publishers.

Bhattacharya, R. (2014) "Amra Nischito Chilam, Chanda Parbe" (We Were Certain That Chanda Would Succeed), *Anandabazar Patrika Online*, 26 May, Available at: anandabazar.com (Accessed: 8 September 2021).

Biswas, B. (2001) *Parbater Mahakshetra* (The Realm of the Mountains). Kolkata: Bharati Publishing.

Biswas, D. (2013) *Everest: Shirshe Bangali* (Everest: A Bengali on the Summit). Kolkata: Ananda Publishers.

Biswas, D. (2014) *Aparupa Annapurna: A Bengali on the Summit* (The Beautiful Annapurna). Kolkata: Ananda Publishers.

Biswas, D. (2016) *Dhaulagiri O Makalu: Romanchakar Abhijatra* (Dhaulagiri and Makalu: An Adventurous Expedition). Kolkata: Ananda Publishers.

Biswas, D. (2022) Interviewed by Anandarup Biswas, 7 January 2022.

Boardman, P. (1985) *The Shining Mountain: Two Men on Changabang's West Wall*. New York, NY: Vintage Books.

Boukreev, A. and DeWalt, G.W. (2002) *The Climb: Tragic Ambitions on Everest*. London: Pan Books.

Burton, S. (2013) *Travel Narratives and the Ends of Modernity*. Cambridge: Cambridge University Press.

Giri, A. (2014) "Nepali officials say Indian climber 'reportedly' killed", *Business Standard*, May 23. Available at: https://www.business-standard.com/article/news-ians/nepali-officials-say-indian-climber-reportedly-killed-114052301324_1.html (Accessed: 19 October 2021).

Chatterjee, A. and Naha, S. (2014) "The Muscular Monk: Vivekananda, Sports and Physical Culture in Colonial Bengal", *Economic and Political Weekly*, 49(11), pp. 25–29.

Chaudhuri, R. (2014) *The Literary Thing: History, Poetry and the Making of a Modern Cultural Sphere*. New York: Peter Lang.

Das, S. (2006) *Himalaya Bhraman O Bhabna* (The Himalaya in Travels and Thought). Kolkata.

Dutta, S. (2016) "Flirting with Danger Puts Bengal Climbers at Risk on Everest", *Hindustan Times*. 10 June. Available at: https://www.hindustantimes.com/india-news/withering-heights-bengal-s-climbers-die-as-they-flirt-with-risk-on-mt-everest/story-LYcK5sGPNnqBbuZABU6zPL.html (Accessed: 15 January 2022).

Ellsworth, S. (2020) *The World Beneath Their Feet: Mountaineering, Madness and the Deadly Race to Summit the Himalay*. New York, NY: Hachette Books.

Ghosh, G.K. (2001) *Nandakanta Nandaghunti* (The Beautiful Nandaghunti). Kolkata: Ananda Publishers.

Hansen, P. (2013) *The Summits of Modern Man: Mountaineering After Enlightenment*. Cambridge, MA: Harvard University Press.

Hatcher, B.A. (2008) *Bourgeoisie Hinduism or the Faith of the Modern Vedantists.* New York, NY: Oxford University Press.

Holland, P. and Huggan, G. (2003) *Tourists with Type Writers: Critical Reflections on Contemporary Travel Writing.* Ann Arbor, MI: The University of Michigan Press.

Hooker, J.D. (1854) *Himalayan Journals or Notes of a Naturalist,* vol. 2. London: John Murray.

Hunt, J. (1954) *The Ascent of Everest.* London: Hodder and Stoughton.

Isserman, M. and Weaver, S. (2008) *Fallen Giants: A History of Himalayan Mountaineering from the Age of Empire to the Age of Extremes.* New Haven, CT and London: Yale University Press.

Jayal, N.D. (2006) "Early Years of Indian Mountaineering", *The Himalayan Journal,* 62(16), pp. 219–238.

Krakauer, J. (1998) *Into Thin Air: A Personal Account of the Everest Disaster.* London: Pan Books.

Mazumder, D. (1988) *Sahasha Himalaya* (Suddenly, the Himalaya). Kolkata: Ananda Publishers.

Mukhapadhyay, S. and Mukhapadhyay, A. (1995) *Sujaler Diary* (The Diaries of Sujal). Kolkata.

Said, E. (2001) *Orientalism.* New Delhi: Penguin Books.

Mukhopadhyaya, U. (2006) *Bhraman Omnibus* (Travel Omnibus). Kolkata: Mitra and Ghosh Publishers.

Ray, R.K. (1995) "Introduction", in Ray, R.K. (ed) *Mind, Body and Society: Life and Mentality in Colonial Bengal.* Calcutta: Oxford University Press, pp. 1–45.

Reader, I. (2015) *Pilgrimage: A Very Short Introduction.* New York, NY: Oxford University Press.

Sen, J. (2005) *Himalaya Samagra* (Collected Writings on the Himalaya). Kolkata: Pritha Publishing.

Siddhanta, S. (2022) Interviewed by Anandarup Biswas, 9 January 2022.

Singh, U. (2017) *A History of Ancient and Early Medieval India.* Noida: Pearson.

Shipton, E. (2014) *Nanda Devi.* Sheffield: Vertebrate Publishing.

Som, V. (2020) "Fifty Years Ago, 3 Women Summited a 20,000-Foot Peak. 2 Never Returned", *NDTV,* 4 August. Available at: https://www.ndtv.com/india-news/50-years-ago-3-women-summited-a-20-000-feet-peak-2-never-returned-2274061 (Accessed: 11 October 2021).

Sunirmalananda, S. (ed.) (2009) "The Message of Mayabati", in *The Charm of Mayabati Ashrama.* Kolkata: Advaita Ashrama, pp. 14–25.

Tagore, R. (1974) *Chithipatra,* vol. 11 (Collected Letters). Kolkata: Viswabharati.

Tagore, R. (1912) *Jeevansmriti* (Memoirs). Kolkata: Viswabharati.

Waddell, L.A. (1899) *Among the Himalaya.* Westminster: Archibald Constable.

Younghusband, Sir F. (2000) *The Epic of Mount Everest: The Historic Account of Mallory's Expeditions.* London: Pan Books.

"Upon the whole I expect he took me for an aventurière"

British Women Grand Tourists' Accounts of Mountains and Mountaineering

Emma Gleadhill

Introduction

Mountaineering, like the Grand Tour, is a cultural activity that men were invested in framing as only undertaken (or at least, only undertaken correctly) by themselves. Based on the long body of the scholarship on the Grand Tour and on mountaineering, it seems that they succeeded (for summaries see Naddeo, 2005; Gilchrist, 2013). Over the last two decades, however, scholars and professional writers have worked hard to bring women into the historical record (Brown, 2002; Robertson, 2003; Colley, 2010, pp. 101–144; Walchester, 2018). This chapter will build on this scholarship to explore how female and male Grand Tourists experienced and wrote about mountains and mountaineering. It will show that the Grand Tour was important to climbing aesthetics for elite British men and women, and that their accounts do differ.

In the seventeenth century, the British felt repulsion or displeasing irregularity at the sight of mountains, exemplified by John Evelyn's comment en route to Rome in 1646 that "nature had here swept up the rubbish of the earth in the Alps" or John Dryden's "I should like the Alps very much, if it were not for the hills" (quoted in Charlton, 1984, p. 42). The eighteenth century marked a new appreciation of mountain environments amongst the British and Europeans as they sought to classify and map plants, minerals and geological features (Schaumann, 2020). By the late eighteenth century, British men not only sought knowledge in the mountains, but also to prove their authority as heads of family, landowners and statesmen through the association with power

In practice, however, elite women also went on Grand Tours (Sweet, Verhoeven and Goldsmith, 2017; Dolan, 2001; Gleadhill, 2022). "It is now all the fashion for the ladies to travel", Grand Tourist Joseph Spence observed to his mother as early as 1733, after seeing a surprising number of Englishwomen in Florence (Spence, 1975, p. 138). In addition, professionals (including diplomats, artists and musicians) undertook these journeys, as did the tutors and servants (some of them women) who catered to the tourists' needs.[1] And the social elite did not stay static but expanded as the century progressed; indeed, increasing numbers of nouveau riche merchant and colliery families, keen to cement their newly landed status, undertook their own Grand Tours.

Elite women Grand Tourists were not expected to return home transformed into patriarchs or statesmen and they travelled at a wide range of stages in their lives; whether as students, newlyweds, matriarchs or widows. Rather than dwelling on danger and grand vistas, therefore, many women focused on the mineral and botanical aspects of mountain environments in which they were readily interested through their polite education in botany and minerology (Gleadhill, 2021). Women also frequently wrote of the social aspects of climbing because they were raised to be hostesses and conversationalists (Sweet, 2012, pp. 38–45). Taking a close look at British women Grand Tourists' accounts, then, shows that the development of climbing aesthetics was more nuanced than a self-glorification and elevation of a male protagonist over nature.

In the analysis that follows, I draw from some of the published accounts and manuscript journals written by those British women who undertook Grand Tours to Italy between 1770 and 1800. Prior to 1770, just two travelogues were published by women, but between 1770 and 1800 over twenty were published, reflecting the prosperity enjoyed by a growing social elite and advances in the tourism and publishing industries (Turner, 2001, pp. 25–26). However, most women Grand Tourists' journals and letters remained in manuscript form and the social unacceptability of claiming authorship and commercialising oneself led women writers to limit their authorial voice with the feminine modesty topos – that is, the Early Modern women's literary trope of humility through the profession of apology, inadequacy or self-denigration (Pender, 2012).

---

[1] In 1808, a poor maidservant from Chamonix, Marie Paradis (1778–1839) climbed Mont Blanc. She is believed to be the first woman to have done so, but was certainly not the only female servant to work for travellers or mountaineers.

those women who had the privilege to undertake Grand
ositions of authority as salon hostesses or patrons and their
ournals and letters were more widely read than has been
generally recognised (Kinsley, 2005, p. 614, note 10; Justice and Tinker,
2002). Many of their travel accounts were also subsequently published
and popularised in the nineteenth and twentieth centuries. These women's
influence on the development of climbing aesthetics, therefore, should not
be underestimated.

In the following pages, I will consider some of these women's narratives
of their experiences of mountain environments, the acts of ascent and
descent, and the people who guided them through their vertical feats.
Taking British women Grand Tourists' accounts of mountains and
mountaineering into consideration sheds new light on some of the ways
in which gender influenced climbing aesthetics as part of the development
of a British imperial subjectivity.

Sublime Danger: The Ascent of the Alps and Vesuvius

In the latter part of the eighteenth century the British and Europeans
began to ascend mountains for pleasure, rather than for transitory,
economic or military purposes. In 1741 a group of male Grand Tourists
known as the Common Room climbed the Mer de Glace in Savoy simply
for the purpose of reaching the top, rather than to overcome a barrier to
get to another destination (Martel, 1744). By the 1770s Alpine riding,
walking and climbing were established tourist activities (Goldsmith,
2017, p. 6). Within Britain, the Romantic poets clambered on the crags
and cliffs of the Lake District (Bainbridge, 2020). After returning home
from a nine-day tour there, in a letter to his friend Robert Southey dated
9 August 1802, Samuel Taylor Coleridge noted that he had "spent the
greatest part of the next day mountaineering" (Coleridge, 1956, p. 846)
(the first recorded use of the word) ("Oxford English Dictionary Online",
2021). As Simon Bainbridge has outlined, the cultural identity of the
"mountaineer" emerged in this period: long used by the British to denote
"a person who is native to or lives in a mountain region", it now came to
be used as a self-descriptor by "a person who engages in or is skilled at
mountain climbing" (Bainbridge, 2012, p. 1).

Grand Tourists of the eighteenth century had the choice to travel into
Italy either on land or by sea. The Alpine route was more popular because

Figure 7.1: Christian von Mechel, Descent from Mont-Blanc in 1787
by H.B. de Saussure, copper engraving, coloured, 380 x 483 mm.
Collection Teylers Museum, Haarlem, The Netherlands. (Image
permission at: https://www.teylersmuseum.nl/nl/collectie/kunst/
kg-16892-afdaling-van-de-mont-blanc-door-prof-de-saussure-1787)

it was safer, more reliable and travellers could break up their journeys
(Figure 7.1). The most common route was from Lyons to the Franco-
Savoyard frontier at Pont-de-Beauvoisin. From there, tourists crossed
the Alps over the Mount Cenis pass to Susa and then continued onto
Turin. The Mount Cenis pass was not suitable for wheeled vehicles until
the following century, so tourist's carriages had to be dismounted at the
foot of the mountain and then transported on mules, while the tourists
themselves were carried in a type of sedan chair by porters (Black, 2003,
pp. 27–28). Once the tourists were well past the Alps, in Naples they
found one of the great sights of the century: the natural phenomenon of
Mount Vesuvius. They enjoyed viewing the volcano at a distance at night,
often from the British diplomat Sir William Hamilton's famed villa, and
also ascended it by mule and on foot to take a close look at the crater.

Figure 7.2: Giovanni Battista Lusieri, Mount Vesuvius by Moonlight (The Eruption of 1787), 1787, Watercolour on paper, 595 x 830 mm, Attingham Park, Shropshire (Accredited Museum). (Purchase image permission at: https://www.nationaltrustcollections.org.uk/object/607881)

The increased popularity of the Alps, Vesuvius and other mountains in eighteenth-century British culture as destinations in and of themselves and not just natural barriers was inspired by the sublime aesthetic, popularised by Edmund Burke's 1757 publication, *A Philosophical Enquiry into the Origin of Our Ideas of the Sublime and Beautiful.* "When danger or pain press too nearly," Burke explained, "they are incapable of giving any delight, and are simply terrible; but at certain distances, and with certain modifications, they may be, and they are delightful" (Burke, 1764, p. 60). Margaret Grenville experienced the sublime viewing Vesuvius while spending the winter of 1761–1762 in Naples en route to Constantinople, where her husband was taking his post as ambassador. "There was a magnificent eruption at Mount Vesuvius," she wrote in her journal, "which created two streams of lava that winded down the hill a considerable length and from our windows at night, it was really a glorious sight, perfectly answered Mr Burke's idea of the Sublime" (quoted in Black, 2003, p. 55). Margaret's understanding and representation of Vesuvius was shaped by paintings of the volcano erupting at night, such as Giovanni Lusieri's *Mount Vesuvius by Moonlight (The Eruption of 1787)* (Figure 7.2). By viewing the volcano nocturnally like a painting and by positioning herself at the requisite safe distance that allowed it to be terrifying in her imagination, but not in reality, Margaret found the sublime.

Both male and female Grand Tourists wrote about their experiences of the sublime, but they were positioned in different ways towards it (Pratt, 2008; Bohls, 1995; Chard, 1999; Kinsley, 2008). According to Sarah Goldsmith, in the second half of the eighteenth century, elite male Grand Tourists sought more and more physically demanding and dangerous encounters in mountain environments to test the limits of Burke's principal of the sublime as a form of distanced terror, in order to better demonstrate their "hardy masculinity" which advanced their "claims of emotional hegemony and fitness for leadership" (Goldsmith, 2017, p. 3). "The climbing up is the hardest work I ever did in my life," declared William Bentinck after climbing Vesuvius in 1727, "not only the steepness, but the quantity of cinders and hot ashes which make one fall back again above three quarters of each step one takes" (quoted in Black, 2003, p. 54). "I must inevitably have been dashed to pieces," George Legge, Viscount Lewisham wrote on 9 September 1777 about his slip on a precipice (quoted in Goldsmith, 2017, p. 6). Goldsmith has explored how these men and others driven by notions of chivalry, martial and sporting masculinity, actively courted danger and hardship in the mountains, placing themselves in deliberately dangerous situations requiring courageous responses. It was from the 1760s that rising incomes and more reliable transport led to a demographic shift from landed to nouveau riche tourists, and from tutors and their elite male pupils to family groups of men, women and children (Towner, 1985, p. 312). Demonstrations of hardy masculinity therefore may have become more important to men as they vied for the Tour's cultural capital within an ever-larger group of male and female tourists from merchant, colliery and 'millocracy' families whilst at the same time seeking to distinguish themselves from the men of the nations and states they were visiting.

In looking at elite male Grand Tourists' narratives of danger in the mountains, Goldsmith has reflected:

> Within particular conventions, such as 'hardy' masculinities, the Grand Tour appeared to demand both the actual experience of

danger and an effective narration of this experience. Reliant on these narrations, it is difficult to evaluate how dangerous these experiences truly were. Several Grand Tourists and tutors reported receiving or witnessing injuries from hunting, mountain climbing and other physical pursuits. Despite this, there is a surprisingly low serious injury and mortality rate, which could suggest that the severity of danger was rhetorically enhanced. More research is needed to explore the physical dimension of eighteenth-century masculinity, but this leads us to question to what extent the construction of masculinity and the significance of danger lay in objective experience and physical activity or in subsequent rhetorical construction and textual representation. (Goldsmith, 2017, p. 7)

Reading women's accounts of their experiences of the same mountain environments provides us with a different perspective from travellers who were not as invested in seeking and demonstrating physical hardship and danger. Though the women's accounts were no less carefully constructed to demonstrate a particular narrative, when placed against the accounts of elite male Grand Tourists they provide a more diverse understanding of the mountain experience.

British women tourists certainly experienced the physicality of the climb and wrote about it, but not in the romantic manner we have come to expect from men of the period. "About four o'clock the rain abating – went upon mules to see the source of the Arveron (a small river which joins the Arve at Chamouni), in the Glacier de Boisson", Mary Berry wrote in her journal on 13 August 1783. "Our mules carried us to within a quarter of a mile of the ice. We then clamoured over a number of large pieces of rock, left by former glaciers, to the edge of the water, where we stood upon large blocks of ice" (Berry, 1865, p. 31). While Mary described the physicality of the climb, she did not dwell on the danger or romance of standing on the edge of a glacier. Women also wrote of the economy of physical expenditure and reward involved in climbing a mountain, with Dorothy Wordsworth commenting in her account of climbing Scafell Pike: "Scafell and Helvellyn being the two mountains of this region which will best repay the fatigue of ascending them" (Wordsworth, 1846, p. 101). Here Dorothy referred to the physical effort of climbing the mountain, along with the relief at having reached the top, but did not mention any dangerous situations causing the fatigue. Perhaps the women were less likely to romanticise danger because they did not seek out the dangerous routes and conditions of their male counterparts, or they may have been less invested in demonstrating courage and hardiness as markers of fitness for rule and so wrote more objectively about the physical experience of the climb. A comprehensive literary and historical study of the women's accounts against those of the men in combination with a scientific study of the routes taken, the clothing and equipment worn and used, and how they were worn and used would shed further light on the male and female experience and its representation.

British men and women alike undertook the physically demanding task of ascending and descending the steep and difficult terrain of Vesuvius, despite William Forbes noting it was conventional for most women to go no further than a view point near the bottom of the mountain (quoted in Sweet, 2012, p. 55).[2] In 1788, the artist and former school teacher Ann Flaxman ascended the volcano with her sculptor husband and a group of men. Stopping halfway up for refreshments she worried that she would not be able to continue "but woman like when they offer'd to return and send the mules away I began to be asham'd of my weakness and resolutely resolv'd at all Events to go forward. I took an additional draught of strong Beer was plac'd on my Mule and brought up the rear most gallantly singing the old song of when I was a Young one no girl was like me" (Flaxman, 1787–1789, p. 71). The group followed their guide on foot when the terrain became too sandy for the mules. Finding her feet sinking into the sand and fearful of losing her shoes, Ann wrote in her journal that she "mounted Heroically alone with the help of a Club but in others I was forc'd to submit and lay hold of the Guides Girdle and let him lug me up resting for Breath & Strength but never for Courage" (Flaxman, 1787–1789, p. 71). After conquering the volcano, she and the others ran and slid down it on their backsides.

In Ann's account of ascending and descending Vesuvius we see that while they did not have the same level of demand for showing physical stoicism placed on them as their male counterparts, climbing still provided women Grand Tourists with an opportunity to demonstrate a robust constitution that set them apart from other women. When she was offered additional assistance because of her sex, Ann felt "asham'd" to succumb to physical exhaustion and so "resolutely resolv'd" to continue

---

[2] Mrs Patrick Home, Hester Piozzi, Catherine Wilmot, Mary Berry, Miss Derbishire and Elizabeth Gibbs amongst others climbed Vesuvius.

the ascent by hook or by crook. The song she chose to sing about being an exception from other girls suggests that keeping up with the men made Ann feel heroic and even superior to other women. The loss of her shoes indicates that Ann had to contend with clothing that was impractical for mountain climbing. The fact Ann chose to note this in her travel account suggests that it was an added hurdle she faced as a woman and one she found rather vexing.

While she did not make any national or class distinctions, nationalistic attitudes of the time likely gave Ann a sense of superiority amongst her male travelling companions as a British woman. By contrast, British men often noted that Italian women had weak constitutions and refused to walk anywhere. Frances Drake complained that the ladies of Florence preferred to "loll in their chariots" rather than walk through the Boboli Gardens (Sweet, 2012, p. 55). In his published journal entry of 7 April 1766, Samuel Sharp, meanwhile, regretted that Italian women "hardly know what it is to walk" (Sharp, 1767, p. 208). Indeed, Ann and other women who climbed Vesuvius were somewhat exceptional amongst their sex, whether Italian or British, because the volcano was one of the few climbs that a woman could undertake without having to make an expedition on unkept roads or staying in scarce and poorly kept inns or monasteries which were barriers for women participating in mountaineering in other locations.

It was, however, not only the physical exertion of the climb, but its combination with "a little sprinkling of terror" that was seen to prove "manliness" and strengthen character by allowing male mountaineers to enter a sublime state (Bainbridge, 2013, p. 250). As demonstrated already, the women's accounts do not generally dwell long on danger and, indeed, sometimes express surprise at not having encountered it, or a similar sense of amusement as Ann's at the idea of it. In 1783, at Montanvert, for instance, Mary Berry noted in her journal that her party "were not stopped by any of those dreadful chasms so much talked about by travellers" (Berry, 1865, p. 33). How women may have perceived themselves in relation to danger and the sublime in comparison to their male counterparts is captured in Lady Bruce's description of her and her husband's encounter with Mount Etna. "How grand and sublime is Etna and its accessories!" she commented in her journal:

> Lord Bruce scaled the very summit and stood on the edge of the crater whilst it projected showers of red hot scoria and ashes to a much greater height than we had seen from Vesuvius... do not

however expect a description from me – it is far beyond it. It is not the first sight of Etna which is striking… but when you approach nearer, when you find little excrescences on the surface to be all vast craters of old eruptions, when you travel a whole day without getting more than half round him and begin to measure by surer indices than sight, the conception swells with the progressive discoveries and you are lost exactly in the same manner as in meditations on infinite and eternity. (Quoted in Black 2003, p. 215)

Here Lady Bruce described her husband scaling the mountain to deliberately stand in a precarious location amid "projected showers of red-hot scoria and ashes" while she held back. Not expected to return home as a paterfamilia or statesman Lady Bruce likely did not experience the same level of pressure to both court danger – and narrate that experience – as her husband. With her polite female education in minerology and botany, it was instead through looking down at the ground beneath her feet to discover and measure the details of the mountain's surface that Lady Bruce chose to represent her experience of the mountain's elevating philosophical qualities. For her the sublime was not about narrating danger and a grand view, it was about narrating the new sensations and experiences produced by paying close attention to the details of the mountain environment.

Mountain Environments: Minerology and Natural History

Many women Grand Tourist's journals and letters show an interest in studying and collecting the flora and strata of the mountains they climbed. "The rocks and stones lying on all sides of the road have many of them the appearance of marble, with beautiful veins, of different colours," Lady Anna Miller observed on the Mount Cenis pass in her published letter of 3 October 1770, "there are also large lumps of spar, which glisten with great brightness in the sun. I picked up some fragments that are incorporated with ore" (Miller, 1776, p. 48). Visiting Vesuvius in 1794, Lady Elizabeth Holland carefully noted that the "stratum of fresh lava" at Tora del Greco was "of a peculiar texture, more charged with metallic particles than any of the other strata from Vesuvius, though not equal in specific gravity to that at Ischia" and that "the density of the atmosphere marks the source of the lava" (Holland, 1908, p. 143). She would return home with a collection of its volcanic eruptions, along with those of Lipari and Ischia, that would form part of her and her Whig politician second husband's immense natural history collection with specimens drawn from across the globe (Faulkner and West, 1820, p. 92).

Mary Berry was more interested in plants than rocks. "The whole way from Terracina most beautiful", she wrote on 15 January 1784 at Sta. Agata:

> the mountains all covered with myrtle bushes; the road, great part of the way, through hedges composed of myrtle, laurestinas, arbutus, phyllarea, a broad-leaved jasmine, and a bush I was not acquainted with. Picked crocuses and anemones by the road-side, and observed in a grass-field the polyanthus, narcissus in full bloom, and in the hedges several eglantine roses in bloom. (Berry, 1865, p. 75)

On 14 August 1784 in Montanvert, Mary gathered the bilberries, cranberries and strawberries that adorned the side of the mountain (Berry, 1865, p. 33). While it may not immediately seem it, picking the berries was an adventurous activity. Cranberries and bilberries (wild blueberries) could not be found in English landscape gardens, only in the wild, and they were not easy to pick. Mary took care to note down the correct names and details of all the rare alpine plants she saw and collected. By studying minerology and natural history in the mountains and collecting specimens Mary and other women Grand Tourists contributed to the empirical classification of the world. They were part of this early stage of the imperial project, for according to Mary Louise Pratt "alongside the frontier figures of the seafarer, the conqueror, the captive, the diplomat", there was "the benign, decidedly literate figure of the 'herbodizer,' armed with nothing more than a collector's bag, a notebook, and some specimen bottles" (Pratt, 2008, p. 25). This was Mary's "view from the top".

Society on the Mountain: Other Mountaineers and Local Guides

Despite the impression given by Romantic mountaineering accounts, British men and women of the eighteenth century did not climb mountains alone. Not only did they enlist the services of many local guides and porters, but mountain climbing was a sociable event, involving groups of likeminded travellers drinking copious amounts of brandy, rum and whisky. Raised to be social orchestrators, women's narrations of their mountain experiences relate mountaineering as a social activity, rather than a solitary endeavour. On 19 October 1783 at Mount Cenis, for instance, Mary Berry noted running into "a gentleman whom I immediately knew to be Cozens the painter's son" and noted that "An unexpected meeting in such a place, even with a person in whom one is little interested or acquainted, is very pleasant" (Berry, 1865, p. 36). The following year, Mary and her climbing group "dined upon the very edge of the crater" of Vesuvius "where we could look down into the fiery gulf and enjoy the noble fireworks with which it continued to treat us". Here, and in the earlier account of Ann Flaxman, we see something of the mixed-gender sociability of mountaineering.

Grand Tourists were assisted by local guides from the mountain areas who supplemented their income from manual or farming work by assisting expeditions and guiding tourists over difficult passes. Sarah Goldsmith has explored how these figures formed "others" against which elite male Grand Tourists showed their superior emotional self-control on a journey that was otherwise framed as a solitary endeavour (Goldsmith, 2017, p. 9). While it is clear from Mary's comment above that women Grand Tourists also viewed their guides as "others", being less invested in demonstrating an ability to face danger (and bound by the feminine modesty topos), they often wrote of how much their guides had assisted them and prevented them from experiencing danger. "About eleven o'clock, the weather clearing up a little, we mounted our mules, accompanied by two guides on foot, to ascent Montanvert," Mary Berry wrote on 14 August 1783, "but as I had before heard of their sagacity and steadiness when left to themselves, I did not experience the least degree of fear even in those places where a slip would have been fatal" (Berry, 1865, p. 32). Mary thus attributed her lack of fear to the skill of her guides, rather than any innate courage or stoicism on her part.

Educated in accomplishments (Pollock, 1989), it is evident that women also thought a great deal about how their guides perceived them and their mountaineering efforts. For example, Lady Elizabeth Holland wrote in Lucca in September 1794:

> I went in a chaise-à-porteurs into the quarries at Carrara. They produce the finest marble after that found at Paros. My royal Greek was very careful of me. He escorted me through all difficulties, torrents, chasms, precipices, etc. Upon the whole I expect he took me for an aventurière; indeed, he well might, though my suite

rather imposed on him, for I went in my own chaise, my maid with me, and on the seat my cook and a footman, and André was on horseback. I am sure he thought there was something mysterious at least, about me. (Holland, 1908, p. 128)

Here Elizabeth, like Mary, took care to note the assistance of her guide provided in helping her to avoid the danger of "torrents, chasms, precipices, etc". One of the wealthiest and most powerful women in Britain at that time, she, however, also sought some sort of endorsement from him. She considered herself as a burden "imposed on him", but at the same time believed that he viewed her in a positive light as a "mysterious" "aventurière". Elizabeth also wondered how her Italian travelling party viewed her and decided that they likely saw "a strange person, young, pretty, and alone" and considered her mountaineering activity as "perhaps an odd freak" (Holland, 1908, p. 127). In this, as in Ann Flaxman's account, we see something of an imperial femininity. Like Ann, Elizabeth viewed herself as exceptional and expected the "others" she encountered to view her as such. This was also how male British mountaineers viewed themselves and represented themselves against the "other", but they expressed this in different ways that were reflective of gender's ordering of social relations and cultural production.

Conclusion

Mountaineering has largely been framed as a male imperial enterprise with women's involvement only brought into the record during the last two decades. This chapter has built on this scholarship to explore some of the historically contingent gendered meanings through which male and female mountaineering subjects were produced on the Grand Tour. It has shown that it was through the cultural practice of the Grand Tour as a British rite of passage, in combination with the development of the sublime aesthetic and Enlightenment empiricism, that mountains became representations of British imperial power. Elite British women and men each carefully constructed their Grand Tour narratives to portray themselves in particular ways that demonstrated a connection to power. Though their descriptions of their experiences of mountains need to be interpreted carefully in a way that acknowledges individual positioning and proclivities, these accounts can shed light on the play of gender in the Grand Tour as a dress rehearsal for British imperialism.

Bibliography

Bainbridge, S. (2012) "Romantic Writers and Mountaineering", *Romanticism*, 18, pp. 1–15.

Bainbridge, S. (2013) "Writing from 'the perilous ridge': Romanticism and the Invention of Rock Climbing", *Romanticism*, 19, pp. 246–260.

Bainbridge, S. (2020) *Mountaineering and British Romanticism: The Literary Cultures of Climbing, 1770-1836*. Oxford: Oxford University Press.

Bayers, P.L. (2003) *Imperial Ascent: Mountaineering, Masculinity, and Empire*. Denver, CO: University Press of Colorado.

Berry, M. (1865) *Extracts from the journals and correspondence of Miss Berry: from the year 1783 to 1852*. London: Longmans Green.

Black, J. (2003) *Italy and the grand tour*. New Haven, CT: Yale University Press.

Bohls, E.A. (1995) *Women travel writers and the language of aesthetics, 1716-1818*. Cambridge: Cambridge University Press.

Brown, R. (2002) *Women on High: Pioneers of Mountaineering*. Boston, MA: Appalachian Mountain Club Books.

Burke, E. (1764) *A Philosophical Enquiry Into the Origin of Our Ideas of the Sublime and Beautiful*. London: J. Dodsley.

Cellauro, L. (2003) "Iconographical aspects of the Renaissance villa and garden: Mount Parnassus, Pegasus and the Muses", *Studies in the History of Gardens & Designed Landscapes*, 23, pp. 42–56.

Chard, C. (1999) *Pleasure and guilt on the grand tour: travel writing and imaginative geography, 1600–1830*. Manchester: Manchester University Press.

Charlton, D.G. (1984) *New Images of the Natural in France: A Study in European Cultural History 1750-1800*. Cambridge; New York: Cambridge University Press.

Cohen, M. (1992) "The Grand Tour: constructing the English gentleman in eighteenth-century France", *History of Education*, 21, pp. 241–257.

Coleridge, S.T. (1956) *Collected Letters of Samuel Taylor Coleridge*. Oxford: Clarendon Press.

Colley, A.C. (2010) *Victorians in the Mountains: Sinking the Sublime*. Farnham: Ashgate.

Dolan, B. (2001) *Ladies of the Grand Tour*. London: HarperCollins.

Faulkner, T. and West, B. (1820) *History and antiquities of Kensington*. London: T. Egerton.

Flaxman, A. (1787–1789) "An Uninteresting Detail of a Journey to Rome", in McAllister, M.E. (ed.) *Romantic Libraries, Romantic Circles*. Available at: https://romantic-circles.org/editions/flaxman/editions.2014.flaxman.flaxman.html (Accessed: 11 October 2022).

Gilchrist, P. (2013) "Gender and British Climbing Histories: Introduction", *Sport in History*, 33, pp. 223–235.

Gleadhill, E. (2021) "'For I Asked Him Men's Questions': Late Eighteenth-Century British Women Tourists' Contributions to Scientific Inquiry", *Eighteenth-Century Life*, 45, pp. 158–177.

Gleadhill, E. (2022) *Taking travel home: the souvenir culture of British women tourists, 1750–1830.* Manchester: Manchester University Press.

Goldsmith, S. (2017) "Dogs, Servants and Masculinities: Writing about Danger on the Grand Tour", *Journal for Eighteenth-Century Studies*, 40, pp. 3–21.

Goldsmith, S. (2020) *Masculinity and Danger on the Eighteenth-Century Grand Tour.* London: University of London Press.

Hansen, P.H. (2013) *The Summits of Modern Man: Mountaineering after the Enlightenment.* Cambridge, MA: Harvard University Press.

Holland, E.V.F. (1908) *The Journal of Elizabeth Lady Holland (1791–1811).* London: Longmans Green.

Justice, G.L. and Tinker, N. (2002) *Women's Writing and the Circulation of Ideas: Manuscript Publication in England, 1550-1800.* Cambridge: Cambridge University Press.

Kant, I. (1798–1799) *Essays and treatises on moral, political, and various philosophical subjects. By Emanuel Kant ... from the German by the translator of The principles of critical philosophy.* London: Printed for the translator; and sold by William Richardson.

Kinsley, Z. (2005) "Dorothy Richardson's manuscript travel journals (1761–1801) and the possibilities of picturesque aesthetics", *The Review of English Studies*, 56, pp. 611–631.

Kinsley, Z. (2008) *Women Writing the Home Tour, 1682-1812.* Aldershot: Ashgate.

Lassels, R. (1670) "A Preface to the Reader Concerning Travelling", in *The voyage of Italy, or a compleat journey through Italy. In two parts.* London: John Starkey.

Martel, P. (1744) *An Account of the Glaciers Or Ice Alps in Savoy, In Two Letters: Illustrated with a Map, and Two Views of the Place, & C as Laid Before the Royal Society.* London: Printed for Peter Martel.

Middleton, C. (1752) *The Miscellaneous Works Of the late Reverend and Learned Conyers Middleton ... Containing all his Writings Except the Life of Cicero ... In Four Volumes.* London: Printed for Richard Manby, and H.S. Cox.

Miller, A.R. (1776) *Letters from Italy, describing the manners, customs, antiquities, paintings, &c. of that country, in the years MDCCLXX and MDCCLXXI, to a friend residing in France.* Dublin: W. Watson.

Naddeo, B.A. (2005) "Cultural capitals and cosmopolitanism in eighteenth-century Italy: the historiography of Italy and the Grand Tour", *Journal of Modern Italian Studies*, 10, pp. 183–199.

"Oxford English Dictionary Online" (2021) Oxford University Press. Available at: https://www-oed-com.simsrad.net.ocs.mq.edu.au/view/Entry/239553 (Accessed: 18 November 2022).

Pender, P. (2012) *Early Modern Women's Writing and the Rhetoric of Modesty.* Basingstoke; New York: Palgrave Macmillan UK.

Pollock, L. (1989) "'Teach her to live under obedience': the making of women in the upper ranks of early modern England", *Continuity and Change*, 4, pp. 231–258.

Pratt, M.L. (2008) *Imperial Eyes: Travel Writing and Transculturation.* London: Routledge.

Redford, B. (1996) *Venice and the Grand Tour.* New Haven, CT: Yale University Press.

Robertson, J. (2003) *The Magnificent Mountain Women: Adventures in the Colorado Rockies*. Lincoln, NE: University of Nebraska Press.

Schaumann, C. (2020) *Peak Pursuits: The Emergence of Mountaineering in the Nineteenth Century*. New Haven, CT: Yale University Press.

Sharp, S. (1767) *Letters from Italy: Describing the Customs and Manners of that Country in the Years 1765, and 1766. To which is Annexed, and Admonition to Gentlemen who Pass the Alps, in Their Tour Through Italy*. London: Henry and Cave.

Spence, J. (1975) *Joseph Spence: Letters from the Grand Tour*. Montreal; London: McGill-Queen's University Press.

Sweet, R. (2012) *Cities and the Grand Tour: The British in Italy, c.1690–1820*. Cambridge: Cambridge University Press.

Sweet, R., Verhoeven, G. and Goldsmith, S. (2017) *Beyond the Grand Tour: Northern Metropolises and Early Modern Travel Behaviour*. London; New York: Routledge.

Towner, J. (1985) "The Grand Tour: A Key Phase in the History of Tourism", *Annals of Tourism Research*, 12, pp. 308–312.

Turner, K. (2001) *British Travel Writers in Europe, 1750-1800: Authorship, Gender, and National Identity*. Aldershot; Burlington: Ashgate.

Walchester, K. (2018) "Alpine guides, gender, and British climbers, 1859-85: The boundaries of female propriety in the British periodical press", *Victorian Periodicals Review*, 51, pp. 521–538.

Wordsworth, W. (1846) *A Complete Guide to the Lakes: Comprising Minute Directions for the Tourist with Mr. Wordsworth's Description of the Scenery of the Country, &c*. Kendal: J. Hudson.

Chapter 8

"The Woman Business"

Dorothy Pilley's *Climbing Days*

Sarah Lonsdale

Introduction

The mountaineer Dorothy Pilley became an overnight celebrity when, in July 1928, with her husband I.A. Richards and two guides, Joseph and Antoine Georges, her party made the first successful ascent of the north ridge of the Dent Blanche (Lonsdale, 2020, p. 127). The razor-toothed peak, near Zermatt in Switzerland, rising to 14,318 feet was notoriously challenging and Pilley and her team's climb was still being described as "one of the great mountaineering achievements of the century" some 50 years later (Williams, 1973, p. 107). The achievement was not only celebrated in the mountaineering press, but in the popular *Daily Mail*, notably emphasising Pilley's gender as the only woman in the party ("Englishwoman Climber: First to perform Alpine feat", *Daily Mail*, 25 July 1928, p. 13).

Later that year, and no doubt cognisant of the publicity value in a mountaineering book written by a woman, the publisher George Bell and Sons commissioned Pilley to write a memoir of her first ten years as a climber. Published in 1935, *Climbing Days* became an "alpine classic" (Williams, 1973, p. 109), enthusiastically reviewed in the *Journal of the Fell and Rock Climbing Club* as "intensely alive and the sense of adventure always present, sometimes so poignantly…that one holds one's breath as one reads".[1] *Climbing Days* is particularly relevant today, not only as a female-authored text published at a time when mountaineering was still

---

[1] Display Advert, *Observer* 5 May 1935, p. 4.

an intensely masculine activity (Schaumann, 2020) but also for the light it sheds on contemporary readings of historical mountaineering texts: Pilley's evocations of the mountain are very different from the masculine "drive to conquer nature" (Schaumann, 2020, p. 22) and are more a meditation of mountain travel as "the quest for encounter with the self" (Dhar, 2019, p. 347). The memoir has gone into two further editions with a fourth currently being planned by Pilley's great great nephew, the travel and exploration writer Dan Richards. Despite its success and longevity, *Climbing Days* had a slow and painful birth, both in the writing and in the publication, and Pilley's difficulties in asserting her authority and authorship illustrate both her publisher's, and her own, lack of confidence in herself as a woman writer. This chapter will begin by outlining women's progress and status in the very masculine sport of mountaineering in the early twentieth century, before going on to discuss the evolution of Pilley's book and the sometimes painful negotiations with the publishers George Bell and Sons. Finally, I will analyse some distinct themes that emerge from *Climbing Days*, including Pilley's ideas on the relationship between the body and the mountain, and her attitudes to exploration and adventuring. At its heart *Climbing Days* asserts women's rights to access the mountain and to write about the wild outdoors on their own terms.

Dorothy Pilley had made a name for herself since just after the end of the First World War, achieving some spectacular female "firsts" including being the first woman to climb the sheer "Devil's Kitchen" chimney in Snowdonia and the north-east side of Mount Baker in the Rockies. In a frenzy of activity in the second half of 1925, she climbed a record-breaking 25 north American peaks in 19 days ("English Girl of Alpine Fame is in Nelson", *Nelson Daily News*, 30 September 1925). Equal to her climbing abilities was her gift for writing, something she shared with other climbers – mountaineering has many times been called "the most literary of all sports" (Dhar, 2019, p. 346). She eloquently described her unique relationship with the mountains in terms of a love affair that represented escape and female freedom. The first time she experienced mountain climbing, in Wales in 1914, aged 20, "It was like waking up from a half sleep with the senses cleared, the self released...I was distraught by the feelings that arose" (Pilley, 1965, 2). She wrote both in her private diaries and for newspaper and climbing journals, about the "feeling of unity" that holding her body close to the rocks provoked. When a group of women climbers formed the world's first women's rock climbing club, the Pinnacle Club, in 1921, Pilley became editor of the club's journal, the *Pinnacle Club Journal*, commissioning and curating a uniquely female-authored collection of nature writing at a time when the vast majority of texts on the wild and on mountains, were considered the preserve of the "lone, enraptured male" (Mills, 1993; Jaimie, 2008). In an article she wrote for the journal's first issue, published in 1924, she described a snow-drenched climb into Spain across the Col du Boucharou in the Pyrenees in epic, fabular terms, two young women and their ancient guide alone in the elements. The article, called "Into Spain and Back Again", contains no information about hand-holds, equipment or practical uses of different kinds of rope, just the humans toiling over a mythically terrifying mountain:

> Two thousand-foot-high cataracts of snow dust…every few moments the blast which roared endlessly overhead would drop upon us, and the slope would dissolve into a race of white, writhing smoke that seemed to eat one's skin. (Pilley, 1924, p. 43)

"Manless Climbing": Women and the Mountain in the Early Twentieth Century

Increasing numbers of middle-class and elite women began serious mountaineering in the second half of the nineteenth century, challenging Victorian notions of women's physical weakness and lack of stamina (Roche, 2013). Many of the British women climbers were either well-connected aristocrats or the wives and daughters of established and respected male climbers, for example Lucy Walker, daughter of Alpine Club founder-member Francis Walker, Elizabeth Le Blond, the daughter of a baronet and the wife of traveller and explorer Aubrey Le Blond, and Mary Mummery, who accompanied her mountaineer husband Alfred on many of his Alpine ascents in the 1880s and 1890s (Birkett and Peascod, 1989, pp. 18–24). While women were tolerated, they were never allowed to climb using ropes without a male guide or escort. The focus of Victorian climbing culture in Britain centred on the men-only Alpine Club and its journal, which maintained severe and negative views of "insane" and "foolish" women climbers until well into the twentieth century (Lonsdale, 2020, p. 99). The sober and dark green covered *Alpine Journal*, published twice yearly, was a space where men could publicly record their achievements, "a way of cementing their position in society, giving credence to their authority, strength, power" as well as their literary prowess (Roche, 2013, pp. 251–252). The absence of women's names for at least the first 60 years of the journal's existence often gave rise to the inaccurate impression that very few women were either interested in, or engaged in, mountaineering (Lonsdale, 2020, p. 113). By the early twentieth century however, three clubs for women mountaineers were established: the mixed-sex Fell and Rock Climbing Club (1906), the Ladies Alpine Club with Elizabeth Le Blond as its first president (1907) and the Ladies Scottish Climbing Club (1908). The Ladies Alpine Club was very much a conscious subordinate to the men's club. It produced its own annual report of women's climbing activities, a list of peaks ascended, but originally with none of the narrative contributions that, as mountaineer and man of letters Leslie Stephen acknowledged, was what brought great mountaineers "immortality" (Roche, 2013, 17). The *Journal of the Fell and Rock Climbing Club* (known as *Fell and Rock*) contained few entries by women but they did, at least, begin to assert women's presence in the hills. The 1921 volume of *Fell and Rock*, for example contains an article by Dora Benson, "A Day on the Arran Hills", where she recounts climbing Ben Nuis, Ben Tarsuinn and Cir Mohr, all between 2,500 and 3,000 feet on a "mellow, crisp and golden" September day (Benson, 1921, 253). In understated fashion, she makes light of traversing a narrow ledge, "squeez[ing] down a little chimney" and "a little more scrambling" involving "hand and foot work" (p. 255).

Dorothy Pilley was part of a younger generation of women who began to challenge the patriarchal structures of post-First World War Britain across a wide range of activities (Beddoe, 1989; Evans, 2019; Holloway, 2005; Curnock, 1917 & 1918). Pilley's diaries are filled equally with expressions of love and excitement that walking in the mountains gave her, and of frustration at being treated differently by her climbing companions because she was a woman. In one entry, for the summer of 1921, her second Alpine season, she wrote, with disdain, of seeing in the lobby of a Zermatt hotel the "A.C. [Alpine Club] dotards with green ties who sit at a table and talk to no one. What a fatuous set of mandarins" (quoted in Lonsdale, 2020, p. 116). These "mandarins" represented the suffocating repression that she had hoped climbing would help her escape from and here they were, men still controlling her movements. In March of that year, 43 founding members had launched the Pinnacle Club, a rock climbing club for women tired of never being allowed to lead climbs, or to conduct serious ascents with women-only parties (Angell, 1988). An objective of the club was to "foster the independent development of rock climbing amongst women" (Clennett, 2009, p. 7); their journal provided a public platform for women to record their ascents. One of the first activities conducted by three members of the club – Pilley and fellow climbers Lilian Bray and Annie Wells – was a "manless" ascent, or *"cordée feminine"*, using ropes, of the Mittaghorn and a traverse of the Egginergrat ridge, climbing above 10,000 feet, including a difficult 300-foot "chimney" (Bray, 1924). These days such an ascent by women would barely raise an eyebrow but in the summer of 1921, this ascent was a radical and subversive act, although Bray did not use the word "manless" in her 1924 account of the climb in the *Pinnacle Club Journal*: the first recorded use of the term "manless" was in a piece published in the *Alpine Journal* in 1931 by Miriam O'Brien (later Underhill), an American climber and fellow pioneer of women-only climbs (O'Brien, 1931). The men-only mountaineering clubs of France, Britain and Switzerland, as well as the conservative group of Swiss Alpine Guides had long proclaimed that only men should lead a climb that required ropes (Ottogalli-Mazzacavallo and Boutroy, 2020). Pilley and her friends had travelled across Switzerland by train dressed in frilled skirts and only when they had arrived at a remote Alpine train station, did they secretly exchange their skirts for breeches and nailed boots, their ladies' travelling trunks for sturdy rucksacks: "Out came tins of herrings in tomato sauce, worn corduroys, woolly mufflers, battered aluminium saucepans and spirit stoves, a box of Keating's and mud-stained leather gloves" (Pilley, 1965, 131). For the next few years Pilley would continue to break records and break the rules, and in July 1928 she achieved an eight-year ambition to ascend the Dent Blanche by way of the treacherous North Ridge, with her husband I.A. Richards and two guides. Both this famous ascent, as well as the less famous, subversive manless ascent of the Mittaghorn, are recorded in her memoir *Climbing Days*. I will now turn to the volume's development and publication.

Climbing Days: From Commission to Publication

After the First World War, the arrival of the first women MPs and successive pieces of legislation such as the Sex Disqualification (Removal) Act (1919), newspapers began reporting on women's growing achievements in the world of work, science and exploration. From the first women magistrates in 1919 and Amy Johnson's solo flight to Australia in 1930 to the entomologist Evelyn Cheesman's insect-collecting trips in the South

Pacific ("Woman collects 42,000 insects", *News Chronicle*, 16 June 1934), women doing things was reported in the news, and helped sell books and newspapers (Bingham, 2004). No doubt on the hunt for guaranteed sales and headline-making material, Alan Harris of publishers George Bell and Sons approached Pilley on 11 December 1928, regarding the possibility of her writing a personal memoir on her mountaineering adventures (Lonsdale, 2020, p. 127). While women's accounts of exploration and even mountaineering had been published before, these were still fairly rare although when they were published, often sold very well. Mary Kingsley's humorous and proto-feminist *Travels in West Africa* (1897) had been an immediate best-seller. In 1907, Mary Hall's *A Woman's Trek from the Cape to Cairo* became an Edwardian publishing sensation as did, a year later, Mina Hubbard's *A Woman's Way Through Unknown Labrador*, both books' titles making it clear this was something new, a woman explorer's story. In 1904, Elizabeth (calling herself Mrs Aubrey) Le Blond, had published *Adventures on the Roof of the World*, implying within it would be contained her climbing memories. This book however is mostly a descriptive account of great men mountaineers' exploits. The book does record the account of another woman's adventures on the Rosetta in the Dolomites. The anonymous reflection records, on first beginning the ascent, "At this point I took off my skirt and removed my boots, putting on tennis shoes instead. The rubber soles of these are far safer than nails on the smooth and slabby Dolomite rock" (quoted in Le Blond, 1904, p. 182). Rope climbing safely and competently required women to wear breeches which, until later in the twentieth century, was seen as unladylike. Another woman climber, the novelist E.H. Young, described in an early issue of the *Pinnacle Club Journal* how this transvestism was greeted in remote and mountainous communities. Here she is describing a climb near Ogwen in North Wales: "A woman in knickerbockers was an object of derision or shame...the skirt was decently worn for as long as possible, then hidden under a rock or carried in a neat bundle...just before the [First World] war, people on the road near Ogwen would walk backwards for quite a long way, in astonishment and mirth at the sign of my sister and me in our corduroy breeches" (Daniell, 2009, pp. 28–29).[2] Not only was the woman traveller prone to wearing strange outfits, in the late nineteenth and early twentieth centuries she went against the social structures that placed the ideal woman in the home. The truly solitary

[2] Emily Hilda Daniell was the "real" name of the novelist E.H. Young.

mobile woman was a focus of suspicion and carried with her a whiff
of scandal: her vulnerability and thus suspected sexual availability and
untrustworthiness would suggest she was either destitute, a prostitute,
or a spy (Boittin, 2014). Working-class women have always been forced,
through financial necessity, to leave the protection and confines of home
to seek employment. The middle-class woman who chose to leave the
protection of her father's home and make a spectacle of herself was seen as
perverse but was also a symbol of social change and modernity and thus
something to fear by the forces of reaction (Evans, 2019).

Pilley's response to the request from the publisher was initially guarded.
She told Harris she detested many types of climbing book, and enquired
the terms on which the proposal was being made (Richards, 2016, 177).
This was not because she was publicity-shy. Pilley, who had worked as a
journalist in the 1920s had a knack for self-promotion, writing stories
about leaving her ice axe in London restaurants, her first ascent of the
Devil's Kitchen and, on her arrival in Canada in 1925, initiating a slew
of articles about herself in local newspapers (Lonsdale, 2020, pp. 103,
105 & 127). Perhaps it was because Harris's letter suggests that while the
publishers wanted to make the most out of her being a woman ("there is
still something striking and original in such a book being written by a
woman at all"), they wondered if it might be "jointly authored" between
Pilley and her husband I.A. Richards who had already published several
books on literary criticism (Richards, 2016, p. 176).

Harris wrote again in March 1929: "It is of course an important fact
that you are a woman climber but I don't think too much attention
should be drawn to the woman business in the book." He once again
stressed "we should awfully like it" if Richards could share authorship,
"so I hope you will have a good try" (Richards, 2016, 177). What is not
clear is whether the publishers felt a joint book would add to its sales and
interest, or whether they doubted Pilley's capacity to write a book on her
own. Pilley had her own doubts too. Her diaries and letters, from the
moment she met her husband, stress her lack of education and erudition
compared to Richards's Cambridge education and ease of expression:
her perceived intellectual inequality between them was one of the main
reasons she refused his proposal of marriage many times over many years.
On 19 May 1929, Pilley sent Harris a synopsis and her "Into Spain and
Back Again" article that would eventually form part of Chapter Ten of
her book. She added: "I haven't been able to persuade my husband to
join me yet." Again, it is not clear whether Pilley wanted her husband to

be a co-author or not. Although in that same letter she wrote she hoped to have a manuscript finished by the autumn of 1930, the book took another five years to write. Travels and illness played their part in the delay but there may also have been troubles over the joint authorship. In 1932, while the publishers were tentatively calling the book "A memoir of two mountaineers" Dorothy wrote "we have pooled our memories and discussed all the incidents and indeed written a good deal of it together" (Richards, 2016, p. 179). In August I.A. Richards, named in the contract as joint author, wrote to the publisher that the manuscript was "now within a day or two of being ready for typing" (Richards, 2016, p. 180). This letter tells the publisher that the two of them had been "collaborating" on the book, although Richards says that from a commercial point of view, it would be better if Pilley claimed sole authorship on the cover. After a gap of six months, two letters from the publisher to Richards first thank him for extracts "*from Mrs Richards'* MS" and then looks forward to the possibility that his wife "may be able to get *her* MS in trim by about the end of April".[3] The language of these two letters suggests that Pilley had by now taken sole authorship of the book, which was still two years away from eventual publication, in May 1935. Certainly, entries in Pilley's diary during these years refer to her writing the manuscript and then Richards reading over it and suggesting edits or corrections, but not his wholesale writing of passages or chapters. Another diary entry refers to Richards helping her arrange the index, and of providing the sketch maps of the mountain ranges referred to in the book, which appear inside the front and back covers (Richards, 2016, p. 185).

There is plentiful evidence for Pilley's sole authorship of the actual text. The chapter "Into Spain and Back Again" is practically verbatim the same piece of writing as appeared in the *Pinnacle Club Journal* some ten years earlier and it's highly unlikely that Richards had any hand in writing it as this was before they were married and when they were spending more time apart than together. Other passages in the book echo pieces of writing she had produced for the *Alpine Journal*. In addition, Pilley's diaries, from her first visit to Snowdon in 1914, strongly echo the language, and themes of the book: the sense of liberation, both bodily and socially, that mountaineering brings, and the difficulty of transcribing these sensations into mere words.

---

[3] Letters to I.A.R. from G. Bell and Sons 3 February and 24 February 1933, emphasis added.

The book, smartly covered in bottle green fabric and adorned with 64 photographic plates, priced at 16 shillings, "by Dorothy Pilley (Mrs I. A. Richards)", was published in May 1935 at the high point of British fascination for the mountains. Interwar interest in mountaineering was part of a new modernity of the outdoors. For the wealthy, developments in air travel and technological breakthroughs led to repeated attempts on Himalayan peaks throughout the 1920s and 30s. At the other end of the social scale, the growth in wages and working-class leisure time led to the creation of working-class ramblers' clubs and, ultimately to the mass trespasses on upland moorlands and the creation of the National Parks (Lowerson, 1980). The outdoors was, however, very much understood as being an extension of the "masculine public sphere", and the vast proportion of mountaineering and rambling was undertaken by men (Tebbutt, 2006). After 1933, mountaineering took on a further masculine dimension as the German National Socialist "need for heroes" charac-terised rival British and German Himalayan attempts as a symbolic battle between the two European super-powers (Hobusch, 2009). Combining imperialism, racism, aggression, competition and brute strength, and dramatized and emphasised by a new genre of German "Berg Film", this symbolic war was no place for a woman (Hobusch, 2009; Ireton and Schaumann, 2020). The year following *Climbing Days'* publication two of Britain's leading writers, Christopher Isherwood and W.H. Auden published their play *Ascent of F6*, a satirical commentary on an English nationalism that was prepared to sacrifice the flower of the country's youth on vainglorious colonial escapades. Mountaineering was in vogue, but it was a hyper-masculine, macho form of mountaineering into which dropped a female-authored memoir that discussed, as we will see, hairpins and flower-filled valleys but in an original, radical and, as reviewers agreed, charming way.

On publication *Climbing Days* received warm reviews in the *Manchester Guardian, Times Literary Supplement, Liverpool Post* and *Time and Tide*. The *Guardian* review likened "the charm of her writing" to that of Gertrude Bell (Smyth, 1935, p. 8). Writing in *Time and Tide* V.S. Pritchett said: "She has a dangerous ability to communicate her fever...and I can see this book claiming many victims."[4] The *Observer* put it on

---

[4] This section of Pritchett's review is contained in a display ad in the *Observer*, 19 May 1935, p. 8.

its recommended summer reading list for that year ("What to Pack?" *Observer*, 11 August 1935).

Climbing Days: Themes and Issues

Climbing Days was republished in 1965 by Secker and Warburg, with Pilley writing a new "Retrospection" at the front, and again by the Hogarth Press in 1989. In the 1965 "Retrospection", Pilley looks back over the previous 30 years, and of her own contribution to women's climbing. She is modest as to whether her book represented a revolutionary contribution to women's gradual acceptance in the mountains although she does acknowledge that in the 30 years since its first publication, "Both in the Alps and in the greater ranges the advances in women's climbing have fulfilled all expectations" and that "*cordées feminines*" are found as a matter of course (Pilley, 1965, pp. xxi–xxii).

The book, dedicated to "I. A. R." and Joseph Georges is a straight chronological account, in 16 chapters, beginning in 1914 with "Initiation" in Wales and ending, in 1928, with "The Great Year" and the Dent Blanche ascent. The chronology is uneven, however, with a full five chapters devoted to Pilley's early years climbing in the British Isles: Skye, the Lake District and Wales. Only one chapter, "The Wander Years" (1925–1927), covers her vast and ranging travels and multiple ascents across Canada, the United States, Japan, China and the Himalayas. It was in these two years that she first ran from, and then finally married I.A. Richards, in Honolulu in December 1926 (Lonsdale, 2020, p. 127). In the first chapters Pilley communicates the sheer joy of encountering nature first hand: the footholds, the waterfalls foaming over precipices, the moss under her fingernails, and, most of all, to enjoy this beauty alone:

> To lie on the summit of Moel Hebog *alone* with aneroid, compass and map and successfully identify all the mountains in my sight, was better than being given the freedom of any city…to find the top of the Bristly ridge of Glyder Fach in the mist, at dusk, *alone*, was an adventure that nothing in later mountaineering could surpass. (Pilley, 1965, p. 11, emphasis added)

Only when one reads Pilley's diaries in conjunction with these passages does it become clear that this intoxicating feeling of freedom comes from its contrast with her stifling and repressed life at home. For Dorothy Pilley, writing and mountaineering represented the twin routes of escape from the repressive expectations of a well-to-do family in the early interwar years. Returning from a weekend of climbing in north Wales, to the "gloves and high-heeled shoes, pavements and taxicabs" having the day before lain "munching a dry sandwich on a rocky ledge, plucking at a patch of lichen" put so much stress on her that "with a little more strain one would become a case of divided personality" (p. 36).

As the book continues she emphasises her difference from the hegemonic masculinity of the Alpine Club both in her status as a woman, and in her relationship with the mountain. In the extract below, from "An Alpine Novitiate" (Chapter 10), about her first season in the Alps, she first describes an arduous and beautiful climb before being brought back to earth by her gendered reception at the hut where she arrives, sweating and panting:

> The waves of ice near to are not like the water's waves. These towers, split and splitting, and leaning forward one behind the other in close-packed ranks over the valley, were all the more terrifying for their beauty of clear white and palest greens and blues against the sky...I had never seen so many tramp-like figures of all nationalities – ragged, dirty and unshaven – as were lolling about the platform, smoking and gossiping, as we trudged up the wooden steps towards them...The reason for Mr Solly's extra special welcome was at once made plain. He had a big pipe and it was unconquerably blocked. What he most needed in life was a hairpin, and what use was woman on the mountains unless she could instantly provide one? (pp. 109 & 112)[5]

Unusually, this passage reveals a woman meditating on the beauty and vastness of "the wild", attempting to understand the urge to propel oneself to the limits of physical strength to participate in it. There is a long tradition of women writing about "the wild", although much is private or overlooked (Mills, 1993, pp. 40–42). The vast proportion of the literary mountaineering canon, from classical period to the interwar years presented the masculine point of view: we can go as far back as Jerome's letters, finding in the craggy spurs of the Syrian mountains a balm for his unhappy flesh and Petrarch's celebrated ascent of Mont Ventoux: more than two thousand years of the male point of view of how the mountains

---

[5] Godfrey Solly (1858–1942) had been a member of the Alpine Club for more than 50 years, and had completed several first ascents of Alpine peaks.

are intricately linked to the sublime (Hansen, 2013; Hollis and Konig, 2021; Schaumann 2020). No wonder, then that the passage above also expresses "woman's" sense of being out of place, an intruder, and only of use to supply a hairpin to help unblock a male mountaineer's pipe. Yet she resisted, and challenged, male climbers' attempts to make her feel she didn't belong. Pilley, perforce needed to face her apparent trespassing on such masculine terrain, both in her snowy footprints, and in her writing, head on. The book is in fact peppered with references to male attempts to make her feel an outsider and to others' views of her as a woman out of place: "a local guide at the summit amused me by saying it was very unfit for a lady because of the cornices [ice overhangs], though why feminine feet should disturb them more than masculine weight it was hard to guess" (Pilley, 1965, 272). On another occasion, this time in the Pyrenees, she writes about a particularly difficult climb, the first winter ascent, in fact, of the Pic du Midi d'Ossau. Afterwards, lying "like seals for some time on a warm boulder" she and her companions discuss "sardines and Feminism", a casually thrown away remark before admitting that on the mountain her favourite food is bread dipped in the oil of a sardine tin, and jam, something she would never eat at sea level (256). Although the substance of the discussion on feminism is never revealed, her simple mentioning of the word is a reminder to the reader that women's equality, even thousands of feet up a mountain, was very much on her mind.

If we turn to Pilley's use of language, we can see clearly how she made deliberate efforts to avoid the aggressive and militaristic written style of the *Alpine Journal* where peaks were "laid siege" to and "defeated", virgin territory was "attacked" great campaigns (Lonsdale, 2020, p. 113). Englishmen, it seemed to readers of the journal, were the first to go, or discover anywhere: "Englishmen had the field more or less to themselves…Cecil Slingsby did single-handed for Norway what Packe and Count Henry Russell had done for the Pyrenees" (Mumm, 1921, pp. 12–13). The journal referred to the Alps as the club's "playground", denoting domination, pleasure and ownership and club members were almost mythically superhuman – unless of course they died heroic deaths (Collie, 1923, p. 1). Peter Hansen's study on mountaineering since the Enlightenment also shows how the dominant theme of much mountaineering memoir was inextricably linked with sovereignty, colonialism and masculinity and the obsession to be the first above any other consideration (Hansen, 2013). Women's voices were initially absent from the *Alpine Journal*, as might be expected, although American climber Meta

Brevoort published under her nephew's name in 1872 (Gifford, 2013, p. 98). Gradually, as editors canvassed for contributions beyond the membership, articles by women began appearing in the interwar period. A survey of the journal during the years 1904–1914 shows not a single woman-authored piece, although in the 1904 volume there is a review of Mrs Aubrey Le Blond's book *Adventures on the Roof of the World*. The February 1908 number notes the establishment of the Ladies Alpine Club with Mrs Aubrey Le Blond as president. It is described as a "child" of the Alpine club "of unique character and formidable dimensions…many of whose members have every qualification for our own Club, except that of sex" (Collie, 1923, pp. 10–11).

Dorothy Pilley's name first appeared in the journal in the November 1921 issue, in a short note in the "New Expeditions" section, of her ascent, with I.A. Richards, of the Pointe Sud des Bouquetins (12,000 feet).[6] One of her first articles on the Alps appeared in the May 1923 issue, detailing her summer 1922 ascent of the Jungfrau, as well as other climbs she accomplished, along with her friend Dorothy Thompson and I.A. Richards, without a guide. Pilley led one climb up the Rothorn, something that caused "surprise" and "amusement" among other climbers on the mountain that day (Pilley, 1923, p. 162). Her written style in the article is noticeably different either from the matter-of-fact technical articles about the use of ice axes or the relative strengths of different ropes, or the triumphalist genre of attack and victory. There is a lyrical, philosophical quality to her writing, and always, nature is respected, admired and trod upon only with her consent:

> To go up by a route unknown to the party, to come down over slopes never seen before into valleys where the rocks, the trees, the houses, the very flowers are different, seems to us the way to wring the best joys from mountaineering…The Trift glacier itself, as the crystal clearness of the sunrise crept down upon it was a thing *almost too exquisite to walk upon*. (Pilley, 1923, p. 165)

Pilley echoes this earlier image – of the walker fearing to disturb original and perfect nature – in *Climbing Days*, about an excursion to the Pointe de Bricolla, in training for the Dent Blanche climb: "Below the Moiry Hut the Alp was carpeted with purple Violas and sharp Blue Gentians so that it was hard to walk for fear of crushing them" (Pilley,

---

[6] "New Expeditions", *Alpine Journal* vol. 34, no. 223, p. 476.

1965, p. 310). Pilley can make these feminine observations without fear of being dismissed because she had done what only three other men had ever done, climb the northern arete of the Dent Blanche. Unusually for this kind of memoir, she also regularly referred to her physical frailty in the book, especially her frequent bouts of severe sunstroke out on the blazing snow, once causing her to slip into a coma (Pilley, 1965, p. 300). To combat this, she wrote, she would experiment with different kinds of scarves and later, would pack her hat with snow to keep her head cool (p. 319). As a young child Pilley suffered from severe debilitating headaches and poor eyesight, which meant her missing many days of school (Lonsdale, 2020, p. 130). She also suffered regular bouts of pleurisy in her left lung that left her breathless and bedridden (p. 107). Despite these severe health setbacks, one family friend described her as having "great strength" and T.S. Eliot, a friend of I.A. Richards referred to "the muscular development of her calves" (Luckett, 1990, p. xvii; Eliot quoted in Richards, 2016, p. 183).

Conclusion

A final theme of the book, and the one, I would argue that has made *Climbing Days* a book to be treasured by mountaineers, is her ability to express that mystical union between the mountaineer and the mountain, which other later women climbers, particularly Nan Shepherd, have also done. In the "Introduction" to the original edition to the book, she warned serious mountaineers that they would not find much technical advice, and in fact, they may find "too little climbing". This modest remark is open to interpretation – there is much climbing in the book (although there is very little on technique) and it would be impossible to use the book as a guide to difficult ascents. However, she has a gift of putting into words how, as Peter Hansen describes it "the modern self is haunted by mountains" (Hansen, 2013, p. 148) and how getting high up in the midst of a vast range comes as close as is humanly possible to transforming the body into something immaterial. Her descriptions of ranges as beloved friends, their great spines permitting the traveller to cross multiple boundaries – of gender, of element, of states, of contours, of social expectation – all told with a woman's voice, is her legacy. In *Climbing Days*, unlike the slightly skittish reminiscences of Elizabeth Le Blond, Pilley never once apologises for her femininity; in fact she embraces and elevates it. Far from feeling a trespassing outsider, which was the intention of Alpine Club "dotards", the book reveals woman as not only equal to men in skill and fortitude, but in complete harmony with the nature around her (Lonsdale, 2020, p. 116). Her publisher may have wanted to steer clear of "the woman business" but she stuck to her original vision, placing woman, sometimes panting, sometimes suffering, always enraptured, at the centre of the book.

Dorothy Pilley enjoyed the privileges of a comfortable middle-class upbringing (although her father, she wrote in her diaries, "wouldn't supply a penny" for her mountaineering travels; this she paid for herself from her income as a journalist [quoted in Lonsdale, 2020, p. 106]). However, in the 1920s and 30s, in the masculine world of mountaineering she was still on the margins and fought hard both head on, and, sometimes subversively, to be accepted as a serious climber. It is clear from her correspondence with her publisher that while they wanted the commercial advantage of a woman-authored volume at a time when women's experiences were in vogue, they didn't seem to trust her to deliver a full manuscript without her husband's help. *Climbing Days*, however, when it was published, was welcomed as an important contribution to women's experiences in the mountains, and its long afterlife is evidence of its original and fresh approach that still enchants readers today.

Bibliography

Angell, S. (1988) *Pinnacle Club: A History of Women Climbing*. The Pinnacle Club.

Auden, W.H. and Isherwood, C. (1936) *The Ascent of F6*. London: Faber.

Beddoe, D. (1989) *Back to Home and Duty: Women Between the Wars 1918-1939*. London: Pandora.

Benson, D. (1921) "A day on the Arran Hills", *Journal of the Fell and Rock Climbing Club*, 5(3), pp. 253–256.

Bingham, A. (2004) *Gender, Modernity and the Popular Press in Interwar Britain*. Oxford: Oxford University Press.

Birkett, B. and Peascod, B. (1989) *Women Climbing: 200 years of achievement*. London: A and C Black.

Boittin, J. (2014) "Adventurers and Agents Provocateurs: A German Woman Travelling Through French West Africa in the Shadow of War", *Historical Reflections*, 40(1), pp. 111–131.

Bray, L. (1924) "Three Pinnaclers in the Alps", *Pinnacle Club Journal*, 1(1), pp. 25–29.

Clennett, M. (2009) "Introduction", *Presumptuous Pinnacle Ladies*. Hinckley: Millrace, pp. 5–14.

Collie, J.N. (1923) "Valedictory Address", *Alpine Journal*, 226, pp. 1–5.

Curnock, G. (1917) "Khaki girls in France: the goddesses of secrets", *Daily Mail*, 21 November, p. 5.

Curnock, G. (1918) "Princess Mary: life with our girl army", *Daily Mail*, 6 December, p. 3.

Daniell, E. (2009) "Reminiscences", *Presumptuous Pinnacle Ladies*. Hinckley: Millrace, pp. 27–34.

Dhar, A. (2019) "Travel and Mountains", in Das, N. and Youngs, T. (eds) *The Cambridge History of Travel Writing*. Cambridge: Cambridge University Press, pp. 345–360.

Evans, E.F. (2019) *Threshold Modernism: New Public Women and the Literary Spaces of Imperial London*. Cambridge: Cambridge University Press.

Gifford, T. (2013) "Early Women Mountaineers Achieve both Summits and Publications in Britain and America", in Gomez Reus, T. and Gifford, T. (eds) *Women in Transit through Literary Liminal Spaces*. Basingstoke: Palgrave Macmillan, pp. 91–106.

Hansen, P. (2013) *The Summits of Modern Man: Mountaineering after the Enlightenment*. Cambridge, MA: Harvard University Press.

Hobusch, H. (2013) "A Triumph of the Will? Andre Marton's *Der Dämon des Himalaya* and the National Socialist Need for Heroes", *Sport in History*, 29(4), pp. 623–645.

Hollis, D. and Konig, J. (eds) (2021) *Mountain Dialogues from Antiquity to Modernity*. London: Bloomsbury Academic.

Holloway, G. (2005) *Women and Work in Britain since 1840*. London: Routledge.

Ireton, S. and Schaumann, C. (eds) (2020) *Mountains and the German Mind: Translations from Gessner to Messner*. Rochester, NY: Camden House.

Jamie, K. (2008) "A Lone Enraptured Male", *London Review of Books*, 30(5), 6 March.

Le Blond, Mrs A. (1904) *Adventures on the Roof of the World*. London: T. Fisher Unwin.

Lonsdale, S. (2020) *Rebel Women Between the Wars: Fearless Writers and Adventurers*. Manchester: Manchester University Press.

Lowerson, J. (1980) "Battles for the Countryside", in Gloversmith, F. (ed.) *Class, Culture and Social Change: A new view of the 1930s*. Brighton: Harvester.

Luckett, R. (1990) "Introduction", in *Selected Letters of I.A. Richards*. Oxford: Clarendon Press.

Mills, S. (1993) *Discourses of Difference: an analysis of women's travel writing and colonialism*. London: Routledge.

Mumm, A.L. (1921) "A History of the Alpine Club", *Alpine Journal*, 223, pp. 1–18.

O'Brien, M. (1931) "In the Mont Blanc Massif and the Oberland", *Alpine Journal*, 43(243), p. 231.

Ottogalli Mazzacavallo, C. and Boutroy, E. (2020) "Manless Rope Team: A socio-technical history of a social innovation", *International Journal of the History of Sport*, 37(9), pp. 791–812.

Pilley, D. (1923) "The North-East arete of the Jungfrau and other Traverses", *Alpine Journal*, 226, pp. 161–180.

Pilley, D. (1924) "Into Spain and Back Again", *Pinnacle Club Journal*, 1(1), pp. 38–46.

Pilley, D. (1960 [1935]) *Climbing Days*. London: Secker and Warburg.

Richards, D. (2016) *Climbing Days*. London: Faber and Faber.

Roche, C. (2013) "Women Climbers 1850-1900: A challenge to male hegemony?" *Sport in History*, 33(3), pp. 236–259.

Schaumann, C. (2020) *Peak Pursuits: The Emergence of Mountaineering in the Nineteenth Century*. New Haven, CT; London: Yale University Press.

Smyth, F.S. (1935) "A Woman Mountaineer", *Manchester Guardian*, 2 June, p. 8.

Tebbutt, M. (2006) "Rambling and Manly Identity in Derbyshire's Dark Peak, 1880s–1920s", *The Historical Journal*, 49(4), pp. 1125–1153.

Underhill, M. (1956) *Give Me the Hills*. London: Methuen.

Williams, C. (1973) *Women on the Rope: the feminine share of mountain adventure*. London: George Allen and Unwin.

Chapter 9

Wanda Rutkiewicz and Ewa Matuszewska

Deliberations on the Auto/Biographical
Na jednej linie [*On One Rope*]

Agnieszka Kaczmarek

Introduction

Before Wanda Rutkiewicz (1943–1992) landed at Kathmandu Airport as a member of the German-French Mount Everest Expedition of 1978, led by Karl Herrligkoffer, her passport had been invalidated due to the accusation of smuggling sheepskin coats across the Polish-Czechoslovakian border. When leaving Poland for Nepal, she was suffering from anaemia, and during the expedition, while fighting off bronchitis, Rutkiewicz was regularly subject to sexist slurs from male team members, who constantly diminished her mountaineering achievements, and openly claimed she was not capable of climbing the mountain. In the milieu of antagonism and with impaired health, the self-described "ascending machine",[1] Rutkiewicz scaled Everest, recollecting the climb in *Na jednej linie* [*On One Rope*] (1986), an autobiographical work written in close collaboration with journalist Ewa Matuszewska (1945–2018). In a foreword to *Karawana do marzeń* [*A Caravan to Dreams*], with reference to Rutkiewicz's proposal to collaborate on another book, Matuszewska (1994, p. 5), half in jest, half seriously, refused the climber the erection of "a little statue in the form of another book". Still bantering, Rutkiewicz (cited in Matuszewska, 1994, p. 6) responded that "It seems to me you will have to get on this statue. After

[1] All the quoted fragments derived from Polish-language sources have been translated by the author of the paper. The article's section on collaborative life writing was partially written thanks to the author's Fulbright grant received for the 2020–2021 academic year.

all, I think I am friends with a journalist for something?" As Rutkiewicz's cooperation with Matuszewska constitutes a contentious issue, the paper aims at defining what roles each of them performed in preparing, writing and editing the *On One Rope* manuscript while attempting to clarify the authorship of the autobiographical account. Since primary and secondary sources related to the Polish climber have not been translated into English, the article also intends to provide more information on Rutkiewicz's ascent of Everest, a pivotal chapter of *On One Rope*.

Collaborative Life Writing

Among all possible trajectories that life narrative research may take (Smith, 2016, p. xviii), one of the trends in the realm of auto/biographical studies is the exploration of *collaborative life writing* (Howes, 2020). As noted by Amy Culley (2014, p. 7), "Collaboration is a helpfully capacious term for an ambiguous practice that complicates our ideas of authorship and ownership, self and other", and not only in life narratives co-written by women writers the scholar scrutinizes. How complex the analysis of a collaboratively written text may be is also exposed by Lynn Linder (2016, p. 122), who poses a myriad of thought-provoking questions for studying a mutually constructed life narrative; for example, "Do such texts represent a cooperative construction of subjectivity and therefore irrevocably blur the distinction between self and 'Other'?" Given that, an attempt to systemise the ambiguous practice text collaboration may invoke is made by Sidonie Smith and Julia Watson (2010, pp. 264–265), who define *collaborative life writing* as:

> A term that indicates the production of an autobiographical text by more than one person through one of the following processes: the as-told-to narrative in which an *informant* tells an *interviewer* the story of his or her life, as in *Black Elk Speaks*; the ghostwritten narrative recorded, edited, and perhaps expanded by an interviewer, as in many political and celebrity autobiographies; a coproduced or collectively produced narrative in which individual speakers are not specified or in which one speaker is identified as representative of the group. (Emphasis added)

With reference to the aforementioned types of collaborative process, the composition of a mutually written and produced life narrative involves at least two agents: "one is the *investigator*, who does the interviewing and assembles a narrative from the primary materials given; the second is the *informant*, who tells a story through interviews or informal conversations" (Smith and Watson, 2010, p. 67; emphasis added). In the appendix, in which sixty genres of the life narrative are defined, Smith and Watson (2010, p. 265; emphasis added) also use the names *recorder / editor* and *teller* respectively, highlighting that power relations between collaborators frequently turn out to be "asymmetrical, with the literarily skilled editor controlling the disposition of the *informant*'s narrative material". In addition, extending Ken Plummer's 1995 research[2] on the agents engaged in the process of creating life stories, Smith and Watson (2010, p. 64) also point out *coaxer / coercer* among possible components of autobiographical acts, defining this particular agent as "any person or institution or set of cultural imperatives that solicits or provokes people to tell their stories". Interestingly, in his study on the memoir, Thomas Couser (2012, p. 94) appears to elevate the role of Smith and Watson's investigator, who could evolve into other roles in the process of composing the narrative to the level of a creator, and further indicates complications resulting from collaborative authorship:

It might seem that the collaborators' contributions are quite distinct: the *subject* provides the content, the *life experience*; the *writer*, the *narrative*, the text. But while the subject "*had*" the experience, he or she can only provide it *as* narrative. Thus, who the true *author* is depends on how one defines that term and the circumstances of the particular collaboration. (Some emphasis added)

Hence, Philippe Lejeune's model and editor (1980, pp. 160–161), with their roles explained in his 1980 essay "Qui est l'auteur?" [Who is the Author?], could also be referred to, respectively, as *informant / teller / subject* and *investigator / interviewer / recorder / coaxer / coercer / writer*, depending on the role they play in structuring the life narrative and on their input into the text's composition as well as edition, which should lead, at least in theory, to the response to the question of who stands for the author of a particular narrative, an extremely difficult task as hinted above by Linder.

As a result, collaboration may raise at least a few further issues. Firstly, when considering only each collaborator's contribution to the process

---

[2] Smith and Watson make a reference to Ken Plummer's *Telling Sexual Stories: Power, Change and Social Worlds*. London: Routledge, 1995.

of composing a text and producing a publishable product, there may be ethical issues between the parties involved (Couser, 2012; Linder, 2016). To refer to Linda Peterson's (2005, p. 178) pioneering work on familial collaborative life writing, collaboration is possible when "its subjects share ideology in order to share narrative". Otherwise put, the partnership between those involved may turn out to be beneficial for all collaborators, if they agree with the narrative's version of events being released, or it may turn out to be destructive to them in the end for various reasons. Secondly, fully acknowledged collaboration imprinted on a book cover with all co-partners' names and surnames may induce "incredulity and dismay" (Laird, 2000, p. 2). As claimed by Lejeune (1980, p. 170), the work of the editor, also referred to as *nègre* (Negro), *scapegoat*, or even *prostitute*, implying the meaning of an exploited ghostwriter, is usually marginalised and their contribution to the production of the text is regarded unfavourably. On the other hand, Smith and Watson (2010, pp. 68–69) assert that the critical reader may wonder whether collaboration, by any means, has not become coercion, thereby influencing the reception and interpretation of the life story. Therefore, they suggest, first of all, "specifying the roles of various coaxers in making the autobiographical text" and secondly, they call for attention to "the widespread notion that indigenous texts produce a kind of unmediated authenticity" that needs to be discussed.

Smith and Watson's final specification regarding the circumscription of the roles that it is feasible for diverse coaxers to play – as well as by any other types of collaborators regardless of which term from the ones cited above one will decide to employ – may be difficult to reveal. In effect, the scholars themselves provide the critical reader with an explanation why it may be problematic to concretise each collaborator's contribution to the publishable work. When pertaining to *the producer of the autobiographical "I"* representing another component of autobiographical acts, Smith and Watson claim (2010, pp. 71–73 & 76) that the speaker audible in the work may be "composed of multiple 'I's" including: (1) the *real/historical* "I" identified as "a flesh-and-blood person"; (2) the *narrating "I" / narrator* grasped as "The 'I' available to readers", or "the 'I' who tells the autobio-graphical narrative"; (3) the *narrated "I"* being "the protagonist of the narrative, the version of the self that the narrating 'I' chooses to constitute through recollection for the reader"; and (4) the *ideological "I"* that is embedded in a particular system of culturally conditioned beliefs at a given historical time and place. And now, if we only think about two collaborators that may construct each of the aforementioned "I"s to different degrees, it is simply inconceivable to arrive at a set number of possible, clearly defined, collaborative patterns of producing the autobiographical "I".

Still, extending the already complex terminology, Smith and Watson digress and pertain to another researcher's nomenclature. When speaking of the narrating 'I' expressing different voices, they invoke the term used by James Phelan, who asserts (2005, p. 69) that in the process of telling the story, one needs to perceive *the implied author*, i.e., "another, knowable agent involved: the one who determines which voices the narrator adopts on which occasions–and the one who also provides some guidance about how we should respond to those voices". Following the definition of the implied author in Wayne C. Booth's *The Rhetoric of Fiction* (1961), Chris Baldick (2008, p. 166) defines the agent as the "source of a work's design and meaning which is inferred by readers from the text, and imagined as a personality standing behind the work". Grasping both definitions and the explanations provided previously, *the implied author* could be Couser's *writer* or Lejeune's *editor*. Still, invoking Phelan's explanation and drawing a clear line between the implied author and the flesh-and-blood one, Smith and Watson (2010, p. 75) summarise that for them "the implied author performs the functions of editing, arranging, and shaping the experience that a narrating 'I' reconstructs of a narrated 'I'", which implies the roles ascribed by the scholars to their *interviewer / recorder/ editor*, or even *coaxer / coercer*. Consequently, regardless of the terms one is inclined to use or marginalise, how may the critical reader attempt to specify the roles performed by particular collaborators and the input they made to a given autobiography?

The responses worth considering are provided by various scholars. Bearing in mind Western book culture, in which the editor's job has been characteristic of "housewifely" and "midwifery" obligations, involving cleaning a text and assistance to produce a book, Alison Ravenscroft (2016, pp. 169, 170 & 172) discusses "the hidden nature of the editor's interventions" which, resembling colonial mechanisms, are to remain invisible to the reader. As a result, demystifying Edith Somerville and her cousin Martin Ross's accomplishable partnership, Nicole Greene (2016, p. 204) asserts that, first of all, "collaboration is the normal mode of writing, and, second, that writing is communal and, therefore, according to Ede and Lunsford, dialogic".[3] Laird (2000, p. 4) infers that it is hardly

---

[3] Nicole Greene refers to Lisa Ede and Andrea Lunsford's 1990 article "Rhetoric in a New Key: Women and Collaboration".

ever possible to differentiate who and to what extent someone contributed to a manuscript, and, also with reference to Somerville and Ross's collaboration, claims that "it does not matter 'which of us held the pen' – what matters is the process behind and around it of conversation, revision, more conversation, and more revision".[4]

Given that, despite the impossibility of marking the clarity as regards authorial and editorial contribution, but still trying to make any scholarly analysis as in-depth as possible, it seems appropriate to go beyond the primary text. As too much academic attention has been paid to supposedly individually composed works, forgetting that mentoring, literary inspiration and text editorial work also exemplify collaboration, Daniel Cook and Amy Culley (2012, p. 3) encourage studying women's life writing through the prism of "complex relationships between author(s) and text", the theme further extended by Culley (2014, p. 7), who showcases that life writing displays "the influence of familial, social, religious, and political networks on female identity and authorship". Furthermore, going beyond the text additionally means cross-referencing to other sources that may widen the reader's perspective by zooming in the lens through which the interpretation of a given passage may be conducted. In her analysis of *The History of Mary Prince, a West Indian Slave. Related by Herself* (1831) to Susanna Strickland when living in England, Sara Salih (2004, p. 132) also argues that the text is "best described as a concatenation of mutually validating and interlinked documents and not a single-authored, autobiographical narrative". Thus, other sources may not only help scholars verify the credibility of a related story when necessary but also assess and, in the long run, make readership appreciate the other collaborator's contribution, although a clearly-cut degree of collaboration may be very hard to specify and demonstrate.

The Everest Time

To the Polish readership and journalists, recently more and more interested in mountaineering literature, the salient primary source of information on

---

[4] In Martin Ross and Edith Somerville's *Irish Memories* ([1917] 2020, p. 134) one reads: "The question put by this lady, as to which of us held the pen, has ever been considered of the greatest moment, and, as a matter of fact, during our many years of collaboration, it was a point that never entered our minds to consider".

Wanda Rutkiewicz's thoughts and feelings as well as the events regarding the momentous ascent of Everest she is remembered for is her life narrative *Na jednej linie* [*On One Rope*], first edited in 1986. The retrospective autobiographical account embraces a few family reminiscences; the origins of Rutkiewicz's fascination with the mountains in the Rudawy Janowickie; experience-gaining climbs in the theatres of the Tatras, Alps, Hindu Kush, Pamir Mountains, and first Himalayan expeditions; and then the "Everest time", the last, almost forty-page, chapter of the narrative unveiling the experiences weaving the story of her 1978 ascent of the world's highest peak. Otherwise put, the publication does not include the post-Everest period of her life, which was mostly devoted to her successful or failed attempts to reach the highest summits on earth.

The contemporary principal secondary source, frequently quoted in publications of different kinds easily accessible on the Internet, is her biography *Wanda* (2017) penned by Anna Kamińska. A much more comprehensive guide to Rutkiewicz's life history, it portrays to the audience interested in the climber's mindset the intriguing personality reconstructed in Kamińska's imagination on the grounds of the scrupulously collected material. Where Rutkiewicz's autobiographical work mainly describes her climbs and barely touches upon her private life, Kamińska's biography fills up the space between the expeditions, answering the questions the reader may ask when reading *On One Rope* and wishing to know more about the Everest climb. Given that, Rutkiewicz's biography authored by Kamińska is frequently quoted nowadays, as it presents one of the most recent, reliable and comprehensible sources unfolding the story of the climber's life. However, there are other references worth scrutinising, and those were written by Matuszewska, the main chronicler of Rutkiewicz's life when she was still alive. Their close, although sometimes turbulent, cooperation began after Rutkiewicz's historic ascent of Everest, so even if there are sources narrating the climb before their encounter – for instance, a New Delhi-based article "Polish Woman Atop Mt. Everest" containing the mountaineer's primary impressions of the scaling and Rutkiewicz's chapter composed for Herrligkoffer's 1979 collective publication recounting the German-French Mount Everest undertaking – the analysis of these texts is beyond the scope of this chapter.

The last chapter of *On One Rope* entitled "Everest Time" presents the background information including Rutkiewicz's preparations for the expedition and circumstances that led to her participation in the climb. Invited by Herrligkoffer to take part in the expedition, Rutkiewicz seemed to be favoured by the leader. Although she claims (2010, p. 203) that during the expedition he neither singled her out nor intervened when she fell out with other team members, she received a few treats from Herrligkoffer. Instead of the minimal rate of six thousand German marks for expedition participation required from every team member to pay, Herrligkoffer agreed that Rutkiewicz (2010, p. 163) would pay for the participation by bringing twenty-five down jackets and trousers, an easily fulfilled demand by the citizen of Poland being well-known for manufacturing high-quality down commodities. Impressed by her achievements on Gasherbrums, in Norway, and on the Matterhorn, he appointed Rutkiewicz a second deputy leader and camera person (Rutkiewicz and Matuszewska, 2010, p. 166) – recognition not welcomed by her team members. On the way to Everest Base Camp, she did not need to trek in the pouring rain, as together with Herrligkoffer and his partner, she travelled to Lukla by helicopter, a treat not offered to other members of the German team (2010, p. 165). After the ascent, the leader also offered her a return alternative: helicopter transportation or the possibility of early leaving Base Camp with cameraman Horst Schumann and expedition doctor Horst Laube, whereas the other climbers were to wait until all the porters descended the slopes of the mountain (Rutkiewicz and Matuszewska, 2010, p. 203).

As Rutkiewicz (1987, p. 147) confesses in a 1987 interview, it was during the Everest undertaking that she had experienced the most explicit gender discrimination. Hence, in *On One Rope*, Rutkiewicz gives vent to her long-harboured resentment over the highly oppressive atmosphere during the expedition and antagonism addressed to her, she claims, by the selected team members. After meeting Rutkiewicz (2010, p. 166), Hubert Hillmaier asserted that "women at expeditions are nonsense". Adding some details of the quarrel with Sigi Hupfauer over oxygen masks, unnecessary in her opinion as there were enough masks for the climbers to use already, Rutkiewicz cites his comment criticising her behaviour: "These are Polish methods", and adds that the situation caused her "to feel contempt for another human being" (2010, p. 189). The chapter also confirms that Rutkiewicz's negligence to film the climbers' activity on Everest's slopes became a bone of contention in the team. Her failure to record Bernd Kullmann and Robert Allenbach's ascent to Camp Three made Hupfauer scorn Rutkiewicz with the words: "You are nothing, such a little, not great, Wanda!" (cited in Rutkiewicz and Matuszewska, 2010, p. 177). According to Józef Nyka (2003), Hupfauer's antagonism toward

Rutkiewicz was hardly understandable, since his wife, Gabriele, aimed to be the leading figure of mountaineering ten years later. In fact, the year before her husband scaled Everest with Rutkiewicz, Gabriele Hupfauer and Rita Allramseder had become the first German women to top Denali in Alaska, thus Sigi Hupfauer had been familiar with high female aspirations. Furthermore, according to team member Kurt Diemberger, it was Herrligkoffer's mistake to designate two leaders above Base Camp, equally strong-minded, as the party might have avoided strong friction with only one manager on the slopes of the mountain (cited in Kamińska, 2017, p. 267).

Nevertheless, in the passages depicting the conflicts, the reader hardly hears Rutkiewicz's verbal responses, thus her conversations are not recorded faithfully and appear incomplete. We do hear her inner thoughts and feelings related to ensuing circumstances, albeit it is necessary for the reader to remember that they have been transformed by the flow of time, as this first edition of the life narrative was published in 1986, eight years after Rutkiewicz's ascent. Regarding the chauvinism displayed by Hubert Hillmaier, Sepp Mack and Georg Ritter, the leading mountaineers in the team, the Polish climber (2010, p. 166) admits she is "inured to such a situation", although in the account there are numerous passages showcasing her worries, anger and resentment over the clashes within the group. When recounting the quarrel with Hupfauer over the oxygen masks, we hear his comment on the Polish methods of solving a problem yet there is no statement given by Rutkiewicz (2010, p. 189), only her inner thoughts and emotions about feeling disregard for the team member. When trudging up to the South Col, Rutkiewicz cites Sepp Mack's words buzzing in her head that she needs to digest: "You shouldn't dream about climbing Everest! You won't make it. You shouldn't even try because you'll be a threat to others" (cited in Rutkiewicz and Matuszewska, 2010, p. 193). However, there is no context given: we do not know when Mack made the statement and in what situation, and Rutkiewicz makes no reference to her reaction, either.

In contrast to the first publications issued in India and the account prepared for Herrligkoffer, in which we hear about Hupfauer's phlebitis and Marianne Walter's sleeping problems (Rutkiewicz, 2003), in the "Everest Time" chapter, Rutkiewicz touches upon her health issues before and during the expedition for the first time. In order to validate her sportsperson identification card, she had been obliged to go through a physical examination, and after a regular check-up, she was diagnosed with anaemia just before the flight to Kathmandu in August 1978. To solve the problem, she asked the medical personnel to forget about her visit, taking to Nepal supplements and appropriate medicaments to produce haemoglobin (2010, p. 164). In the middle of September, after participating in establishing the first camps, Rutkiewicz suffered from bronchitis (2010, p. 174). On September 25, she resumed her mountaineering activity, and loaded up on antibiotics, left Base Camp to reach Camp One to restart the acclimatisation process. Whatever one thinks of her decisions concerning her medical condition at the foot of Everest and intention to scale the world's highest mountain, the fact that she ultimately reached the mountaintop, after having suffered from anaemia, bronchitis and dissension sapping her of physical and psychological immunity, just confirms the numerous stories about Rutkiewicz's legendary resilience. As Kamińska (2017, p. 254) asserts, Rutkiewicz not only managed "to fight anemia with injections [containing iron] and regulate the level of hemoglobin in the mountains. Her expedition to Mount Everest . . . [was] also an injection of energy for Polish climbers to reach this summit in winter". Although colleagues affiliated with the Polish Mountaineering Association sent warm congratulations on her Everest accomplishment, unofficially, Andrzej Zawada, a legendary Polish expedition leader, who in the meantime was working on obtaining a permit to climb Sagarmatha in winter, expressed his jealousy by saying: "I said not to send a bloody woman to Everest" (cited in Kamińska, 2017, p. 267). The events that unfolded afterward also made history, because even if Rutkiewicz, in Zawada's words, "solved our problem" (cited in Winter, 2020), his team scaled Sagarmatha in February 1980, an unprecedented climb of an eight-thousand-meter peak in the coldest season, thus beginning a new chapter in the history of Himalayan exploration.

In the story of Rutkiewicz's resilient ascent of Everest depicted in *On One Rope*, it is also possible for the reader to notice her dependence upon Sherpas' support and her careful attention paid to the availability of supplemental oxygen. Commenting upon organisational issues, Rutkiewicz notes that "the expedition is poor; we have too few oxygen bottles and few Sherpas" (2010, pp. 171–172), repeating the information on the following page. Under the entry of October 13, her commentary showcases that the Sherpas were the backbone of the expedition to a great extent, revealing how important the information about the Sherpas' positions on the mountain's slopes was to Rutkiewicz. She also mentions (2010, p. 187) that a group of the Sherpas was to be a back-up for their summit attempt by setting up tents at the South Col and bringing food and fuel to their highest camp: "We cannot go without the tent and the provisions and equipment they were supposed to bring up" (Rutkiewicz and Matuszewska, 2010, p. 191). On the one hand, Rutkiewicz's impaired health may partially explain her dependence upon Sherpas' support when scaling Everest. On the other hand, her attitude and dependence upon the Sherpas' portering services were not uncommon among professional mountaineers at that time, as Hillmaier's reminiscences, cited in Rutkiewicz's life narrative, also confirm. The then widely accepted attitude among European and North American mountaineers towards usually nameless Nepalese climbers is even imprinted in the name of one of the Sherpas called "Hilton Boy". Interestingly enough, Rutkiewicz (2010, p. 169) also mentions the help of "German Sherpas" who paid less for their participation in the expedition just to grab a chance to be in the Everest region, with no opportunity to join a summit team.

The fragments about the Sherpas' support are sometimes intertwined with the passages showing Rutkiewicz's concern (2010, p. 182) about supplemental oxygen, which she treated as one of the pivotal factors that could enable her to stand on Everest: "The number of people who can reach the top depends on the number of oxygen cylinders and tents there [on the South Col]". Before the expedition, Rutkiewicz (2010, p. 192) had never used an oxygen face mask, bottle or regulator, as she claims, and was apprehensive of the oxygen equipment failure on the day of the ascent; therefore she made sure that she knew how to handle the gear when trudging up to the South Col. Relating in detail the story of the quarrel with Hillmaier over her asking one of the Sherpas to carry an additional oxygen bottle for her for additional remuneration, she comments: "I suddenly felt a panic of failure for a reason as stupid as the lack of a cylinder full of oxygen" (2010, p. 197). Bearing in mind the aforementioned quotations, and further perusing the chapter "Everest Time", the reason does not seem to be as trivial as Rutkiewicz asserts. Moreover, that the dependence upon oxygen constituted a considerable issue for the Polish mountaineer is also confirmed by her admiration for those climbers that managed to reach the top with no supplemental oxygen, voiced in the article published in India and in the chapter written for Herrligkoffer, as well as in the passages in her life narrative ("Polish", 1978, pp. 10–11; 2003; 2010, p. 199). Additionally, Rutkiewicz's admiration might have been fed by the first ascent of Everest with no supplemental oxygen achieved by Peter Habeler and Reinhold Messner in May 1978, just a few months before Rutkiewicz's attempt.

Rutkiewicz's Collaboration with Ewa Matuszewska

The most vivid and comprehensive picture of the climber's ascent of Everest is presented in her life narrative *On One Rope*, nevertheless, the question remains whose statements the reader peruses when following Rutkiewicz's steps. At the moment of issuing this paper, *On One Rope* has been released three times, in 1986, 1996 and 2010. All the editions' bibliographical information enlists the "author cooperation" of journalist Ewa Matuszewska, introduced in Kamińska's biography as Rutkiewicz's friend and an author of mountain-travel works (2017, p. 54). This cooperation was pejoratively evaluated by reputable Tatra Mountains historians and guides Witold Paryski and Zofia Radwańska-Paryska, the editors of *Wielka Encyklopedia Tatrzańska* [*The Great Encyclopedia of the Tatra Mountains*], who deduced that "the narration [in *On One Rope*] was sometimes expressly distorted by another person's inappropriate intrusion" (1995, p. 1044) bearing in mind Matuszewska's involvement. In an introduction to the 2010 edition of the climber's life narrative, Matuszewska (2010, p. 5) strongly denies any possible distortion of Rutkiewicz's text on her side or by any other person, adding that any accusations of inappropriate interference in the climber's wording indicate that Paryski and Radwańska-Paryska did not know Rutkiewicz's personality. Given that, in the same introduction, Matuszewska (2010, p. 5) touches upon "writing the book together", a first-time experience for the climber and the journalist, which, as well as their uneasy friendship, commenced after Rutkiewicz's ascent of Everest. In addition to helping the climber write the account, she assures the reader of Rutkiewicz's authentic story, admitting that "There is not a single word in this book that she would not accept, sometimes after heated discussions" (Matuszewska, 2010, p. 5).

In her biography on Wanda Rutkiewicz, *Uciec jak najwyżej* [*Escaping to the Highest*], originally published in 1999 and treated by the journalist as a farewell to their friendship, Matuszewska unveils further nuances of their collaboration of *On One Rope* as well as over a dozen interviews conducted with the mountaineer. Matuszewska (2007, pp. 16, 45–46 & 49) admits that *On One Rope* constituted a cooperative effort, referring to it as their "joint book". Rutkiewicz put the idea forward to the journalist in 1980 on the phone, after the climber had failed to submit subsequent chapters to a publishing house, with the latter having suggested the solution to the problem of Rutkiewicz's inability, or notorious lack of time, to keep up with set-up deadlines. As stated in an afterword to the first edition of *On*

One Rope, Matuszewska's role (1982, p. 198) was also to assist Rutkiewicz with "the literary smoothing of the text". In a legal contract confirming their cooperation on the book, Matuszewska's input (2007, p. 46) was stipulated as "author cooperation", the statement that appeared on the title page of the following editions. Furthermore, she was to be paid half the royalties, thus following Lejeune's inference (1980, p. 167) on book authorship, stating that the claim of a text's authorship is confirmed by publishing rights that commercially ascribe a given author to a particular text. Under such a framework Matuszewska should be recognised as the co-author of Rutkiewicz's autobiographical work.

Their joint authorship appears to be confirmed by the method applied in the process of working on the manuscript. It was Matuszewska who first recorded their conversations on tapes, posing questions and imagining herself as a future reader willing to get acquainted with the icon of Polish mountaineering, and then copy-edited the audio materials. Rutkiewicz read and reviewed the edited texts, introducing alternations to make the future manuscript sound the way she intended to see it in the printed version. The phase when they were attempting to smooth the text was quite formidable to both of them, as it happened that their work turned into "heated discussions, sometimes over one sentence or term" (Matuszewska 1982, p. 199). In her biographical farewell to Rutkiewicz, Matuszewska recollects (2007, p. 67): "When writing the book, she [Rutkiewicz] made sure that it was *her* book. She insisted on some phrases that seemed awkward to me and changed the word order, claiming that in this way it was closer to her speaking and writing style. I fought with her at first, acting like a typical editorial secretary, and then relented." Given that, it is worthwhile to mention that the title *On One Rope* was, in effect, Matuszewska's idea willingly accepted by Rutkiewicz.

From the 1982 afterword (Matuszewska 1982, p. 199), it is also known that the result of their joint efforts was an over three-hundred-page manuscript, "a very personal text, sometimes even exhibitionistic, not hiding the bad sides of mountaineering and the people who practice it". In contrast, the three subsequent editions of Rutkiewicz's life narrative number approximately two hundred pages, so even if a different layout or font was employed, a certain part of the text had been omitted in the final printed versions. Furthermore, as Matuszewska testifies (2007, p. 97), "when we were working on the book together, she wiped out everything in the text that seemed intrusively sentimental". Regarding Rutkiewicz's words (cited in Matuszewska 2007, p. 98), every reader of the mountaineer's narrative needs to be cognisant of her "inner censorship", which usually prevented the climber from revealing her thoughts and emotions with the intention of presenting a balanced point of view, partially stemming from her apprehension of being criticised. Consequently, *On One Rope* constitutes a personal text, however, the conclusively published manuscript cannot be designated as "exhibitionistic", i.e., as revealing too many private issues, since it displays the controlled flow of her feelings and reasoning. With the text in hand, Rutkiewicz began to auto-censor the manuscript, willing to shape her public image that the book – as well as other articles, interviews, and movies – was to sell. Unfortunately, to the best of my current knowledge, it is impossible to compare the audio materials with the printed account of *On One Rope*, since many tape recordings (including two sixty-minute cassettes constituting their first Everest interview carried out approximately one month after the 1978 ascent of Sagarmatha), nor the letters received from Rutkiewicz were retained by Matuszewska (2007, p. 29), the irretrievable loss of their authentic voices neither subjected to editorial proofreading nor distorted by the flow of time and fading memory.

With the flow of time, Rutkiewicz's auto-censorship began to wane. After the phase of authorising every interview and article written by Matuszewska, Rutkiewicz did not even read the texts to be published (Kamińska, 2017, p. 345). Moreover, in her biography on the Polish mountaineer, Matuszewska (2007, p. 15) recollects that "It happened that I conducted an interview with her [Rutkiewicz], writing it from beginning to end, asking questions, and responding on her behalf. Then Wanda was reading it, adding something or not, and everyone was satisfied." Of significant importance is also Rutkiewicz's decision to publish a long interview in cooperation with Barbara Rusowicz, not Matuszewska (2007, pp. 15–16), which turned out to be one of her last testimonies recorded before her death on the slopes of Kangchenjunga in 1992. Nevertheless, Rutkiewicz felt some moral obligation to her long-standing friend and eventually requested Matuszewska proofread the extended – not as auto-censored as the earlier texts – interview conducted by Rusowicz, which due to the lack of time on Matuszewska's side was not read and corrected insightfully by the climber's personal editor and member of her public relations team. To sum up, Rutkiewicz's editorial contributions to her printed legacy allow the reader interested in the mountaineer's mindset to familiarise themselves with her vision of the world, but it is worth invoking Kamińska's commentary (2017, p. 345) on Rutkiewicz's modus operandi exhibited during her exchanges with media representatives:

When she starts working with Ewa [Matuszewska], Wanda [Rutkiewicz] has already been playing a game with journalists. She does what she wants with them. She says what they want to hear, and during authorization she throws out her statements or refuses to grant permission to publish the text at all. If she wants an interview to come out and someone sent to her from the editorial office asks silly questions, she maneuvers the conversation so that the question becomes quite right. Over the years, she does more soul-baring and talks about herself more and more. She does not shun interviews when she sees the need to remind the press of herself. She knows that journalists build up her legend.

Conclusion

In an interview published in May 1987, responding to Matuszewska's questions, Rutkiewicz (1987, p. 144) spoke about her fondness for cooperation with women in both the mountainous and the literary landscape, claiming that she liked "to organize expeditions, to write books". However strong her taste for writing was, which appears difficult to verify, in reality, her claim about her liking for verbal composition is rather unsubstantiated – the rationale being that Rutkiewicz simply had no time to focus on collecting her memories on paper. As Matuszewska notes (cited in Kamińska, 2017, p. 357), the mountaineer had "neither patience nor time to write . . . She rushed from expedition to expedition". Therefore, for the above-mentioned reasons, it may be concluded that Matuszewska did the jobs of the *interviewer, recorder, writer,* and *editor* as she interviewed the climber, recorded their conversations on tapes, copy-edited the audio materials, wrote the manuscript, edited, and re-edited *On One Rope* and other texts published under Rutkiewicz's surname. Willing to hear about the climber's experiences, to a certain degree, she was even the *coaxer / coercer* since she tried to persuade Rutkiewicz to meet a publisher's deadlines. Rutkiewicz was certainly Lejeune's *model* as well as the *subject, informant, teller,* and also *editor* to a certain extent because she proofread and tailored the manuscript to her taste and vision the published book was to carry. Furthermore, concerning Smith and Watson, it may be inferred that the *narrating I* in *On One Rope* embodies both Rutkiewicz and Matuszewska as the voices telling the autobiographical narrative since both of them collaborated on the content of what would ultimately become the published manuscript. The *narrated I*, being the protagonist of the tale is clearly Rutkiewicz, since the life narrative comprises her recollections and she ultimately resolved what she intended the reader to know about her personality and climbing experiences, shaping the preferred version, or versions, of her complex identity for the reading audience. Having performed the functions of transcribing the verbal text as well as arranging and editing the written account to make the climber's memories comprehensible for the reader, Matuszewska is also cast in the role of the *implied author* of *On One Rope*, signified in the editions of the book by including the designation of "author cooperation" next to her name and surname on the title page of *On One Rope*. Nevertheless, her role in the writing process as the narrating I together with all the jobs she performed should elevate Matuszewska to the position of co-author included on the cover, beside the name of Wanda Rutkiewicz, which is not the case in any of the three editions of *On One Rope*. It is the case in *Karawana do marzeń* [*A Caravan to Dreams*], a 1994 publication with both surnames on the cover, although the journalist's name is printed in a smaller font than the climber's. The work comprises two parts: one being the manuscript of *On One Rope*, and the other, Matuszewska's text exclusively recounting Rutkiewicz's expeditions after scaling Everest in consecutive chapters penned after the Kangchenjunga tragedy. Otherwise put, Matuszewska's considerable input and her active participation in the writing process of Rutkiewicz's life narrative *On One Rope*, her editorial work, and even her willingness to meet deadlines have significantly contributed to preserving Rutkiewicz's legacy, enabling the readership of mountain-travel literature to have access to the climber's stories. Therefore, Matuszewska's intensely personal and professional involvement in the composition of *On One Rope* should not be regarded as the "inappropriate intrusion" Paryski and Paryska deduced it to be.

Wanda Rutkiewicz was a very controversial mountaineering figure arousing extreme emotions not only in Polish climbing circles, but also in the international arena. Remembered for her resilience and goal-achievement ability, and by some for denoting unmitigated stubbornness bordering with blind egoism, she did not follow the paths designed by mainstream society, and was thus ahead of her time by several decades. When she was dismantling gender barriers, Jerzy Kukuczka said that she led "an abnormal lifestyle", for "a normal woman" dedicates her life to a husband, children and home (cited in Rutkiewicz, 1987, p. 148). The General Secretary of the Polish Mountaineering Association from 1974 to 2005, Hanna Wiktorowska, on the other hand, stated that "Rutkiewicz could give out her ambition and tenacity not to five, or ten women, but twenty-five" (cited in *Polskie Himalaje* [*The Polish Himalayas*], 2008). Most probably, it is unlikely for the reader willing to believe in the authenticity of the account recounted in *On One Rope* to reach definitive conclusions as to what extent Rutkiewicz altered the manuscript Matuszewska had prepared and written, apparently spending more time on the publication of the book. Given that, it appears very probable that without Matuszewska, or any other person in her position, there would be no life narrative by Rutkiewicz, therefore Matuszewska's authorship should not be marginalised.

Bibliography

Baldick, C. (2008) *The Oxford Dictionary of Literary Terms*. Oxford: Oxford University Press.

Cook, D. and Culley, A. (2012) "Introduction: Gender, Genre and Authorship", in Cook, D. and Culley, A. (eds) *Women's Life Writing, 1700-1850: Gender, Genre and Authorship*. Basingstoke: Palgrave Macmillan, pp. 1–8.

Couser, G.T. (2012) *Memoir: An Introduction*. Oxford: Oxford University Press.

Culley, A. (2014) *British Women's Life Writing, 1760–1840: Friendship, Community, and Collaboration*. Basingstoke: Palgrave Macmillan.

Greene, N.P. (2016) "Demystifying and Resituating the Somerville and Ross Writing Partnership, 1889-1915", *The Canadian Journal of Irish Studies*, 39(2), pp. 196–217.

Howes, C. (2020) "Life Writing", in *Oxford Research Encyclopedia of Literature*. Available at: <https://oxfordre.com/literature/view/10.1093/acrefore/9780190201098.001.0001/acrefore-9780190201098-e-1146> (Accessed: 28 October 2022).

Kamińska, A. (2017) *Wanda. Opowieść o sile życia i śmierci* [*Wanda: A Story About the Power of Life and Death*]. Kraków: Wydawnictwo Literackie.

Laird, H.A. (2000) *Women Coauthors*. Urbana, IL: University of Illinois Press.

Lejeune, P. (2001 [1980]) "Kto jest autorem" [Who is the Author]. Translated from French to Polish by Jaworski, S. In Lubas-Bartoszyńska, R. (ed.) *Wariacje na temat pewnego aktu: O autobiografii* [*Variations on a certain act: On autobiography*]. Kraków: Universitas, pp. 155–176.

Linder, L.M. (2016) "Co-Constructed Selves: Nineteenth-Century Collaborative Life Writing", *Forum for Modern Language Studies*, 52(2), pp. 121–129. Available at: doi: 10.1093/fmls/cqw008 (Accessed: 23 October 2022).

Matuszewska, E. (1982) "Posłowie" [Afterword], in Rutkiewicz, W. and Matuszewska, E. (1986) *Na jednej linie [On One Rope]*. Warszawa: Krajowa Agencja Wydawnicza, pp. 198–201.

Matuszewska, E. (1994) "To nie miało być tak . . ." [It was not supposed to be like this . . .], in Rutkiewicz, W. and Matuszewska, E. (eds) *Karawana do marzeń [A Caravan to Dreams]*. Londyn: Wydawnictwo At, pp. 5–7.

Matuszewska, E. (2007) *Uciec jak najwyżej: nie dokończone życie Wandy Rutkiewicz [Escaping to the Highest: The Unfinished Life of Wanda Rutkiewicz]*. Warszawa: Iskry.

Matuszewska, E. (2010) "Powrót do czasu zaprzeszłego" [Back to the Past], in Rutkiewicz, W. and Matuszewska, E., *Na jednej linie [On One Rope]*. Warszawa: Wydawnictwo Iskry, pp. 5–6.

Nyka, J. (2003) "Introduction", in Rutkiewicz, W., "Mój Everest" [My Everest]. Translated by Józef Nyka. *Biblioteczka Historyczna Głosu Seniora [The Historical Little Library of the Senior's Voice]*, [e-journal] 12. Available at: http://nyka.home.pl/bibl_his/pl_ascii/12.htm. (Accessed: 18 March 2022).

Paryski, W. and Radwańska-Paryska, Z. (1995) *Wielka Encyklopedia Tatrzańska [The Great Encyclopedia of the Tatra Mountains]*. Poronin: Wydawnictwo Górskie.

Peterson, L.H. (2005) "Collaborative Life Writing as Ideology: The Auto/biographies of Mary Howitt and Her Family", in Huff, C. (ed.) *Women's Life Writing and Imagined Communities*. London: Routledge, pp. 176–195.

Phelan, J. (2005) *Living to Tell About It: A Rhetoric and Ethics of Character Narration*. Ithaca, NY: Cornell University Press.

"Polish Woman Atop Mt. Everest" (1978) *Polish Facts on File* issued by the Information Centre of Poland in India, 390, November, pp. 10–11.

Polskie Himalaje: Część 4. Panie w górach [The Polish Himalaya: Part 4. Ladies in the Mountains]. 2008. [DVD] Warszawa: Agora. (Script written by M. Giero, directed by A. Filipow and K. Wielicki).

Ravenscroft, A. (2016) "Recasting Indigenous Lives Along the Lines of Western Desire: Editing, Autobiography, and the Colonizing Project", in Chansky, R.A. and Hipchen, E. (eds) *The Routledge Auto/Biography Studies Reader*. London: Routledge, pp. 168–174.

Ross, M. and Somerville, E. (2020 [1917]) *Irish Memories*. [e-book] New York: Longmans. Available at: Project Gutenberg <https://www.gutenberg.org/cache/epub/61336/ pg61336-images.html> (Accessed: 3 November 2022).

Rutkiewicz, W. (2007 [1987]) "Kobiecość kontrolowana" [Controlled Femininity], in Matuszewska, E. (ed.) *Uciec jak najwyżej: nie dokończone życie Wandy Rutkiewicz [Escaping to the Highest: The Unfinished Life of Wanda Rutkiewicz]*. Warszawa: Iskry, pp. 142–148.

Rutkiewicz, W. (2003) "Mój Everest" [My Everest]. Translated by Józef Nyka. *Biblioteczka Historyczna Głosu Seniora [The Historical Little Library of the Senior's Voice]*, [e-journal] 12. Available at: http://nyka.home.pl/bibl_his/pl_ascii/12.htm. (Accessed: 18 March 2022).

Rutkiewicz, W. and Matuszewska, E. (1994) *Karawana do marzeń [A Caravan to Dreams]*. London: Wydawnictwo At.

Rutkiewicz, W. and Matuszewska, E. (2010) *Na jednej linie* [*On One Rope*]. Warszawa: Wydawnictwo Iskry.

Salih, S. (2004) "*The History of Mary Prince*, the Black Subject, and the Black Canon", in Carey, B., Ellis, M. and Salih, S. (eds) *Discourses of Slavery and Abolition: Britain and its Colonies, 1760–1838*. Basingstoke: Palgrave Macmillan, pp. 123–138.

Smith, S. (2016) "Foreword", in Chansky, R.A. and Hipchen, E. (eds) *The Routledge Auto/Biography Studies Reader*. London: Routledge, pp. xvii–xix.

Smith, S. and Watson, J. (2010) *Reading Autobiography: A Guide for Interpreting Life Narratives*. 2nd edn. Minneapolis, MI: University of Minnesota Press.

"Winter Mount Everest Expedition 1979/1980" (2020) *The Andrzej Zawada Memorial Foundation*. Available at: https://andrzejzawada.pl/muzeum/expeditions/mount-everest-1979-1980/ (Accessed: 17 March 2022).

Chapter 10

Julie Tullis

Gender and the Emotional Labour of Climbing the "Mountain of Mountains"

Jenny Hall

Introduction

Julie Tullis was a formidable mountaineer and the world's first female high-altitude mountaineering filmmaker, forming the "highest film team in the world" (Tullis, 1987, p. 6), with accomplished mountaineer and filmmaker Kurt Diemberger. Together they produced a roster of awarding winning films that covered the first French and Austrian expeditions to the Himalayan peak Nanga Parbat (8,126m) in 1982 and 1985. Tullis and Diemberger also filmed the 1983 Italian ascent of K2 (8,611m) in the Himalayas and made their first summit attempt of the mountain. Despite failing, it sealed Tullis's love of K2 as her "mountain of mountains" (Tullis, 1987, p. 199). Julie was the first British woman to climb Broad Peak (8,051m) in the Himalayas during the 1984 Swiss expedition to K2, which for the second time Kurt and Julie failed to summit. Her growing celebrity and reputation resulted in being the first British woman to be invited to climb Everest (8,849m) by the unclimbed Northeast Ridge in 1985. The Everest expedition was frustrated by poor weather and fatalities, leading Julie to feel a lack of fulfilment and strong desire to return. Kurt and Julie made two further attempts to climb K2 during the black summer of 1986, making her the first British woman to summit the mountain, on 4 August. However, Julie was unable to descend and it was to prove fatal. Despite Tullis' achievements and significant public profile, like many elite women mountaineers, she has not received the recognition of her male contemporaries. Nor, has her 1986 autobiography *Clouds from Both Sides* been recognised as a mountaineering classic. Gender is consequential in mountaineering and "for more than two centuries, ideas of what good climbing is, have had the effect of policing who gets to be a climber" (Rak, 2021, p. 5), and shapes how adventurous and heroic feats are recorded, represented and published.

The reasons for this reside in abstract concepts associated with "gender and nature" founded on imperialism and colonialism in Western culture that have evolved into a "narrow version of masculinity...writ large in hundreds of accounts of classic mountaineering expeditions", no less the mountain memoir, in a discourse of "heroic masculinity...remarkably resistant to imagining any other kind of identity for its participants" (see Rak, 2021, pp. 5–6). Despite significant social change, mountaineering remains a hypermasculine environment, where women are considered outliers (Evans & Anderson, 2018; Frohlick, 2006; Hall & Brown, 2022; Ortner, 1999). Women's mountaineering is systemically under-represented in publishing and marginalised "by the overwhelming male-ness of popularised mountain-eering" (Hunt, 2019, p. 6). Moraldo's (2013) analysis of French and British mountaineering memoirs highlights that 94 percent of all mountain autobi-ographies are written by men, and in a systematic survey of 32 climbing guidebooks, covering the major mountain areas in the United Kingdom, only one had received editorial contribution from a woman (Hall, 2018b). Rak (2021, p. 14) attributes this to several reasons, notably an insatiable desire for "real-life" adventure stories founded on acts of bravery, suffering, adversity and heroism that maintain a pervasive discourse of "romantic masculinity", a factor that is often absent in literary accounts authored by women. Despite a prevalence of travel writing and scholarship exploring the experiences of women adventurers, there is paucity that explores emotional labour and politics in the mountaineering memoir authored by women (Hall & Brown, 2022; Torland, 2011). Gifford (2006, p. 158) illustrates the cultural impact that British climbing writing had during the post-war macho working-class "Rock and Ice era" that rejected all things feminine, such as poetry. Literary representations of open emotion were suppressed through stories "told with a terse humour of understatement...a distracting curtain drawn across the full expression of the emotions" (Gifford, 2006, p. 159). Although the work of women mountaineers such as Arlene Blum (1983) decry such machismo, their contributions remain marginalised in the literary representations that shape our understanding of mountain spaces and places as sporting and leisure destinations (Hunt, 2019). Such factors provide fresh impetus for interrogating how inequality in the apparatus of mountaineering literature pervades.

How Julie Tullis navigated this environment so successfully is intriguing, particularly the way she managed emotional politics. Through the lens of emotional politics, Julie's experiences expressed in her memoir *Clouds from Both Sides,* offer insight into the different ways she represents her mountaineering achievements and the emotional labour she experienced. This deepens our understanding of how women negotiate power-laden relations in high-altitude environments to create different spaces of adventure. The implications for identifying inequalities offer insight for diversifying the mountain memoir by problematising this "singular white history" and call for different heritages in mountaineering to be recognised (Hunt, 2019, p. 3). What follows is a brief historical exploration of emotional politics and labour in mountaineering and how this impacted representation through published accounts.

Emotional Labour: Affective Emotional Politics in Mountaineering

The idea that bodies are "inscribed" with gendered meanings that represent social, cultural, economic and political experience is not new (Wearing, 1996, p. 80). Ahmed (2010b, p. 29) considers how emotion is in constant flux and "happening", functioning "as a promise that directs us toward certain objects, which then circulate as social goods" that stick to bodies like the masculine trope of the heroic adventurer, to the exclusion of femininity. Ahmed's (2010a) conceptualisation of the cultural politics of emotion asks us to consider the connections within communities and why/how some bodies are marginalised. Such approaches show how emotions have histories that are shared and replicated, assuming a bodily life that affect us (Ahmed, 2004). For example, the mountaineering hero is imbued with an imperialist vision of masculine histories, memories and emotions that are intrinsic to being a good mountaineer (Beedie, 2015). The mountaineering hero is emotionally objectified circulating in an atmosphere that is shared across social and psychic fields, unconsciously affecting bodies (Ahmed, 2010a). This vision of heroism forms an atmosphere where certain types of emotions and sensory perceptions become a form of social capital that is felt, impressed and expressed through masculine senses and emotions, such as, anger, risk, bravery, aggression and powerful or technical bodily movements. The affective atmosphere of heroism in mountaineering is exclusive to masculine ways to be, where femininity is alien and masked consciously and unconsciously, producing emotional labour that is often (tacitly) at work in generating alignment with and within communities (Hall, 2018b).

The emotional labour that female mountaineers experience when accessing adventure spaces is significant. Emotional labour shows "how people, within their working lives, mask their true feelings and emotions to meet others'" expectations (Hochschild, 1979, p. 7). It leads to significant emotional dissonance or discomfort that women mountaineers may "experience as result of incongruence between their displayed and felt emotions" (after Torland, 2011, p. 370). Strategies to manage such feelings or "rules" are expressed verbally and non-verbally and signify the ability to manage sensations of risk and perform "the cultural ideal" of the adventure hero (Sharpe, 2005, p. 34). Dilley and Scraton (2010) argue that women are subject to different kinds of responsibility and care founded on familial social values, governing the expectation that women should exercise greater risk-aversion than men (also see Frohlick, 2006). When women transgress their traditional familial role, the reaction can be extreme, epitomised in the sexist media backlash following Alison Hargreaves's death on K2 (see Frohlick, 2006). The media cast her as selfish for putting mountaineering before her two small children, demonstrating the incongruency of mountaineering and motherhood and the emotional labour it can produce (Frohlick, 2005).

Writing and Emotional Labour: Women and the Mountaineering Memoir

Women had a significant place within the Alpine Golden Age (1854–1865), claiming many first and daring ascents (McNee, 2017; Roche, 2013; Stockham, 2012; Colley, 2010; Brown, 2002; Mazel, 1994). Gifford (2013) argues that early women mountaineers' achievements went largely unrecorded because they had little control over, or inclination to transgress social norms during the Victorian period. A rush to make first ascents during this era evolved into a conceptual space that required adherence to gentlemanly rules such as the production of evidence through written reports, publications, photographs, films and memoirs and is why, Gifford (2013) argues, mountaineering "has such a strong literary heritage" (Gifford, 2013, p. 92). Prior to the use of tools such as photography and film, mountaineers reported their successes based on "their word as a gentleman" and so trust was embodied in masculine ideals that contrasted sharply with notions of femininity (Gifford, 2013, p. 92). The gendered nature of emotion and behaviours meant women who openly expressed masculine traits such as strength, fitness and competitive ambition risked transgressing traditional ideas of femininity and morality (Gifford, 2013). When women did write about their experiences, their stories would be devoid of emotional content and self-promotion, preferring to use bland matter-of-fact language as a way of deflecting criticism; they would often put their successes down to other reasons, such as good weather, as a way of preserving hard-won space. Tragedy or accidents were "dealt with in a perfunctory, dismissive, even joking, manner" (Roche, 2013, p. 252). Women conformed to social convention and took a diminutive and modest approach to avoid social shaming (Williams, 1973; Mills, 1991). Thus, men dominated the pages of mountaineering journals, newspaper articles and publications, securing recognition for their achievements. In contrast, nineteenth-century women's literary contributions were significantly constrained and largely absent.

Historians have revealed how a small number of female mountaineers did transcend social conventions and publish accounts of their exploits, however women had little control over the reception and distribution of these works (McNee, 2017; Gifford, 2013; Roche, 2013). Early accounts both published and unpublished often took the form of intimate diaries diminishing their status as works of serious merit. Elizabeth Le Blond's books were the exception, taking a more technical and professional tone that chronicled her achievements. Even though, Le Blond's achievements rivalled that of her male contemporaries, they were belittled by critics, who attributed her startling ascents, of Alpine Peaks in the winters of 1882 and 1883, to the skill and judgement of her guides alongside her own perseverance. Le Blond experienced significant emotional labour, enduring constant ridicule and shaming from her family, friends and peers that meant she climbed in secret and alone (with her male guide). Modesty and secrecy were the tactics employed by significant numbers of Victorian women, enabling them to make extraordinary ascents; these were evidenced through the registers from remote mountain huts that contain the signatures of women mountaineers, along with the führerbücher in which female clients of individual (male) guides wrote testimonials (Roche, 2015; Williams, 1973). In contrast, male counterparts published their exploits regularly in the mountaineering club journals. The first journal dedicated to mountaineering, *Peaks, Passes and Glaciers*, was published in 1859, later becoming *The Alpine Journal*. The journal was popular with the British public and spawned a proliferation of publications from the other mountaineering clubs during the 1890s. Women rarely featured in these journals and when they did, they were reported through a male voice, such as Meta Brevoort's 1872 account of ascending the Bietschhorn that was published under her nephew's name, W.A.B. Coolidge (Birkett & Peascod, 1989). For men, recording their achievements was a public affair that secured their place and position, making them more visible to historians, contributing to mountaineering evolving as a "male space" (Roche, 2013, p. 251).

Women are marginalised in mountaineering literature and mountaineering more generally, their difference contrasts sharply in a hypermasculine heroic atmosphere in which their presence invades a space not designed for them (after Puwar, 2011). Women mountaineers are often cast as super women (Warren, 2016) in mountaineering literature and filmmaking, something Ortner (1999) refers to as a kind of gender radicalism attributed to women operating outside of normal gender roles. The radical is not, however, a role model of resistance but perceived as an act of deviancy or what Moraldo (2013, p. 3) describes as "double deviancy", which is transgressive of femininity and familial gender norms. The representation of women mountaineers as radical, exceptional or inspirational further marginalises them by casting their difference as alien both to everyday life and within mountaineering communities. Taylor (2006) observes that female climbers have historically internalised and reproduced imperialist, colonial and masculinist values in mountaineering, which I later argue, is a strategy for survival that produces significant emotional labour. Through Tullis's memoir questions concerning the construction of feminine subjectivities are raised to explore how exclusion is manifest and impacts on bodies (Hunt, 2019). Through exploring how Julie negotiated the complex environment of high-altitude mountaineering I aim to nuance the emotional labour and politics she experienced.

Climbing the Mountain of Mountains: Emotional Labour and the Politics of Difference and Care

Julie embraced caring and empathetic values that were fundamental to her life as a climbing instructor and mountaineer. From her earliest days of learning and then teaching others to climb at the sandstone outcrops in Sussex, Julie had worked with adults and young people with disabilities. She appreciated how climbing unlocked something in her students, "bringing them to life" through engaging with new physical experiences like vertical movement and uneven ground (Tullis, 1987, p. 77). Her expertise in working with people with physical impairment proved invaluable during her first high-altitude expedition, in 1978, to the Peruvian Andes with double amputee Norman Croucher. Undoubtedly, Julie's vicarious experience of physical impairment had well equipped her to help make the expedition a success, summiting several mountains including Huascarán (6,768m) in the Cordillera Blanca. However, the expedition was not always met favourably by other mountaineers. On ascending Huascarán they encountered an Austrian mountaineering team and Julie reflected how "The poor Austrians were confused by our strange little group; the woman, a somewhat scruffy man and Norman with his crutches, walking slightly awkwardly" (Tullis, 1987, p. 100); their difference marked them as strange and after a short exchange with the Austrian team (who inquired about Norman's disability), Julie noted this confirmed the Austrians' worst fears that "we were quite mad and definitely to be kept at a safe distance" (Tullis, 1987, p. 100). Julie's team did not fit the heroic "cultural ideal" (Sharpe, 2005 p. 34), and were ostracised by the Austrians who returned to their tent and "firmly closed the door" (Tullis, 1987, p. 100). Julie reflected that help from the Austrians would not be offered and, although treated with good humour, the emotional labour of such exclusion was marginalising and produced feelings of isolation.

The expedition experienced other challenges, for example, Norman's prosthetic legs meant his speed when descending was slow, which increased the risk of an exposed overnight camp high on the mountain. Julie considered abandoning the climb, but felt guilt and intense emotional labour at the loss this would represent for her companions, her inner voice asked "how could I voice such a thought to this incredibly courageous man? How many future opportunities would he have to reach such heights. No, he was strong and fit and today was his day, the summit should be his" (Tullis, 1987, p. 101). Julie led the technical sections of the climb enabling Norman to successfully ascend the highest altitude recorded by a double amputee. The sense of achievement Norman and Julie felt was shared in a moment of silence, that rendered it "difficult to speak, such strong emotion welled up in me" (Tullis, 1987, p. 102). Although the ascent of Huascarán was an outstanding achievement, the care and compassion Julie afforded Norman does not fit with the cultural ideology of heroic mountaineering. Julie's representation of the expedition creates a different discourse founded in care, empathy and selflessness, where Norman's needs superseded her own. As such, her memoir contrasts sharply with classic *real life* heroic adventure storytelling and, I argue, one of the reasons why it has not been lauded as a mountaineering literary classic.

Managing Emotional Labour Through Spirituality

To manage the emotional labour and psychological demands of her dual life as mountaineer and housewife Julie turned to Japanese martial arts to positively channel her emotions, which was to prove invaluable throughout her mountaineering career. Becoming a black belt in martial arts in 1981 in her early 40s, Julie understood how important it was to harmonise mind and body as one entity; "I know that even when I have felt that I have reached the limits of my endurance I could go on for a long time by co-ordinating mind, body, breathing and spirit" (Tullis, 1987, p. 55). It helped her to physically endure the rigours of the harshest of high-altitude climates and social environments as well as deal with the tragic loss and disappointment that featured heavily in her brief yet spectacular mountaineering career. After successfully ascending Broad Peak in July 1984 (her first 8,000m peak) Julie and Kurt were swept away by an avalanche falling over 120m; at 7,600m, Julie's training in martial arts undoubtedly enabled her to co-ordinate mind and body to survive:

> I had the sensation of being in a fast lift, my stomach went up as my body went swiftly down and the snow engulfed me with such force that I felt as if I were trapped inside a waterfall. Somehow I knew that I was falling the right way up and that gave me comfort. I was also aware that I must get some air, or I would suffocate, and I punched out strongly with my right arm as I had done so often in my martial arts practice...a hole appeared...I was upright and I had air. (Tullis, 1987, p. 4)

Martial arts helped Julie survive, enabling her to access masculinities, such as harnessing aggression into technical strength and emotional/physical self-control, learned through her practice. It also enabled her to develop a sense of self care and bodily awareness, developing techniques that allowed her to regulate her mind, bodily movements, and systems such as oxygen reserves to navigate high risk situations psychologically and physically. For example, when descending from Broad Peak in harrowing conditions:

> I knew I must be calm and in control of my mind and movements. To try to rush to safety was pointless we would just become exhausted in no time at all, and probably then lose our sense either of reason or of balance. One of the rules for movement at altitude is to start off slowly and give the heart and lungs time to adjust to the exertion. I began to consciously control my breathing in time to my steps. One foot forward … breathe in! Two, weight forward … then breathe! Three, next foot forward … breathe out! (Tullis, 1987, pp. 3–4)

The pressures of the environment were not the only challenge Julie faced. She also cared immensely for others and worked hard to meet their expectations. The pressure of becoming a public figure so quickly was compounded when, as the first British woman to climb on Everest in 1985, she became the focus of intense press attention. However, joining the first British expedition to climb the Northeast Ridge (the last unclimbed ridge at the time) from the Tibetan side, proved to be traumatic and deeply frustrating. The season was marred by ferocious storms that precipitated several tragic accidents that led to the expedition being cut short, news that shattered both Kurt and Julie. Feeling the pressure to produce a decent film Julie and Kurt felt they needed further footage to fulfil their contract to the expedition sponsors and meet public expectations: "We had a responsibility to the film and expedition's sponsors to do everything possible. I was the first British woman to make an attempt on Everest, and so far, circumstances had not given me a chance to prove my worthiness for that privilege" (Tullis, 1987, p. 280). The emotional labour produced by the pressure to perform for a public hungry for success left Julie with an intense feeling of failure on returning to England:

> I crept in quietly. It would have been difficult to explain publicly how I felt about this adventure … This time something was missing, hunger pains still remained. The whole thing seemed inconclusive, and I felt frustrated. I had never come back home feeling this way before. (Tullis, 1987, p. 283)

On reflection she realised "My frustration lay with myself. I had worried only about what I had not seen or achieved instead of truly appreciating what I had experienced". She had applied the psychological self-care developed through her martial arts training to reconcile the disappointment she felt. Yet, the desire for success meant she still longed "to go back to Everest" (Tullis, 1987, p. 283) – evidence of the emotional labour driven by the Western normative politics of success.

Shortly after returning from Everest Julie and Kurt were on their way to join Peter Habeler's 1985 Austrian expedition to Nanga Parbat (8,126m) in the Himalayas. Kurt and Julie made two unsuccessful summit attempts, on reaching 7,600m the first time, they were forced to retreat due Kurt feeling unwell. Julie's acute disappointment was once again expressed in terms of care for others, it was "disappointing to have to go down from our high point ... especially as it was Lindsay's birthday and I wanted to reach the top as a special present for her" (Tullis, 1987, p. 291). Julie's sense of loss of being absent from home and missing her daughter's birthday was intensified by not summiting. Offering a summit success as a present to her daughter, I argue, was a way to alleviate the emotional labour of being absent from home. The sense of failure was acute. The greatest "mountain of mountains" she faced was navigating the emotional labour produced by the expectations of and care of others ... family, friends, press and peers (Tullis, 1987, p. 222).

Emotional Labour: Incongruity of Motherhood, Domesticity and Mountaineering

Like many women pursuing adventurous lives either professionally or for leisure, Julie faced the incongruity of motherhood and familial responsibilities with pursuing a professional mountaineering career (Frohlick, 2006; Dilley & Scraton, 2010). However, this was significantly alleviated by the unerring backing of her husband Terry Tullis, who selflessly supported Julie's mountaineering career, providing childcare, running the business and many other things domestically, in her absence. This was partly precipitated by the tragic events that led to Terry being unable to fulfil his mountaineering dreams, suffering a significant injury to one of his legs. Such male allyship and support was fundamental to Julie's success as a mountaineer. Even so, Julie delayed her mountaineering career until her children became more independent and was 38 when she began high-altitude mountaineering. In 1978, she joined an expedition to the

South American Cordillera Blanca in the Andes, and reflected on her newfound freedom:

> I had spent many years sheltering under the ideas of others; now the children did not rely on me so much, I wanted to think my own thoughts, and even if they were not successful, try out my own ideas. (Tullis, 1987, p. 129)

The emotional labour associated with women being linked to "reproduction and thus as gendered, maternalised 'other' in contrast to the fraternal geographies and normative white sporting bodies of the mountaineering hero" (Frohlick, 2006, p. 481) is evident in the way Julie had suppressed her own thoughts and ideas. Although Julie's husband Terry was enormously supportive Julie grappled with the emotional labour of leaving her family behind. Expressing how on her invitation to join Kurt Diemberger on a second trip to the Himalayas to film a French K2 expedition, in 1983, she mused, "Most husbands would have said once was enough …knowing … that [she was] going to tackle one of the most demanding routes in the world on such an enormous and dangerous mountain" (Tullis, 1987, p. 171). Frohlick (2006) notes how "maternal bodies trouble mountaineering terrains" but in doing so produce significant emotional labour that Julie felt she could not "allow the mountains to become a dominating passion. Even though Terry is the most understanding husband I could have, every time I go away we have problems with our relationship" (Tullis, 1987, p. 218). The guilt produced by her prolonged absences is illustrated by her empathy shown for the emotional labour that Terry experienced, created by "waiting interminably for news". "I try so hard to keep him up-to-date", she writes, intensifying the emotional labour she felt. This collision of mountaineering discourses concerning the fraternal escape from domesticity, in contrast to motherhood discourses that bind women to the home (Frohlick, 2006) produced emotional labour when transitioning between two contrasting worlds:

> My travels cause us to live very different lives … it is harder perhaps for my husband as I walk back into his everyday routine, feeling a little resentful that I am immediately plunged back into the routine of a housewife. The initial difficulty is that I do need time alone to come back from one world to another, which appears very anti-social when I have been away for so long. (Tullis, 1987, p. 218)

Julie had to contend with not only a personal sense of guilt but also social shaming, where on more than one occasion she had been "accused of being self-indulgent, even though I limit my climbing to expeditions" (Tullis, 1987, p. 219). This, however, was not a view held by Terry who was fully supportive of her mountaineering career. When Julie did receive media attention it was not always her achievements as a mountaineer that drew focus, but her difference as woman and mother. Being the first British woman to be invited to climb Everest, in 1985, she received lot of press attention that led to an invasion of her private family life. Lindsay her daughter answered the phone and was asked live on air by a Radio 4 presenter, "How do you feel about your mother going to climb Everest? … Does your mother climb mountains…and put up tents in the kitchen when she is cooking the Sunday lunch?" (Tullis, 1987, p. 262). Such an invasion illustrates the gendered nature of mountaineering where wife and mother are cast as outliers and doubly deviant for abandoning their familial duties (Moraldo, 2013). The affective emotional undertone of the interview with Lindsay intensified the emotional labour associated with feeling a "mother's guilt" and shame for causing hurt and loss to her children.

To avoid such debilitating emotional labour, Julie reduced her space to mountaineer geographically by remaining in Suffolk and declined opportunities to train in the British mountains for future overseas expeditions, unlike her male peers. Despite Terry's support, gender was consequential in reducing her space to climb and produced conflictual feelings concerning the inequalities she experienced:

> We both know that a sacrificial end to my mountaineering and filming is not the answer…After all, if it had been Terry's vocation that took him away from home there would be less of a problem. It has always been socially acceptable for husbands to go off on business trips – or to climb mountains – while the wife sits patiently waiting at home. It is genuinely far more difficult for a woman. (Tullis, 1987, pp. 218–219)

Julie also recognised the temporal differences between the professional lives of men and women expressing how men pursue and fulfil their professional ambitions much earlier in life. Whereas women by their 40s and 50s "have just become free from the responsibility and ties of caring for children and are ready to take up the challenge of life again, to spread their wings", she acknowledges sadness at the imbalance this creates in life and relationships (Tullis, 1987, p. 219). Yet Julie resisted the dominant discourse to "sacrificial motherhood" and foregoing her life to the selfless nurturing of her children; she deviated from the white middle-class normative expectations of motherhood (Frohlick, 2006, p. 477), creating, I argue, the double bind of being different in everyday life and different in mountaineering communities. Shame is central to this discourse for women who leave their children and are cast as wrongdoers (after Ahmed, 2010a, p. 101): the "we" – women mountaineers – are shamed by the recognition that leaving behind children creates pain, hurt and loss. This is illustrated by the public vilification of British mountaineer Alison Hargreaves, which precipitated a media frenzy that reinforced the shaming of the collective "we", perpetuating the emotional labour in an affective atmosphere of guilt that constrains women's access to spaces of adventure and risk. Male mountaineers are not subject to this atmosphere of guilt (Frohlick, 2006).

To manage the intensity of emotional labour women like Julie developed numerous coping strategies. One such strategy is to assume a sense of modesty by not overstating her ambitions or achievements.

Emotional Labour of Fitting the Masculine Norm

Even though women had been claiming their right to be mountaineers since the creation of the first all-women's climbing clubs such as the Ladies Alpine Club in 1907, women still preserved their modest silence. As the only woman and Brit on her second 1984 expedition to K2, Julie mused that she "could never see herself as part of a 'feminist' expedition", such as the all-female Polish expedition led by Wanda Rutkiewicz. Julie was careful to ensure she "fitted in" to her all-male expedition and conform to the social norms expected. She notes how Wanda's team "had attached themselves to our enterprise. They called themselves an 'all women's expedition' but shared our base camp and camps on the mountain" (Tullis, 1987, p. 227). Julie's statement questions and undermines the authenticity of a claim to be a women's only expedition, because the women were in receipt of support from male teams' equipment and labour; a criticism that was not levelled at the other all-male teams using the same resources. The very presence of all-women's clubs and expeditions is evidence of how hard women had to fight for the right be mountaineers and have their achievements recognised. Wanda was aware that accusations of male-help were ever present and felt the need to protect the legitimacy of her team through a women-only expedition (Loomis, 2005). Even though Julie had experienced extreme chauvinism at the hands of the French expedition in 1982 on Nanga Parbat and prevented from leaving Camp 1 because she was a woman, she observed the politics of silent modesty as a means of preserving acceptance in her all-male team. In doing so, Julie conformed/ reproduced social norms by rejecting feminist/different approaches to mountaineering. In part, this was due to Julie feeling compelled to present a credible identity as a (heroic) mountaineer and not be labelled first as a mother or wife who *also* mountaineered, nor a feminist troublemaker.

Male allyship was crucial to Julie's mountaineering career, in particular the supportive relationship with her husband Terry Tullis was fundamental, along with male peers. Her climbing partnership with Kurt Diemberger was built on a powerful bond forged through experiencing great hardships that proved foundational to their success as high-altitude mountaineers and award-winning film makers. The partnership opened a doorway for Julie to become the first woman to reach 8,000 meters, the first woman to climb Broad Peak (12th highest mountain, 8,051m) and the first to reach the summit of K2. On making the first female ascent of Broad Peak, she wrote how climbing the summit was for Terry and her family, and the film was "for Kurt who had put in so much effort and, because this was his special mountain. But most of all, I wanted to reach the top" (Tullis, 1987, p. 241). Julie's first thoughts were to others. The relationship between Julie and Kurt was based on a deep mutual admiration and friendship, yet subject to a significant power imbalance. Diemberger was an acclaimed veteran high-altitude mountaineer and filmmaker, being one of the first people to summit an 8,000m peak with Hermann Buhl on Broad Peak (8,051m) in 1957, and one of only two people to make first ascents of two 8,000m peaks (1960, Dhaulagiri, 8,167m). Although highly accomplished as a climber, the incongruity between Tullis and Diemberger is stark, producing complex questions at the intersection of class, sex and gender. Arguably, Diemberger's mountaineering career was hindered by gender-based prejudice through his partnership with Julie, for example, on Nanga Parbat leader Pierre Mazeaud's refusal to let a woman ascend beyond Camp 1 seriously impacted the filming. Deeply frustrated, Julie expresses significant emotional labour: "I was desperately disappointed and upset...Why did Pierre have to be so chauvinistic? I was not a threat to his success on the mountain. I felt terribly sorry for Kurt" (Tullis, 1987, p. 153). Again her first thoughts are for Diemberger and not the injustice she suffered. Despite this, the deep bond between them did not falter and to do justice to the complexities of their relationship is beyond the scope of this chapter. Tragically, the partnership ended when Julie succumbed to altitude sickness on K2, and on the descent to base camp Kurt expressed his anguish to fellow climber and writer Jim Curran, "'I've made it yes. But, she … Julie … she is up there. I've lost Julie,' I tell Jim. There's nothing else to say" (Diemberger, 2017, p. 229). Traumatised it took Kurt many years to recover and return to mountaineering.

Writing about the death of Ginette Harrison in 1999, Britain's then high-altitude record holder, fellow mountaineer Sue Black wrote, "It is really only since her death that much has been written about her achievements … one of her most endearing traits – her genuine and unassuming modesty – meant that she made light of her achievements" (Black, 2001, p. 101). Yet, Harrison's achievements were astounding, being the first woman to climb Kangchenjunga (third highest in the world, 8,586m) and the third woman to climb all seven of the highest mountains on seven continents. Although more than a century had passed, women were still reticent to promote their achievements, and when they did they risked public shaming, which was compounded by the limited exposure of published works. Like their antecedents the fear of breaking social norms silenced women's space from which to promote and share their achievements. Modesty was a political tool Victorian women mountaineers used to keep their mountaineering activities hidden to minimise the social risks and maintain space to mountaineer. I argue that the politics of modesty perpetuated into the twentieth century, evidenced by Julie's reaction to the Polish all-women's mountaineering team.

Emotional Labour: Death and Spiritual Belonging

In 1985, after living above 6,000 meters on the mountain for ten days, both Kurt and Julie were exhausted. That year, Kurt and Julie had "lived above 20,000 feet for 52 days" (Tullis, 1987, p. 291). Their second attempt on Nanga Parbat was once again thwarted by a storm which meant a dangerous and harrowing descent, being engulfed in many small avalanches. However, this time Julie did not experience the emotional labour of disappointing others; she just felt relief and joy:

> I looked back at Nanga Parbat sitting peacefully in the later afternoon sun and uncontrollable tears rolled down my cheeks … it's like coming back to the world, and life. The flowers seem brighter the sun warms me to the core, and inside I am myself again, able to smile from the heart. (Tullis, 1987, pp. 299–300)

Julie expressed an embodied deep connection with the mountains and mountaineering, which held profound meaning that was more than just sport and "was about trying to achieve a harmony with nature" (Tullis, 1987, p. 220). Julie meticulously recorded her joy at the small things around her: the wildlife, flora and fauna, and the beauty of the high-altitude landscapes she encountered. After reaching base camp after their second retreat from Nanga Parbat she recalls:

> That evening we sat by our tent amongst the forget-me-nots and buttercups, with the birds singing and the marmots whistling to each other in the background, I felt content. 'I don't mind not getting to the top…It doesn't really matter…You see, it was like reaching the summit, just to get down safely. This time this is our summit…to be here.'

> I turned and looked back up at Nanga Parbat, painted mauve and red by the rays of the dying sun. I had reached the clouds and climbed through them, going up and coming down. We had met the evil spirits of Nanga Parbat and had survived; we had a future. This time I was content. 'There are no winners or losers', is a martial arts philosophy. 'The challenge is only within yourself'. (Tullis, 1987, pp. 299–300)

Her martial arts training provided a safety net of self-care. She had overcome, in that moment, the pressure of meeting the demands of others, and felt a more-than-human connection to the mountains. Julie connected mind-body-environment to become "an extension of that force of nature [mountains] of which my body and spirit are a part" and explored her desire to know more about *being* in high-altitude places:

> You learn to push yourself through a desire to want to know more…and this is what draws me back to the mountains time after time. Even though I know the odds of injury and survival must be shortening, I have to go back. (Tullis, 1987, p. 222)

Following the avalanche on Broad Peak Julie had reconciled the probability that she would die at high altitude, reflecting on her experience of descending the mountain:

If I could choose a place to die, it would be in the mountains. When we were falling in the avalanche on Broad Peak, I knew that I would not mind dying that way. There have been a number of other occasions in the mountains, when just to sit still and drift into an eternal sleep would have been an easy and pleasant thing to do... hopefully the circle of nature will not close too soon. I have a lot to live for. Injury worries me far more especially being damaged in a senseless accident (Tullis, 1987, p. 276)

The mountains gave Julie the freedom and space to express and feel her own thoughts and desires, she was free to choose how she would want to die. In that moment of reflection her thoughts are her own – not owned by her family, peers or media. She alludes to having a lot to live for and is situated in her physical health and capacities, not her familial duties. In this moment Julie's thoughts embodied the mountain and her connection within it:

at 25,700ft ... I sat in the evening sunshine looking out over the thousands of golden peaks stretching as far as I could see, I felt so deeply happy and contented. I climb mountains for moments like this, not only to reach the summit – that is an extra bonus, a special gift ... I felt in complete harmony with my surroundings ... I was not a passive observer; mountains offer the ultimate human experience – to be involved physically, mentally and spiritually ... here I was sitting high up on the mountain that had filled my dreams ... the joy was overwhelming. (Tullis 1987, p. 209)

It took nearly a century for women mountaineers to not only overcome the right to publish but also to claim a mode of expression where their emotional and sensory lives were shared in intimate detail. By the twentieth century it was no longer considered a weakness to express such emotional experiences. The pithy matter-of-fact modest descriptions of Mary Mummery and Elizabeth Le Blond were giving way to a new style of expressing what mountaineering meant to women like Julie Tullis, perhaps preceded by a shift in the writing of male mountaineering peers, in particular influential climbers like Reinhold Messner, who wrote in a more spiritual way expressing how he "wanted to climb high again in order to see deep inside myself" (Messner, 1978/1999, p. 1). For Julie the experience of climbing K2 offered her "the ultimate human experience", to achieve a sense of embodied connection to the mountain world "physically, mentally and spiritually" (Tullis, 1987, p. 209). Yet, such expression is gendered and does not fit the cultural ideology of the mountaineering adventure that consigns such classic literature to the shelves of curiosity.

Conclusion

Julie Tullis's autobiography offers a different understanding of the world of high-altitude mountaineering by exploring her experiences of successfully navigating this gendered environment. The emotional labour of managing power-laden politics has offered appreciation of the tactics that women mountaineers in this period adopted to survive the social battleground of high-altitude adventure spaces. Julie's approach to managing this through her modest, emotional, empathetic and spiritual writings offers new insight into the mountain memoir as a genre of emotional and sensory storytelling beyond the cultural ideology of heroic mountaineering. She shows us how fluidity between masculinities and femininities offers different ways to be in the mountains and to appreciate how mountain environments are spaces of transformation. Her care for others, the environment and her family all shape diverse ways to imagine the life of elite mountaineering at the intersection of gender, dis/ability, class, race, age and sexuality, illustrated by her experiences with disabled climbers. Yet, hypermasculinity pervades, governing how mountain places and spaces are performed, produced and reproduced. Moreover, mountains and mountaineering are gendered, codified and valorised through masculine literary expressions of heroism in an atmosphere of masculinities that renders femininity invisible (Rak, 2021; Colley, 2010). Yet, I argue, Julie Tullis's autobiography is a mountaineering classic that broadens our understanding of life in extreme high-altitude environments and a call to scholars, publishers and the mountaineering literary community to recognise works like *Clouds from Both Sides* as "classic" texts that provide valuable insight into the different ways we engage in spaces of risk and adventure.

Bibliography

Ahmed, S. (2004) "Affective Economies", *Social Text*, 22(2), pp. 117–139.

Ahmed, S. (2010a) *The Cultural Politics of Emotion*. Edinburgh: Edinburgh University Press.

Ahmed, S. (2010b) "Happy objects", in Gregg, M. and Seigworth, G.J. (eds) *The Affect Theory Reader*. Durham, NC: Duke University Press, pp. 29–51.

Beedie, P. (2015) "A history of mountaineering tourism", in Musa, G., Higham, J. and Thompson-Carr, A. (eds) *Mountaineering Tourism*. London: Routledge, pp. 40–54.

Birkett, B. and Peascod, B. (1989) *Women Climbing: 200 Years of Achievement*. London: A & C Black Publishers Ltd.

Black, S. (2001) "Women and the mountains: Ginette Lesley Harrison", *Alpine Journal*, pp. 99–104.

Blum, A. (1983) *Annapurna: A Woman's Place*. San Francisco, CA: Sierra Club Books.

Brown, R.A. (2002) *Women on High: Pioneers of Mountaineering*. Boston, MA: Appalachian Mountain Club Books.

Colley, A.C. (2010) *Victorians and the Mountains: Sinking the Sublime*. Farnham: Ashgate Publishing Ltd.

Diemberger, K. (2017) *The Endless Knot*. Sheffield: Vertebrate Publishing.

Dilley, R.E. and Scraton, S.J. (2010) "Women, climbing and serious leisure", *Leisure Studies*, 29(2), pp. 125–141.

Evans, K. and Anderson, D.M. (2018) "'It's never turned me back': female mountain guides' constraint negotiation", *Annals of Leisure Research*, 21(1), pp. 9–31.

Frohlick, S. (2006) "Wanting children and wanting K2: The incommensurability of motherhood and mountaineering in Britain and North America in the late twentieth century", *Gender, Place and Culture*, 13(5), pp. 477–490.

Frohlick, S. (2005) "'That playfulness of white masculinity': Mediating masculinities and adventure at mountain film festivals", *Tourist Studies*, 5(2), pp. 175–193.

Gifford, T. (2013) "Early women mountaineers achieve both summits and publication in Britain and America", in Gomez Reus, T. and Gifford, T. (eds) *Women in Transit Through Literary Liminal Spaces*. London: Palgrave Macmillan, pp. 91–106.

Gifford, T. (2006) *Reconnecting with John Muir: Essays in Post-Pastoral Practice*. Athens, GE: University of Georgia Press.

Hall, J. (2018a) "Women mountaineers and affect: Fear, play and the unknown", in Saul, H. and Waterton, E. (eds) *Affective Geographies of Transformation, Exploration and Adventure*. Oxon: Routledge, pp. 147–164.

Hall, J. (2018b) *Women Mountaineers: A Study of Affect, Sensoria and Emotion*. [Doctoral Thesis, York St John University]. https://ray.yorksj.ac.uk/id/eprint/3793/.

Hall, J. and Brown, M.K. (2022) "Creating feelings of inclusion in adventure tourism: Lessons from the gendered, sensory and affective politics of professional mountaineering", *Annals of Tourism Research*, 97, 103505.

Hochschild, A.R. (1979) "Emotion work, feeling rules, and social structure", *The American Journal of Sociology*, 85(3), pp. 551–575.

Hunt, R. (2019) "Historical geography, climbing and mountaineering: route setting for an inclusive future", *Geography Compass*, 13(4), e12423.

Loomis, M. (2005) *Going Manless: Looking Back, Forward and Inward.* American Alpine Club. Available at: http://publications.americanalpineclub.org/articles/12200509900/Going-Manless-Looking-Back-Forward-and-Inward (Accessed: 22 January 2018).

Mazel, D. (1994) *Mountaineering Women: Stories by Early Climbers.* College Station, TX: A&M University Press College Station.

McNee, A. (2017) *The New Mountaineer in Late Victorian Britain: Materiality, Modernity, and the Haptic Sublime.* London: Palgrave Macmillan.

Messner, R. (1999 [1978]) *Everest: Expedition to the Ultimate.* Seattle, WA: The Mountaineers.

Mills, S. (1991) *Discourses of Difference: An Analysis of Women's Travel Writing and Colonialism.* London: Routledge.

Moraldo, D. (2013) "Gender relations in French and British mountaineering", *Revue de Géographie Alpine.* Available at: https://doi.org/10.4000/rga.2027 (Accessed: 22 January 2018).

Ortner, B.S. (1999) *Life and Death on Mount Everest: Sherpas and Himalayan Mountaineering.* Oxford, CT: Princeton University Press.

Puwar, N. (2004) *Space Invaders: Gender and Bodies Out of Place.* London: Bloomsbury Publishing Plc.

Rak, J. (2021) *False Summit: Gender in Mountaineering Nonfiction.* Canada: McGill-Queens's University Press.

Roche, C. (2015) *The Ascent of Women: How Female Mountaineers Explored the Alps 1850–1900.* PhD thesis, Birkbeck, University of London.

Roche, C. (2013) "Women climbers 1850–1900: A challenge to male hegemony?" *Sport in History*, 33(3), pp. 236–259.

Sharpe, E. (2005) "'Going above and Beyond': The emotional labor of adventure guides", *Journal of Leisure Research*, 37(1), pp. 29–50.

Stockham, K. (2012) *"It went down into the very form and fabric of myself": Women's Mountaineering Life-Writing 1808–1960.* Unpublished PhD Thesis. University of Exeter.

Taylor, J. (2006) "Mapping adventure: a historical geography of Yosemite Valley climbing landscapes", *Journal of Historical Geography*, 32(1), pp. 190–219.

Torland, M. (2011) "Emotional labour and job satisfaction of adventure tour leaders: Does gender matter?" *Annals of Leisure Research*, 14(4), pp. 369–389.

Tullis, J. (1987) *Clouds from Both Sides.* 2nd edn. London: Grafton Books.

Warren, K. (2016) "Gender in outdoor studies", in Humberstone, B., Prince, H. and Henderson, K.A. (eds) *Routledge International Handbook of Outdoor Studies.* Abingdon: Routledge, pp. 360–368.

Wearing, B. (1998) *Leisure and Feminist Theory.* London: Sage Publications Ltd.

Williams, C. (1973) *Women on the Rope.* London: George Allen & Unwin Ltd.

III. EMBODYING THE MOUNTAIN

Chapter 11

The Total Mountain

Nan Shepherd and the Virtual Qualities of Landscape

Ben Garlick

Abstract

The work of author Nan Shepherd explores the relationships between nature, culture, landscape and bodies. Increasingly regarded as an important figure in early twentieth-century Scottish literature for her poetry and fiction, Shepherd's work received renewed attention following the re-publication (in 2009) of her nonfiction treatise *The Living Mountain*, and its celebration by writers such as Robert Macfarlane. A meditation on place that draws upon experiences of the Cairngorm mountains in Scotland, Shepherd explores the different ways in which the environment and body meet, affording multiple "ways in" to the plateau. This chapter develops her notion of "the total mountain", introduced within *The Living Mountain*, as a concept figuring the "virtual" in an ontology and epistemology of landscape: always excessive and alive with potential.

Introduction: The Invitation of Landscape

"Certain books, [...] like certain landscapes, stay with us even when we have left them, changing not just our weathers but our climates." (Macfarlane, 2015, p. 12)

In his experimental novel-memoir *Here is Where We Meet* (2006), author John Berger traverses a series of haunted urban landscapes – Geneva, Lisbon, London, Krakow, among others – animated by past relationships and encounters. Presenting places alive with the spectres of personal and shared histories, he demonstrates the capacity of literary writing to reflect and respond to the enticement of geography. He writes, "I love the landscape's invitation, wherever it may lead" (2006, p. 173). Thus, his novel exemplifies landscape as both a theoretical concept – in its concern with how environmental perception unfolds – and empirical subject – in its desire to attend to the material, lived character of place – with enduring, animating trans-disciplinary allure (Rose and Wylie, 2006). In meeting them, landscapes both draw us into their capacious folds, and cast us outward towards other sites, situations and times (see Rose, 2010).

Landscape – both a defined portion of the earth, and a question of how such environments are experienced within specific cultural contexts – has long been a staple of thinking in human geography, environmental history and anthropology; not to mention literature, art history and, increasingly, the interdisciplinary environmental humanities (e.g., Tsing, 2005, 2015; Reinert, 2014). A protean "shuttle", the term weaves disparate works and approaches into a shared project concerned with the human-environment relationship (Matless, 2003). Serving as the primary inspiration and departure point for this chapter are recent discussions in cultural geographies approaching landscape through attention to its more-than-human, material, bodily and affective dimensions, mobilising practices of creative and literary writing in the process. Such interest in writing place has stimulated expanded engagement with literary texts as part of a reenergised "literary geography" that goes beyond the analysis of works as solely *representations* of the environment, reflecting on the "geographical event" of their formation and reception; and the potential of literary engagements with place to capture their more-than-representational aspects (Hones, 2011).

This chapter discusses a celebrated piece of "mountain literature": *The Living Mountain* by Nan Shepherd. In doing so, it elaborates Shepherd's conceit of the "total mountain" as a working metaphor for the excessive nature of landscape. Notably, Shepherd's work has not gone unexamined by geographers (see Carter, 2001; della Dora, 2016a; Hall, 2018; Hunt, 2019). Moreover, poet and literature scholar Samantha Walton (2020) has recently offered a detailed ecocritical analysis of Shepherd and her output, making clear just how much her writing resonates with current academic enthusiasms for the more-than-human, ecological thought and ethical status of the environment amidst a current age of crisis. Such efforts are continued here, teasing out those aspects of Shepherd's writing offering a means to articulate the "virtual" qualities of the landscape-event, alive with the potential to be otherwise. Thus, through her writing, Shepherd provides what, after Brian Massumi (2002), are understood as vital "parables for the virtual" with regard to landscape's becoming, affects and materiality. The next section briefly elaborates thinking on landscape and "the virtual", comprising the conceptual basis for this chapter. The chapter then introduces Nan Shepherd and the presence of landscape in her work, before turning specifically to *The Living Mountain* (hereafter, *TLM*). Finally, "the total mountain" is examined as both an ontology and epistemology for engaging with (mountain) landscapes in geography, and beyond.

The Potential of Landscape

For geographer David Matless, landscape is a mobile concept, shifting "between paint and ground, people and rock, vegetable and animal, profit and emotion, the wistful and the earthed" (2014, p. 6). Work on mountains in geography and cognate disciplines – "the first features to capture our attention in the landscape" (della Dora, 2016b, p. 147) – showcases such variety. As well as considering mountains as objects of power and representation (della Dora, 2016a), scholars have directed the insights of bodily, material, affective and decolonising 'turns' towards these environments (Hunt, 2019). Mountain landscapes, traditionally constructed as unpeopled "wildernesses", are increasingly recast as lived spaces (Wall-Reinus et al., 2020) differently assembled via legal, scientific, bodily and more-than-human practices (Vannini and Vannini, 2016). Works by Sarah Nettleton (2015), Hannah MacPherson (2008) and Jenny Hall (2018), among many others, examine how environments including the Scottish Highlands and Lake District are "brought to hand" by different bodies (running or walking; able or partially sighted; male or female) engaging multiple activities. The practical, material business of mountain wayfinding has also been discussed (e.g., Lorimer and Lund, 2003), with recent work attending to the manner in which recent techno-logical advancements mediate the ways such landscapes are seen and sensed by – or for – a range of individuals (see Smith et al., 2020; Stanley, 2020). Thus, as Veronica della Dora (2016a) emphasises, mountainous landscapes have long hosted knowledge-making acts, being imbricated into our perception and experience of space and time (see also Cosgrove and della Dora, 2009). Collectively, then, such mountain scholarship showcases "a body-subject whose ambit is involvement and engagement rather than a detached gaze in which materiality stiffens into objectivity" (Anderson and Wylie, 2009, p. 324).

This chapter draws from phenomenological, post-phenomenological and posthumanist work on landscape, foregrounding its materiality, embodiment and more-than-human composition (see Wylie, 2006; Pries, 2018; Wylie and Webster, 2019; Garlick, 2019; Rush-Cooper, 2020). Increasingly, geographers and others conceptualise landscapes as unstable, emergent, changeable. Abiding in the tension between immersion and detachment, one is liable to get *lost* in the landscape, empirically and conceptually (Nancy, 2005). Post-phenomenology opens questions of subject's and environment's co-constitution via the specifics of encounter, highlighting the emergent qualities of perception and materiality (Rush-Cooper, 2020). As something sensed with (Wylie, 2006), the actions of inhabitants call landscape forth in different ways as the "engine" of its being (Rose, 2002, pp. 456–457). Therefore, whilst the world unfolds as landscape (Wylie, 2006), it is never solidified, stable, nor a matter of harmonious dwelling (Wylie, 2012). As lively, more-than-human event-spaces (Garlick, 2019), landscapes – such as mountains – are "enacted" and brought to hand (Rose, 2002) in particular ways (and under particular conditions) – for example, as sites of conservation, heritage, leisure, aesthetic appreciation or practical living.

Thus, we encounter the landscape less as coherent, bounded spatial entity; more as a "multiplicity of narratives and perceptions" (Lorimer and Wylie, 2010, p. 7). One of multiple states in flux, it names an untidy discontinuity realised in the specifics of entanglement between perception and materiality (Barad, 2010, p. 251). Echoing shifts towards thinking space topologically in geography – as a manifold, rather than in terms of Euclidean geometry – landscape becomes an entity that is "bent, stretched or rotated" into different expressions (Martin and Secor, 2014, pp. 423–424). Thought this way, as "future-oriented, always open and ongoing" (Wylie, 2012, p. 376), discussions of landscape necessitate a reckoning with its "virtual" dimensions. As Mitch Rose argues, "the source of landscape's presence is excess", it's "overabundance", continuously called forth as it is differently "put to task" (2002, pp. 460–462). For Rose, a "labyrinth" of practices conjoins the actualised structures of society and culture (termed "pyramids", after George Bataille) – that (materially and conceptually) explain, organise, represent and act within the world – and the plane of immanence or possibility (the "plateau"), that underlies all. The practices, or labyrinths, that we engage in, and trace, both manifest and sustain the constructions through which we live our lives out of the virtual domain of otherness, difference and potential. Landscapes are therefore (re-)made through labyrinthine acts that conjure and sustain modes of encountering the world. The task of landscape interpretation becomes to examine how "it is both cared for and put to task", following the threads of its actualisation into particular versions of itself (Rose, 2002, p. 463). This "movement from reading to tracing" (p. 463) enables "analysis to roam" (p. 465) amidst endless labyrinths, rather than seek "hidden order":

> In this sense the only thing that the landscape ever *is* is the practices that make it relevant. While it appears as a definable material space, its materiality is constituted by the totality of possible performances immanent within it [...] Thus, the interesting question for landscape is not what (i.e. what is it? what is its nature?) as much as what for (i.e. what is it used for?). (Rose, 2002, pp. 462–3 & 465)

The question of the virtual is thus central to theorising landscape. Conceptualised here in the vein of Brian Massumi (2002), drawing on the work of Giles Deleuze (and Felix Guattari), the virtual names the excessive, multiplicitous and ever-emergent properties of existing relations, arrangements and assemblages. Offering a means of thinking about the vitality of existence, Deleuze's thinking suggests that the way things – subjects, entities, spaces, collectives – are, how they exist or are experienced now, is only one possible "actualisation" of multiple potential possibilities, constituting a plane of immanence that accompanies existence. Indeed, the virtual is "super empirical": "too large to fit into a perception since it envelops a multiplicity of potential variations" (Massumi, 2002, p. 16). It is simultaneously "real but abstract": the unrealised or not currently realised aspect to present existence. As Massumi puts it: "Actually existing, structured things live in and through that which escapes them" (2002, p. 35). Perception of the world's vitality arises from a cognisance of this escape. Actual states of affairs are but one, contingent resolution of the swirling dynamic agencies and relationships currently in play, or yet to emerge. In *Parables for the Virtual* (2002), Massumi elaborates by way of examples from popular culture, neuroscience, literature and everyday life, the affective qualities of human existence. His desire, as the title suggests, is to offer a series of empirical "ways in" to its dynamic excess.

Such qualities are, he argues, excised by "static" modes of thinking that seek only to address a snapshot of social relations at a particular moment in time and proffer explanation with recourse to abstract structures and forces like "the market", "culture" or "power". For a world always in process, such "freeze-frame" critique fails to engage the dynamic, unstable, vibrant differences and processes of the becoming-otherwise characteristic of life's *liveliness*.

For geographers, the virtual proposes a conceptualisation of space as dynamic, lively and topological. That is, spatial configurations become defined by the relationships between the entities and agencies that affect them, and are liable to change and reconfigure. It matters less what a space *is* than *what it does*: what it enables, sustains, forecloses or opens onto. For Massumi, the virtual is in itself "inaccessible to the senses". However, empirical encounters rendering moments of change, of difference, of becoming otherwise, can allow it to "fleetingly appear" and disrupt any sense of a singular perspective on the world (2002, p. 133). The matter of landscape, as we find it, is therefore always an empirical question, provocative and open to interrogation (Anderson and Wylie, 2009, pp. 330–332). As I discuss below, Shepherd's work offers one way to conceptualise the mountain landscape on these terms. The Cairngorm landscape, as it appears through Shepherd's writing, is "super empirical": we only ever actualise, or experience, one part of it. The mountain plateau coheres as any number of possible landscapes, depending on the means, or by which subjects, it is encountered. *TLM* thus provides a store of parables and place-portraits that facilitate a way into the virtual dimensions of landscape.

A Note on Writing Landscape

Much work on landscape in cultural geographies has been concerned with the question of how to write and represent, as much as theorise, it (Merriman et al., 2008). As Sean Pries notes: "As a concept, landscape is an attempt to distil phenomenological experience and embodied knowledge into stories that, at their best, successfully analyse and contextualise a slice of the earth" (2018, p. 2). Small stories can conjure the "spirit of place" whilst also offering ways into larger ontological and epistemic debates (Lorimer, 2019). The challenge of the more-than-representational prompts experiments with new forms of writing and reflections on how the "unrepresentable" dimensions of existence have been encountered within literature (see Kneale, 2011). Kathleen Stewart, in her efforts to trace regional landscapes in terms of their "ordinary affects" characterises writing as "an energetics of what happens and also a carapace of spent and living forms", with the expending "writerly effort" freeing up space for the "non-obvious" by way of "descriptive detour or lyrical evocation" (Stewart, 2013, p. 284).

Thus, amidst recent disciplinary turns, geographers have taken ever more seriously the potential of literary expression (Sharp, 2000). Literary works, especially recent examples of place or nature writing, showcase alternative approaches for thinking, and conveying, the landscape (Wylie, 2012). Here, language is mobilised as a domain of connection, practice, materiality, and affect, as well as representation, performing worldly arrangements into being as much as reflecting them (Daya, 2019). As Hayden Lorimer recently noted, "Asking how place-stories work, why we tell them and what we might yet make them do is to press an ancient currency of cultural exchange into renewed service, where shared environmental challenges are more effectively addressed and affectively articulated" (2019, p. 333).

There is also political dimension to the matter of landscape's articulation, as writer Robert Macfarlane has championed. "Language deficit leads to attention deficit" with the consequence that "fungibility has replaced particularity" (Macfarlane, 2015, pp. 24–25), undermining the relations of intimacy that lead to acts of care. Relatedly, common critiques of scholarship in the affective, neovitalist vein – much of which informs this paper – take aim at its often obfuscatory, inaccessible or dense character. As Robbins and Marks write, "the complexity in writing assemblage geographies can invite sloppiness" (2010, p. 192). A turn to the literary is proposed by many to both enliven, and make tangible, the significance of landscape in scholarly discussion. Work within geography's "telling turn" advocates the power of "the written word" in animating the significance of place (Lorimer and Parr, 2014, p. 543). Contemporary cultural geography writing increasingly seeks to affect and conjure emotion; create a sense of immersion; mobilise description as a mode of conceptualisation, rather than in support of it; present experimental or open-ended accounts; and gather words into an evocation of geo-poetics. The well-crafted story or narrative, figured as "a question, or a generator of questions", manifests critical space between theoretical "rhetoric" and the "reality" of specific geographies (Daniels and Lorimer, 2012, p. 5). Experimentation can include parables, fables and other archetypal narrative forms (as well as genres such as poetry – e.g., Eshun & Madge, 2016). In light of such efforts, the chapter turns to consider Nan Shepherd's writing as a vital resource for theorising landscape and its virtual qualities.

Nan Shepherd's Landscapes

Anna 'Nan' Shepherd (1893–1981) was born and lived most of her days in Cults – then a small village on the outskirts of Aberdeen. Much of her adult life was spent working at a teacher training college in the city, as well as exploring the mountains of her native region. As a writer, she published three novels, a collection of poetry, and several critical and creative essays, reviews, and commentaries of various lengths (see Shepherd and Peacock, 2018) as well as editing *The Aberdeen University Review*.

Early in her writing career, Shepherd emerged as part of the Scottish modernist literary scene, alongside contemporaries Lewis Grassic Gibbon and Neil Gunn. She presented a rich, materialist, unromantic account of Aberdeenshire living in contrast to the cliched depictions of "kailyard" life (Peacock, 2015). Her first novel, *The Quarry Wood* (1928), told the story of Martha Ironside, a young farmer's daughter living at the edge of Aberdeen, who attends university, suffers unrequited love and domestic strife, before ultimately finding fulfilment in a teaching career and the care of an adopted son. Her subsequent two novels, *The Weatherhouse* (1930) and *A Pass in the Grampians* (1933), likewise centred upon strong, active female protagonists. Meanwhile, Shepherd's attention to landscape shifted in altitude: first to the foothills, and the fictional community of Fetter Rothnie; then further upward, to the more remote croft of Boggiewalls. Each text offered a different perspective onto her beloved Aberdeenshire's landscapes, and the communities, relationships and tensions that animated them. Following these novels, Shepherd published a book of poetry, *In the Cairngorms*, in 1934. Though she would write *TLM* – her mountain 'prose poem' (Macfarlane, 2011, p. xiv) and love-letter to the highlands of Deeside and Speyside that she had explored and walked in so often – in the latter years of the second world war (though not published until 1977), in later life she seemed unwilling, or unable, to write much else beyond shorter essays and reviews.

For Roderick Watson, "It is difficult not to make connections between Shepherd's personal history and some aspects of the lives of her characters".

Her work depicts strong female protagonists who "have learned to strike a balance between challenging and accepting the roles allocated to them by society" (Watson, 1997, p. 416). Shepherd's particular "bio-geography" (after Lorimer, 2015) reveals a life spent involved with place, and a relationship with the environment shaped through engagements with the thinking of Buddhism, Taoism and Zen philosophy as much as the Scottish literary scene, as revealed by the traces that comprise her archive (Macfarlane, 2015; Peacock, 2015; Walton, 2020). Across her work is an attention to the empirical specificity and material metaphysics of landscape, manifest as meditations on the seasons, flora and fauna, and the transmutation of perception. Her places of Aberdeenshire are not static backgrounds, but dynamic worlds amidst which characters live, love, labour and explore their corporeal capacities. She was, as Gillian Carter observes, first and foremost concerned with mapping a lived (and lively) *geography*:

> In all Shepherd's work, the regional landscape is an important feature, so important, in fact, that the title of each of her books is named for a place, and not a person or event. This would suggest the narrative arrangement of her work is spatial rather than temporal, and that the individual is not, in fact, central, but exists as part of a place and part of a community. (2001, p. 29)

Indeed, Shepherd's writing offers "metaphysical insight into [...] the puzzle of being", exceeding social commentary to muse upon the material: "air, light, water, darkness and stone" (Watson, 1997, p. 426). A consistent feature of much of her prose and poetry – the latter, she considered "the purest of art forms" (Macfarlane, 2011, p. xi) – is the transformative effects of encountering the excessive qualities of matter. Her world is "a universe of livingness" (Walton, 2020, p. 21). In *The Quarry Wood* (Shepherd, 2018), the protagonist Martha, after a fractious childhood encounter with foster-sister Dussie, is taken to observe the "Merry Dancers" of the northern lights by her father, reorienting her perspective and sense of scale with regard to self and world. Both *The Weatherhouse* (Shepherd, 2017), and Shepherd's short story "Descent from the Cross" (in Shepherd and Peacock, 2018), present individuals who, in the wake of wartime experience of war, achieve the realization that their personal trauma has opened them onto being affected in altogether different ways by once familiar landscapes. As Watson remarks, *The Weatherhouse* consistently "evokes the unknowability of things" (1997, p. 427), regarding both our relations to other people and those to the world around us. Such examples reveal Shepherd's characters inhabiting, and interrogating, surroundings composed of solid earth and rock; turbulent skies and winds; streams and rivers. Her texts are thus alive, and excessive, with elemental force (Anderson and Wylie, 2009).

One of Shepherd's most well-known modern-day advocates, Robert Macfarlane (2015), sees her writing as a vital resource for "rewilding" our landscape lexicon. Shepherd, Macfarlane argues, exists alongside figures such as J.A. Baker, Jaquetta Hawkes and Tim Robinson in inspiring different ways to capture and commune with landscape. Her writing deploys "precision of utterance as both a form of lyricism and a species of attention" (Macfarlane, 2015, p. 11), inculcating an expanded way of seeing the Cairngorms. Macfarlane views *TLM* as an exemplar, foregrounding the promise of a careful place attention. Shepherd was, he argues, "a localist of the best kind", a crucial touchstone for the contemporary geographical "portraiture" characteristic of much new nature writing (Lorimer, 2019). Across her output, the landscapes of her native Aberdeenshire are called forth to propose a relational, emergent ontology of the body-in-landscape by way of an "intense empiricism" figured as "the first step to immanence" (Macfarlane, 2015, p. 66).

Therefore, from her novels to the non-fiction, yet poetic, geographical writing of *TLM*, Shepherd demonstrates an enduring consideration of the excessive qualities of landscape. There is a consistent effort to write the ways in which landscapes can *become different, be otherwise,* change and transform, and coalesce in a variety of ways and as part of a variety of experiences. The remainder of the chapter emphasises the ways in which Shepherd's work offers geographers (and others) an ontological and epistemological route to reckon with the virtual dimension of landscape amidst wider (re)turns to storying the character of place. As elaborated below, these concerns are arguably most succinctly conveyed via her concept of *the total mountain.*

The Total Mountain

Written in the early 1940s, but not published until 1977, when Shepherd rediscovered the manuscript in a drawer of her home, *TLM* can be read as the realisation of a geographical project implicit throughout her earlier writing. Finding herself, at last, wandering the upland slopes, high tops and deep recesses of the Cairngorm plateau, Shepherd's attention to landscapes and their material immanence – expressed in the lowland rural surroundings of Aberdeen, the upland environs of Fetter Rothnie, the highland setting of Boggiewalls croft and lyrically through her poetry – is given space for full expression in a text that combines intense empirical attentiveness, personal reflection and a kind of transcendental existentialism.

The book comprises her effort to render the Cairngorm plateau from multiple different angles. Each of its twelve chapters – with titles such as "Water", "Air and Light", "Life: The Plants", "The Senses", "Sleep" – exist as almost self-contained meditations on the corporeal and elemental qualities of place. This is a text that is "exhilaratingly materialist, and almost animist […] both a geo-poetic quest into place, and philosophical enquiry into the nature of knowledge". Its "parochial" precision treats the Cairngorm plateau as an "aperture" opening onto broader questions, rather than a focal object that gathers her concerns into narrow coherence (Macfarlane, 2015, p. 62). At the same time, as Macfarlane emphasises, the chapters do not present their subject(s) as "distinct facets" of the Cairngorm landscape, separate to each other. *TLM* is "a transverse descriptive weave – the prose equivalent of a dwarf juniper forest". Its form performs Shepherd's "central proposition": "that the world will not fall into divisible realms […] but is instead an unmappable mesh of interrelations" (2011, pp. xxiv–xxv). As Walton writes, *TLM's* form and content emphasise that "the lives and elements described in the chapters cannot be easily disentangled" (2020, p. 78).

It is apt that Shepherd talks of the Cairngorms in terms of a "plateau", rather than as a collection of individual glens and summits, or even definable ridges or ranges. Although written several decades before, this term evokes the neovitalism of Giles Deleuze and Felix Guattari, and their text *A Thousand Plateaus*. Composed not of chapters but "plateaus", each exists – after Gregory Bateson – as "a continuous, self-vibrating region of intensities whose development avoids any orientation toward a culmination point or external end" (2013, p. 23). For Deleuze and Guattari, writing through the plateau offers a way "to attain the multiple" and hold onto the virtual qualities of their subject matter: "A plateau is always in the middle, not at the beginning or end. A rhizome is made of plateaus […] Each plateau can be read starting anywhere and can be related to any other plateau (2013, pp. 22–23)."

Thus, the chapters of *TLM*, like those of *A Thousand Plateaus*, fit together "like a set of split rings" that can be combined in multiple ways, each retaining "its own climate, its own tone or timbre" appropriate to the particular "modes of individuation" (Deleuze, 1995, pp. 25–26) that characterise different becomings of the Cairngorms-as-landscape. They also serve to mobilise, in literary form, Shepherd's central ontology of landscape. The text produces a "multiplex effect" as she refuses any single vantage, in favour of a kaleidoscopic multiplying version of the mountain (Macfarlane, 2015, p. 69). Hers is an "ecological vision" of the Cairngorms, rendered from multiple, situated perspectives – an approach likewise taken in her previous poetry collection named for the massif (Walton, 2020). Those aspects of the region which she has experienced are but a minute part of an ever-excessive whole. In recalling days spent hiking through the Lairig Ghru, the pass connecting Braemar and Aviemore; efforts to locate the source of rivers amidst rocks and moss; the taste of blaeberries and the cool water of mountain burns; the sounds of animal life such as dotterel, rutting stags and ptarmigan; the weathered visage and hardy corporeality of the mountain "characters" she has come to know on Deeside or Speyside; or even – in later life – the ways in which humans continue to find new ways into the plateau via the development of tourism, skiing and infrastructure; Shepherd animates a landscape that continuously escapes her.

Shepherd consciously seeks to decentre any notion of a single, authoritative, scientific way of seeing space as a domain of measurement and control, instead emphasising the multiplicity of experience and aesthetic encounters as of more importance than practices of listing or ordering the environment (Carter, 2001). The mountains that she knows so well are unknowable in their entirety in part because each excursion allows her to better realise the capacities of herself as "paramount [...] essential body" (Shepherd, 2011, p. 106); but also, because the plateau is host to "life in so many guises" (p. 74), and matter in so many forms. She concludes: "Knowing another is endless [...] the thing to know grows with the knowing" (p. 108). In capturing this fundamental excessiveness of the mountain, Shepherd arrives in the conclusion of her text at the concept of "the total mountain":

> So there I lie on the plateau, under me the central core of fire from which was thrust this grumbling grinding mass of plutonic rock, over me blue air, and between the fire of the rock and the fire of the sun, scree, soil and water, moss, grass, flower and tree, insect

bird and beast, wind rain and snow – *the total mountain*. Slowly I have found my way in. If I had other senses, there are other things I should know. [...] There must be many exciting properties of matter that we cannot know because we have no way to know them. (p.105, emphasis added)

As Macfarlane cautions, the "total" of "the total mountain" is "distinct from the 'total' of 'totalising' or 'totalitarian'" but "total insofar as it exceeds the possibility of our capacity to ever know it entirely" (2011, p. xxvi). Thus, the text of *TLM* elaborates a way of appreciating landscape in its virtuality. It is a philosophical work that understands landscape as a matter of "circumstances rather than essences" (Deleuze, 1995, p. 32), diagrammed through its intersecting chapters – each capturing a different "way in" through the capacities of the body, learning to be affected anew. The sensing body-in-landscape is manifest here as "a space of productive indeterminacy, in which sensing and sensed, point of view and landscape, pass into and through each other, substitute and exchange, coil and recoil … [in] a productive process of questioning and provocation" (Anderson and Wylie, 2009, p. 325). In this sense, the total mountain – or total landscape – is an aporetic entity, like Tim Robinson's "good step" (Wylie, 2012). One can never grasp this whole, but its excessiveness proves inspirational, invitational; incitement and incentive to continue to explore, the engine of mountain feyness.

The Total Mountain as Epistemology for Landscape

Shepherd's concept of *the total mountain* crystallises the idea that the landscape is a multifaceted event space, actualised through the intersection of bodies, affects and materialities; never exhausted, always with more to give. One might refer to the *total landscape* as the entirety of one's surroundings – its immanent potential – available, and unavailable; both present and absent, ready to be called forth like the mysterious blue peak glimpsed in the heat haze of a day on the high tops (p. 2). In turn, Shepherd's ontology proposes a way of *knowing* landscape as an open-ended and uncertain project. It is therefore worth considering the ways in which Shepherd's "total mountain" is offered not merely to understand the mountain landscape, but as a lure to engage with and know the mountain differently.

For Massumi, parables of the virtual do epistemological, and ultimately political, work in rendering discernible the excess of actualised existence. As he writes:

> Concepts of the virtual [...] are important only to the extent to which they contribute to a pragmatic understanding of emergence, to the extent to which they enable triggerings of change (induce the new). It is the edge of the virtual, where it leaks into actual, that counts. For that seeping edge is where potential, actually, is found. (Massumi, 2002, p. 43)

The total mountain is a provocation to seek alternative encounters beyond the familiar or privileged. Shepherd is, by her own admission, "compelled by the massif's excesses, its unmappable surplus" (Macfarlane, 2015, p. 71). *TLM* is "a text which moves beyond habitual means of charting the world and unsettles habitual ways of perceiving a landscape" (Carter, 2001, p. 28). Shepherd's text expresses a desire, and lifetime project, to know the mountain by way of a slow, accumulated, exploratory project: "the knowledge that is a process of living" (Shepherd, 2011, p. 1). At the same time, she is explicit about the futile, necessarily partial nature of this project: "one never quite knows the mountain, nor one's self in relation to it" (Ibid.). Its "elemental" character is neither "governable" nor containable – always excessive. Indeed, the experience of affective joy and exhilaration that Shepherd terms "feyness" (pp. 6–7) – a state of desire to seek out and engage with the mountain landscape, to indulge in its "invitation" – appears conditional on this undetermined character.

Shepherd champions a slower, more open-ended passage across the plateau, one that descends into its recesses – such as her beloved Loch Avon – and pauses to savour its sensory milieu, rather than marching ahead with the object of "bagging" peaks. Likewise, those tourists, landowners and sporting tenants who drive land rovers or ride "funiculars" to reach "the startling view, the horrid pinnacle" (p. 15) miss too much. Not adverse to the company of good hill companions, she savours the opportunity to meditate on the landscape in (relative) silence, bemoaning the "talking tribe" of walkers, whose inane conversation distracts from the environment. She gives similar short shrift to the scientists and surveyors who record species or sound lochs. Such work, for her, "serves no purpose" (p. 67) when it comes to really knowing the land in terms of the encounters it affords.

Whilst some writers might harbour an ambition for "the total description of landscape" (Wylie, 2012, p. 366), Shepherd does not. For her, "haste can do nothing for these hills" (p. 12). The compulsion to list birds or "bag" Munros, following a rigidly planned itinerary or route, is anathema to moments of discovery or joy emergent from walking "the unpath" (p. 51). Hers is a concern with the "minor experiences" (Walton, 2020, p. 196) that accumulate into an understanding of regionality (see Stewart, 2013). She moves slowly, traversing familiar ground along new lines, spending time in favoured places, even sleeping on the hull. Shepherd conveys "a necessity to feel immersed, co-joined and an integral part of a mountain through wandering" (Hall, 2018, p. 154), seeking out and examining the fine-grained specifics of slopes, screes and streams. She celebrates acts of playful, childlike engagement, as well as moments of exposure and openness. As Hall argues, "Her vulnerability is a space of play ... [revealing] a potentially different kind of feminine mountaineering practice" (2018, p. 155). This is a politics of exploration and attunement that resists efforts to colonise or control the land around. Place-love is performed via acts of careful attention and an openness to surprise.

Such an epistemology of landscape is realised in startlingly simple ways. Practices such as half closing her eyes; looking at the world through her legs, upside down; or tilting her head this way and that see her challenge "habitual vision" in ways that involve "adopting a childlike, playful view of the world" (Carter, 2001, pp. 30–31). As she describes:

> The static things may be caught in the very act of becoming. By so simple a matter, too, as altering the position of one's head, a different kind of world may be made to appear. [...] As I watch, it arches its back, and each layer of landscape bristles – though bristles is a word of too much commotion for it. Details are no longer part of a grouping in a picture of which I am the focal point, the focal point is everywhere. Nothing has reference to me, the looker. This is how the earth must see itself. (Shepherd, 2011, pp. 10–11)

TLM documents a variety of ways to "look creatively" (p. 102), engaging the full sensory array. As della Dora has argued, contrasting Shepherd's writing on mountain landscapes with the long history of "high places" bound up with a revelatory gaze or "god trick" (see also Cosgrove and della Dora, 2009), such an attention to the poetics of landscape asks us to look "*into* and *through*" the mountain as a *lens* onto alternative perspectives. Rather than a site actualising of "the modern dream of omniscience", the mountain sojourn as a "creative act" plays host to "an infinite act of learning, an enriching but always unfolding process" (della Dora, 2016a, pp. 137–138).

Lying face down in the heather to look through the undergrowth. Peering over precipices into the depths of a corrie, falling asleep, and then waking to the full force of the mountain's depth. Half closing the eyes to blur her vision. Taking the time to trace the diverse effects that the "weatherworld" (Ingold, 2015) can have on one's surroundings: a smur of drizzle, or patch of snow, refracting sunshine; the heat haze conjuring a mysterious "blue peak" where no hill is known to exist. The "continuous creative act" of striving to see the mountain anew works to "widen the domain of being" (Shepherd, 2011, p. 102). In opening oneself onto the possibilities of landscape, one comes to better understand its potential store of encounters, and what the body might be made to do. As Shepherd writes:

> Such illusions, depending on how the eye is placed and used, drive home the truth that our habitual vision of things is not necessarily right: it is only one of an infinite number, and to glimpse an unfamiliar one, even for a moment, unmakes us, but steadies us again. It's queer but invigorating. It will take a long time to get to the end of a world that behaves like this if I do no more than turn around on my side or my back. [...] How can I number the worlds to which the eye gives me entry? (p. 101)

More than the eyes are deployed to find new ways in. Shepherd uses all her bodily capacities to "thirl" herself to the mountain: "Each of the senses is a way in to what the mountain has to give" (p. 97). In her discussion of silence (or its absence) Shepherd foregrounds its rarity and celebrates the ear as a means to attune to the multiple nonhuman presences, forces and rhythms animating the landscape of the plateau (see Archer, 2018). Anticipating the arguments of more-than-representational scholarship, Shepherd encourages the use of taste, smell and touch, not least because such sensations "mean nothing at all in words" (p. 98) and are aspects of the landscape that can *only* be understood through direct experience. She frames touch as "the most intimate" way into the mountain; reflecting on the surface of the skin and body braced against the wind, the "infinity of pleasure" (p. 102) available to the hands, the "small enchantment" (p. 104) of a flower stem caught between the toes, and her time spent learning how to place each foot to walk barefoot across the heather.

Particularly intense experiences – such as plunging oneself into a cold mountain pool – are so intense that they "disintegrate the very self" in a moment of extreme sensation. After a moment, feeling lost, "life pours back" (p. 104) and Shepherd finds herself reterritorialized by the material impress of the landscape: "Flesh is not annihilated but fulfilled" (p. 106). In this way, just as learning new skills of seeing landscape – via painting or drawing – can attune one to the materiality of the air or the light, so Shepherd's experimenting with her own body is intended to open onto new experiences and appreciations of the plateau environment.

Collectively, then, *TLM* conveys both an account of the mountain landscape's vitality and Shepherd's lived efforts to learn – or trigger – alternative ways of sensing; "and in so doing to be drawn out, drawn in" to landscape features, "to be aware of them anew" (Wylie and Webster, 2019, p. 38). For Jenny Hall, Shepherd thus reconfigures the landscape as "a polysensorial space in which to play" (2018, p. 156); wherein such play "enables a connectedness to journey into the unknown, formed of rock, air, human and the non-human" (2018, p. 160). In this spirit, cultural geographers and others might draw upon *the total mountain* as both ontology for landscape – simultaneously actual encounter and virtual potential – and an epistemological invitation to consider an alternative, slower knowing of landscape in creative, careful and attentive ways.

Conclusion: Approaching the Total Landscape

For Deleuze, philosophy as a practical exercise is above all else concerned with acts of creative intervention "in the realm of concepts" (1995, p. 26). A concept, for Deleuze, is "full of critical, political force" and they operate best as "singularities […] acting on the flows of everyday thought" (1995, p. 32) to make new connections, suggest new lines of approach, or challenge ossified patterns of discourse. Or, to quote Massumi, "A concept is a brick. It can be used to build a courthouse of reason. Or it can be thrown through the window" (1987, p. xi).

Landscape, as a concept, acts to gather works together – those with an interest in the meeting of people and places, and the relationship between perception and environment – as much as it diffracts and distributes a whole host of theoretical questions. It is at once a domain of representation and the unrepresentable; lively, corporeal possibilities and unsettled absence or dissonance; detached vantage and deep immersion. It is a series of tensions, drawing in, and casting outwards (Wylie, 2007; Rose, 2010). This chapter has aimed to show how Nan Shepherd's celebrated text, *The Living Mountain*, offers and elaborates a concept of that which escapes us in attending to the landscape of the mountains, and beyond.

Shepherd, as an unashamed "localist", demonstrates a way of attending to the specifics of landscape across her writing that takes the virtual qualities of the environmental encounter as a lure to continue to return, and explore, place anew. Her experiences reveal efforts to seek out alternative "angles of approach" amidst familiar surroundings, revealing the mountain as at once "a loved place, an ecological whole, a vast geologic entity and living landscape" (Walton, 2020, p. 26). Moreover, Shepherd's text, as Macfarlane has strongly argued, showcases the promise of "word magic": "the power that certain terms possess to enchant our relations with nature and place" (Macfarlane, 2015, p. 4). Learning a new vocabulary "opens prospects" and unsettles familiar landscapes. Equally, "There are experiences of landscape that will always resist articulation, and of which words offer only a remote echo" (2015, pp. 6–10). For Macfarlane, linguistic precision – not as objective, scientific accounting but the expression of patient attention – is, following poet Marianne Moore, "best enabled by metaphor" (2015, p. 33). If we lack a precise, deep appreciation of landscape it is because we have eroded our metaphorical toolkit.

In sum, this chapter has sought to show how Shepherd's notion of "the total mountain" – perhaps elaborated into a concept for "the total landscape" – offers both an ontological and epistemological framework for approaching landscape, slowly and with a desire to stray onto the "unpath". *TLM,* understood as a work of theorising landscape, pre-empts more recent calls to embrace the ethical implications of becoming uncertain, disorientated, and acknowledging the unfathomable gulf between what is and what could be (Bissel and Gorman-Murray, 2019). The total landscape offers an invitation to follow, without disclosing as to where it might lead. It is a concept that embodies the fey impulse that sees so many "possessed" by mountain places (della Dora, 2016a, p. 226), as much as it denies any possibility of our possessing *them*. As Shepherd remarks, knowledge continues to grow, and there is much that will, always, remain beyond our sensory capacity. There are as many landscapes as there are combinations of bodies, matter and affective forces. The total mountain as ontology for landscape challenges us to seek difference amidst environments that we may be tempted to see as repetitively familiar.

Bibliography

Anderson, B. and Wylie, J. (2009) "On geography and materiality", *Environment and Planning A*, 41(2), pp. 318–335.

Archer, A. (2018) "The men on the mountainside: An ethnography of solitude, silence and sheep bells", *Journal of Rural Studies*, 64, pp. 103–111.

Berger, J. (2006) *Here Is Where We Meet*. London: Bloomsbury.

Bissell, D. and Gorman-Murray, A. (2019) "Disoriented geographies: Undoing relations, encountering limits", *Transactions of the Institute of British Geographers*, 44(4), pp. 707–720.

Carter, G. (2001) "'Domestic Geography' and the Politics of Scottish Landscape in Nan Shepherd's *The Living Mountain*", *Gender, Place and Culture*, 8(1), pp. 25–36.

Cosgrove, D. and della Dora, V. (2009) *High Places: Cultural Geographies of Mountains, Ice and Science*. London: I.B. Taurus.

Daniels, S. and Lorimer, H. (2012) "Until the end of days: Narrating landscape and environment", *cultural geographies*, 19(1), pp. 3–9.

Daya, S. (2019) "Words and worlds: textual representation and new materialism", *cultural geographies*, 26(3), pp. 361–377.

Deleuze, G. (1995) *Negotiations, 1972–1990*. New York, NY: Colombia University Press.

Deleuze, G. and Guattari, F. (2013) *Capitalism and Schizophrenia Vol. 2: A Thousand Plateaus*. London: Bloomsbury.

della Dora, V. (2016a) *Mountain: Nature and Culture*. London: Reaktion.

della Dora, V. (2016b) *Landscape, Nature and the Sacred in Byzantium*. Cambridge: Cambridge University Press.

Eshun, G. and Madge, C. (2016) "Poetic world-writing in a pluriversal world: a provocation to the creative (re)turn in geography", *Social & Cultural Geography*, 17(6), pp. 778–785.

Garlick, B. (2019) "Deceptive Landscapes: Ornithological Hide Work and the Perception of Ospreys on Speyside, 1957–1987", *GeoHumanities*, 5(1), pp. 215–236.

Hall, J. (2018) "Women mountaineers and affect: Fear, play and the unknown", in Saul, H. and Waterton, E. (eds) *Affective Geographies of Transformation, Exploration and Adventure*. Abingdon: Routledge, pp. 147–163.

Hones, S. (2011) "Literary geography: the novel as a spatial event", in Daniels, S., DeLyser, D., Entrikin, J.N. and Richardson, D. (eds) *Envisioning Landscapes: Making Worlds*. Abingdon: Routledge, pp. 279–287.

Hunt, R. (2019) "Historical geography, climbing and mountaineering: route setting for an inclusive future", *Geography Compass*, 13(4), p. e12423, pp. 1–9.

Kneale, J. (2006) "From beyond: H. P. Lovecraft and the place of horror", *cultural geographies*, 13(1), pp. 106–126.

Lorimer, H. (2015) "Standards of Beauty: Considering the Lives of W. A. Poucher", *GeoHumanities*, 1(1), pp. 51–79.

Lorimer, H. (2019) "Dear departed: Writing the lifeworlds of place", *Transactions of the Institute of British Geographers*, 44, pp. 331–345.

Lorimer, H. and Lund, K. (2003) "Performing facts: finding a way over Scotland's mountains", *The Sociological Review*, 51(2), pp. 130–144.

Lorimer, H. and Parr, H. (2014) "Excursions – telling stories and journeys", *cultural geographies*, 21(4), pp. 543–547.

Lorimer, H. and Wylie, J. (2010) "LOOP (a geography)", *Performance Research*, 15(4), pp. 6–13.

Macfarlane, R. (2011) "Introduction", in Shepherd, N., *The Living Mountain*. Edinburgh: Cannongate, pp. ix–xl.

Macfarlane, R. (2015) *Landmarks*. London: Hamish Hamilton.

MacPherson, H. (2008) "'I don't know why they call it the Lake District they might as well call it the rock district!' The workings of humour and laughter in research with members of visually impaired walking groups", *Environment and Planning D: Society and Space*, 26(6), pp. 1080–1095.

Martin, L. and Secor, A. (2014) "Towards a post-mathematical topology", *Progress in Human Geography,* 38(3), pp. 420–438.

Massumi, B. (2013 [1987]) "Translators Foreword: Pleasures of Philosophy", in Deleuze, G. and Guattari, F., *Capitalism and Schizophrenia Vol. 2: A Thousand Plateaus.* London: Bloomsbury, pp. ix–xv.

Massumi, B. (2002) *Parables for the Virtual: Movement, Affect, Sensation.* Durham, NC: Duke University Press.

Matless, D. (2003) "Introduction: Landscape", in Anderson, K., Domosh, M., Pile, S. and Thrift, N. (eds) *Handbook of Cultural Geography*. London: SAGE, pp. 227–232.

Matless, D. (2014) *In the Nature of Landscape: Cultural Geography on the Norfolk Broads.* Oxford: Wiley-Blackwell.

Merriman, P., Revill, G., Cresswell, T., Lorimer, H., Matless, D., Rose, G. and Wylie, J. (2008) "Landscape, mobility, practice", *Social & Cultural Geography*, 9(2), pp. 191–212.

Nancy, J.-L. (2005) "Uncanny Landscape", in Nancy, J.-L., *Ground of the Image*, trans. Jeff Fort. New York, NY: Fordham University Press, pp. 51–62.

Nettleton, S. (2015) "Fell-runners and walking walls: towards a sociology of living landscapes and aesthetic atmospheres as an alternative to a Lakeland picturesque", *British Journal of Sociology*, 66(4), pp. 759–778.

Peacock, C. (2015) *Into the Mountain: A Life of Nan Shepherd.* Plymouth: Galileo.

Pries, S. (2018) "A geographer looks at the landscape, once more: Toward a posthumanist political ecology approach", *Geography Compass*, 2018e12401, pp. 1–12.

Reinert, H. (2015) "The Landscape Concept as Rupture: Extinction and Perspective in a Norwegian Fjord", in Soovāli-Sepping, H., Reinert, H. and Miles-Watson, J. (eds) *Ruptured Landscapes: Landscape, Identity and Social Change*. Dordrecht: Springer, pp. 41–54.

Robbins, P. and Marks, B. (2010) "Assemblage Geographies", in Smith, S., Pain, R., Marston, S. and Jones III, J.P. (eds) *The SAGE Handbook of Social Geographies*. London: SAGE, pp. 176–194.

Rose, M. (2002) "Landscape and labyrinths", *Geoforum*, 33(4), pp. 455–467.

Rose, M. (2010) "Back to back: a response to 'Landscape, absence and the geographies of love'", *Transactions of the Institute of British Geographers*, 35(1), pp. 141–144.

Rose, M. and Wylie, J. (2006) "Animating landscape", *Environment and Planning D: Society and Space,* 24, pp. 475–479.

Rush-Cooper, N. (2020) "Nuclear landscape: tourism, embodiment and exposure in the Chernobyl Zone", *cultural geographies*, 27(2), pp. 217–235.

Sharp, J. (2000) "Towards a critical analysis of fictive geographies", *Area,* 32(3), pp. 327–334.

Shepherd, N. (2011 [1977]) *The Living Mountain.* Edinburgh: Canongate.

Shepherd, N. (2017 [1930]) *The Weatherhouse.* Edinburgh: Canongate.

Shepherd, N. (2018 [1928]) *The Quarry Wood.* Edinburgh: Canongate.

Shepherd, N. and Peacock, C. (2018) *Wild Geese: A Collection of Nan Shepherd's Writing.* Cambridge: Galileo.

Smith, T.A., Laurier, E., Reeves, S. and Dunkley, R.A. (2020) "'Off the beaten map': navigating with digital maps on moorland", *Transactions of the Institute of British Geographers*, 45(1), pp. 223–240.

Stanley, P. (2020) "Unlikely hikers? Activism, *Instagram*, and the queer mobilities of fat hikers, women hiking alone, and hikers of colour", *Mobilities,* 15(2), pp. 241–256.

Stewart, K. (2013) "Regionality", *The Geographical Review,* 103(2), pp. 275–284.

Tsing, A. (2005) *Friction: An Ethnography of Global Connection.* Oxford, CT: Princeton University Press.

Tsing, A. (2015) *The Mushroom at the End of the World.* Oxford, CT: Princeton University Press.

Watson, R. (1997) "'To know Being': Substance and Spirit in the Work of Nan Shepherd", in Gifford, D. and McMillan, D. (eds) *A History of Scottish Woman's Writing.* Edinburgh: Edinburgh University Press, pp. 416–427.

Wall-Reinus, S., Prince, S. and Dahlberg, A. (2019) "Everyday life in a magnificent landscape: Making sense of the nature/culture dichotomy in the mountains of Jämtland, Sweden", *Environment and Planning E: Nature and Space,* 2(1), pp. 3–22.

Walton, S. (2020) *The Living World: Nan Shepherd and Environmental Thought.* London: Bloomsbury.

Wylie, J. (2006) "Depths and folds: on landscape and the gazing subject", *Environment and Planning D: Society and Space,* 24(4), pp. 519–535.

Wylie, J. (2007) *Landscape.* Abingdon: Routledge.

Wylie, J. (2012) "Dwelling and displacement: Tim Robinson and the questions of landscape", *cultural geographies*, 19(3), pp. 365–383.

Wylie, J. and Webster, C. (2019) "Eye-opener: Drawing landscape near and far", *Transactions of the Institute of British Geographers,* 44(1), pp. 32–47.

Vannini, P. and Vannini, A. (2016) *Wilderness.* Abingdon: Routledge.

Chapter 12

The Representation of Play in Joe Simpson's *Touching the Void* and Paratexts

Anna Holman

Introduction

At the age of fourteen, Joe Simpson picked up a copy of Heinrich Harrer's *The White Spider*, a classic book of mountaineering recounting his and others' exploits on the north face of the Eiger. Of that experience, Simpson (2005, p. i) recalls, "When I closed the book my head was filled with grim black-and-white images of men fighting for survival in a ferociously steep and unrelentingly dangerous landscape. I could not imagine any more frightening way to die." Yet, something compelled Simpson to read the book again. Stories like Harrer's successful ascent and Toni Kurz's tragic demise on the Eiger left Simpson with an insatiable curiosity about climbing mountains. "There must be something very special about mountaineering for these people to think that such risks are worth it. I became a mountaineer inspired by the most gripping and frightening mountaineering book I have ever read" (Simpson, 2005, p. i). A decade later, at twenty-five, Simpson wrote his own memoir of a frightening, near-death experience in the mountains. In 1985 Joe Simpson and his partner Simon Yates summitted a remote mountain in the Peruvian Andes called Siula Grande. On the descent, Simpson fell, breaking his leg. Yates attempted to lower his partner to safety, descending thousands of feet in a snowstorm, only to inadvertently lower Simpson over the edge of a cliff just a few hundred feet from the bottom of the mountain. With Simpson incapable of climbing up and Yates unable to lower him further, with deteriorating conditions and frostbit fingers, Yates cut the rope connecting him to his partner. Simpson fell over two hundred feet into a crevasse. Left for dead, Simpson climbed out of the crevasse and crawled for three days back to base camp. *Touching the Void*, Simpson's story, has since been captured in memoir, a documentary, and a play. Although Harrer's memoir inspired Simpson to take up climbing, he finds himself "astounded by the number of young people who tell me that my account of this survival epic in Peru, *Touching the Void*, inspired them to take up climbing" (Simpson, 2005, p. i).

What compels new climbers to take up mountaineering after encountering stories of risk and suffering like *Touching the Void*? I argue that mountaineering stories are set within a cultural narrative of mountains as playgrounds and climbing as a game, a narrative that entices new players into the game. Risk and suffering contribute to the game's appeal, or as Simpson contends at the beginning of the *Touching the Void* documentary (2004), "We climb 'cause it's fun". Climbers engage in this "fun" with an embodied performance that I explore through the concept of play. Mountaineering play captures the childlike freedom of movement on the playground but also "deep" and "dark" play, play that involves a significant amount of risk. Unique to alpinism, the best in the sport often face the most serious consequences, and climbers at the top of their game die young and at startling rates. From the mid-1800s, climbers' stories have made this rate of attrition an accepted part of mountaineering, couching the risk of death in the language of winning or losing a game as on a childhood playground. In addressing how the risk of death in mountaineering stories inspires rather than deters future climbers, I look at the representation of play in Joe Simpson's *Touching the Void* as told through three different mediums: Simpson's memoir (2004) first published in 1988, director Kevin Macdonald's documentary (2004), and David Greig's play (2018) with director Tom Morris's 2021 theatrical staging.

Mountains as Playgrounds

Leslie Stephen, the first president of London's Alpine Club, argues (1894, p. 39) that the 1760s ushered in a new era that saw the Alps "inaugurated [...] as a public playground". This definition of mountains as playgrounds, and thus mountaineering as play, dominated the European climbing narrative. By the late nineteenth century, mountains had become havens from industrialised society, places where men (and almost exclusively men) were freely able to express themselves (Magdalinski, 2004). During this so-called "golden age of climbing", guide companies and alpine clubs commodified risk and developed rules, contributing meaning to the conquest of mountains (Donnelly, 2004). Mountain climbing became a game. In his memoir, Joe Simpson and his partner Simon Yates inherit this mountaineering-as-play legacy. Writing about an acclimatisation climb in Peru prior to his Siula Grande summit, Simpson (2004, p. 21) says, "For the first time in my life I knew what it meant to be isolated from people and society. It was wonderfully calming and tranquil to be here. I became aware of a feeling of complete freedom." After several failed attempts to reach smaller summits during their acclimatisation process, Simpson (2004, p. 26) recalls telling Yates, "I wouldn't mind winning the next one. So far it's mountains three, climbers nil." Within the first chapter of the memoir, Simpson touches upon the basic premise of mountains as playgrounds: places of freedom from society, and climbing as a game to be played and won against the mountains.

Mountains as playgrounds provokes images of movement, the physicality of play. In the opening sequence of Macdonald's documentary, Brendan Mackey, Simpson's reenactor, climbs towards a clear blue sky, the sound of his heavy breathing mingling with the satisfying crunch of ice axes and crampons on snow and the snap of the rope passing through a carabiner. Macdonald couples shots of the reenactors competently climbing a steep snow slope with voiceovers from Simpson and Yates describing the joy of mountaineering:

Joe: Starting doing it was brilliant. This is what we live for. I love the actual movement of climbing. When you're climbing well it just feels brilliant. It's like a combination between ballet and gymnastics. It's that mixture of power and grace.

Simon: For me, mountains are the most beautiful places in the world. When I go into these places I feel an amazing sense of space, an amazing sense of freedom, when I get away from all of the clutter that we have in the world.

The documentary grounds Simpson and Yates's continued assertion of climbing as a freeing and empowering endeavour in visual imagery with playful camera movements. The mountains *feel* like playgrounds as the camera swings down over the lip of a snow cliff to focus on the two tiny figures of the climbers below, then suddenly focuses in on ice axes and crampons biting into snow before quickly looking up at the climbers from below, warm orange rays of sun peaking over the top of the cliff. These swooping shots, combined with the soundtrack of wildly pounding drums, creates a frenetic, exhilarating atmosphere. Macdonald makes mountaineering look like fun.

David Greig's play introduces his audience to the thrill of climbing when the character of Simon teaches Joe's sister Sarah how to climb. Director Tom Morris's 2021 staging of Greig's *Touching the Void* has actor Fiona Hampton (Sarah) scaling tables and chairs and clambering up the theatre's proscenium arch. Under Morris's direction, the set and the theatre building itself become a playground-like representation of mountains. Sarah experiences the pleasure of climbing through a movement sequence with the characters of Joe and Simon where the three stand on tables to symbolise climbing a pitch on the "Grandes Jorasses A thousand foot up – a thousand to go" (Greig, 2018, p. 18). Repeating the lines "Hit – hold – hit – hold, Kick – push – kick – breathe" the three mime placing ice axes above their heads and kicking into the side of the mountain with cramponed feet. Together, the characters' movements on the tables-turned-mountains capture the physicalised act of climbing. Later in Act I, Joe and Simon clamber over and around a pipe and foam Siula Grande that reviewer Elisabeth Vincentelli (2021) likened to "monkey bars". Finally, to reinforce the mountain-as-playground image, Joe tells Sarah:

> Climbing's what humans *do*. Have done for a hundred thousand years – it's what we did since before we were human – since we were just apes – We evolved to put our hands on stone or branches and feel for a hold to pull ourselves up – just look at any kid – any girl or boy in the playground – on a wall in the street – what are they doing? Climbing. (Greig, 2018, p. 17)

If Macdonald's film visualised mountain play, Greig and Morris's theatrical production turns the set itself into a mountain playground.

Each *Void* text's depiction of mountaineering as play allows the reader/audience to imagine themselves as part of the game. Through the character of Sarah, an outsider to the world of climbing, the audience can understand the thrill of climbing by proxy. Similarly, Macdonald's camera work puts the viewer in the position of the climber. Close-ups of the climbers' movements combined with quick shots of stunning scenery allow the audience to imagine themselves climbing Siula Grande. Simpson's technical explanation of their ascent in the memoir becomes all absorbing, inviting the reader into the two climbers' world. When told through different mediums, mountaineering stories like *Touching the Void* give audiences an alluring taste of the childlike freedom of climbing without the actual risk. Without the physical presence of danger, mountains read as playgrounds and climbing as recreation.

Framing mountains as playgrounds casts Simpson and Yates as children at play, and like children, they shrug off the serious consequences their actions might provoke. In the memoir, Simpson reports Yates laughing off his concerns and writes off his own fear of the mountain as "healthy", priming his body for the exertion ahead (p. 25). At this stage of the book, the mountain is still a playground with each section of the climb a puzzle to work through. However, once Simpson breaks his leg, the mountains take on a different character. Following the accident, Simpson (2004, p. 140) states, "This was not the playground we had walked into so long ago". He begins to describe the mountains as "malevolent" and filled with "tangible hostility". Writing from the perspective of Yates, Simpson then anthropomorphises the mountains after the rope-cutting. Simpson-as-Yates describes the mountains as watchful, waiting, and evil, stating, "I hated the place for its cruelty, and for what it had made me do" (Simpson, 2004, pp. 106, 118 & 150). As the game of mountaineering shifts from school-yard shenanigans to survival in a hostile environment, Simpson casts the mountain as an antagonistic bully disrupting their play.

Sarah Thomson (2004, p. 75) argues that the freedom of play on the playground is "only a relative freedom from the physical boundaries and constraints of the classroom". Playgrounds still exist under the watchful eyes of authority figures who determine what kind of play is allowed (Thomson, 2004). During Simpson's ordeal, his own mind became the authority figure dictating the way he should play the game. As he writes in his memoir, Simpson imagined a voice separate from himself, a coldly rational part of his psyche ordering him to keep moving: "It was as if there were two minds within me arguing the toss. The *voice* was clean and sharp and commanding. It was always right, and I listened to it when it spoke and acted on its decisions" (p. 141). In order to cross the eight-mile distance over rugged terrain back to base camp, Simpson follows the *voice's* commands and makes a game of crawling to specific boulders within a certain amount of time. Failing to reach the next landmark left Simpson "sob[bing] with annoyance" (p. 163). The authoritative *voice* became part of the game, allowing Simpson to move past the antagonistic mountains:

A couple of times I looked back at the ice cliff as I hobbled away down the rocks. Each time they grew smaller and I felt that I was shutting the door on something intangible but menacing that had been with me for so long. Those cliffs were the doors to the mountains. I grinned when I glanced at them. I had won a battle of some sort. (Simpson, 2004, p. 165)

Even in the midst of desperate circumstances, Simpson evokes the idea of following the authority of the *voice* in order to win against the mountain. In so doing, he felt he had won the battle against the "bully" on the playground, the mountains themselves.

In Greig's play, the *voice* is both authority figure and bully embodied in the character of Sarah. Greig structures the events of the play, and thus the other characters, as figments of Joe's injury-delirious mind. Sarah appears as a hallucination as Joe pulls himself out of the crevasse, a physicalisation of the *voice* from Simpson's memoir. Unlike Simpson's written account, Sarah as the *voice* is sadistic as well as commanding. Crawling towards each landmark boulder, the stage directions indicate that "*With each rock, she tortures him*" and "*Sarah beats Joe's leg hard, a number of times, with the pool cue*" to simulate the pain of Joe's broken leg (Greig, 2018, p. 82). Sarah torments Joe but also urges him onward; she suggests Joe break up the journey back to basecamp into "achievable tasks", the timing/landmark game Simpson set himself in the memoir (Greig, 2018, p. 76). Externalising the voice shifts the concept of play away from the mountains and into the realm of a childhood spent with siblings. Greig states (2018, p. i) that he based the character of Sarah on Joe's portrayal of her in his second book, *This Game of Ghosts*. As Simpson explains in *This Game*, Sarah engaged Joe in many hours of "mad schemes" that often left him injured or in trouble with authority. For Simpson, Sarah represents an "innocent, seemingly fearless childhood" (Simpson, 1994, p. 47). To include the character of Sarah, in what was originally Simpson's isolated journey back to camp, activates the kind of "innocent, fearless" play found in childhood and born out of sibling rivalry. Joe pushes himself to continue down the mountain, not to win a game against himself or the mountains, but to prove himself to his feared but beloved older sister.

The title of his second memoir, *This Game of Ghosts*, from which the character of Sarah emerges, indicates Simpson's changing of perspective towards mountaineering after his accident on Siula Grande. Mountaineering remains a "game", but one that often ends in death.

Simpson admits that once the "innocent, seemingly fearless childhood" with Sarah ended, it was "replaced with something much more confusing which I never fully took on board – learning to be an adult" (1994, p. 47). For Simpson, being an adult meant taking responsibility for the consequences of the "game" he chose to play. Produced fifteen years after the publication of *Touching the Void* and ten after *This Game of Ghosts*, Macdonald's documentary features this more mature Joe Simpson. Although Simpson still refers to the "malign presence" of the place of his accident during the film's narration, his description of the mountains makes no mention of playgrounds or games. For an older Simpson, the mountains made him feel small and vulnerable. He reflects on the "game" of timing himself to the next landmark, saying, "I don't know why I did it, I think I knew the big picture of what had happened to me, and what I had to do was so big I couldn't deal with it". With the distance of time, the Simpson of the film sees the game for what it was: a survival strategy for a seemingly insurmountable task.

As the game changes for Simpson following his accident, so too does the representation of play in the three mediums. The memoir exteriorises Simpson's relationship with his accident into other "players". The mountains perform as his antagonist and the *voice* as the authority figure urging Simpson to continue the game. This manifestation reflects Simpson's mindset during and shortly after his trip to Peru that, as stated in *This Game*, adulthood was a distant prospect far from the child-like freedom of climbing. In the film, Simpson has had time to reflect on the accident and recognises that the external forces he assigned in his memoir were coping mechanisms for his traumatic experience. Combining both *Touching the Void* and *This Game of Ghosts*, Greig's dramatic interpretation includes both the childish sentiments of the younger Simpson and his later awareness of how his death in Peru might have affected his family. The three *Void* texts represent how Simpson understands mountaineering at different stages of his life.

Deep Play and Accountability

Simpson's opening narration in Macdonald's documentary begins with him saying, "We climb 'cause it's fun" but ends with "It *was* just brilliant fun. And every now and then it went wildly wrong. And then it wasn't" (emphasis mine). In *Performing Mountains*, Jonathan Pitches

(2020, pp. 238 & 242) expands upon Richard Schechner (1993; 2006), Clifford Geertz (1972), and Diane Ackermann's (1999) theory of "deep play", based on Jeremy Bentham's 1840 term, to describe "an addictive attitude toward risk-taking", primarily the kind of voluntary risk with high consequence (death) and low reward (standing on top of a mountain for a few moments). Pitches (2020, p. 242) characterises deep play as occurring between actor and spectator and involves "acts of witnessing, presentation and emotional investment at-a-distance". In other words, deep play is addictive, seemingly unreasonable voluntary risk-taking, *with a performance/audience component.* The embodied repetition of climbing, witnessed through story-telling in various mediums since the mid-1800s, has embedded risk into the culturally constructed narrative of mountain climbing. The performance of deep play like mountaineering for an audience has made that narrative an expected part of mountaineering reality.

Simpson (p. 121) uses the idea of deep play himself in *This Game of Ghosts* as he wrestles with the deep play conundrum of mountaineering: voluntarily risking your life or your friends' lives to climb landscape features. However, when Simpson touches on climbing risk in *Touching the Void*, written shortly after his accident in Peru and before he began climbing again, he evades the conversation, instead falling back on the metaphor of climbing as a game:

> We took the customary summit photos and ate some chocolate. I felt the usual anticlimax. What now? It was a vicious circle. If you succeed with one dream, you come back to square one and it's not long before you're conjuring up another, slightly harder, a bit more ambitious – a bit more dangerous. I didn't like the thought of where it might be leading me. As if, in some strange way, the very nature of the game was controlling me. (Simpson, 2004, p. 53)

Simpson gives agency to outside forces (i.e., the game or the mountain) to avoid taking responsibility for his part in the dangers of climbing. The body of the book ends with Simpson in a hospital in Lima, succumbing to anaesthesia before surgery. His last line (p. 199) reads, "Darkness slipped over the lights and slowly all sounds muffled down to silence", leaving his reader to wonder, what did Simpson learn from his ordeal? Although Simpson performed a remarkable act of seemingly super-human survival to which the readers of his memoir bear witness, Simpson's narrative of mountaineering as an addictive game perpetuates the lack of accountability for undertaking such risk. A brief epilogue, set in 1987, written about one of Simpson's first climbing expeditions after Peru, suggests he was aware of the consequences of mountaineering but was not quite ready to accept them: "Somewhere out in those serried peaks lay the bodies of two of my friends, alone, buried in the snows on different mountains. That was the dark side of this beauty which for this moment, I could close from my mind" (Simpson, 2004, p. 202). Simpson "closes his mind" to the depth of mountaineering's play, at least in writing, until *This Game of Ghosts*. In the 2004 edition of *Touching the Void*, Simpson (p. 204) includes a "Ten Years On…" section where he freely admits that at first he believed he had made no mistakes on Siula Grande. Only with the benefit of time and hindsight did Simpson hold himself responsible for the accident and the suffering his death might have caused his loved ones.

Grieg's play presents the risk of death in mountaineering during the very first scene due to the presence of Sarah. Richard, a traveller Joe and Simon picked up in Lima to act as base camp manager, introduces himself to Sarah at the pub following Joe's funeral. He tells her, "I haven't been to many funerals" to which Sarah replies, "Not a climber then?" (Greig, 2018, p. 5). Sarah's quip is a recognition of the staggering amount of death involved in climbing. Her following tirade against climbers reveals her frustration and grief over what she sees as a needless loss of life. Grieg's play shifts the consequences of deep play away from the primary actor, Joe, and focuses on the family members and friends left behind. Sarah becomes a witness, first to the joyful play of mountaineering as Simon shows her how to climb, and later to Joe's agony as she becomes the *voice*, tormenting and cajoling Joe to survive. In Sarah's last scene in the play, she reads a letter from Joe written before he began his summit attempt that Simon gives to her after the funeral. In the letter Joe writes,

So, I'm sorry I'm dead
I really am, sis,
But I want you to know.
I died laughing
On top of the fucking world. (p. 101)

In response (p. 101), Sarah *"crunches up the letter and throws it in the bin"*, angrily rejecting Joe's apology. As a combination of both *Touching the Void* and *This Game of Ghosts*, Grieg's play wrestles with the consequences of mountaineering as deep play. From the memoir, Grieg takes Simpson's unremitting belief that, risk and all, mountaineering is play, hence his line, "I died laughing on top of the fucking world". However, pulling the character of Sarah from *This Game of Ghosts* introduces Simpson's later thoughts on climbing during a time when he himself is grappling with the "deep" aspect of mountaineering play. Having witnessed many funerals of his climbing friends, along with his accident in Peru, Simpson questions whether the joy of climbing is worth the danger.

Neither the memoir nor the film refers to the effect of a climber's death on their friends and family. These mediums confine the danger of climbing in the *Void* story to the climbers themselves. While Simpson often interjects humour and a recognition of the absurdity of his situation into the book's narrative, Macdonald's documentary grimly captures Simpson's suffering. Macdonald condenses Simpson's two-hundred-page book into an hour and forty-seven-minute film, during which Simpson and Yates stoically narrate their story to shots of mostly dialogue-less reenactment. Compressing the story into short bits of narration with accompanying shots of the mountains, some filmed on location at Siula Grande, lends an intensity to the film that sensorily evokes the deep play of mountaineering. There is no need for long descriptions of the menace and danger of the mountains from Simpson and Yates; Macdonald shows the mountains as both beautiful and deadly with aerial shots of razor-thin snow summits and ground shots taken from below the climbers looking upwards, emphasising the impossible steepness of the mountain they are climbing. When Simpson awakens after the rope has been cut, Macdonald reveals reenactor Mackey perched on a narrow ice ledge in the terrifying blue-black dark of a crevasse. The camera drops far below Mackey into the bowels of the crevasse to show that the tiny pinprick of his headlamp barely makes a dent in the gloom. Deathly silence replaces the howling storm above, the eerie quiet only broken by Simpson's (Mackey's) frightened sobbing. The film is the only medium to visually portray the sense of scale of Simpson's climb, from the towering mountain to the nightmarish bottomless crevasse and then over the long miles of harsh terrain back to camp. In Macdonald's film, the risk of climbing in such a dangerous environment feels wildly out of proportion to the few happy moments the climbers spend on the summit.

Dark Play and Self-Deception

In mountaineering, deep play exists alongside dark play, play that Richard Schechner defines as occurring when "contradictory realities coexist, each seemingly capable of canceling the other out [...] Dark play subverts order, dissolves frames, breaks its own rules, so that the playing itself is in danger of being destroyed" (1993, p. 36). The game of mountaineering skirts the fine line between life and death. Mountaineering can feel like "life times a thousand" (Greig, 2018, p. 19), but can also end with the destruction of that life, thus ending the play. Dark play involves a level of deception when, as Schechner (1993, p. 36) argues, not all the players know they are playing, or not all the players have the same information. I contend that mountaineering is dark play involving *self*-deception. The climbers, like Simpson and Yates, believed they were playing a game where the mountains were a playground to be ruled over, but in reality, mountains are indifferent landscapes where climbers in their prime often lose their lives. This self-deception only reveals itself when the game goes awry, or when climbing is put in front of a witness who fails to see climbing as a game.

In Macdonald's documentary, Simpson reveals that the accident fundamentally changed who he thought a climber should be:

> I felt very, very alone. And I was very scared. I was also 25, you know, I was fit, I was super ambitious. And this was the first trip I'd been on. I wanted to climb the world, and it just didn't seem... this hadn't been part of our game plan. [...] As a climber you should always be in control, you have to be in control. So in [losing control], you could be seen as half a failure. You lost it. It was just childish. I just cried and cried. I thought, I'd be tougher than that.

Simpson acknowledges his "childish"-ness at that time of his life. Climbing was supposed to be a proving ground for control and conquest, but in reality, could very well end in the loss of his life. In the memoir, Simpson recognises that serious and possibly fatal injury were part of the game, but held the "childish" belief, perhaps through surviving other accidents in his early climbing career, that death would continue to miss him. Despite his assumption in 1994 that he never fully took on adulthood, the Joe Simpson featured in the 2004 documentary has left his childhood behind. While shooting on location in Peru in 2003, Simpson (2004, p. 209) writes:

Then I saw the West face of Siula Grande and felt a tremor of fear. It was bigger and meaner and so much more threatening than I remembered. It made me wonder at the person I had been all those years ago. I must have been bold, ambitious, or even a little crazy to have considered such an undertaking.

For a twenty-five-year-old Simpson, mountain climbing was a game to be played and won, a game not yet filled with ghosts.

Greig highlights the self-deception of mountaineering dark play with the introduction of Toni Kurz's story as a source of inspiration for Simpson. Joe tells his sister Sarah the story of Kurz struggling to stay alive alone on the north face of the Eiger before finally succumbing to the elements. Joe call Kurz's death "beautiful" and heroic (pp. 29 & 27). However, the reality of freezing to death at the end of a rope or dying in a crevasse after days of agony lacked the beauty and heroism that Simpson had imagined. Instead, his accident unveiled the actual consequences of deep play. The fictional mountaineer that Simpson was happy to play when circumstances were favourable gave way to a completely different sense of self, one that no longer saw climbing with the void as a game. Sarah, as the audience stand-in, also disrupts Joe's "beautiful" vision of Kurz's death saying, "No, Joe, not beautiful. Ugly. Horrible. Ugly and cold" (Greig, 2018, p. 29). In the second half of the play, Joe tells *voice* Sarah that he is dying of dehydration to which she replies, "That doesn't seem very glamorous. Not very Toni Kurz" (p. 78). The reality of Joe's death in the mountains reveals how he has deceived himself into believing that a heroic and beautiful end was part of the game.

If the accident shifted how Simpson envisioned himself as a climber, Yates cutting the rope and leaving Simpson for dead in a crevasse presents another side of the self-deception of mountaineering dark play. Simpson and Yates fooled themselves into believing in the "brotherhood of the rope", the concept that a climber would, and sometimes did, sacrifice themselves for their partner (Isserman, 2017). As Simpson writes (2004, p. 206), "The rope cutting had clearly touched a nerve, transgressed some unwritten rule". *Touching the Void* exposed the performative aspect of what climbing partnerships entailed. The climbing community, since the late nineteenth century and emphasised during WWII with the creation of mountaineering companies, would have climbers behave more like comrades in arms, a band of brothers willing to lay down their lives for their partners (Isserman, 2017). If the brotherhood of the rope no longer applied, as the *Void* story suggests, the risk involved in mountaineering becomes that much more unreasonable. Even more disturbing, the narrative of mountains as playgrounds where climbers play games with set rules and ethics comes into question. Mountaineering is no longer a game if the other climbers do not play by the rules.

In stressing that Yates's actions on the mountain were justified, Simpson's memoir exposes the dark play of mountaineering, the self-deception climbers engage in in order to ignore the deep play element of the sport. Simpson wrote *Touching the Void* when he learned that a member of the Mount Everest Foundation Selection Committee attempted to bar Yates from receiving funding due to the rope-cutting incident in Peru (Simpson, 1994, p. 213). The "authorities" had deemed Yates a rule-breaker. Wanting to tell the story "straight" (p. 206) Simpson's memoir (p. 19) describes Yates as "an easy friend: dependable, sincere, ready to see life as a joke". Of their descent from the mountain, as Yates tried to lower Simpson several thousand feet to safety, Simpson (2004, p. 92) writes:

> For a short moment on the storm-swept belay we had accepted a warm sense of friendship. It felt like some cliché from a third-rate war movie – We're all in this together, lads, and we're all going to make it home.

Drawing on the brotherhood of the rope's own allusion to brothers-in-arms, Simpson implies that Yates's attempt to rescue Simpson from the mountain was a heroic effort in line with how climbing partners should behave. After discovering Yates had cut the rope, Simpson's memoir holds no recrimination, only the thought that "I shouldn't even have got this far. He should have left me on the ridge" (p. 114). Simpson argues that in choosing to put themselves into such dangerous conditions, anything Yates did to ensure his own survival was reasonable. However, in justifying Yates's actions, Simpson also calls attention to the absurdity of climbing mountains in the first place. In believing in the sanctity of the brotherhood of the rope, mountaineers deceive themselves into thinking that mountaineering is play with rules based on shared ethics. *Touching the Void* shows how in its deceptions, the dark play of mountaineering disrupts order and breaks its own rules.

Simpson is very careful not to cast blame on Yates in the memoir, however Macdonald's film presents a more ambiguous take on their relationship. Macdonald chooses to never show the real Simpson and Yates on screen together. Instead, each man tells his side of the story directly to the camera with no one else in frame. This narrative device emotionally distances the two climbers from each other. The sparse dialogue between the reenactors introduces an aloofness to the relationship that a hug and a few back slaps during the summit shot fail to overcome. Even more telling, in narrating his side of the story Richard Hawking (Simpson and Yates's base camp manger) says that if only one climber returned from the mountain, he hoped it would be Yates. The inclusion of Hawking's callous admission not only complicates the audience's feelings about Yates but also involves Hawking in the dark play of mountaineering where betting on which climber to survive becomes part of the game. Additionally, Macdonald's editing foreshadows the rope-cut, introducing a sense of foreboding into the relationship even before the reenactors begin climbing the mountain:

> Simpson: The rope can be something that rather than save your life, could kill you. If your mate falls off then all this gear rips out, you're dead, you're going go with him. If you're going do that sort of climbing at some point you're going have to rely wholly on your partner.

With Simpson's line, Macdonald establishes the idea that climbers must be able to rely on their partners for safety, however this reliance could prove fatal if your partner makes a mistake or, as the documentary reveals, your partner chooses their life over yours. Yates's retelling of the rope cutting for the camera is matter-of-fact, his delivery at times slightly rushed as though to forestall questions about his decision. Intercut with his explanation are shots of actor Nicholas Aaron as Yates cutting the rope and then letting his helmeted head fall back into the snow with a sigh of relief. Yates's narration continues with him saying that the "overriding memory" of the night after the rope cut was one of feeling "desperately thirsty" in the snow cave he made for himself. Taken together, Yates' logical but almost-defensive delivery, Aaron's sigh of relief, and Yates's admission of thirst being the main memory from that night paint him as an unsympathetic character, or at least less sympathetic than Simpson who, when seeing the cut rope, says he felt "pleased" that Simon was still alive. While the reenactors are recognisably putting on a performance as the characters of Joe and Simon, Macdonald plays with his representation of Simpson and Yates to cast Yates in a more questionable light than portrayed in Simpson's memoir.

Unlike the memoir or film, in Greig's theatrical version Joe blames Simon for cutting the rope. As Joe (Greig, 2018, p. 62) says to his hallucination of Sarah after discovering the cut rope, "Simon killed me". The other characters then try to convince Joe that Simon was not at fault. This reversal from Simpson trying to persuade others of Yates's innocence to himself in need of convincing creates a level of distance in their relationship not seen in either film or memoir. Greig portrays their relationship as relatively detached from the beginning of the play in a conversation between Simon and Sarah:

> Simon: Look, Sarah, I didn't really know Joe that well. We were just –
> Sarah: I know –
> Simon and Sarah: Climbing partners.
> Sarah: Just.

With Sarah's line, "Just", the character highlights how Simon's guarded depiction of their relationship belies the long-held understanding that a climber should be a brother-in-arms to their partner. In this version of *Touching the Void*, Joe is the one who deceives himself into believing in the brotherhood of the rope, and feels betrayed when that concept proves to be little more than a fiction. Although Greig and Morris consulted with Simpson, the play is the only version of *Touching the Void* in which Simpson did not actively participate. Knowing that he wrote his memoir in defence of Yates, Simpson's lack of involvement in the play allowed Greig and Morris the freedom to represent Simpson in the character of Joe without being protective of Yates's reputation. Joe's anger at Simon performs another version of the *Touching the Void* story, a dark play on the deep play of mountaineering.

Conclusion

Touching the Void itself is a performance of dark play. Stories that cast mountains as playgrounds and mountaineering as play deceive future climbers into believing the risk of death is a necessary part of the game. Through stories like Simpson's, injury and death have become accepted outcomes of mountaineering deep play with little accountability on the part of the climber. The dark play aspect of *Touching the Void* manifests in the fact that even if Simpson had died, his play would still have been successful because death is part of the game. Making a game of mountain-eering in which either outcome, life or death, furthers the narrative of risk produces a compelling win-win situation for future climbers. However, Macdonald's documentary and, to a further extent, Greig's play demonstrate that this narrative is mutable. Macdonald presents a less-than-brotherly relationship between Simpson and Yates. The film asks its viewers, would you take up mountaineering if you had to kill your partner to survive? Is climbing a mountain worth that risk? Similarly, with the character of Sarah, Greig's play questions Joe's valorisation of death. Despite experiencing the joy of mountaineering for herself, Sarah never deceives herself into thinking that climbing is a game, and therefore never engages in its dark play.

Exploring *Touching the Void* as play has broader implications for the study of risk. Dark play accompanies deep play, this essay's model of risk in performance, but the self-deception of dark play could also apply to other theories of risk such as Stephen Lyng's (2012) "edgework" or Peter Simmons's (2003) "performing safety/risk". At some level, all risk is contingent upon self-deception that can be fostered and perpetuated through the repetition of stories of its embodiment, like *Touching the Void*. As long as mountaineering narratives perform the self-deception of dark play, stories like *Touching the Void* will continue inspiring new players to enter the game.

Bibliography

Donnelly, P. (2004) "Playing with Gravity: Mountains and Mountaineering", in Vertinsky, P.A. and Bale, J. (eds) *Sites of Sport: Space, Place, Experience.* London: Routledge, pp. 131–144.

Greig, D. (2018) *Touching the Void.* London: Faber and Faber Limited.

Isserman, M. (2017) *Continental Divide: A History of American Mountaineering.* New York, NY: W.W. Norton and Company.

Lyng, S. (2012) "Existential Transcendence in Late Modernity: Edgework and Hermeneutic Reflexivity", *Human Studies*, 35(3), pp. 401–414.

Magdalinski, T. (2004) "Homebush: Site of the Clean/sed and Natural Australian Athlete", in Vertinsky, P.A. and Bale, J. (eds) *Sites of Sport: Space, Place, Experience.* London: Routledge, pp. 101–114.

Pitches, J. (2020) *Performing Mountains.* London: Palgrave Macmillan UK.

Schechner, R. (1993) *The Future of Ritual: Writings on Culture and Performance.* London: Routledge.

Simmons, P. (2003) "Performing safety in faulty environments", *The Sociological Review*, 51(2), pp. 78–93.

Simpson, J. (1994) *This Game of Ghosts*. New York, NY: Vintage.

Simpson, J. (2004) *Touching the Void: The True Story of One Man's Miraculous Survival*. Revised. New York, NY: Harper Perennial.

Simpson, J. (2005) "Introduction", in Harrer, H., *The White Spider*. New York, NY: Harper Perennial.

Stephen, L. (1894) *The Playground of Europe*. Harlow: Longmans, Green and Co.

Thomson, S. (2004) "Just Another Classroom? Observations of Primary School Playgrounds", in Vertinsky, P. A. and Bale, J. (eds) *Sites of Sport: Space, Place, Experience*. London: Routledge (Sport in the Global Society), pp. 73–84.

Touching the Void (2004) [Film] Directed by Kevin Macdonald. MGM Studios.

Vincentelli, E. (2021) "'Touching the Void' Review: Choices That Shape a Life on the Edge", *The New York Times*, 28 May, p. 5.

Chapter 13

Walking Mountains

Zen Practice and Ecological Awareness in Peter Matthiessen's *The Snow Leopard*

Christopher Kocela

This chapter examines the representation of mountaineering as a form of ecological Zen practice in Peter Matthiessen's *The Snow Leopard*. Winner of two National Book Awards for non-fiction in 1979 and 1980, Matthiessen's account of the two-hundred-and-fifty-mile expedition he made across the Dolpo region of Nepal with field biologist George Schaller in 1973 has proven enormously influential in popularising mountain climbing and trekking as forms of spiritual seeking. A 2018 *Guardian* article commemorating the fortieth anniversary of *The Snow Leopard* identified it as "the inspiration for more hippy trails and backpacker expeditions to Kathmandu and beyond than any other volume" (Adams, 2018); later that year *The New Yorker* portrayed *The Snow Leopard* as "a prescient exploration of how we might confront the dire reality of climate change without shying away from either nature's profound beauty or our own sadness" (O'Connor, 2018). Yet despite Matthiessen's frequent characterisation by literary critics as a nature writer in the American tradition of Emerson, Thoreau, and Aldo Leopold, little scholarly attention has been paid to Matthiessen's use of Zen practice to shape the form and ecological argument of *The Snow Leopard*.

In this chapter I argue that *The Snow Leopard* draws heavily on the de-anthropocentric representation of mountains "walking" and "flowing" in Zen master Dōgen's *Mountains and Waters Sutra* (1240). Matthiessen echoes Dōgen's medieval Zen insights in depicting a new spiritual and ecological awareness which he portrays as essential to arresting the human exploitation and destruction of the natural environment. He also draws on Dōgen to establish that any heightened form of awareness is inseparable from careful attention to one's day-to-day activities – in this case, the rigors of mountaineering. Although *The Snow Leopard* enjoys a well-deserved reputation for inspiring readers to take up hiking and mountain climbing, this reputation obscures the fact that Matthiessen, at the time of his famous trek, had never done strenuous climbing before and was critical of what he regarded as the egocentric motivations of mountaineers. Through its depiction of Matthiessen's conflicted attitude toward mountaineering, *The Snow Leopard* becomes a form of ecological life writing in which the climbing and walking of mountains reflect what Dōgen defines as the unity of practice and realisation. Representation of this unity helps to explain the ongoing relevance of *The Snow Leopard* for contemporary readers interested in mountaineering and trekking as forms of sustainable tourism.

Walking Through Dōgen's Zen

In his 1985 memoir, *Nine-Headed Dragon River*, Matthiessen makes clear that *The Snow Leopard* was the product of a definitive change in his Zen practice that occurred in the four years following his 1973 journey across the Himalayas. Although he had been warned by his Zen teacher not to seek spiritual attainment during his travels in Nepal, Matthiessen confesses that "I had clung to the hope that the great clarity and insights of hard snow mountain samadhi would culminate in a profound enlightenment. When this failed to occur, I was cast down" (1998, p. 47). Returning to New York, he participated in intense periods of group meditation known as *sesshin* which, in the Rinzai Zen tradition, are considered the most effective way of bringing about a spiritual awakening. But after two and a half years of such practice he had a falling out with his teacher in 1976 while revising his Himalayan journals for publication; six months later, he visited a prominent Zen centre in California and was exposed to a different form of meditation that placed much less emphasis on the enlightenment experience. Inspired by this new approach, Matthiessen became a Soto Zen student while completing revisions to his Himalayan journals; *The Snow Leopard,* in his words, came to "represent a period of transition between Rinzai Zen and the Soto Zen studies that commenced with my first sesshin at the Zen Center of Los Angeles in 1977" (1998, p. 72). The most significant aspect of this transition was Matthiessen's exposure to the writings of Eihei Dōgen (1200–1253), the founder of the

Soto Zen school in medieval Japan. Matthiessen quotes liberally from Dōgen's works throughout *Nine-Headed Dragon River* and uses portions of Dōgen's *Mountains and Waters Sutra* as the epigraph to the chapter on his Himalayan trek. Although scholars have largely ignored Dōgen's influence on Matthiessen, the *Mountains and Waters Sutra* sheds considerable light on the spiritual and ecological themes of *The Snow Leopard.*

The *Mountains and Waters Sutra* was first delivered by Dōgen as a sermon to his community of Zen monks in 1240 and later collected as a fascicle of his *Shobo Genzo* or *Treasury of the True Dharma Eye.* Although labelled a "sutra", the text, like many fascicles of the *Shobo Genzo*, consists of Dōgen's original and often unorthodox reinterpretation of passages taken from previous Zen literature. In the *Mountains and Waters Sutra*, Dōgen's exegetical jumping-off point is a line from a Chinese Ch'an koan in which Priest Daokai (1043–1118) of Mount Furong tells his students, "The green mountains are always walking; a stone woman gives birth to a child at night". In Dōgen's reading, the image of "mountains walking" becomes a powerful expression of Zen practice which he explicates on at least two levels.

On one hand, Dōgen uses the notion of "mountains walking" to illuminate the inseparability of practice and realisation. Dōgen was aware that canonical Zen literature tended to give a false impression of enlightenment or *satori* as a permanent transformation that eliminated the need for practice and put an end to deluded, unenlightened views. In the *Mountains and Waters Sutra* he takes direct aim at this textual tradition. Alluding to Zen texts in which students achieve *satori* through a spontaneous communion with nature, he writes: "Even if you understand mountains as the realm where all buddhas practice, this understanding is not something to be attached to. Even if you have the highest understanding of mountains as all buddhas' wondrous characteristics, the truth is not only this" (2010b, p. 156). In Dōgen's view, restricting an understanding of enlightenment to moments of sudden epiphany overlooks the embeddedness of realisation in mundane daily activities that do not produce such emotional or intellectual highs. Enlightenment for Dōgen is not a transcendent exit from the mundane or from unenlightened views; instead, it is always embedded in and inseparable from those activities and views. Accordingly, he reconsiders the seemingly incongruous image of "mountains walking" as a challenge to reflect on the up-and-down, back-and-forth vicissitudes of everyday Zen practice: "Clearly examine the green mountains' walking and your own walking.

[…] If walking had stopped, buddha ancestors would not have appeared. If walking ends, the buddha dharma cannot reach the present. Walking forward does not cease; walking backward does not cease" (2010b, p. 155). As this passage makes clear, there can be no enlightenment without the continuous walking that is daily practice. Such practice is experienced not as a steady progression from delusion to realisation but as a series of forward and backward steps, breakthroughs and setbacks, which form the dynamic unity of what Dōgen calls "practice-realization": "All mountains walk with their toes on waters and make them splash. Thus, in walking there are seven vertical paths and eight horizontal paths. This is practice-realization" (2010b, p. 158).

On a second level, Dōgen also employs the image of "mountains walking" to emphasize that the most important practice is compassion. In Mahāyāna Buddhist traditions such as Zen, the ideal practitioner is the bodhisattva who, while enlightened to the ultimate truth of emptiness or formlessness, nonetheless remains in the discriminating world of relative truth to work for the liberation of all. The first of the bodhisattva's four great vows is "However innumerable sentient beings are, I vow to save them" (Kim, 2004, p. 204). But Dōgen greatly expanded the reach of the bodhisattva's compassion by breaking down conventional distinctions between sentient and insentient beings. In Dōgen's view, sentient and insentient beings are alike in that all are impermanent; as such, they all embody the buddha nature which is none other than ultimate reality. In the *Buddha Nature* fascicle of his *Shobo Genzo* Dōgen writes: "Grass, trees, and forests are impermanent; they are buddha nature. Humans, things, body, and mind are impermanent; they are buddha nature. Land, mountains, and rivers are impermanent, as they are buddha nature" (2010a, p. 244). To recognise "mountains walking" is to practise the wisdom and compassion of the bodhisattva who reconciles dualities of sentience and insentience, self and other, form and emptiness (Kim, 2004, p. 208). Compassionate practice of this kind means stepping beyond anthropocentric views to acknowledge alternative animal, vegetable and mineral perspectives:

> Not all beings see mountains and waters in the same way. […]
> Some beings see water as wondrous blossoms, but they do not see blossoms as water. Hungry ghosts see water as raging fire or pus and blood. Dragons and fish see water as a palace or a pavilion. […] Human beings see water as water. (Dōgen, 2010b, pp. 158–159)

Alternating among such a variety of views, one comes to appreciate the many forms of mountains and oceans while also recognising their fundamental emptiness or formlessness. "Mountains walking" emerges out of this respect for differing perspectives that together reveal the impermanence or buddha nature of all beings.

Dōgen's *Mountains and Waters Sutra* has proven important to the work of contemporary eco-Buddhists such as Gary Snyder and Joanna Macy as well as to philosophers and activists in the deep ecology movement. Wirth portrays Dōgen's Zen as a key influence on Snyder's view that "[e]cological policies would also be a question of practice, not just the rational and bureaucratic execution of tasks" (2017, p. 21). Devall and Sessions present Dōgen's *Mountains and Waters Sutra* alongside Aldo Leopold's *The Sand County Almanac* (1949) as texts which dramatize *self-realisation*, the first "ultimate norm" of deep ecology in which one recognises affiliations beyond the human sphere. In this vein Dōgen's ability to see mountains walking illustrates a form of "questing [toward] appreciation of nonhuman self" (Devall and Sessions, 1985, p. 67). Yet although several critics have commented on Matthiessen's Buddhism or aligned him with the deep ecology movement, none has examined the specific impact of Dōgen's Zen on his ecological vision. Both Campbell and Jenkins interpret *The Snow Leopard* as a deep ecological text, but Campbell reduces Zen to a form of "mysticism" equivalent to the "great lessons of Emerson and Thoreau" (1988, pp. 139–140), while Jenkins interprets Matthiessen's meditative insights as examples of Leopold's "thinking like a mountain" (2000, pp. 268–269). Dowie acknowledges Matthiessen's commitment to popularising Dōgen's writings in *Nine-Headed Dragon River* but reads *The Snow Leopard* as a form of spiritual autobiography whose essential tropes are established by Thoreau's *Walden* (1991, pp. 107 & 110). Allister examines *The Snow Leopard* with reference to Emerson and the Ten Oxherding Pictures of Chinese Ch'an Buddhism, concluding that Matthiessen's book constitutes a form of "relational life writing" in which a therapeutic relationship with nature develops out of religious pilgrimage (2001, pp. 141–142). Finally, Oh refers briefly to Dōgen in the introduction to his study of Matthiessen's fiction but locates the significance of Zen in its perceived similarity to Native American spiritual traditions (2010, pp. 20–22). Apart from their tendency to equate Zen with other ecological visions, several of these readings exhibit what Sponberg identifies as a critical tendency to romanticise ecological self-realisation while downplaying Buddhism's traditional emphasis on moral and physical discipline (1997, pp. 370–371).

In contrast to previous critics, I take seriously Matthiessen's claim that *The Snow Leopard* represents his transition to Soto Zen between 1976 and 1978. The transitional status of the text emerges out of the fact that, while Matthiessen wrote his Himalayan journals before his exposure to Dōgen's Zen, he edited and prepared them for publication with a view of Dōgen's writings firmly in mind. Rather than revise his earlier view of enlightenment as a transcendent escape from the challenges of day-to-day practice, Matthiessen published those views in a form of ecobiography that encourages readers to see the interdependence between his ecological insights and his frustrations as an inexperienced mountaineer.

The Snow Leopard as Zen Ecobiography

In *Reading Autobiography*, Smith and Watson define ecobiography as life writing in which "internal terrain is mapped onto and illuminated by natural setting, as an intimate relationship between them is developed" (2010, 160). Environmentalists such as John Muir, Edward Abbey, and Al Gore have used ecobiography to highlight the degradation of the natural world while also establishing a "textual place from which to call for an ethic of care for the environment" (Smith and Watson, 2010, p. 161). *The Snow Leopard* clearly qualifies as ecobiography in the terms defined by Smith and Watson. At the outset Matthiessen portrays his journey across the Himalayas as both "a true pilgrimage, a journey of the heart" (2008, p. 2) and an effort to help his friend, the field biologist George Schaller, collect data on the Himalayan blue sheep that populate the mountains around Crystal Monastery. Schaller hopes that information on the rutting habits of the blue sheep, or bharal, will clarify their evolutionary relationship to goats and substantiate his report to the Nepalese government about the need for a wildlife preserve in Inner Dolpo. For Matthiessen, the journey to Crystal Mountain also affords an opportunity to experience a profoundly altered relationship to the natural world. Early on he reminds the reader of the Buddha's spiritual wisdom (in Sanskrit, *prajna*) that overcomes the seeming dichotomy between self and nature:

> A true experience of *prajna* corresponds to "enlightenment" or liberation—not change, but transformation—a profound vision

of his identity with universal life, past, present, and future, that keeps man from doing harm to others and sets him free from fear of birth-and-death.

In the fifth century B.C., near the town of Gaya, south and east of Varanasi, Sakyamuni attained enlightenment in the deep experience that his own "true nature," his Buddha-nature, was no different from the nature of the universe. (2008, pp. 15–16)

To realise one's "true nature" is to break free from the egotism and anthropocentrism that drives human exploitation and destruction of the environment. Referencing celebrated figures in Buddhist history (Bodhidharma, Milarepa) who have achieved liberation from the bounds of the ego (2008, pp. 31–32 & 85–86), Matthiessen hopes for a transformative realisation of buddha nature while traveling in the Himalayas. The prospect of seeing the elusive snow leopard, which preys upon the blue sheep at Crystal Mountain, unites the ecological and spiritual aspects of his quest: "If the snow leopard should manifest itself, then I am ready to see the snow leopard. If not, then somehow (and I don't understand this instinct, even now), I am not ready to perceive it" (2008, p. 238). Interweaving details of Matthiessen's spiritual development with the events of hiking and climbing in the Himalayas, *The Snow Leopard* constitutes what Schwalm calls *peripatetic life writing,* a form of ecobiography that "entwines 'live' philosophical reflection, didactics/dialogue, and the physical effort of moving along by foot" (2016, p. 76).

Yet while *The Snow Leopard* conforms to several features of ecobiography, it also differs in one crucial respect. As Schwalm notes of peripatetic nature writers, "walking, especially mountain walking, constitutes the crucial mode of experience and reflection" (2016, p. 78); walking and climbing are therefore valued as practices which generate biographical detail and intimacy with the environment. By contrast, Matthiessen frequently portrays mountain climbing as an egotistical practice that elevates human aspiration above respect for the natural environment and is thus at odds with the extinction of ego which he seeks. Citing Lama Govinda's explanation of the religious appeal of Crystal Mountain, he writes: "the worshipful or religious attitude is not impressed by scientific facts, like figures of altitude [. . .] Nor is it motivated by the urge to 'conquer' the mountain" (2008, p. 182). In the same vein he argues that approaching mountains "respectfully" is the antithesis of the mountaineer's desire to "challenge" them (2008, pp. 244–245). To be sure,

Matthiessen's characterisation of the difference between spiritual practice and traditional mountaineering is not without precedent. As Schaumann observes, Leslie Stephen advocated in the late nineteenth century for a practice of climbing in the Alps that emphasized "intense contact and communication with one's environment" rather than "the frenzied activity of mountain conquest" (2020, p. 222). Matthiessen's spiritual aspirations for his quest also resonate with Western attitudes of the time. Isserman and Weaver portray the 1960s as a turning point in the evolution of Himalayan mountaineering owing to the celebration and promotion of Eastern spirituality by cultural influencers such as Allen Ginsberg, Jack Kerouac, and the Beatles (2008, p. 383). As travels in India, Nepal and Tibet became synonymous, for many Westerners, with spiritual seeking, "Western mountaineers increasingly spoke of their own endeavors in the Himalaya not in the traditional terms of conquest or national glory but as a kind of transcendent personal experience" (Isserman and Weaver, 2008, p. 350). In this vein Robert Pirsig's bestselling *Zen and the Art of Motorcycle Maintenance* (1974) distinguishes between the "ego-climber" and the "selfless climber": where the former is motivated by self-glorification, the latter climbs "with as little effort as possible and without desire" (2005, pp. 205 & 211–213). In *The Snow Leopard* the tension between the goals of spiritual transformation and mountaineering manifests in a recurring pattern. Matthiessen repeatedly experiences a sense of oneness with his environment akin to the "true nature" of his Buddhist predecessors; but those insights disappear when confronted with the day-to-day challenges of mountaineering in the Himalayas. An inexperienced climber, Matthiessen is humbled not only by altitude sickness and fear of falling but also by the anger and hostility he feels toward his more skilled companions, on whom he becomes increasingly dependent as they ascend higher into the mountains. The result is a text which, alternating between depictions of epiphanic insight and the trials of mountaineering, represents not only the transcendent "flowing" of mountains described by Dōgen, but also the continuous "walking forward" and "walking backward" of Dōgen's practice-realisation. Like the *Mountains and Waters Sutra*, *The Snow Leopard* challenges its reader to recognise that spiritual and ecological enlightenment cannot occur independently of the trials and delusions that attend working with others in the real world.

Enlightenment and Travelling Light

Dōgen's influence on *The Snow Leopard* emerges most clearly in Matthiessen's repeated awakening to the flowing and walking of the mountains. Pausing to meditate at 14,000 feet, he remarks that "no doubt high altitude has an effect, for my eye perceives the world as fixed or fluid, as it wishes. The earth twitches, and the mountains shimmer" (2008, p. 100). Two weeks later he describes the mountains as "a mirror to one's own true being, utterly still" and yet "moving, full of power, full of light" (2008, p. 170). These passages reflect the compassion of Dōgen's bodhisattva who sees both emptiness and form, buddha nature and individual beings: "Do not remain bewildered and skeptical when you hear the words *Mountains flow*; but study these words with buddha ancestors. When you take up one view, you see mountains flowing, and when you take up another view, mountains are not flowing" (Dōgen, 2010b, p. 162). In keeping with this principle, Matthiessen later portrays Crystal Mountain as forging (2008, p. 182), breathing (2008, p. 194), and dancing (2008, p. 208), and he experiences a sense of communion with animals who thrive in radically different circumstances from his own. Recall that, for Dōgen, "[s]ome beings see water as wondrous blossoms" while others see it as "raging fire or pus and blood" (2010b, pp. 158–59). At one point Matthiessen transports himself into the mind of a lizard sunning itself on a rock: "My head is the sorcerer's cup full of blood, and were I to turn, my eyes would see straight to the heart of chaos, the mutilation, bloody gore, and pain that is seen darkly in the bright eye of this lizard" (2008, p. 223). According to Gary Snyder, one of the chief strengths of Dōgen's *Mountains and Waters Sutra* is that it does not confine ecological awareness to blissful experiences of peace and emptiness; on the contrary, it also asserts that "other orders of beings have their own literatures" (Snyder, 2000, p. 136) rooted in decay, fermentation, and cannibalism. Like Snyder, Matthiessen suggests that breaking through one's anthropocentric worldview requires direct experience of the ways that nature humbles us through its beauty, mundanity and violence.

To date, scholars interested in the spiritual and ecological themes of *The Snow Leopard* have focused almost exclusively on Matthiessen's transcendent moments of identification with nature. Dowie argues that *The Snow Leopard* qualifies as spiritual autobiography because, like Thoreau's *Walden,* it depicts Matthiessen's escape from civilisation into "union with creation as the archetypal religious experience" (1991, p. 110).

Jenkins compares *The Snow Leopard* to Aldo Leopold's *Sand County Almanac* on the basis that, for each author, "the burst into ecological enlightenment forever changes his perception of his own place in the natural world" (2000, p. 269). But these critics gloss over the fact that Matthiessen's spiritual and ecological epiphanies are always short-lived and often followed by doubt and despondency derived from climbing at high altitudes. Early on Matthiessen laments that his elation at the natural scenery gives way so suddenly to "reeling with the altitude, with a bad headache, and a face baked stiff by the sun" (2008, p. 96). At several points he wonders whether his epiphanies are simply products of being "silly with the altitude" (2008, pp. 110 & 165) and he occasionally blames the altitude for his irritability toward Schaller and the Tibetan Sherpas and porters (2008, pp. 171 & 293). These frustrations and disappointments are not merely incidental to his moments of higher awareness; on the contrary, they are important because they undercut Matthiessen's own assumption that he can achieve spiritual and ecological enlightenment independently of the rigors of mountain climbing.

Matthiessen not only distrusts mountaineers for what he regards as their egotistical motivations; he also seems to believe that his spiritual transformation depends on circumventing the challenges faced by other climbers. Like most peripatetic nature writers (Schwalm, 2016, 77), Matthiessen frames his narrative through intertextual references to those who have travelled the area before him. In the opening pages of *The Snow Leopard* he contrasts his quest with that of David Snelgrove's *Himalayan Pilgrimage* (1961) noting that, while Snelgrove was unable to find the Lama of Shey at Crystal Monastery, "surely our luck would be better" (2008, p. 2). Later he cites a passage from Maurice Herzog's mountaineering classic, *Annapurna* (1953), in which Herzog describes "groping" for freedom on the side of the mountain (2008, p. 107). In Matthiessen's view, Herzog's existential frisson is the antithesis of real freedom, which he defines as "traveling light, without clinging or despising, in calm acceptance of everything that comes" (2008, p. 107). For Matthiessen, "traveling light" becomes a metaphor for enlightenment that also indicates his belief in the separability of realisation and practice. For Dōgen, as we have seen, the danger of such a belief is that it can obscure the vital importance of one's daily activities. Matthiessen wrestles with this problem throughout the text. Disappointed at the fading of one of his early visions, he tells himself: "'Expect nothing.' Walking along, I remind myself of that advice; I must go lightly on my way, with no thought of attainment" (2008, p. 125). But despite this reminder, his hope of going "lightly" continues to reinforce his belief that awakening to his true nature in the mountains can occur independently of the practice of mountain climbing. Nowhere is this belief more fully expressed than in the dream that recurs throughout his trip:

> In a dream I am walking joyfully up the mountain. Something breaks and falls away, and all is light. Nothing has changed, yet all is amazing, luminescent, free. Released at last, I rise into the sky... This dream comes often. Sometimes I run, then lift up like a kite, high above the earth, and always I sail transcendent for a time before awaking. (2008, p. 172, ellipses in original)

As this passage makes clear, Matthiessen's quest for spiritual and ecological awakening is predicated on a naïve assumption that he will be able to experience his true nature unimpeded by the obstacles that have challenged other mountaineers in Nepal. Of course by the time Matthiessen completed the manuscript of *The Snow Leopard* he was acquainted with Dōgen's teachings and was able to see the limitations of this view of Zen practice. But rather than simply correct his earlier view, which would have resulted in misrepresentation of his thoughts at the time, Matthiessen challenges the reader to see the unity of Dōgen's practice-realisation in the oscillation between epiphany and frustration that defines the form of *The Snow Leopard*.

Walking Forward, Walking Backward

Where Matthiessen's fantasies of traveling lightly and joyfully across the Himalayas imply a disconnect between enlightened awareness and mountaineering practice, his actual experience of climbing undercuts those fantasies by revealing how he comes to regard climbing as, itself, a form of spiritual practice. Initially Matthiessen goes out of his way to distinguish himself from his friend and travelling companion George Schaller, who is not only a field biologist and wildlife advocate but also a "mountaineer" (2008, p. 93). Although Matthiessen respects Schaller, he is critical of his technical approach to their journey which places more emphasis on efficiency and speed of travel than on appreciating the landscape and culture of the area. Matthiessen writes of his friend: "I am an inspired walker, but he is formidable; were it not for the slow pace of the porters, he would run me into the ground" (2008, p. 22). When Schaller complains that the "damned porters" (2008, 25) stop too often to rest, Matthiessen reflects: "The porters' pace just suits me [. . .] I am happy in this moment" (2008, 25). The first argument between the two men occurs in Darbang where Schaller leaves his used cans in the schoolyard for the villagers to collect. Although Matthiessen understands that the locals value the cans as containers, he criticizes Schaller for "littering the place" (2008, p. 33) rather than making a more aesthetically pleasing offering. Like his characterisation of Herzog, Matthiessen's description of Schaller casts the mountaineer as a figure driven by a future goal that renders him insensitive to the joys of living in the present.

As hiking and climbing becomes more difficult, however, Matthiessen begins to recognise that it is he, rather than Schaller, who is the odd man out when it comes to maintaining equanimity in the mountains. At Jaljala Ridge, Schaller and the Sherpas and porters are all able to cross flooded streams by walking upright on fallen trees, but Matthiessen is forced to "hitch ignominiously across the worst of them on my backside" (2008, p. 46). Humiliated, he attempts to compensate for his lack of technical skill by adapting Buddhist practices to the task of mountaineering. At one point he tries to steel himself against his fear of heights through the Tibetan practice of *chöd*, or directly confronting that which he most fears. While walking along high narrow ridges, he pauses every so often to look down over the precipice in the hope that "hardening myself might make less scary some evil stretch of ledge in the higher mountains" (2008, p. 88). This effort is partially successful. Soon after taking up this practice he becomes comfortable enough at high altitude to experience the sense of flowing and moving mountains cited above. Yet Matthiessen's fears also persist and lead him to wonder about his oscillation between epiphany and doubt. Contemplating with dread a narrow ledge he must travel around the western cliffs of Phoksundo Lake, he asks himself: "What am I to make of these waves of timidity, this hope of continuity, when at other moments I feel free as the bharal on those heights, ready for wolf and snow leopard alike?" (2008, p. 144). The next day he is reduced to climbing much of this two-mile ledge on his hands and knees, at which point his humiliation and anger take a particularly revealing form. When Schaller remarks on the technical interest of the climb, Matthiessen considers pushing his friend off the cliff (2008, p. 146). Watching the fearless Sherpas and porters make their way along the ledge, Matthiessen sees in them the lightness he had hoped would characterise his own climbing: "On they come, staring straight ahead, as steadily and certainly as ants, yet seeming to glide with an easy, ethereal lightness, as if some sort of inner concentration was lifting them just off the surface of the ground" (2008, pp. 145–146). Later that day he wonders whether the remarkable agility of the Tibetans derives from the "Tantric discipline called *lung-gom*, which permits the adept to glide along with uncanny swiftness and certainty, even at night" (2008, p. 147). The possibility that these men are superior climbers *and* more accomplished Buddhists than Matthiessen is more than he can handle. When the Sherpas and porters demand extra rest before setting out the next morning, he is outraged and reflects that "[p]erhaps we should adopt the imperial methods of dealing with unruly Tibetans" (2008, p. 150). He goes so far as to cite a passage from A. Henry Savage Landor's *In the Forbidden Land* (1899) in which Landor kicks and beats a Tibetan man for contesting British claims on his country (2008, pp. 150–151).

Whitney argues that Matthiessen's romanticising of his Tibetan companions and his invocation of Landor cast *The Snow Leopard* as an "Orientalist travel chronicle" that caters to Western fantasies of imperial domination (2014). In Whitney's view Matthiessen was an earnest Buddhist and nature writer who knew better than to exoticise the East; but he depicted magical Tibetans and a fantasy of colonial discipline because "they are what the reader of this kind of text wants. It is the classical Orientalism Said delineated, the genre of Western conquest, at least subtextually" (2014). Whitney's charges of Orientalism are irrefutable; but I disagree that Matthiessen includes these passages out of conformity to perverse genre conventions. Instead, Matthiessen's violent Orientalist fantasy reflects perhaps the hardest lesson of Dōgen's practice-realisation: enlightenment is not separate from, but always intimately bound up with, delusion. As Dōgen reminds us: "Walking forward does not obstruct walking backward. Walking backward does not obstruct walking forward" (2010b, p. 155). Much as one might like to believe that enlightenment puts an end to selfishness, bigotry and hostility, it tends instead to heighten awareness of these constitutive elements of the self. Glossing Dōgen's representation of enlightenment as "radiant light", Kim observes: "The radiant light penetrates and unfolds the depths of delusion—in brief, human nature and the human condition—that have hitherto been unnoticed, unknown, or unfathomed by practitioners, who in turn become aware of their own emotional, existential, and moral anguishes, doubts, and ambiguities" (2007, p. 4). As the most egregious examples of Matthiessen's delusion, his fantasies of murdering Schaller and beating the Tibetans highlight the painful development of self-awareness that necessarily accompanies the dissolution of self which he experiences, at other moments, through communion with nature. At the same time these passages also suggest how enlightenment can overcome delusion even if it cannot eliminate it. By projecting his fantasy of "light climbing" onto the Tibetans, Matthiessen begins to separate himself from that fantasy and the belief that he can attain his spiritual and ecological goals without attention to the practice of mountaineering. His anger at the Sherpas the next morning also indicates his realisation that he is utterly dependent on them to reach Crystal Mountain – a realisation that angers him because it cuts through his notions of individualism and self-sufficiency. Here Matthiessen begins to intuit that the dissolution of self obtains not only in solitary moments of meditation among the elements, but also through the shared labours of others with whom one must work to achieve worldly and spiritual ends.

Conclusion: Mountaineering as Practice-Realisation

In *The Snow Leopard* Matthiessen never completely abandons his view of enlightenment as transcendent "lightness", but at one point he clearly perceives the unity of Dōgen's practice-realisation while climbing at Crystal Mountain:

> My foot slips on a narrow ledge: in that split second, as needles of fear pierce heart and temples, eternity intersects with present time. Thought and action are not different, and stone, air, ice, sun, fear, and self are one. What is exhilarating is to extend this acute awareness into ordinary moments, in the moment-by-moment experiencing of the lammergeier and the wolf, which, finding themselves at the center of things, have no need for any secret of true being. (2008, p. 245)

In sharp contrast to his recurring dreams of levitating above the mountain, here he achieves a new spiritual and ecological awareness by attending carefully to his climbing. He also recognises that it is practice itself, rather than concern for an abstract "true nature", that best prepares him to study and appreciate the animals he has come to observe. According to Wirth, the most radical aspect of Dōgen's ecological vision today may be its insistence on taking satisfaction in mundane practices that support global ecological initiatives. Commenting on efforts to curb pollution and cruelty created by industrial farming and fast food, Wirth observes: "If you cannot take the time to clean your own dishes and to learn to relish doing so, the forests, oceans, wetlands [...] will continue to languish" (2017, p. 22). Despite the power of Matthiessen's realisation while climbing, however, his insight, like each of those that precedes it, is momentary and quickly forgotten. While returning to Kathmandu he regards a Japanese mountaineering expedition as a modern intrusion on the natural beauty around him (2008, p. 284). He also continues to wrestle with his own attachment to transcendent awareness:

> As I walk along, my stave striking the ground, I leave the tragic sense of things behind; I begin to smile, infused with a sense of my own foolishness, with an acceptance of the failures of this journey as well as of its wonders [...]. I know that this transcendence will be fleeting, but while it lasts, I spring along the path as if set free; so light do I feel that I might be back in the celestial snows. (2008, p. 296)

Amused by his tendency to veer between epiphany and doubt, Matthiessen reverts, at this moment of acute self-awareness, to his long-held fantasy of lightness and easy travel. If enlightenment fails to overcome delusion in this instance, however, the form of *The Snow Leopard* continues to affirm "mountains walking" by depicting the progression and pitfalls that necessarily comprise Dōgen's practice-realisation.

Ultimately Matthiessen does not achieve either of the goals he sets for himself at the start of his journey: he never sees a snow leopard nor does he experience lasting spiritual transformation. Yet his quest can hardly be regarded a failure. Beyond the critical respect accorded *The Snow Leopard* since its publication, Schaller's and Matthiessen's recommendations were instrumental in the creation of Shey Phoksundo National Park, established in 1984 and still the largest National Park in Nepal. Despite Matthiessen's reservations, at the time of his trek, about the motives of mountain climbers, *The Snow Leopard* has inspired many to regard trekking and mountaineering as vital spiritual and ecological practices. Of course such enthusiasm is no guarantee that mountain spaces will not fall prey to destructive commercialism. As well-known mountaineer and Zen practitioner Yvon Chouinard observes, "The opposite of the Zen approach is climbing Everest if—like many a plastic surgeon or

CEO—you pay $80,000 and have Sherpas put all the ladders in place and 8,000 feet of fixed rope" (2019, p. 223). But since 1996 tourism activities in Shey Phoksundo National Park have been regulated in accordance with standards of "ecotourism" or sustainable tourism (Garver-Hume, 1998, p. 24) that aims to promote conservation while contributing economically to local communities. Of the numerous Inner Dolpo treks advertised as recreations of Matthiessen's and Schaller's 1973 journey, several are run by companies with strong commitments to environmental protection and preservation. In 2020 *The Nepali Times* featured an article on Tshiring Lhamu Lama, a researcher and conservationist born in Phoksundo who was inspired by Matthiessen's book to accompany Schaller when he retraced his original trek to Crystal Mountain in 2016 (Lama, 2020). Afterward she founded Snow Leopard Journeys, a trekking company that channels many of the profits of wildlife tourism to local herders who are deeply ambivalent about trekking and the protection of snow leopards who kill their yaks and sheep. Rooted in conservationist ideals and local economics, Tshiring Lhamu Lama's efforts reveal the ongoing relevance of Matthiessen's spiritual and ecological Zen message.

Bibliography

Adams, T. (2018) "Zen and the art of the following in your father's footsteps", *The Guardian*, 4 April [online]. Available at: https://www.theguardian.com/books/2018/apr/04/zen-following-fathers-footsteps-peter-matthiessen-snow-leopard-40-years (Accessed: 14 September 2020).

Allister, M. (2001) *Refiguring the Map of Sorrow: Nature Writing and Autobiography.* Charlottesville, VI: University of Virginia Press.

Campbell, S.E. (1988) "Science and Mysticism in the Himalayas: The Philosophical Journey of Peter Matthiessen and George Schaller", *Environmental Review* 12(2), pp. 127–142. Available at: https://www.jstor.org/stable/3984437 (Accessed: 5 August 2021).

Chouinard, Y. (2019) *Some Stories: Lessons from the Edge of Business and Sport.* Ventura, CA: Patagonia.

Devall, B. and Sessions, G. (1985) *Deep Ecology: Living as if Nature Mattered.* Layton, UT: Gibbs Smith.

Dōgen, E. (2010a) "Buddha Nature", in Tanahashi, K. (ed) *Treasury of the True Dharma Eye: Zen Master Dōgen's Shobo Genzo.* Boston, MA: Shambhala, pp. 234–259.

Dōgen, E. (2010b) "Mountains and Waters Sutra", in Tanahashi, Kazuaki (ed.) *Treasury of the True Dharma Eye: Zen Master Dōgen's Shobo Genzo.* Boston, MA: Shambhala, pp. 1541–1564.

Dowie, W. (1991) *Peter Matthiessen*. Boston, MA: Twayne.

Garver-Hume, J. (1998) "People in the Park: Reconciling Residents, Tourism, and Conservation in Shey-Phoksundo National Park, Nepal". Western Washington University Honors Program Senior Projects 142. Available at: https://cedar.www.edu./wwu_honors/142 (Accessed: 6 August 2021).

Isserman, M. and Weaver, S. (2008) *Fallen Giants: A History of Himalayan Mountaineering from the Age of Empire to the Age of Extremes*. New Haven, CT: Yale University Press.

Jenkins, M. (2000) "'Thinking Like a Mountain': Death and Deep Ecology in the Work of Peter Matthiessen", in Tallmadge, J. and Harrington, H. (eds) *Reading Under the Sign of Nature: New Essays in Ecocricitism*. Salt Lake City, UT: University of Utah Press, pp. 265–279.

Kim, H.J. (2004) *Eihei Dōgen: Mystical Realist*. Boston, MA: Wisdom.

Kim, H.J. (2007) *Dōgen on Meditation and Thinking: A Reflection on His View of Zen*. Albany, NY: State University of New York Press.

Lama, S.C. (2020) "Trekking to save Nepal's snow leopards", *Nepali Times* 23 October [online]. Available at: https://www.nepalitimes.com/banner/trekking-to-save-nepals-snow-leopards (Accessed: 6 August 2021).

Matthiessen, P. (1998 [1985]) *Nine-headed Dragon River: Zen Journals*. Boston, MA: Shambala.

Matthiessen, P. (2008 [1978]) *The Snow Leopard*. New York, NY: Penguin.

O'Connor, M.R. (2018) "Peter Matthiessen's 'The Snow Leopard' in the Age of Climate Change", *The New Yorker* 30 December [online]. Available at: https://www.newyorker.com/science/elements/peter-matthiessens-the-snow-leopard-in-the-age-of-climate-change (Accessed: 6 August 2021).

Oh, I. (2010) *Peter Matthiessen and Ecological Imagination*. New York, NY: Peter Lang.

Pirsig, R.M. (2005 [1974]) *Zen and the Art of Motorcycle Maintenance: An Inquiry into Values*. New York, NY: Harper.

Schaumann, C. (2020) *Peak Pursuits: The Emergence of Mountaineering in the Nineteenth Century*. New Haven, CT: Yale University Press.

Schwalm, H. (2016) "Literary Configurations of the Peripatetic", in Kilian, E. and Wolf, H. (eds) *Life Writing and Space*. Surrey: Ashgate, pp. 75–88.

Smith, S. and Watson, J. (2010) *Reading Autobiography: A Guide for Interpreting Life Narratives*. 2nd edn. Minneapolis, MN: University of Minnesota Press.

Snyder, G. (2000) "Blue Mountains Constantly Walking", in Kaza, S. and Kraft, K. (eds) *Dharma Rain: Sources of Buddhist Environmentalism*. Boston, MA: Shambhala, pp. 125–141.

Sponberg, A. (1997) "Green Buddhism and the Hierarchy of Compassion", in Tucker, M.E. and Williams, D.R. (eds) *Buddhism and Ecology: The Interconnection of Dharma and Deeds*. Cambridge, MA: Harvard University Press, pp. 351–376.

Whitney, J. (2014) "Imperial Methods: Peter Matthiessen's Orientalism", *Boston Review*, 7 May [online]. Available at: https://bostonreview.net/books-ideas/joel-whitney-matthiessen-snow-leopard-orientalism (Accessed: 5 August 2021).

Wirth, J. (2017) *Mountains, Rivers, and the Great Earth: Reading Gary Snyder and Dōgen in an Age of Ecological Crisis*. Albany, NY: State University of New York Press.

Chapter 14

Fatherhood, Emotional (Dis)Entanglements and Adventurous Masculinities

Ben Fogle on Everest

Paul Gilchrist

Going *Up*: The Everest Dream of an Accidental Adventurer

Two soft toys are held aloft by an outstretched arm from the summit of Everest. They belonged to Iona and Ludo, the young children of British broadcaster and adventurer Ben Fogle. This "most important photo", as Fogle described it on his *Instagram* account (17 May 2018), completed a personal mission and fulfilled a promise made to his children. As the bright orange carrot and hug-worn panda bear gazed out across the Everest massif, an unmasked Fogle tried to catch his breath in the rarefied atmosphere of the summit. He called his wife on a satellite telephone and, overwhelmed with emotion, told Marina, "It's really hard. It's the hardest thing I've ever done … I love you so much, I can't wait to get back. I think I'm done with mountains now" (CNN, 2018).

Fogle is no stranger to tough challenges. His early life was by all admission not academically accomplished and he was "positively allergic" to sport (Fogle, 2011, p. 13). He credits a gap year journey to Amazonia and Ecuador for turning around his fortune and igniting a passion for nomadic adventure (Fogle, 2018, 2020). In 2000 he took part in the BBC's *Castaway* programme, living for a year on the Hebridean island of Taransay in a journey of self-sufficiency and self-realisation (Dunn, 2006) that "created an unshakeable relationship with the wilderness" (Fogle, 2018, p. 44). As the breakout star from *Castaway*, Fogle landed a series of TV presenting roles, primarily fronting programmes on rural life, animals, wilderness lifestyles and adventure, and he continues to work in this area. Fogle classifies himself as an "accidental adventurer" (Fogle,

2011). For nearly two decades, his career has been punctuated by televised spectacles which fit within the genre of "celebrity-suffering" through extreme journeys of physical adventure, simultaneously raising money and garnering public exposure for charitable causes (Lim and Moufahim, 2015; Gilchrist, 2020). In 2005–2006 he partnered with British Olympic rower James Cracknell to complete the Atlantic Rowing Race, which was subsequently televised in the BBC series *Through Hell and High Water*. Fogle then accomplished the six-day Saharan ultramarathon the Marathon des Sables and teamed up with Cracknell once again in 2008 for the Amundsen Omega 3 South Pole Race, competing against five other teams to cross the Antarctic Plateau. This aired on BBC in summer 2009 as *On Thin Ice*.

Climbing Everest was the big one. Fogle had dreamt of summiting Everest when as a young boy he saw a picture of the mountain in *National Geographic* magazine (Fogle, 2018, p. 13). The opportunity to climb Everest came in 2016 via Anything is Possible, a charitable foundation established by Princess Haya Bint Al Hussein, daughter of King Hussein of Jordan, who had attended the Dorset-based boarding school Bryanston with Fogle in the early 1990s. Fogle teamed up with former Olympic cycling champion Victoria Pendleton and they were accompanied by world-renowned mountaineer Kenton Cool, who was making his thirteenth ascent of Everest (Gilchrist, 2020). The celebrity cachet of Fogle and Pendleton meant that their Everest journey gathered widespread media coverage, documented on social media too via *Instagram* posts. The British press, in particular the *Daily Express*, which published Fogle's weekly Everest Diary, remained intrigued by their unlikely pairing. Award-winning photographer and mountaineer Mark Fisher filmed the climb for a CNN documentary *The Challenge* which aired in June 2018. Fogle subsequently penned an account of the journey, *Up: My Life's Journey to the Top of Everest*, published by William Collins, an imprint of HarperCollins.

Up was Fogle's tenth book. His previous books have included best-sellers and popularly acclaimed accounts covering his adventurous travels. *English: A Story of Marmite, Queuing and Weather* (2017) offered Fogle's reflections on English national character and he has also written on those staples of English middle-class respectability: the Labrador and Land Rover (Fogle, 2015, 2017). His accounts of the Atlantic and Antarctic crossings were co-written with James Cracknell and provide a dual perspective on key moments in the planning, training and eventual success of the endeavours (Cracknell and Fogle, 2006; Cracknell and Fogle, 2009). *Up* can be placed in the wider body of autobiographical narrative (Smith and Watson, 2002). It merges the genres of celebrity autobiography and climbing memoir in its combination of biographical details and personal anecdote, key life events, meditations on vocational and family dynamics, access to an interior monologue of doubts and concerns, and general account of high-altitude expeditioning (Lee, 2014; Yelin, 2016; Rak, 2021). However, *Up* is written and marketed as dual-authored as it includes passages written by Fogle's Austrian-born wife, Marina. Their contributions are unequal. The central focus is on Ben's personal experience of preparation, departure, travel, performance and return, and the narrative arc largely follows the literary conventions of the heroic journey (Campbell, 2008 [1949]). Ben intersperses his reflections with wider concerns that have influenced his thinking and motivations – the therapeutic value of being in wilderness, the appeal of alternative lifestyles, the nature of risk in society – but the primary focus is upon communicating the lived experience of the Everest quest. Marina contributes just over 10 percent of the text, echoing the themes developed by Ben and offering her own reflections on living with her husband's Everest dream and the family's role in supporting Ben's adventurous desires. There are paratextual elements too (Genette, 1991) – acknowledgements; recognition of sponsors and charitable causes; and reportage on the environmental condition of Everest as part of Fogle's role as UN Patron of the Wilderness. Nigerian writer Ben Okri's poem "Everest" appears towards the end, and we learn this was read aloud by Ben Fogle on Everest, establishing an intertextual continuity of romanticism and mountains (Bainbridge, 2020; Hollis and König, 2021) which burnishes Fogle's self-identification as a "romantic dreamer" (Fogle, 2018, p. 24). These fringe elements beyond the main text underscore and extend the authorial commentaries, offering a zone of transaction for readers to better understand the collaborative effort and the benefits of the endeavour.

This chapter employs literary methods of analysis through a close textual reading of *Up* to determine its cultural meanings and contextually informed discursive subjectivities. Fogle makes possible an analysis of the phenomenon and literary form of the "celebrity-climber", a task made more complex as Fogle is constituted by and contributes to multiple representative subject positions grounded in his vocation as a broadcaster, positionality as a father and husband, and interpolation as belonging to a romantic tradition of the adventurous traveller. The chapter reveals the ways in which these subjectivities are encountered during Fogle's Everest challenge and reflected upon through *Up*. Fogle's complex subject positionings, I will show, are consolidated and accommodated by his wife and co-author whose contributions to the text provide access to the emotional repercussions of an Everest quest. Furthermore, I argue that Fogle's image as doting father and loving husband is strengthened in contrast to the military masculinity performed and communicated by another British climber on Everest during the same 2018 climbing season, the former UK Special Forces operative and reality TV star, Ant Middleton. The analysis interweaves Fogle's negotiation of his celebritised "father-mountaineer" subjectivity and its emotional entanglements with Middleton's rearticulation of a heroic militarised masculinity and its emotional disentanglements. I will argue that these negotiations and positionings provoked by Middleton's presence on Everest are informed by their respective approaches to risk and fear, their media personas, and are shaped too by the sub-genres of celebrity autobiographical narrative and reality TV that they produce and work within. *Up* is therefore read not as a historically accurate account, for this can never be established, but as a text, focusing on the narratives and discourses established by its authors. The insights into fatherhood, emotion and adventurous masculinities are embellished with consideration of selected press materials, Middleton's contemporaneously published memoir and the documentaries that followed the celebrity climbers on Everest.

Manning *Up*: Bodies, Mindsets and Adventurous Masculinities

The quest commences. Chapter 2 of *Up* entitled "Preparations" sees Fogle, Pendleton and Cool engaged in training exercises in Bolivia, developing their climbing skills and honing their team dynamics. The chapter prefigures themes and events that would play out on Everest. Fogle emphasises the suffering and exhaustion that comes with climbing high peaks and the need for endurance and a positive mental attitude. Frustrations with Pendleton begin to emerge. We learn she is a camping virgin, vegan, and when she faltered near the summit of Bolivian peak Illimani (6,438m), only metres from the top, Fogle and Cool are "incredulous". Pendleton's "irrational" decision-making is explained as resulting from insufficient food consumption for the task at hand (Fogle, 2018, p. 27). Yet, Fogle also sees concerns ahead given Pendleton's oxygen saturation levels and inability to complete the training challenges both in Bolivia and Nepal (Fogle, 2018, pp. 27 & 30). Fogle observes Pendelton's gnawing self-doubt. Compared to his childhood dream to conquer Everest, he labels her motivations "slightly more rudderless" (Fogle, 2018, p. 34). Fogle's approach by implication remains true: to fulfil romantic dreams and Everest quests one must demonstrate capacities to endure. Doubts surface over Pendleton's suitability as a climbing companion. Her motivations to climb Everest were more to do with a post-Olympic exorcism of being told what to do born from the years of disciplining performance management exacted by British Cycling (Fogle, 2018, pp. 27 & 155). She had been, in the words of Fogle, "institutionalised" by the training regime of the Olympic performance cycle and was now, troublingly for Fogle and Cool, asserting a post-Olympic independence of mind that could prove deadly on Everest (Fogle, 2018, p. 153; Fogle, 2020, p. 211; see also, Gilchrist, 2020). As will become apparent, the qualities that Fogle had honed through his years of televised adventuring and wilderness survival valorise a masculine ideal of self-reliance. As Davidson writes, the genre of survival television teaches its contenders that "'Real' men…do not need to rely on technological shortcuts or intercommunal support; they are able to face the full force of nature without mediation" (Davidson, 2020, p. 480). Pendleton was able to cope with the velodrome but to deal with the unpredictability of mountains required a positive self-belief (Fogle, 2018, p. 31; Fogle, 2020, pp. 216–218), not "performance loathing" and an "Eeyore-like pessimism" (Fogle, 2018, p. 154).

The Everest climb would realise Fogle's anxieties. Pendleton is evacuated from the mountain suffering from low levels of oxygen saturation. She had proven her determination in making it to Camp 2 (6,400m), but her physiological inability to cope with the hypoxic conditions of high altitude meant that the team would experience 'Different Endings', the title to Chapter 9. Several chapters of *Up* work through the narrative conventions of Himalayan mountaineering ascent in reverentially detailing the power of nature and the risks posed to the remaining all-male team (Purtschert, 2018). These are experiences common to many Everest expedition accounts: the nerve-racking trial of passing the Khumbu Icefall and its deadly seracs and yawning crevasses; thundering electrical storms higher up; and a mountain that was ogre-like and seemingly alive. An assortment of fears are confided: the threat of oblivion through avalanche, lightning strike, oxygen depletion, or misstep; the threat of life-altering injury through frostbite. Fogle's body encounters the discomforts of the extreme environment and the mundane hardships of camp: sleep deprivation, frozen clothes and defecating into plastic bags. As if to underline his difference to Pendleton, Fogle writes that he drew upon experiences of previous close-shaves with death to quell the negative voices encountered on Everest. He remembers confronting crocodiles in Botswana and surviving a mid-Atlantic capsize (Fogle, 2018, p. 120). This is more than the endurance shown by the average Everester; the affordances of a television career and the incidents of "celebrity suffering" (Lim and Moufahim, 2015) have endowed Fogle with hyperauthentic masculine reserves which can be released on Everest (Alexander and Woods, 2019).

The 2018 Everest climbing season saw an especially long period of eleven straight days of calm weather which enabled a record 807 climbers to reach the summit (BBC, 2019). Amongst their number was another celebrity-climber: Ant Middleton. An ex-soldier and former member of the UK Special Forces' (UKSF) Special Boat Service, Middleton found fame in 2015 fronting the British reality television series *SAS: Who Dares Wins* (SASWDW) (Middleton, 2019). The series simulates the UKSF selection process with ex-soldiers training civilians through gruelling physical and mental trials. The programme has proven to be a successful format, with over a million viewers and has spawned a celebrity spin-off version. Middleton was hired as one of the Directing Staff on the programme, part of a team of instructors drawn from the UKSF who now subject contestants to a Spartan version of soldiering built around the individual performance of "no pain no gain, mind over matter, training is hell" (Pears, 2022; see also, Champion, 2016). Middleton and his co-stars have published best-selling books within the sub-genre of military chronicles and special forces confessionals detailing their traumatic early lives, the special forces selection process and dangerous operations (Middleton, 2018; Billington, 2019). Their memoirs articulate a model of military masculinity which has fed the mythology of the tough elite troopers (Woodward and Jenkings, 2018; Pears, 2022).

Ant Middleton's presence on Everest was a cause of concern for the Fogles. Ben Fogle was hyper-aware of the fleeting nature of stardom. As a freelance broadcaster and media personality he was conscious that changes in TV commissioner or viewers' tastes could leave him unemployed. "The vulnerability of a TV presenter cannot be underestimated", he pleas, underlining his status as a precarious labourer (Fogle, 2018, p. 12). Middleton's Everest challenge was supported by energy supplement brand Berocca and Channel 4, which broadcast a film of the climb in October 2018 as a one-hour documentary "Extreme Everest with Ant Middleton" (Middleton, 2019; Channel 4, 2022). Middleton's presence on the mountain was a challenge to the publicity value of Fogle's Everest climb and added extra pressure. Both had similar filming arrangements, commissioned by major television networks to produce a documentary of their experiences using single cameramen operators to record their journeys. Both had harboured childhood dreams of making the summit. Both had employed the services of the Seattle-based mountain guide company Madison Mountaineering to support their summit attempts, sharing camps, mess tents, oxygen supplies and Sherpas. And now Fogle faced the "humiliation of being out-summited" (Fogle, 2018, p. 165). Marina's response was one of concern and exasperation. She felt that the presence of Middleton would diminish the value of their media contracts, with the *Daily Telegraph* primed to publish a summit photo (Fogle, 2018, p. 179); the competition might lead Fogle into poor decision-making and "summit fever", a compulsion to reach the summit at all costs which had been credited as the human failing that led to the high-profile 1996 Everest tragedy (Elmes and Barry, 1999; Palmer, 2002). "Having a competitor at your heels might well inspire resolve, bravery and persistence, but it might also spur Ben on to make foolish decisions. I cursed bloody Ant Middleton for being there" (Fogle, 2018, p. 212).

Some of Ben Fogle's fears, however, were allayed on the journey to Base Camp. Word had spread among the multinational trekkers and hikers that a TV personality was in their midst (Fogle, 2018, p. 68). Fogle's regular updates to his social media accounts meant that not only his TV fans could follow his progress, but so could the hordes of tourists making their way to Base Camp. Fogle understood that his fame provided the opportunity to attempt Everest and being recognised was comforting. "It brought familiarity to an unfamiliar landscape. There was something rather reassuring about people stopping to wish us luck and to take a photo with us along the trail" (Fogle, 2018, p. 68). These same mountain tourists posed problems for Ant Middleton. Used to working off-grid and in the shadows, Middleton detoured from the well-worn trekking route to avoid nauseating retired couples completing the Everest trail (Middleton, 2019, p. 92). Middleton was exasperated with the extent of mountain tourism on Everest. Scenes from "Extreme Everest" show his frustrations as he remonstrates with a climber whose Bambi-like inexperience on an ice climb was causing a dangerous bottleneck on the mountain. Plain-speaking and direct, he tells the tourist: "You shouldn't be on the mountain. If you can't even get up that, what makes you think you can get up there?" (Channel 4, 2018). Middleton reads the abilities of the novice climbers through the lens of his military training and the contestant selection process of *SASWDW*. They would not pass muster. Not only did they lack physical ability, strength, and self-reliance, they lacked too the discipline to acknowledge their own limits and the dangers they posed to the collective (Pears, 2022). Middleton's own Everest memoir, *The Fear Bubble*, developed the critique and labelled the naïve and inexperienced tourists "Mr and Mrs Maybe" (Middleton, 2019, pp. 166–167).

The Fear Bubble shows Middleton's journey from thinking Everest would be "just a holiday, really. A camping trip" and a "challenge to tame that warrior ghost inside me", to gaining a respect for the mountain through his embodied experience of high-altitude climbing risk (Middleton, 2019, pp. 28 & 32). Whereas Fogle remained wedded to the expert guidance of Kenton Cool, Middleton suspected non-indigenous commercial guides would be ultra-cautious, not keen on the negative publicity that may accrue from dead or injured clients (Middleton, 2019, p. 77). Middleton preferred to set the pace and call the shots. Mountain tourists would be avoided by taking the earliest possibility to ascend in the summit window, literally on the heels of the Sherpa fixing teams. His Sherpa guide, Dawa Phinjo Lama, he rationalised in a familiar refrain of environmental determinism, "would be more game. After all, [Sherpas] live close to the mountain…They'd known the mysterious lump of ice and rock, and its shifting, deadly moods for thousands of years. It was in their blood" (Middleton, 2019, p. 77). The trials Everest posed were part and parcel of the adventure: crack on. "Get it done" (Middleton, 2019, p. 87). To coin the motto of the SBS, Everest would be won "By Strength and Guile". Middleton privileged mind over matter: no dwelling on near-misses from avalanches; high winds and electric storms were "exciting shit"; feeling frostbite in his feet, Middleton half-quipped, "I could always get fake toes" (Middleton, 2019, pp. 265 & 279). Ant Middleton's climbing bravado reifies the "super soldier" image of the special forces; "stronger, faster, tougher, harder, better and more resilient than normal people" (Pears, 2022, p. 74). Unlike *Up*, which has several pages devoted to Middleton's climb and time spent in his company, Fogle is not mentioned in *The Fear Bubble*. Dawa and Ed were the capable companions who earn Middleton's respect through jointly surviving the trials of the Everest operation in a demarcation of military brotherhood (Middleton, 2019, pp. 318 & 343). One can't help but think that Fogle's absence implies Middleton groups him with the tourists he was trying to avoid. Everest would be a transformational and life-affirming event for both men, but Middleton's account revels in a potent gendered imagery that rearticulates a militarised hypermasculinity.

Ups and Downs: Emotional (Dis)Entanglements on Everest

Climbing Everest was an embodied adventure, but it meted out other types of challenge. Emotional spectres and psychological fears were to be confronted. Four years prior to Everest the Fogles had suffered a stillbirth. Willem Fogle was lost 33 weeks into the pregnancy. Whereas Marina had grieved openly, Ben "held it together" and internalised the grief. Panic attacks, social anxiety and reclusiveness followed (Fogle, 2018, p. 184). Fogle was haunted by the loss and confides to readers that he felt Willem's presence on Everest. At the daunting Lhotse Face, en route to the South Col of Everest, Fogle gained in confidence and purpose as the presence of Willem helped overcome a sense of solitude (Fogle, 2018, p. 186). When he reached the summit on 16 May he whispered a "thank you" to Willem, "the words disappearing into the ether" (Fogle, 2018, p. 216). Fogle's connection with Willem on Everest was not simply a solitary processing of grief; rather Willem emerges as deeply implicated in the vital experience of living and is crucial for the continued production of Ben Fogle's adventurous subjectivity. Throughout *Up* Ben and Marina speak in unison about the importance of risk-taking to a life worth living. Willem is credited as a catalyst for the Everest adventure, the moving preface to the book foregrounding the impact of this event. The injunction to live life more brightly is returned to in several places. Ben implores, "without risk we cannot grow. We cannot improve. We cannot learn. We cannot experience. Without some form of risk, we are in danger of never really living. Can we ever really be ourselves if we don't take risks?" (Fogle, 2018, p. 135). Marina concurs: "a life with no risk is a life not worth living…you don't become so risk averse that it stops allowing you to have any fun" (Fogle, 2018, p. 137). Willem is given a legacy in emboldening Ben and encouraging Ludo and Iona – and all of us – to go in search of risk and adventure. The final words of *Up* hone this message: "Don't be slaves to conformity. Risk a little. Because without it, you can't live, love or experience" (Fogle, 2018, p. 250). In her seminal work *Ghostly Matters*, sociologist Avery Gordon writes of haunting as an affective process,

"Being haunted draws us affectively, sometimes against our will and always a bit magically into the structure of feeling of a reality we come to experience, not as cold knowledge, but as a transformative recognition" (Gordon, 2008, p. 8). What emerges from Fogle's Everest experience and subsequent narrative of loss is an embodied relationship to Willem that operates through and across cognition, affect and intention (Dragojlovic, 2015). Risk-taking is a way of honouring the potentiality of Willem. The agentic modality of journeying to the extreme moves the Fogles from the private grief of traumatic loss to a hauntingly public instruction to "climb your own Everest", the teary message Fogle delivers from the summit.

Death stalked the mountain in other ways. In the assessment of historian Jonathan Westaway, Everest is a "mortuary landscape" and climbers need to negotiate, both literally and emotionally, the proximity to dead bodies and the prospect of death (Westaway, 2019, 2022; see also, Ortner, 1997). Kenton Cool finds a dead body of a Sherpa at the Lhotse Face. Half the head is missing and Cool is left deeply affected by the experience of recovering the body. It is assumed the death was a freak accident, the unfortunate Sherpa struck by a falling piece of ice or rock (Fogle, 2018, p. 128). No critique is offered by Fogle here of the risks to indigenous labour by commercialised mountain tourism, the unnamed Sherpa is simply a victim of nature. Peter Bayers makes a pointed observation on the complicity of Western climbers in these tragedies. "Sherpas…are useful to Western masculine identity not only for their cultural 'raw' materials but also for their bodies; in the process of constructing their masculinity, climbers lay waste to families and friends as little more than discarded commodities" (Bayers, 2003, p. 139). The Himalayan Database recorded that since 1921 and as of 2018, there had been 295 lives lost on Everest, a third of whom were Sherpas. Fogle offered more sober reflection on the impacts of mountaineering accidents earlier in the book as the team first encountered the dozens of stone cairn memorials on the Thukla Pass on the route to Base Camp. "I thought about the families who had mourned those close to them. The families that had waved goodbye to their loved ones, just as I had mine" (Fogle, 2018, p. 74). In perhaps his most critical assessment of mountain tourism in *Up*, Fogle contemplated a memorial to a lost Sherpa and considered their death "especially unfair" as were it not for the "steady stream of dreamers and hopefuls like myself that were drawn to the romance of summiting" Everest the death would not have occurred (Fogle, 2018, p. 74). Contemplating the memorials was "sobering" and produced a wave of doubt (Fogle, 2018, p. 75). "Why was I doing this? Who's to say I wouldn't join these romantics who had lost their lives in the pursuit of their dreams? What made me any different?" (Fogle, 2018, p. 75). What is interesting about these reflections is not just the emotional scars that mourning families must bear (Ortner, 1997) but the point of relatability that is forged between the dead Sherpa and Fogle the Everest neophyte. In their study of perceptions of risk and death experienced by trekkers in the Mount Everest Region, Mu and Nepal found that memorial spaces in the Everest region can be read very differently depending on the intent and prior experience of adventure tourists. Less experienced trekkers generally feel less threatened by the deaths of mountaineers, whereas more experienced trekkers and serious climbers find points of relatability (Mu and Nepal, 2016). For Ben Fogle that point of relatability was one of shared values. Fogle reads the memorials as a final destination for romantic dreamers. This both places him in a heroic tradition but also imposes a universalising cultural ideal that homogenises the motivational drivers of other climbers and in so doing negates more critical reflections concerning the exploitative practices and mortal risks that have derived from Himalayan climbing and adventure tourism.

The ascent of Everest produced other emotional dynamics, which played out high up on the mountain. The CNN documentary presents an exhausted and emotionally drained Fogle at Camp 4 (8,000m). Ben explains to readers that emotional fragility is a physiological response to high altitude (Fogle, 2018, p. 91). Scientific studies have identified altered mood and heightened emotionality under extreme high-altitude hypoxic conditions. Anticipatory emotions congruent with raised cortisol levels can produce beneficial effects in terms of dealing with anxieties and nervousness of a hard climbing day ahead (Aguilar et al., 2018). Yet, worsening states of mood linked to tension and fatigue are also symptoms of cognitive dysfunction and are possible signs of Acute Mountain Sickness and High Altitude Cerebral Oedema (Aquino Lemos et al., 2012). Close surveillance of emotional states is paramount for climber safety. Both Fogle and Cool experienced a swirl of emotions at Camp 4. Fogle writes: "The combination of altitude, exhaustion, worry, fear and stress had worn us all down" (Fogle, 2018, p. 181). Thoughts of family came to the fore as the team sat out a storm and waited for news of Ant Middleton. Middleton completed his mission two days before Fogle would stand on the summit. However, in waiting for the summit to clear of other mountain tourists so he could enjoy a solitary crowning moment, his exit from the mountain was slowed by a bottleneck at the Hilary Step and worsening weather conditions which affected the descent of more inexperienced climbers, in one case with fatal consequences (Middleton, 2019, pp. 305–318). At Camp 4, Fogle turned to Cool and raised his wrists, showing the names of his children scrawled onto his thermal jacket. "That's what it's about, and yours, OK?" (CNN, 2018). Even experienced mountain guides were party to emotional distress. Long hours spent in close quarters gave opportunity for teary stories to be recounted of friends lost to mountaineering accidents (Fogle, 2018, pp. 91–92). The value of this was not lost. In some interesting scenes during "Extreme Everest with Ant Middleton", cameraman Ed Wardle, perhaps cognisant of the vulnerabilities induced by high altitude, pushes Middleton to open up about the death of his father when he was five, a formative event that changed the course of Middleton's life. Such examples reveal high-altitude camps as more than sanctuaries for the weary summiteer; they are emotional spaces where climbers deal with loss and separation, ghostly pasts and anticipated ghostly futures.

The mediation of emotions suggests a managed vulnerability cognisant of their media persona and display of self (Evans, 2009). Passages of *Up* reveal Fogle's distress at the possibility of Ant Middleton's death and having to confront his wife and family on return. The relief shown when Middleton returns to Camp battered and bruised from his ordeal suggest a situational comradeship for both former military men (Fogle was also a former Royal Navy Reservist) (Fogle, 2018, pp. 180–182). Not so for Middleton. *The Fear Bubble* makes no direct reference to the presence of Fogle or even Pendleton on Everest. His comradeship is drawn more tightly. Middleton's brothers-in-arms are his Sherpas and cameraman Ed Wardle, all of whom have demonstrated their hypermasculine credentials to Middleton by gaining the summit. This is not to say that Middleton is a man without feeling. His summit moment also involved a phone call to his wife and heartfelt expressions of love. On arrival at Camp 2 Middleton unexpectedly burst out crying, the first time his wife had heard him do so. But it was purposefully away from the camera's gaze (Middleton, 2019, pp. 281 & 322). Fogle's bouts of crying are caught on camera. They are shown to be an authentic part of his being. Both men place their emotional expressivity within the contexts of the climb; crying is an acceptable part of its trials (see, MacArthur and Shields, 2015). However, Middleton maintains an operational alertness as a soldier on deployment, blocking the "bittersweet sadness" and emotional distraction of separation from his family (Middleton, 2019, p. 69). He is much more self-conscious about the power of tears to disrupt his hypermasculine image. Explicit public displays of emotion are still taboo.

Fogle's image as a sensitive family man permeates his writing. He consistently foregrounds his identity as a father, frequently referring to his children and projects an image as a loving paternal presence. The Fogles, pictured smiling and embracing their children on their doorstep, are the prototypical model of the traditional heterosexual nuclear family. While Ben Fogle's media career affords opportunities for travel which maintain older gender boundaries and divisions of labour within family life (akin to Middleton here), his emotive descriptions of his family show a softer masculinity of paternal care and provision, maintaining commitment and involvement in his children's lives (King, 2015). The age of their children was an important factor, young enough to be "oblivious to the magnitude of what lay ahead. They were still in the sweet spot of innocence, glorious naivety", writes Ben (Fogle, 2018, p. 39). Fogle negotiates his separation from his family in a number of ways on Everest. Of course, there is the tearful summit phone call to his wife (Fogle, 2018, p. 208). But we learn too that Fogle brings to Everest several material reminders of his family: a shark's tooth necklace given by his son to be worn to the summit, and Marina has packed 50 envelopes containing photographs and scribbled messages from the children, one for each day of the trip (Fogle, 2018, pp. 40 & 90–92). Ben maintains an involvement in his children's lives, sending private video messages from camp and broadcasts to a school assembly live from Base Camp to discuss the environmental conditions on Everest. Marina cherishes Ben's thoughtfulness for inviting her recently retired father to join him at Base Camp (Fogle, 2018, p. 51). When his father-in-law struggles to cope with the freezing and hypoxic conditions of Base Camp, Ben shows his caring sensibilities by holding his hand as he vomits and helps him to settle into a sleeping bag (Fogle, 2018, p. 92). The feeling when his father-in-law is evacuated back to Kathmandu is "like cutting my final tie to Marina and my family" (Fogle, 2018, p. 96).

The scale of the challenge raised dilemmas for Marina. In a pre-trip interview, Ben Fogle spoke of knowing the dangers and emphasised placing self-preservation over pride. "Because I've already achieved other physical challenges in my life I don't think I'm going to be blinded by what is often described as summit fever, whereby people become so obsessed with reaching the top of Everest that they do it to the detriment of everything else", he told a reporter (Midgeley, 2018). Fogle evoked polar explorer Sir Ernest Shackleton's line "Better a live donkey than a dead lion". He would not risk his life for some false bravado, he assured. Marina contemplates her fears over "summit fever" in Chapter 11, a counterpoint to the chapter's title of "Positivity". She recalls the stories of Alison Hargreaves on K2 and Rob Hall on Everest; prominent examples of experienced climbers taken by this all-consuming desire (Frohlick, 2006; Osborne, 2022; Krakauer, 1997). "Ben had promised me that he wouldn't succumb to summit fever; he had too much to lose, he insisted. But then so did Rob" (Fogle, 2018, p. 179). For all these assurances and despite Ben's insistence on adopting Shackletonian fortitude in turning back when the risks were too high, arguably this didn't quite manifest. At 8,500m his oxygen regulator fails, potentially imperilling his life. The team are carrying no spares. Kenton Cool requests Ming Dorjee Sherpa hand over his oxygen bottle and regulator, sacrificing his chance to summit and the professional recognition it would bring, though as compensation Fogle offers to pay Ming Dorjee's summit bonus. Fogle pushes on upwards. A second oxygen regulator fails close to the summit and Fogle starts to panic. Kenton Cool surrenders his mask and oxygen in the hope that spares could be found amongst the teams assembled at the summit. Fogle pushes on upwards and fulfils his childhood dream (Fogle, 2018, pp. 195–200). The hierarchies of the client-guide relationship are made all too apparent.

With no news of summit success, Marina rued over the consequences if her husband failed to reach the summit. She composed an email – reproduced in *Up* – to remind Ben of his achievements and to request that he not bring home any sense of disappointment. A list of everyday parental chores is given by Marina who has stoically kept the home going during the absences of her husband. To top it all Marina has endured too, she tells Ben, frequent innuendo posed by journalists at *The Daily Mail* over unfounded suggestions of an affair between Fogle and Pendleton (Shakespeare, 2018a, 2018b, 2018c). The message is not sent (Fogle, 2018, pp. 213–214). It helped to release the anxiety Marina was harbouring. Her reflections alert us to the fact that the psychological strain of extreme adventurous travel is not confined to trekkers and climbers (Pomfret, 2012; Doran, 2016; Wantono and McKercher, 2020): it permeates the domestic sphere, the wider family and especially worried partners who stay at home to care for dependent children.

To much relief, Ben Fogle returned to a hero's welcome. His children had handmade a colourful celebratory banner and the gesture was gratefully received. Yet, Ben struggled to readjust. There were corporeal and emotional legacies of climbing Everest to confront. Ben was able to heal his body over time, but experienced post-expedition depression, which he likened to a solder returning to civilian life (Fogle, 2018, p. 231). His process of re-entry and reunion was handled sensitively and the Fogles communicate the importance of family and home to post-expedition recovery (Doyle and Peterson, 2005). Marina had been there before. She gave him space and time to heal. His colleague, Victoria Pendleton, had fared much worse, suffering clinical depression and contemplating suicide. We are later to learn that her Everest journey had coincided with a period of marital strain and was likely to have catalysed a divorce from her husband (Daily Telegraph, 2019; Gilchrist, 2020).

The narrative arc of the heroic monomyth is completed in the final chapter. Fogle crosses the threshold between heroic and everyday life and accepts, as Joseph Campbell writes, "the passing joys and sorrows, banalities, and noisy obscenities of life". He eventually settles to write his Everest account and the moral lessons of the adventure are foremost in his thoughts. The encouragement to "Climb your own Everests" the book ends upon champions a "freedom to live". Fogle emerges as the "father-mountaineer", master of two worlds, the lessons from Everest translated for would-be risk-takers. The adventurous mask is then put aside to await the next adventure. Fogle would no doubt approve of Campbell's assessment of the successful return from a heroic journey: "The hero is the champion of things becoming, not of things become" (Campbell, 2008, pp. 189 & 209).

Conclusion

Ultimately, *Up* and *The Fear Bubble* confirm the resilience of conquest narratives of Everest – escaping the conventions of modern society, experiencing moments of sublime revelation and homosocial pleasures, forming new friendships and deepening bonds of brotherhood, and testing the moral fibre of the inner self through trials of self-reliance (Ortner, 1997, p. 139). The texts – and the Everest documentaries that followed Fogle and Middleton – do not move us far from Julie Rak's opinion that mountaineering nonfiction is dominated by accounts, both visual and textual, that remain stubbornly wedded to the archetypal white male heroic adventure story and its discourses of heroic masculinity (Rak, 2021, pp. 5–6). However, a further element can now be added. The hyperauthentic masculinities on display from these erstwhile "celebrity-climbers" implicate reality television in this story of mastery. Both men consciously act within the boundaries of their media personas, which pattern the representations and performances of their adventurous masculinities. Their emotional entanglements – or disentanglements – are constituted through the framing of their celebritised discursive subjectivities as "father-mountaineer" and "hard man" special forces veteran.

Fogle strikes an important point when he writes, "Every person who summits Everest will experience powerfully unique sentiments, often products of their own unique lives" (Fogle, 2018, p. 208). With the growth in extreme tourism on Everest following the granting of evermore climbing permits, we might expect these powerfully unique sentiments to be mediated by the hundreds of challengers and summiteers, feeding the voluminous cultural texts of Everest (Birrell, 2007). Each climber will bring their own situated knowledges, personhood, needs and desires, and their complex web of relations to the mountain. Some may even choose the path of familial disconnection as climbing goals come into view. Various positionalities will shape how Everest is done, the narratives that emerge, and will implicate how Everest is experienced. What we learn from the Fogles, Pendleton, Cool, Middleton, their cameramen and Sherpas, is that Everest is spatially promiscuous. It is a site of colonial logic and touristic dreams, a space to both escape and feed the cult of celebrity, a gendered space of survivalist resolve, and a space of fear and desire. The benefit of reading *Up* and listening to its dual voices is that Everests' emotional spaces are laid bare, both on the mountainous front line and at home. Marina's apprehensive moods betray private sensitivities and practised moral support. Fogle's and Middleton's vulnerabilities are made visible as they connect with ghostly remains and haunting presences and confront the shadow of death and their own fear bubbles. Their accounts offer insight into the emotional entanglements and disentanglements that occur for these seasoned white English adventurers, but fundamentally different types of men.

Whether *Up* could pave the way for a rebalancing of the expedition account in ways that are sensitive to the emotional, familial and domestic consequences of pursuing Everest dreams remains a moot point. Fogle's was a "negotiated journey" (Doran, 2016) that understood a life of adventure came with private costs. Global telecommunications made possible an involvement and synchronous emotional presence in his children's lives, but Fogle acknowledged it was Marina that carried the burdens of parenthood. The penultimate paragraph in the acknowledgements underscores the pact they have made:

> Thanks to Marina, my heroine. While I am away, Marina is the one who runs the family. You are the glue that keeps us together when we are apart. My rock, without you I would be half the person I am. While adventure might be in my blood, it is you that makes me, me. You complete me. You have always allowed me to be the person I am. I may have been the one to stand on the roof of the world but it was a true team effort and you were there too. (Fogle, 2018, p. 269)

What emerges from Fogle's Everest quest is an articulation of the social value of the high-altitude climber to the process of childrearing through the demonstration and subsequent advocacy of a life of adventure. Marina is complicit with this choice as a supportive spouse and though she endured nights of worry and anguish, she concludes "that those who are privileged enough to test themselves in the way that Ben did, to push their boundaries to see what is humanly possibly and to reflect on life and what each part, person or experience means to us, have an obligation to share it" (Fogle, 2018, p.228). It is telling that the post-Everest publications of both Fogle and Middleton have entered this terrain. *Inspire* (2020) written during the covid lockdowns, is an anthology of Fogle's life lessons from his various adventures. *Zero Negativity* by Ant Middleton sees the military man turn positivity guru (Middleton, 2020). Further adventures into the world of mental health and wellbeing seem to await these family men and conquerors of Everest.

Bibliography

Aguilar, R., Martínez, C. and Alvero-Cruz, J.R. (2018) "Cortisol awakening response and emotion at extreme altitudes on Kangchenjunga", *International Journal of Psychophysiology*, 131, pp. 81–88.

Alexander, S.M. and Woods, K. (2019) "Reality television and the doing of hyperauthentic masculinities", *The Journal of Men's Studies*, 27(2), pp. 149–168.

Aquino Lemos, V.D., Attunes, K.M., Santos, R.V.T., Lira, F.S., Tufik, S. and De Mello, M.T. (2012) "High altitude exposure impairs sleep patterns, mood and cognitive functions", *Psychophysiology*, 49, pp. 1298–1306.

Bainbridge, S. (2020) *Mountaineering & British Romanticism: The Literary Cultures of Climbing, 1770–1836*. Oxford: Oxford University Press.

Bayers, P.L. (2003) *Imperial Ascent. Mountaineering, Masculinity and Empire.* Boulder, CO: University of Colorado Press.

BBC (2019) *Everest: Three more die amid overcrowding near summit.* Available at: https://www.bbc.co.uk/news/world-asia-48395241 (Accessed: 28 March 2022).

Billington, M. (2019) *The Hard Way: Adapt, Survive and Win.* New York, NY: Simon & Schuster.

Birrell, S. (2007) "Approaching Mt. Everest: on intertextuality and the past as narrative", *Journal of Sport History,* 34(1), pp. 1–22.

Campbell, J. (2008 [1949]) *The hero with a thousand faces.* 3rd edn. Novato, CA: New World Library.

Champion, J. (2016) "Survivor shows and caveman masculinity", *The Popular Culture Studies Journal,* 4(1/2), pp. 240–258.

Channel 4 (2018) *Extreme Everest with Ant Middleton.* Directed by Ed Wardle. London: Parable.

Channel 4 (2022) Reaching new heights with Berocca and Ant Middleton. Available at: https://www.4sales.com/our-work/reaching-new-heights-berocca-and-ant-middleton (Accessed: 28 March 2022).

CNN (2018) *The Challenge: Everest.* Directed by Mark Fisher. London: CNN Vision.

Cracknell, J. and Fogle, B. (2006) *The Crossing: Conquering the Atlantic in the World's Toughest Rowing Race.* London: Atlantic Books.

Cracknell, J. and Fogle, B. (2009) *Race to the Pole.* Basingstoke: Macmillan.

Daily Telegraph (2019) "If he hadn't picked up, I would not be around now", *Daily Telegraph,* 23 January, p. 2.

Davidson, J.P.L. (2020) "'Life can be a little bit fluffy': survival television, neoliberalism, and the ambiguous utopia of self-preservation", *Television & New Media,* 21(5), pp. 475–492.

Doran, A. (2016) "Empowerment and women in adventure tourism: a negotiated journey", *Journal of Sport Tourism,* 20(1), pp. 57–80.

Doyle, M.E. and Peterson, K.A. (2005) "Re-entry and reintegration: returning home after combat", *Psychiatric Quarterly,* 76, pp. 361–370.

Dragojlovic, A. (2015) "Affective geographies: intergenerational hauntings, body affectivity and multiracial subjectivities", *Subjectivity,* 8, pp. 315–334.

Dunn, D. (2006) "Television travels: screening the tourist settler", in Burns, P.M. and Novelli, M. (eds) *Tourism and Social Identities: Global Frameworks and Local Realities.* Amsterdam: Elsevier, pp. 185–194.

Elmes, M. and Barry, D. (1999) "Deliverance, denial, and the death zone: a study of narcissism and regression in the May 1996 Everest climbing disaster", *The Journal of Applied Behavioral Science,* 35(2), pp. 163–187.

Evans, J. (2009) "'As if' intimacy? Mediated persona, politics and gender", in Sclater, S.D., Jones, D.W., Price, H. and Yates, C. (eds) *Emotion.* London: Palgrave Macmillan, pp. 72–84.

Fogle, B. (2011) *The Accidental Adventurer: My Wilderness Years.* London: Bantam Press.

Fogle, B. (2015) *Labrador: The Story of the World's Favourite Dog.* London: William Collins.

Fogle, B. (2017) *Land Rover: The Story of the Car that Conquered the World*. London: William Collins.

Fogle, B. (2018) *Up: My Life's Journey to the Top of Everest*. London: William Collins.

Fogle, B. (2020) *Inspire: Life Lessons from the Wilderness*. London: William Collins.

Frohlick, S. (2006) "'Wanting the children and wanting K2' the incommensurability of motherhood and mountaineering in Britain and North America in the late twentieth century", *Gender, Place & Culture*, 13(5), pp. 477–490.

Genette, G. (1991) "Introduction to the paratext", *New Literary History*, 22, pp. 261–271.

Gilchrist, P. (2020) "Embodied causes: climbing, charity, and 'celanthropy'", *International Journal of the History of Sport*, 37(9), pp. 709–726.

Gordon, A. (2008) *Ghostly Matters: Haunting and the Sociological Imagination*. Minneapolis, MN: University of Minnesota Press.

Hollis, D. and König, J. (eds) (2021) *Mountain Dialogues from Antiquity to Modernity*. London: Bloomsbury Academic.

King, L. (2015) *Family Men: Fatherhood and Masculinity in Britain, 1914–1960*. Oxford: Oxford University Press.

Krakauer, J. (1997) *Into Thin Air*. New York: Villard.

Lee, K. (2014) "Reading celebrity autobiographies", *Celebrity Studies*, 5(1–2), pp. 87–89.

Lim, M. and Moufahim, M. (2015) "The spectacularization of suffering: an analysis of the use of celebrities in 'Comic Relief' UK's charity fundraising campaigns", *Journal of Marketing Management*, 31(5–6), pp. 525–545.

MarArthur, H.J. and Shields, S.A. (2015) "There's no crying in baseball, or is there? Male athletes, tears, and masculinity in North America", *Emotion Review*, 7(1), pp. 39–46.

Middleton, A. (2018) *First Man In: Leading from the Front*. New York, NY: HarperCollins.

Middleton, A. (2019) *The Fear Bubble*. New York, NY: HarperCollins.

Middleton, A. (2020) *Zero negativity*. New York, NY: HarperCollins.

Midgeley, D. (2018) "Explorer and presenter Ben Fogle talks preparing to scale Mount Everest", *Daily Express*, 7 April. Available at: https://www.express.co.uk/life-style/life/942837/tv-presenter-explorer-ben-fogle-scaling-mount-everest-climb (Accessed: 30 August 2021).

Mu, Y. and Nepal, S. (2016) "High mountain adventure tourism: trekkers' perceptions of risk and death in Mt. Everest Region, Nepal", *Asia Pacific Journal of Tourism Research*, 21(5), pp. 500–511.

Ortner, S.B. (1997) "Think resistance: death and the cultural construction of agency in Himalayan mountaineering", *Representations*, 59, pp. 135–162.

Osborne, C.A. (2022) "Injury at the extreme: Alison Hargreaves, mountaineering and motherhood", in Wagg, S. and Pollock, A.M. (eds) *The Palgrave Handbook of Sport, Politics and Harm*. Basingstoke: Macmillan, pp. 187–206.

Palmer, C. (2002) "'Shit happens': the selling of risk in extreme sports", *The Australian Journal of Anthropology*, 13(3), pp. 323–336.

Pears, L. (2022) "Military masculinities on television: Who Dares Wins", *NORMA: International Journal for Masculinity Studies*, 17(1), pp. 67–82.

Pomfret, G. (2012) "Personal emotional journeys associated with adventure activities on packaged mountaineering holidays", *Tourism Management Perspectives*, 4, pp. 145–154.

Purtschert, P. (2018) "White masculinity in the death zone: transformations of colonial identities in the Himalayas", *Culture and Religion*, 21(1), pp. 31–42.

Rak, J. (2021) *False Summit: Gender in Mountaineering Nonfiction*. Montreal: McGill-Queen's University Press.

Shakespeare, S. (2018a) "TV explorer Ben Fogle, who will climb Everest [...]", *The Dailly Mail*, 28 March, p. 36.

Shakespeare, S. (2018b) "Happily married TV adventurer Ben", *Daily Mail*, 4 April, p. 32.

Shakespeare, S. (2018c) "Ben Fogle's father-in-law sent to 'keep an eye' on him and former Olympic cyclist Victoria Pendleton", *Daily Mail*, 17 April, p. 36.

Smith, S. and Waton, J. (2001) *Reading Autobiography: A Guide for Interpreting Life Narratives*. Minneapolis, MN: University of Minnesota Press.

Wantono, A. and McKercher, B. (2020) "Backpacking and risk perception: the case of solo Asian women", *Tourism Recreation Research*, 45(1), pp. 19–29.

Westaway, J. (2019) "Everest: 11 climbers dead in 16 days—How should we deal with the bodies on the mountain?" *The Conversation*, 10 June. Available at: https://theconversation.com/everest-11-climbers-dead-in-16-days-how-should-we-deal-with-the-bodies-on-the-mountain-118374 (Accessed: 10 August 2021).

Westaway, J. (2022) "Bodies of ice: post-mortal (im)mobilities and Mount Everest as a mortuary landscape", Podcast from original talk given to the London Group of Historical Geographers. London: Institute of Historical Research. Available at: https://www.history.ac.uk/podcasts/bodies-ice-post-mortal-immobilities-and-mount-everest-a-mortuary-landscape (Accessed: 28 March 2022).

Woodward, R. and Jenkings, K.N. (2018) *Bringing War to Book: Writing and Producing the Military Memoir*. London: Palgrave Macmillan.

Yelin, H. (2016) "'A literary phenomenon of the non-literate': classed cultural value, agency and techniques of self-representation in the ghostwritten reality TV star memoir", *Celebrity Studies*, 7(3), pp. 354–372.

Chapter 15

Politics of Representation in Mountaineering

Conclusion

Jenny Hall and Martin Hall

The stories we tell, published or otherwise, condition our mountain experiences in practice and reinforce cultural memory and representation. Yet, as this book and the authors within it set out to demonstrate, if we look beyond the boundaries of this "singular white history" (Hunt, 2019, p. 6) there is a rich diversity of stories to tell. This volume contributes to a growing body of scholarship that calls for a heterogeneity of voices in mountain memoir genres. For the first time, this diverse scholarship interrogates how mountaineering literary and media culture impact bodies, spaces and places, in order to nuance how commodification intersects across social categories and is embodied in multi-dimensional ways.

Mountain memoir heritage and traditions remain little changed since their rise to popularity in the mid-1850s. Through historical and contemporary mountaineering experiences, the authors show how the commodification of storytelling is founded within heroic white, class-based, masculine ideologies. The threads that bind these authors together concern how our desire to tell a story catalyses the processes of commodification, which is embodied in a multitude of different ways. This book has demonstrated that these stories of risk, of endurance, of extreme environmental conditions and of personal deprivation, are bound up in heroic imperialism and in addition, are foundational to the way in which bodies experience mountain spaces. Interestingly, such stories make compelling and highly commodifiable reading; that is, if the body in question meets the regulatory heroic ideal. As Fiona Mossman highlights in Chapter One, the growth in mountaineering as a sport is intimately linked to its texts and how books are used both on and off the mountainside, creating a communication circuit connecting "book-experience-place". This communication circuitry has contributed to the ways in which mountains have been shaped and codified for social, political and economic purposes, at both macro and micro levels, via masculinist traditions and social politics in mountain storytelling. The epitome of these traditions manifests in Leslie Stephens's (1832–1904) guide book *The Playground of Europe* (1871) that became an instant classic and is still highly influential through his conceptualisation of mountains as site of play. Stephens's book contributed to the notion of mountains being commodified as playground which pervades in modern accounts such Joe Simpson's memoir *Touching the Void* (1988). Experiencing extreme risk in mountaineering is theorised by Anna Holman, in Chapter Twelve, as a form of dark play, an addictive attitude to extreme risk with high probabilities of death, that is socially constructed as, not only acceptable, but necessary in mountaineering. Holman identifies how risk is embodied as dark play in the practice of, and is foundational to, traditions in mountaineering story-telling. She argues that such masculinist traditions and "Stories that cast mountains as playgrounds and mountaineering as play deceive future climbers into believing the risk of death is a necessary part of the game" (page number confirmed at typesetting stage).

Martin Hall, in Chapter Two, explores how commercialisation underpins the adventure experience and, like Raymen (2019, p. 18), has suggested that climbing as a sub-cultural sport is founded upon neoliberal consumer capitalist forces that drive "cool individualism". Hall has shown that the globalising communication circuitry between film-experience-audience transcends any question of whether it is ethical to film someone who risks their life. He has exposed how commodifying forces ameliorate the masculinities + risk = reward equation, making it palatable to the stakeholders involved; mainly uninitiated audiences are thrilled, and sponsors, filmmakers and climbers capitalise socially and economically. Here again we see the replication and reinforcement of heroic ideologies. Risk in extreme mountain film spaces is globally romanticised through the sublime actions of middle-class white male bodies and is thus exclusive. The romantic bedrock upon which such ideologies are founded can be traced back to early Romantic writers like Jean-Jacques Rousseau (1712–1778). Rousseau wrote that when he was immersed in nature it allowed a loss of all "consciousness of the independent self" and that "our existence is nothing but a succession of moments perceived through the senses" (quoted in Clark, 1982, p. 191).

Rousseau's maxim of "I feel therefore I am" (Ibid.), provided the founding tenet of English Romanticism (1800–1850) that popularised intense emotion as an authentic source of aesthetic experience. Notions of the sublime emphasised emotions such as fear, terror and awe, associating these with mystical and spiritual sensations when immersed in nature. Poets, writers and artists such as Wordsworth, Coleridge, Byron, Turner and Constable transformed ideas of the natural and wild landscape into places for self-discovery and self-actualisation, thus walking and climbing mountains were born as wholesome and intellectual activities. These artists characterised the picturesque sublime, and a "belief in the divinity of nature developed. Mountains became the abode of gods rather than of demons" (Williams 1973, p. 15). Mind-body-environment was inscribed with a social currency that reified sublime risk-taking with mountain spaces; men who climbed them were hailed as demi-gods. This narrative still dominates and is explored by Sarah Ives, in Chapter Five, through an analysis of Instagram posts by the BAME climbing group @melanin-basecamp who critiqued the media storm that followed the release of Alex Honnold's award-winning film *Free Solo* (2018). Anaheed Saatchi posted that the film "took up so much screentime … none of the work around diversity in the outdoor industry is ever going to pan out if we keep bolstering straight, cis-gendered, white men as demigods".

Rak (2021) has argued that mountain writing is culpable in perpetuating such oppression, and memoirs like John Krakauer's bestselling book *Into Thin Air* (1997) reproduce notions of exclusivity. Moreover, she has shown how mountain writing has framed diversity as a threat that represents climbing in decline. The decline of mountaineering, arguably, is due to commercialisation, which has been attributed to the diversification of mountaineering participation by those other than the dominant norm, and not viewed by "real climbers" as authentic. The impact of such traditions is acutely illustrated in Anna Holman's conceptualisation of dark play in Chapter Twelve and Paul Gilchrist's discussion of the celebrity "father-mountaineer" in Chapter Fourteen. He has shown how gender is consequential in the battle for supremacy on the mountainside. The impact of rivalry between Ben Fogle and Ant Middleton's documentary film making crews on Everest reproduces narratives of heroic militarised masculinity and its emotional disentanglements that valorise a masculine ideal of self-reliance to create a form of hyperauthenticity. Fogle embodied gendered hyperauthenticity by sharing his anxiety that he faced the "humiliation of being out-summited" (Fogle, 2018, p. 165):

The hyperauthentic masculinities on display from these erstwhile "celebrity-climbers" implicate reality television in this story of mastery... Everest is spatially promiscuous. It is a site of colonial logic and touristic dreams, a space to both escape and feed the cult of celebrity, a gendered space of survivalist resolve, and a space of fear and desire. (p.284)

As Ives in Chapter Five asserts, to achieve social change and reset the publishing-experience-space in mountaineering we need to decolonise the outdoors, by foregrounding the visibility of people excluded from the narrative in tandem with realigning the histories of mountains themselves. Ives has identified how social media is being used to reappropriate, rename and geotag mountains using their indigenous names rather than the 'colonial name': Sagarmāthā instead of Everest. Ives had demonstrated how social media is playing a significant role in achieving visibility for people of difference by conceptualising Instagram as a "mini-memoir", which enables representation of BAME communities and indigenous people of colour in the outdoors, globally. However, despite the mini-memoir providing a platform for resistance and social change, Ives acknowledges this has its limitations and harbours new forms of oppression such as digital access and literacy. And yet, social media has a globalising power to change the ways in which we embody difference in mountain spaces and thus, processes of commodification.

In Chapter Three David Lombard argues that the romantic ideals of the sublime require revision if we are to build a better embodied relationship with our sensitive mountain environments. This is starkly illustrated further by James Maples and Michael Bradley's chapter wherein they conceptually frame 'dirtbag economics'. Maples and Bradley explore how accidental environmental benefits arose out of the collision between two seemingly diametrically opposed communities. The host community in Red River Gorge, Kentucky, USA wished to destroy a landscape to preserve life and livelihoods by building a damn, whereas incomers (climbers) indirectly became preservers of the environment by offering a new economic opportunity. Through analysing local climber Chris Chaney's (2019) memoir, Maples and Bradley show how class, gender and race intersected to produce local entrepreneurialism that developed "Red" into a highly commodified climbing destination, which in turn now threatens this fragile environment.

Along this environmental theme, Christopher Kocela's analysis of Peter Matthiessen's ecobiography *The Snow Leopard* (1978) within Chapter

Thirteen has conceptualised mountaineering as a form ecological Zen practice. Matthiessen and Schallers's 1973 expedition helped to popularise the idea of trekking and mountaineering as vital spiritual and ecological practice. The research expedition led to the creation of Shey Phoksundo National Park in 1984, the largest in Nepal, an astounding achievement. Although seemingly innocent, the processes of commodification were initiated by their publications and as such, trekking and mountaineering have become synonymised with spirituality and ecological practice, which has not protected the Himalayas from destructive commercialism. Although evolved from culturally different perspectives, connecting natural environments with spirituality and authentic experience echoes with the commodifying influences of the romantic sublime. Thus, embodying spirituality intersects across race, religion, class and gender founded in an ideology of authentic mountain climbing. The shift from militaristic and siege tactics used for achieving high-altitude first and new ascents adopted by mountaineers in the 1950s, notably Sir Edmund Hillary and Tensing Norgay, gave way to what was seemingly a more spiritual and ecological approach. Reinhold Messner and Peter Habeler's first ascent of Everest without oxygen adopted an alpine fast and "light weight" style that they claimed to be a spiritual and purer way to ascend the mountain. Messner has famously asserted that "I wanted to climb high again in order to see deep inside myself" (Messner, 1999 [1978], p. 1). This transition, firmly embedded within traditions associated with white masculinities, worked to the exclusion of those outside the dominant norm. New ways to climb became entangled in notions of spiritual heroics that only the pure, best and brave could perform.

The commodifying forces impact mountaineering bodies both on and off the mountain and are embodied producing and reproducing oppression in multi-dimensional ways, in particular the way voices have been silenced, hidden and ignored (something which is central to this volume). Anandarup Biswas has highlighted, with Chapter Six, the impact Bengali climbers achieved during the 1960s in pioneering access to high-altitude climbing for subsequent generations. Significantly, Biswas explores the spiritual and cultural meaning that has motivated Bengalis to participate in mountaineering; unlike the Western desire to conquer, mountaineering for Bengali climbers, represented a way to test their moral righteousness or *dharma* on the way to heaven (*swarg*) and "bring mountains closer to their private lives". Bengali climbers have faced considerable prejudice from their own communities as well as other foreign climbers and fought hard for recognition. Although widely shared in Asia their stories have been largely ignored in the global north.

Excluding difference has had, however, a long tradition, which Emma Gleadhill has explored through the hidden stories of British women Grand Tourists in Chapter Seven. In contrast to their male counterparts, women Grand Tourists were not obliged to return home having engaged in risky activities, expected of men who were tasked to return transformed to assume positions of power and leadership. In contrast to heroic stories, women Grand Tourists' memoirs and unpublished accounts have focused on facets of the mountain environment such as flora, fauna, and geological features. Gleadhill has argued that women Grand Tourists created a different cultural construction of mountain spaces through narrating new sensations and experiences drawn from paying close attention to the mountain environment. Thus, early women mountain tourists played a role in the development of the "imaginative constructions of the mountain and the activity of mountaineering in relation to the self". Sarah Lonsdale in Chapter Eight, Agnieszka Kaczmarek with Chapter Nine, and Jenny Hall throughout Chapter Ten have emphasised the absence of women mountaineers from mountaineering literature in the twentieth century. Lonsdale has contended that Dorothy Pilley's memoir *Climbing Days* (1935) is a feminist text that was ground-breaking because it asserted women's rights to access mountains and mountaineering. Pilley deliberately chose a style that did not adopt the hyper-masculine approach to jam the book full of militaristic and technical details. Instead, she offers a visceral account of her experiences and feelings, exposing a deep emotional connection to the mountain that finds echoes in the work of Nan Shepherd. Yet, gender was consequential and Pilley expresses how she was subject to sexism and being made to feel an outsider. Similarly, Kaczmarek, in Chapter Nine, has shared the first English glimpse of one of the twentieth century's finest mountaineers, Polish climber Wanda Rutkiewicz. Until now Rutkiewicz's memoir has only been published in Polish, and an English translation, despite her achievements, has yet to appear. Echoing this, Jenny Hall's chapter, through the lens of emotional politics, investigated Julie Tullis's experiences expressed in her memoir *Clouds from Both Sides* (1986). Tullis formed the first high-altitude filmmaking team in the world with mountaineer Kurt Diemberger. Hall highlights the different ways Julie represents her mountaineering achievements and the emotional labour she experienced as result of the sexism and pressures she felt as a mother mountaineer:

Julie's approach for managing this through martial arts and her modest, emotional, empathetic and spiritual writings offers new insight into the mountain memoir as a genre of emotional and sensory storytelling beyond the brave "real life cultural ideal" of heroic mountaineering (Rak, 2021). She shows us how fluidity between masculinities and femininities offers different ways to be in the mountains and understand mountain environments as spaces of transformation. Her care for others, the environment and her family all shape diverse ways to imagine the life of elite mountaineering at the intersection of gender, dis/ability, class, race, age and sexuality, such as her experiences with disabled climbers. (p.206)

Tullis, like Pilley and the Bengali climbers, sought a spiritual way to experience mountains and like Pilley, the women Grand Tourists and Nan Shepherd, Tullis wrote extensively about her emotional connection and joy in being immersed in mountains. Nan Shepherd's *The Living Mountain* (1977) is the antithesis of commodifying forces that she so despised and offers a vision of a private yet inclusive space to be different in the mountains. The fragility of environmental and human experience is explored in Garlick's Chapter Eleven, wherein he has analysed the prose of Shepherd's book. Through a more-than-representational lens, Garlick has invited us to consider an "alternative, slower knowing of landscape". He has argued that, Shepherd's text "combines intense empirical attentiveness, personal reflection, and a kind of transcendental existentialism", creating a different way to embody mountaineering experiences. Garlick's chapter has conceived of Shepherd's writing as a vital source for theorising landscape and its virtual qualities. Notably, her writing creates new spaces and ways to engage in an ancient currency of cultural exchange between human and non-human bodies, fostering a mind-body-environment that could enable ways to tackle pressing environmental challenges.

The resounding call from this diverse range of scholars is a turn to heterogeneity in adventure mountain storytelling. In summation, this book makes an important contribution to the genre of memoir in the context of mountaineering and, further, in expanding our understandings of this mode of representation. By encompassing a wide milieu of perspectives, the authors have engaged with difference through multifaceted methodologies and a range of power geometries. Questioning the scope of the memoir, this book has nuanced dominant narratives of consumption within leisure and tourism spaces by offering sensitive accounts of mountain environments and their communities. We have demonstrated how commodification materialises, how it is embodied and how it is experienced across multiple axes of social distinction. This volume's interdisciplinary approach has helped us appreciate how hyper-masculinities pervade in the commodification and thus, representation of mountaineering in popular culture. Crucially, the authors have highlighted how this normalised experience has reproduced hegemonic mountain environments and has deepened understandings of how Indigenous communities, people of colour and women negotiate power-laden relations in high-altitude environments to create different spaces of adventure. The implications for this volume's identification of inequalities offers insight both for diversifying the mountain memoir by problematising this "singular white history" and in its call for different heritages in mountaineering to be recognised (Hunt, 2019, p. 3).

To begin with, our aim was to open a discussion and to contribute to the emerging field of mountain studies by inviting scholars to the discussion on diversity and difference in publicly consumable mountaineering representations. However, we do acknowledge the dominance of Western academic voices and subjects in this volume and call upon academics to take seriously issues of inclusion across multiple axes of social distinction.

Bibliography

Chaney, C. (2019) *In the Red: Adventures in Kentucky's Red River Gorge*. Stanton, CA: Ascensionist Press.

Clark, K. (1982) *Civilisation*, 3rd edn. London: Penguin Books.

Fogle, B. (2018) *Up: My Life's Journey to the Top of Everest*. London: William Collins.

Hunt, R. (2019) "Historical geography, climbing and mountaineering: route setting for an inclusive future", *Geography Compass*, 13(4), p. e12423.

Messner, R. (1999 [1978]) *Everest: Expedition to the Ultimate*. Seattle, WA: The Mountaineers.

Rak, J. (2021) *False Summit: Gender in Mountaineering Nonfiction*. Montreal: McGill-Queens's University Press.

Raymen, T. and Smith, O. (2019) *Deviant Leisure: Criminological Perspective on Leisure & Harm*. London: Palgrave.

Stephen, L. (1871) *The Playground of Europe*. London: Spottiswoode and Co.

Williams, C. (1973) *Women on the Rope*. London: George Allen & Unwin Ltd.

Index

Adventure 9, 54, 67, 68, 99, 136, 223, 245
aggression 141
Alpine Club 19, 26, 47, 169, 170, 177, 179, 181, 182, 217, 224, 250
Alpine Journal 23, 47, 48, 169, 171, 174, 178, 179, 182, 209, 223
Alps, The 18, 22, 33, 35, 36, 37, 38, 40, 41, 42, 45, 48, 49, 60, 68, 149, 150, 152, 153, 154, 164, 165, 176, 177, 178, 179, 181, 191, 224, 250, 274
Annapurna 32, 39, 49, 109, 123, 142, 146, 223, 276
Anthropocene 72, 73, 85, 86
Auden, W. H. 43, 175, 181
audiences 19, 53, 55, 56, 57, 58, 59, 62, 63, 65, 67, 107, 123, 253, 306
Austrian 205, 211, 214, 287
autobiography 76, 116, 189, 205, 222, 271, 275, 287
avalanche 124, 143, 212, 221, 289

Base Camp 192, 193, 194, 291, 294, 297
BBC 32, 127, 285, 286, 290, 302
Bengal 6, 10, 22, 131, 132, 133, 134, 135, 136, 137, 138, 139, 141, 142, 143, 144, 145, 146, 147

Biswas, Debasish 142, 144
Blum, Arlene 14, 110, 206
body 17, 18, 24, 26, 46, 73, 75, 78, 82, 84, 109, 115, 143, 149, 168, 180, 212, 220, 227, 230, 236, 238, 239, 242, 243, 253, 256, 270, 287, 289, 294, 299, 302, 305, 307, 311
bravery 94, 115, 309, 311
Broad Peak 205, 212, 213, 218, 221
Buddhism 12, 132, 235, 271, 272, 283

California 11, 14, 79, 124, 268
chauvinism 193
Chin, Jimmy 19, 25, 58, 63, 64, 69
Chomolungma 119, 142
class 15, 17, 21, 32, 51, 133, 143, 158, 169, 173, 175, 181, 206, 217, 218, 222, 286, 305, 306, 308, 309, 311
Clouds from Both Sides 23, 205, 207, 222, 224, 310
CNN 285, 286, 295, 296, 302
colonialism 10, 17, 22, 26, 105, 108, 119, 123, 124, 131, 136, 137, 139, 143, 175, 189, 210, 279, 300, 304, 308
community 10, 102, 103, 123, 201
culture 1, 2, 12, 13, 25, 26, 48, 102, 123, 146, 182, 223, 245, 264, 302, 303, 304

Diemberger, Kurt 193, 205, 215, 218, 219, 223, 310
dirtbag 21, 88, 89, 90, 93, 96, 109, 308
diversity 2, 15, 23, 110, 112, 114, 305, 307, 312
documentary 9, 11, 57, 101, 114, 250, 251, 255, 258, 259, 262, 264, 286, 291, 295, 307

economic 10, 21, 33, 40, 89, 99, 101, 152, 207, 306, 308
El Cap 54, 57, 60, 62, 115
embodied 9, 15, 16, 17, 18, 19, 21, 24, 25, 73, 75, 78, 82, 83, 90, 109, 121, 208, 220, 221, 222, 232, 250, 254, 256, 292, 293, 294, 305, 306, 307, 308, 309, 312
emotion 9, 61, 150, 206, 207, 209, 211, 229, 233, 285, 288, 297, 301, 307
endurance 150, 212, 288, 290, 305
enlightenment 268, 269, 270, 272, 273, 274, 276, 279, 280, 281
environment 10, 11, 12, 16, 22, 23, 24, 31, 46, 54, 59, 61, 73, 74, 75, 84, 106, 108, 159, 206, 207, 210, 213, 220, 222, 227, 228, 230, 235, 238, 240, 243, 245, 253, 258, 267, 272, 273, 274, 290, 307, 308, 310, 311
Europe 18, 27, 32, 33, 49, 68, 150, 165, 265, 306, 312
Everest 6, 22, 23, 25, 26, 35, 48, 60, 80, 81, 82, 83, 85, 89, 102, 108, 110, 111, 115, 119, 124, 132, 135, 140, 141, 142, 143, 144, 145, 146, 147, 150, 185, 186, 190, 191, 192, 193, 194, 195, 196, 198, 200, 202, 203, 205, 213, 214, 216, 224, 261, 281, 285, 286, 287, 288, 289, 290, 291, 292, 293, 294, 295, 296, 297, 298, 299, 300, 301, 302, 303, 304, 307, 308, 309, 312
expedition 41, 81, 89, 109, 132, 133, 134, 135, 137, 140, 142, 143, 158, 185, 191, 192, 193, 194, 195, 199, 205, 211, 212, 213, 214, 215, 217, 218, 267, 281, 289, 299, 300, 309

extreme 9, 18, 25, 46, 54, 59, 63, 65, 66, 91, 200, 208, 218, 222, 243, 286, 289, 294, 295, 298, 300, 301, 303, 305, 306

family 25, 31, 37, 51, 79, 88, 95, 99, 112, 113, 149, 155, 177, 180, 191, 209, 214, 215, 216, 218, 221, 222, 255, 257, 258, 287, 295, 296, 297, 298, 299, 301, 311
fatal 142, 161, 205, 259, 262, 296
feminine 151, 161, 171, 178, 180, 183, 206, 210, 241
femininity 22, 38, 162, 180, 207, 209, 210, 222
feminist 23, 27, 111, 117, 122, 172, 217, 218, 310
film 9, 56, 57, 67, 69, 102, 175, 265
filmmaker 63, 205, 218
flow 52, 193, 198, 275
France 150, 163, 164, 171, 182
Free Solo 19, 20, 25, 51, 56, 57, 58, 61, 62, 63, 64, 65, 68, 69, 114, 307
French 17, 26, 181, 185, 191, 201, 205, 206, 215, 218, 224

gender 2, 9, 12, 13, 15, 17, 18, 21, 32, 39, 89, 108, 110, 112, 121, 123, 152, 161, 162, 165, 167, 180, 192, 200, 206, 210, 216, 218, 222, 224, 297, 302, 307, 308, 309, 310, 311
genre 201
geographer 9, 229, 246
geography 13, 26, 163, 224, 228, 229, 230, 233, 235, 245, 246, 312
glacier 77, 156
guides 42, 95, 110, 157, 162, 169, 178, 179, 180, 191, 209, 251, 291, 292, 298, 306
guilt 163, 211, 215, 216, 217

Harding, Warren 62, 90
Hargreaves, Alison 208, 217, 298, 303
harmony 181, 220, 221
heroic 15, 17, 19, 21, 24, 39, 124, 158, 178, 206, 207, 210, 211, 212, 218,

222, 260, 261, 287, 288, 295, 299, 305, 306, 307, 310, 311
Hillary, Edmund 132, 133, 309
Himalaya 48, 133, 134, 136, 137, 139, 140, 142, 144, 146, 147, 182, 202, 274
holiday 35, 36, 40, 42, 43, 134, 292
Honnold, Alex 57, 58, 62, 63, 64, 65, 66, 68, 69, 89, 102, 114, 115, 307
human 9, 11, 85, 246, 264, 270

ideology 2, 17, 81, 110, 188, 212, 222, 309
imperialism 108, 150, 162, 175, 206, 305
imperialist 72, 207, 210
India 10, 131, 132, 133, 134, 135, 136, 141, 142, 144, 147, 193, 195, 202, 274
indigenous 16, 113, 119, 188, 292, 294, 308
injury 20, 52, 156, 214, 220, 254, 259, 263, 289
Instagram 10, 21, 105, 106, 107, 108, 111, 112, 113, 114, 115, 117, 119, 120, 121, 122, 123, 125, 126, 127, 128, 247, 285, 286, 307, 308
intersection 218, 222, 239, 311

K2 25, 61, 68, 205, 208, 215, 217, 218, 219, 222, 223, 298, 303
Kangchenjunga 198, 200, 219, 301
Kant, Immanuel 71, 150, 164
Krakauer, Jon 5, 20, 71, 73, 74, 75, 76, 77, 78, 79, 80, 81, 82, 83, 84, 85, 86, 89, 102, 110, 111, 142, 147, 298, 303, 307

labour 23, 206, 207, 208, 209, 210, 211, 212, 213, 214, 215, 216, 217, 218, 219, 222, 224, 235, 294, 297, 310
Lake District 152, 176, 229, 246
landscape 12, 24, 31, 40, 42, 44, 45, 61, 72, 76, 79, 80, 83, 120, 122, 160, 199, 227, 228, 229, 230, 231,

232, 233, 234, 235, 236, 237, 238, 239, 240, 241, 242, 243, 244, 245, 246, 247, 249, 256, 277, 291, 294, 304, 307, 308, 311
Le Blond, Elizabeth 38, 169, 170, 180, 209, 221
Lyng, Stephen 20, 26, 52, 68, 264

Macfarlane, Robert 39, 52, 227, 233, 236
male 15, 17, 21, 23, 61, 96, 106, 107, 109, 112, 114, 116, 124, 149, 150, 151, 152, 155, 156, 157, 158, 161, 162, 169, 177, 178, 183, 185, 205, 206, 209, 210, 214, 216, 217, 218, 221, 224, 229, 289, 299, 306, 310
Mallory, George 59, 68, 131, 135, 145, 147
masculine 21, 108, 111, 168, 175, 177, 178, 181, 207, 208, 209, 222, 289, 290, 294, 305, 307, 310
masculinity 26, 105, 108, 109, 124, 141, 142, 150, 155, 156, 177, 178, 206, 223, 288, 290, 294, 297, 299, 302, 303, 304, 307
memoir 11, 15, 16, 17, 18, 19, 20, 21, 22, 23, 24, 25, 32, 33, 34, 36, 39, 41, 42, 66, 73, 76, 79, 81, 84, 87, 89, 90, 96, 101, 107, 110, 114, 121, 167, 168, 171, 172, 174, 175, 178, 180, 187, 206, 207, 210, 212, 222, 227, 249, 250, 251, 252, 253, 254, 255, 256, 257, 258, 259, 261, 262, 263, 268, 287, 288, 292, 304, 305, 306, 308, 310, 311, 312
Messner, Reinhold 39, 141, 195, 221, 309
Miguel's Pizza 89, 96, 97, 98
mind 49, 52, 69, 147, 182, 307
moral 65, 81, 136, 164, 198, 272, 279, 299, 300, 309
mother 38, 115, 120, 142, 150, 151, 216, 218, 310
Muir, John 79, 99, 101, 103, 106, 223, 272

Nanga Parbat 205, 214, 218, 219, 220
National Park 57, 62, 105, 281, 282,
    283, 309
Native American 118, 271
nature 12, 13, 16, 17, 18, 22, 26, 31,
    33, 45, 46, 62, 72, 76, 90, 106, 107,
    108, 109, 112, 124, 139, 140, 149,
    151, 168, 169, 176, 179, 181, 189,
    206, 209, 216, 220, 221, 227, 228,
    231, 233, 236, 237, 240, 244, 247,
    256, 267, 269, 270, 271, 272, 273,
    274, 275, 276, 277, 279, 280, 287,
    289, 290, 294, 306, 307
Nepal 124
New York Times 58, 60, 62, 66, 67, 68,
    69, 265
Norgay, Tenzing 132

Olympic 286, 289, 304

photography 105, 120, 285, 291
Pinnacle Club 168, 169, 170, 171, 172,
    174, 181, 183
psychological 64, 212, 214, 293, 298
Pyrenees 169, 178

Rak, Julie 15, 17, 19, 26, 39, 49, 105,
    108, 109, 110, 111, 113, 124, 206,
    222, 224, 287, 299, 304, 307, 311,
    312
risk 20, 22, 23, 26, 33, 38, 46, 51, 52,
    53, 54, 55, 56, 58, 59, 60, 61, 62,
    63, 64, 65, 66, 67, 68, 82, 83, 100,
    105, 114, 146, 207, 208, 211, 213,
    217, 222, 250, 251, 253, 256, 257,
    258, 261, 263, 264, 287, 288, 292,
    293, 295, 298, 299, 303, 304, 305,
    306, 307

Scotland 12, 31, 41, 170, 227, 229,
    234, 235, 245, 247
sensory 26, 74, 82, 207, 221, 222, 223,
    240, 241, 244, 311
sexism 110, 115, 117, 310
sexist 20, 185, 208

Sherpa 127, 133, 142, 292, 294, 295,
    298
soldier 40, 290, 292, 296
spirit 22, 36, 131, 135, 140, 171, 212,
    220, 232, 243
sport 11, 27, 66, 67, 69, 163, 182, 183,
    224, 264, 265, 282, 302, 303
strength 22, 122, 143, 169, 175, 177,
    180, 209, 212, 292
Sublime, The 11, 18, 20, 21, 32, 46,
    62, 71, 72, 73, 74, 75, 76, 77, 78,
    79, 80, 81, 82, 83, 84, 85, 150, 154,
    155, 158, 159, 162, 178, 299, 306,
    307, 308, 309
summit 16, 32, 33, 76, 80, 111, 132,
    134, 135, 140, 142, 143, 145, 158,
    176, 178, 194, 195, 205, 211, 214,
    218, 220, 221, 251, 256, 257, 258,
    262, 285, 288, 290, 291, 292, 293,
    294, 295, 296, 297, 298, 302

Tibet 132, 146, 274
television 2, 25, 285, 288, 290, 291,
    304
Touching the Void 6, 24, 27, 249, 250,
    251, 252, 253, 255, 256, 257, 259,
    260, 261, 263, 264, 265, 306

Vasarhelyi, Elizabeth Chai 19, 25, 58,
    63, 64, 69
Vesuvius 150, 152, 153, 154, 155, 157,
    158, 159, 161
Victorian 18, 26, 33, 35, 36, 49, 86,
    105, 108, 124, 165, 169, 208, 209,
    219, 224
volcano 153, 155, 157, 158

woman 22, 31, 38, 60, 77, 105, 110,
    111, 113, 114, 115, 120, 122, 151,
    157, 158, 167, 168, 170, 172, 173,
    175, 177, 178, 179, 180, 181, 194,
    200, 205, 206, 211, 213, 216, 217,
    218, 219, 269
women 13, 22, 23, 26, 31, 32, 38, 89,
    109, 110, 111, 112, 114, 115, 117,

121, 122, 135, 139, 147, 149, 151, 152, 155, 156, 157, 158, 159, 160, 161, 162, 164, 168, 169, 170, 171, 172, 173, 176, 177, 178, 179, 180, 181, 182, 186, 190, 192, 193, 199, 201, 205, 206, 207, 208, 209, 210, 214, 215, 216, 217, 218, 219, 221, 222, 223, 247, 302, 304, 310, 311, 312

Yosemite National Park 57, 62, 66, 89, 90, 97, 102, 103, 114, 224
youth 22, 95, 97, 99, 133, 143, 144, 150, 162, 169, 180, 210, 234, 250, 285, 286, 297

Zen 6, 24, 25, 235, 267, 268, 269, 270, 271, 272, 274, 277, 281, 282, 283, 309

Printed and bound by CPI Group (UK) Ltd, Croydon, CR0 4YY

13/12/2023

08207823-0001